Identity, Morality, and Threat

Studies in Violent Conflict

Edited by
Daniel Rothbart
and
Karina V. Korostelina

LEXINGTON BOOKS

A division of
ROWMAN & LITTLEFIELD PUBLISHERS, INC.
Lanham • Boulder • New York • Toronto • Plymouth, UK

LEXINGTON BOOKS

A division of Rowman & Littlefield Publishers, Inc.
A wholly owned subsidary of The Rowman & Littlefield Publishing Group, Inc.
4501 Forbes Boulevard, Suite 200
Lanham, MD 20706

Estover Road
Plymouth PL6 7PY
United Kingdom

British Library Cataloguing in Publication Information Available

Library of Congress Cataloging-in-Publication Data

The hardback edition of this book was previously cataloged by the
Library of Congress as follows:

Identity, morality, and threat : studies in violent conflict / edited by
    Daniel Rothbart and Karina V. Korostelina.
       p. cm.
    Includes bibliographical references and index.
    1. Social conflict. 2. Ethnic conflict. 3. Violence. 4. Intergroup relations. 5. Group
    identity. I. Rothbart, Daniel. II. Korostelina, K. V. (Karina Valentinovna).
    HM1121.I34 2006
    303.6—dc22   2006027374

    ISBN-13: 978-0-7391-1618-0 (cloth : alk. paper)
    ISBN-10: 0-7391-1618-5 (cloth : alk. paper)
    ISBN-13: 978-0-7391-1619-7 (pbk. : alk. paper)
    ISBN-10: 0-7391-1619-3 (pbk. : alk. paper)

Printed in the United States of America

♾™ The paper used in this publication meets the minimum requirements of American
National Standard for Information Sciences—Permanence of Paper for Printed Library
Materials, ANSI/NISO Z39.48–1992.

Contents

Acknowledgements

As editors, we never had any doubts that this book would be completed. Our confidence came largely from the chapter authors, from their enthusiasm about the book's major themes, from their cooperation and efficiency in preparing their chapters. It was truly a pleasure working with each author. In the early stages of this project, colleagues inspired us at our home institution, The Institute of Conflict Analysis and Resolution at George Mason University. Their insights into identity-based conflicts were conveyed during in-house meetings, scholarly conferences, and classroom settings. Sometimes we gained knowledge and insight from casual conversations around the 6th floor kitchen. The Institute is always a lively, stimulating and productive working environment, thanks in large measure to the Institute Director, Sara Cobb. We are so thankful to her for encouraging us and supporting this project.

Special thanks go to three of the Institute's graduate students: Joshua Fisher, Meg Kagawa, and Kim Toogood. We are grateful for their editorial skills, calmness under pressure, and good cheer in preparing the camera-ready copy. Daniel Rothbart owes special thanks to his "other home," the Department of Philosophy at George Mason University, for giving him the freedom to work on this project and the encouragement to extend philosophy beyond its traditional boundaries. In addition, we express our gratitude to Dr. Leila Dane who helped us organize the first round table on collective axiology at the 2005 American Psychological Association Convention, Washington, DC.

Finally, we offer special thanks to the editors of Lexington Press for their support, professionalism, and efficiency at various stages of this work.

Daniel Rothbart
Karina V. Korostelina

Let no one be called infidel unless
He seeks to harm another.
Let the curse of idolater be reserved
Only for the self-righteous,
Whose tyrannous faith brings war,
And permits any cruelty
In the serve of its self-deity.
Let the charge of blasphemy fall
Only on the self-anointed,
Ventriloquists of divinities.
Once again, let no god be abominated,
Declared a devil by another's partisans,
Let none be despite, but all honored.

Excerpts from

"Pagan Litany"[1]

By

Patricia Storace

---

[1] Reprinted in *New York Review of Books*, January 12, 2006, p. 30.

Chapter 1

Introduction: Identity, Morality, and Threat: Studies in Violent Conflict

Daniel Rothbart and Karina V. Korostelina

In cases of protracted conflict, an act of violence always has unanticipated consequences. Its effects far exceed the objectives of strategists
and perpetrators. The worst fears and best hopes of any agent of violence never prepare them for the results. Over time, violence can redefine social relationships in unpredictable ways. The threatening Other,
immortalized in various threat narratives, is not only described by their
malicious deeds; they are characterized as vicious and/or depraved.
Questions about "what happened" in a conflict quickly turn to monolithic
explanations of who "they" are, why are "they" malicious, and when
"they" will strike.

How do societies respond to generations of violent conflict? During
periods of crisis, the threatened group denigrates the Other as uncivilized, savage, subhuman, or demonic. Negative images are retrieved
from mythic stories of the past. In turn, such images lend validity to notions of ingroup nobility, skill, and virtue. Via these narratives, violent
actions against a perceived "enemy" become sanctified, and the agents of
such actions glorified. This dynamic is no less true for today's terrorist
threats than for the Corinthians who recounted the threats posed by the
Corcyraeans during the Peloponnesian War.

Even in some peaceful and cooperative communities, group differences can be exaggerated. During times of protracted conflict, such differences foster hatred and fear. Members of the ingroup position themselves positively, while the Other is demonized. Studies have shown that
high salience of ingroup identity promotes negative opinions of outgroups. Ingroup members also share important values and norms (Esses
et. al, 1993). Prejudices or negative attitudes toward other groups are
influenced by attributed differences in such beliefs, including visions of
the ideal society, and the exclusion of the outgroup from such a society.

The chapters below offer the first rigorous study of threat narratives
as a major source of identity-based conflict. In the minds of conflict pro-

tagonists, threats frame the them/us duality in normative terms. Who "they" are is revealed through their vices; who "we" are is revealed through our virtues. "They" are bad, vicious, or unjust; "We" are good, virtuous, or just. In such narrative retellings, the threatening Other rarely, if ever, acts justly. When hatreds intensify, such differences are elevated to the level of a social ontology. The actions of the Other today seal their immorality in perpetuity. In acting justly, "we" do the right thing at the right time for the right reasons, for the sake of what is good. "We" are positioned as morally pure, endowed with virtues that inhere in a birthright connected to a sacred Homeland ("from sea to shining sea"), the legacy of a country's monarchy, and/or a social order established by an approving God.

Threat narratives frequently exploit intense and powerful imagery. The choice and assignment of such imagery are often deeply embedded in fabrications about race, ethnicity, gender, religion, or nationality. Foreign invaders, for example, are characterized as insects, magicians, demons, and predators. The Other is denigrated as vermin, demons, seducers of women, enemy-combatants, or subhuman creatures.

Conflict Theory as Value Theory

One of the great mysteries of human existence centers on a search for "meaning" in the face of life's finiteness, frailty, and finality. For philosophers of Ancient Greece, this search required insight into something beyond the concrete facts of daily life. Thinkers turned their attention to visions of an ideal society. One mission of the polis of Ancient Greece was to offer remembrance of good and bad deeds, to inspire admiration in the present and in future ages (Thucydides 1989, Book ii., 41). In this context the true locus of a polis lies in the virtues that bind individuals together, both living and dead. So, life in the polis served to assure that the deeds and stories, which are their outcome, would become imperishable.

This quest for life's meaning is relevant to today's violent conflicts. Every religious, political and nationalistic group with a highly salient identity finds meaning beyond the here-and-now of daily encounters. Like the Greek polis of the past, these groups strive for betterment in an idealized future. Every group of high salience unites the faithful through its own notion of a polis, blending political realities with aspirations for immortality. As Arendt observes, "There is no politics, no common world and no public realm without aspirations for earthly immortality" (Arendt 1958, 55). For salient groups, politics acquires a moral legitimacy through a vision of an ideal state.

Human life is not just a random, continuous flow, but displays normative patterns, regularities, and characteristic ways of doing and being, of feeling and acting, of speaking and interacting (Pitkin 1972, 132). Of course, every identity group has a sense of its unity, its wholeness among the many. Every social group with high identity salience navigates through life's struggles by aspiring to transcend the finitudes of individual (fleeting) life. Solace from life's frailties and dangers is sought in realms that are presumably permanent, enduring, and potentially universal. Through its value commitments, every identity group distances itself (at least in partial exploratory ways) from the encounters, schemes, and experiences of the present. The collective seeks to reach beyond the immediacy of life, imagining what the future holds, where they want to go, and how they can get there (Emirbayer and Mische 1998, 984). The ways in which a group imaginatively recomposes future possibilities are essential to its self-image. Martin Buber writes that "in the beginning is relation," and such relation has a projective dimension. Members of a religious community long for extension in time and in space, and for a union with their 'god'" (Buber 1986, 107-8).

The collective projects and actions of every group with highly salient identity are political and normative. The group's sociality rests on processes of mutual obligations that compel compliance, and establish duties through the adoption of normative rules. In striving towards a better world, a collective establishes cohesion among individuals. It exerts a force on individuals, and offers guidance for distinguishing right from wrong.

In this respect, the polis of every identity group realizes its unity through the categories of right and wrong, good and bad, virtues and vices. These categories are passed on through storytelling practices, and are used to justify, rationalize, condemn, and denounce specific actions. In recounting episodes of violence and impending threat, storytellers often dwell in the realm of values. A particular episode is situated within a pattern of virtuous or vicious deeds. Negative valuation inheres within the threat, and is inseparable from its significance for the threatened group. Threatening actions are thought to be vicious, wicked, immoral, criminal, uncivilized, reprehensible, blameworthy, scurrilous, felonious, nefarious, infamous, villainous, heinous, atrocious, accursed, satanic, diabolic, hellish, infernal, fiendish, demonic, and depraved. The responses of the ingroup have moral worth, at the very least to thwart the advances of invaders. The ingroup actions are right, commendable, praiseworthy, pure, noble, angelic, saintly, or possibly godlike. Such actions promote and cohere with an idealized vision of "the good." An act deemed heroic, for example, exhibits certain virtues that link past deeds to aspirations for a better world, inspiring later generations to continue along the same "righteous" path.

Of course, every protagonist group declares that its cause is just, and the sacrifices of others are necessary. Over time, such declarations embed a group's collective axiology. For example, national identity often rests on claims of original habitation of the land. Such a claim is often used to legitimize control, rights, and privileges. National identity is inseparable from normative judgments about ingroup virtues and outgroup vices.

Underpinning every social, religious, and national group is a polis, and every polis blends politics with value-commitments that confer a collective axiology on individuals. A collective axiology is a system of value-commitments that define which actions are prohibited, and which actions are necessary for specific tasks. It provides a sense of life and world, serves to shape perceptions of actions and events, and provides a basis for evaluating group members. A collective axiology defines boundaries and relations among groups and establishes criteria for ingroup/outgroup membership. Through its collective axiology, a group traces its development from a sacred past, extracted from mythic episodes beyond the life of mortals, and seeks permanence. Transcending the finitude of individual life, a collective axiology extends retrospectively from the salient episodes of the past to a prospective vision, presumably into the otherwise uncertain future. An individual's identity and values that are acquired at birth and left behind at death exist before that birth and behind that death.

Axiology is an inquiry into the nature, criteria, and conception of value. Of course, such a study of values is legend in the world of philosophy, from it earliest days.[1] In the present study, we explore how the value-commitments underpinning threat-narratives are often converted to a collective axiology of identity and difference, which in turn galvanizes conflict protagonists to resort to extremes forms of violence.

The Totalization of Threat

In many settings, threat narratives can be converted into ideologies of terror. Hannah Arendt reminds us how totalitarian regimes are prepared to sacrifice everybody's vital interests for the sake of so-called historical inevitabilities. Extending Arendt's insights to protracted conflict, we show how a threat-logic can be totalizing. A threat-logic recasts Self and Other within a pre-formed dogma, elevating their roles to a timeless universal Law. All "facts" are ordered, all experiences are explained, and all personal relationships are subject to controls. Group differences need not be validated by actual facts, because such differences cannot possibly be disputed.

For groups with a high salience of identity, the threat-logic becomes sacrosanct, achieving an aura of transcendent truth. The logic is removed from direct contact with the subtleties, complexities, and temporality of daily life. It does not depict the real causal sequences of events. But to its followers, the threat-logic imposes a vice-grip on thought. It separates thought from reality. The struggle against a threatening Other is "necessary" but never completely finalized. In cycles of violence, a threat-logic includes a demand for security that is never actually attained. This fosters the hope for peace through the strategies of perpetual conflict.

Like a Law of History, a threat-logic conveys infallibility. There is no need for critical inspection, because no possible evidence could contradict the dogma. Of course, all so-called neutral observers are dangerous. Any critic of the threat-logic is viewed as disloyal. The critic's true danger lies in the new path opened up for critical investigation, a path that could undermine the totalizing control of the threat narrative. Criticism could expose the contamination of the logic itself. The logic can become an end in itself, growing deeper than a stipulation of certain words, symbols, and ideas.

A threat-logic replaces the familiar modes of understanding with something alien, and contaminates their capacities for understanding and judgment (Arendt 1994, p. 316). In extreme cases, the threat-logic contributes to a tyranny of thought and deed. The totalizing effects of threat-logic rob protagonists of the capacities for genuine understanding, and cut off any access to the very phenomenon that it presumably explains. Followers are severed from contact to actual events "on the ground." One result of this process is blindness to others, to their sufferings, fears, and struggles. A collective axiology can infiltrate into private life, and contaminate even intimate relationships. Over time, the original idea of a threat is devoured by the very mechanisms for preserving the system of controls. Just as unanticipated events simply do not "occur" to those in the grip of threat logic, individuals who cannot easily be categorized within the axiology do not exist.

In our exploration of threat narratives, we examine how collective axiology is defined through categories of right/wrong, good/bad, and/or virtuous/vicious, drawing upon stories of a sacred past and propelled forward in the form of obligations, expectations, requirements, demands, and rights. Although existing studies on identity based conflicts provide adequate empirical information about the effects of salience of identity on attitudes and behaviors, such studies shed considerably less light on the axiological dimensions of group identities. With this volume we launch a new program of research for the analysis of protracted conflicts, stressing the importance of threat narratives as expressions of those value-commitments which are deeply embedded in perceptions of identity and difference.

The following questions are addressed in this study. Through what social and cognitive processes are actions evaluated as good or bad? Is valuation of action reducible to factuality of events, episodes, or social phenomena? Is valuation of individuals or groups reducible to mere feelings? What is the relation between valuing (devaluing) an action and valuing (devaluing) individuals or a group? How does this kind of evaluation, or devaluation, lead to the collective actions and violence? How can negative characterizations be transformed in ways that promotes a sense of positive worth in the Other?

Plan of the Book

By exploring the normative implications of threat narratives in protracted conflict, the authors of this volume are launching a new research field.

This field will bear fruit in nuanced studies of protagonist groups, detailed cases of protracted conflict, and innovative modes of conflict resolution practice. The chapters below are organized into three parts.

Part I: Threat and Collective Axiology

In Part I the authors examine how threat narratives converge around certain normative categories. Such categories contribute to a shared value-system (collective axiology) that determines the range of "permissible" responses to threats. The collective axiology is used to "educate" the faithful to the "true" sources of hostilities, guide them in taking the right course of action, and prepare them for the struggle ahead. The question "Who are they [as a collectivity]?" calls for an understanding of the character, commitments, and plans of the Other. Such an understanding shapes and solidifies beliefs about group differences. As the Other is denigrated, the moral superiority of the ingroup is reinforced.

Even the term "threat" implies negative characterizations of the Other. This term can be used to represent a threatening action or a source of a threatening action, in the form of a person or a group. Similarly, the adjective "threatening" can modify an action or its source. Of course, many terms modify both actions and agents. "Immoral" is another example. This action/agent duality tells us something important about the notion of a threat. Over generations of protracted conflict, threatening actions reinforce the moral denigration of the Other. Group differences are defined by dualities of virtues/vices, good/bad, and/or pure/impure. Of course, these dualities are not fixed. The dynamism of group differences leaves open the possibility for change, recasting the us/them dualities in more or less extreme terms.

In his groundbreaking research on the psychology of social positioning, Rom Harré characterizes a position as a spatial metaphor for the relative placement of individuals or groups. Such a placement is defined by beliefs about the rights and obligations that guide actions, and is revealed through reflection on storytelling practices. A system of normative positions comprises three elements: actions, storylines, and positions (Harré 1999, Chapter 1). For his contribution to this volume, Harré extends his findings in social psychology to a rigorous study of threat ("Threat Narratives" Chapter 2). Associated with notions of danger, malice, and menace, a threat provokes speakers to exaggerate divisions. To declare "He threatened me" is often followed by "He is a threat to me." The shift from describing an action to attributing a characteristic can have stunning consequences. When a person (or group) is said to represent a danger, a system of normative positioning is formed or transformed. The social geography that emerges from this positioning system extends in time. Like the term "enemy," "threat" oscillates between retrospective framing and anticipatory projection. The dangers of the past are thought to continue into an indefinite future.

With this kind of thinking, loyal followers are driven by their perceptions of the "realities" of threats. Followers must carry out policies that are "demanded" by the threat-logic. For example, the alleged leader of the group responsible for the London bombings of July 7, 2005 wrote about the "ethical stance" that he and his fellow soldiers have taken against the governments responsible for "atrocities against my people."[2] He stated that he is engaged in a "war" that is waging in the streets of London against "your democratically elected governments." The rationale for his violent actions is both political and normative.

In "Moral Denigration of the Other" (Chapter 3), Rothbart and Korostelina examine as a source of conflict the mode of thinking associated with global devaluation of the Other. This chapter reveals how the Other is stigmatized and thus devalued, and how character traits of individuals are converted to negativities. In the process of global devaluation, protagonists characterize the outgroup as unjust, immoral, uncivilized, or inhuman. Systems of normative commitments offer groups a means for orienting themselves by their relations with others.[3] Actors of conflict find their place in the world by attributing both causal and moral responsibility to a stigmatized group. In this respect, the purity of the ingroup offers a moral foundation for collective actions and for the sacrifices that lay ahead. How exactly is the characterization of Other-as-enemy essentialized, given an aura of eternal truth? What are the conditions for neutralizing such negativities, and inviting reflection on positive traits of the Other? The authors in this chapter demonstrate that the shift in terms from "he" to "they" in threat-narratives represents a major transformation in the source of hostilities that demands attention to the axiological commitments of the protagonist groups. Global devaluation is a complexity, revealed in certain stages of development, relying on a transition from icon to word, from word to model, and from model to action.

As Chapter 3 stresses, the formation of demonized and devalued images of the Other can galvanize members of the ingroup. The Other is essentialized as morally degenerate. The findings in Chapter 3 are starkly illustrated in the detailed study of apocalyptic terrorism by Dennis J. D. Sandole. In "Identity Under Siege: Injustice, Historical Grievance, Rage, and the 'New' Terrorism" (Chapter 4), Sandole offers insight into the complexity and differences among today's "terrorist" threats. The received categories of terrorist, guerrilla fighter, and military personnel suggest important normative differences in goals, objectives, and strategies. Unlike the guerrilla fighter or the nation's soldier, the "apocalyptic terrorist" is driven by a sense of embattled group identity, and links survival to a neo-"crusader" immersion in global struggles. Sandole explores the cognitive and moral blindness of such an immersion. He advises practitioners of conflict resolution to delve more deeply into the protagonists' motives and intensions through careful study of their worldview commitments.

The chapter "Identity Salience as a Determinant of the Perceptions of the Others" (Chapter 5) by Karina V. Korostelina explores the connections between salient identity and readiness to fight. The results of four studies presented in this chapter show that salient ethnic identity changes the balance of relations between person and ingroup, leading to ingroup primacy. Salience of identity fosters a sense of negativity that in turn creates a kind of a "tunnel consciousness" about the outgroup. Consequently, salient social identity leads to a perception of the Other through exaggerated value differences.

Part II: Multiple Value-Systems

The chapters in Part II explore cases in which protracted conflict is fueled by struggles over competing value-systems. A collective identity often exhibits a tension over two incongruous axiologies. In "Humanitarianism and Intolerance: Two Contemporary Approaches to the Other"

(Chapter 6), Peter N. Stearns documents how the past century has witnessed two dominant narratives in international relations, both of which underpin recent debates over the role of America in the international arena. One narrative retains a humanitarian commitment to universal human rights, based on the tradition of French enlightenment political philosophy. According to this narrative, Western "civilization" becomes protector of "universal" humanitarian values, savior of the oppressed, and advocate of the "rights of man." A second narrative of international relations prioritizes the need for national, ethnic, or religious groups to protect their security in the face of external threats. Security narratives tend to inflate and distort the security-needs of all nations. In so doing, these narratives frame the Other as hostile and dangerous, and promote universal categories of "them" and "us."

Sterns' chapter illustrates how national identity can reflect a struggle over incompatible axiological systems. The norms of interpersonal relations fostered by particular cultures can also produce two diverse types of collective axiology. The chapter entitled "Cultural Differences of Perception of the Others" by Karina V. Korostelina (Chapter 7) shows how threat narratives tend to shift from individual denigration to collective negativity. This chapter examines two types of cultures—collectivistic and individualistic. Each type of culture influences the degree of a person's dependence on the group, the orientation to personal or group values, and the readiness to interact with members of other cultures. Korostelina stresses that in individualistic cultures one's personal orientation is dominant, and the most important narratives reflect personal relationships and achievements. In collectivistic cultures group relations determine perceptions, understandings, and interpretations of the social reality. The transition from multiple identities to a single, dominant group identity can have dangerous consequences in the formation of negativities about the Other.

Another conflict over competing value-systems is documented in the chapter by Lena Tan, entitled "From Incorporation to Disengagement: East Timor and Indonesian Identities, 1975-1999" (Chapter 8). In her study, Tan explores two powerful forms of collective axiology, one grounded in the Indonesian identity of elite policymakers and the other in the ethnic identity of East Timoreans. Emerging from centuries of Dutch colonialism, Indonesian liberation sought as its "true mission" a struggle for national unity. In 1945, when Sukarno enunciated a set of doctrines known as the Pancasila, he attempted to unify the young and heterogeneous nation around five principles: Indonesian unity, humanitarianism, democracy, social justice, and belief in God. These principles were used to solidify the Indonesian nation as such. In the years immediately following 1945, the homogeneity of an Indonesian identity eventually suppressed the heterogeneity of local cultural heritage and religious traditions. The struggle for East Timorese independence in the late 1980s and 1990s grew in reaction to the oppressive nature of the New Order elite. This struggle included demands for justice in recognition of a separate identity.

Of course, some groups do not tie their identity to denunciations of the Other. Consider the humanitarian ethic of many religious traditions. Many scholars have documented how an enlightened reading of the Quran, for example, reveals a commitment to peace and nonviolence. Undermining the recent denunciations of Islam by many Westerners, S. Ayse Kadayifici-Orellana in "Islamic Tradition of Nonviolence: A Hermeneutical Approach" (Chapter 9), reminds us of the rich tradition of nonviolence in the Islamic faith. According to many Islamic scholars, the Quran establishes strict standards for the use of violence. Kadayifici-Orellana explores a particular Islamic community that defined its identity through a renunciation of all forms of violence against civilians. In the eyes of this community, God requires no less.

Part III: The Dynamics of Collective Axiology

The chapters in Part III examine ways in which a collect axiology undergoes change. In some settings a threat-logic is crafted intentionally to prepare for a struggle that lies ahead. This theme is explored in the chapter "'Good Violence' and the Myth of the Eternal Soldier" (Chapter 10) by David G. Alpher and Daniel Rothbart. These authors show that the military world confers on new recruits a "hermetic conceptual framework" that reinforces an internal peace in the face of violent suppression of external threats. Ingroup membership offers absolution and justification for acts of "good violence," which are perceived to contrast sharply with the enemy's "bad violence." This contrast is closely tied to the dualities of scared/profane, good/evil, and virtuous/vicious. Alpher and Rothbart examine how both military systems and fundamentalist religions rationalize personal sacrifice through commitments to ingroup virtues and outgroup vices. Military systems and fundamentalist religious sub-groups provide in their trainings proprietary language and forms of learning that are structured around powerful icons, sacred words, and conceptual models (see Chapter 3 by Rothbart and Korostelina). Birth in the sacred realm (the Homeland) guarantees collective virtues, whereas birth in the enemy region confers a stigmatization linked to a profane foreign territory. The homeland becomes a sacred realm that offers a bounty of riches for potential conquerors.

In "Gender and Violence: Redefining the Moral Ground" (Chapter 11), Sandra Cheldelin also examines how the denigration of one group—women—directly leads to violence. During times of peace, the sexual violence against women is rooted in patterns of discrimination and demonization. Under circumstances of war or armed conflict, such patterns are deepened. The powerful narratives that society produces and repeats through the media reinforce the stereotypes of women as sexual objects. Repetition of such narratives contributes directly to violence toward women. Cheldelin stresses the importance of gendered *re-positioning*. Such a shift leads to new ways of thinking about the sources of sexual violence in times of peace and war.

A clear case of the dynamics of group identities and collective axiology is recounted in the chapter by Marc H. Ross, entitled "Psychocultural Interpretations and Dramas: Identity Dynamics in Ethnic Conflict" (Chapter 12). Ross examines a particularly powerful form of protest in Northern Ireland. Retrieving Victor Turner's notion of social drama, Ross characterizes certain conflictual settings as psychocultural dramas. The performers in the Loyal Order Protestant parades are depicted as morally pure. Such performances have the effect of aggravating tensions in relations between Protestants and Catholics. Ross's study of the Loyal Order Protestant parades shows how ingroup identity can be solidified by affinity to distant groups. The demands of the Loyalists are implicitly communicated by their associations with the traditions of Dutch Protestantism. In many of our chapters, salience of identity is explained by the intersections among distinct identity groups.

A stunning example of the dynamism of ingroup identity is found in the German identity in the second half of the twentieth century. Germany's struggles with its criminal past created normative divisions that were more temporal than geographical. In "Coping with Collective Stigma: the Case of Germany" (Chapter 13), Edward A. Tiryakian examines the so-called "Holocaust Identity" of Germany, as well as the dynamics of German stigmatization on ingroup identity. Tiryakian then offers strategies for Germany to reverse the pattern of post-war images, casting off its negative identity to assume a positive post-modern identity.

An effective methodology for positive change must address the consequences of axiological differences. Amid all the broken peace treaties, unsuccessful shuttle diplomacy, and tiresome speeches by Track I diplomats bemoaning senseless violence, the world continues to witness episodes of stunning devastation and genocide. Joseph V. Montville is a leading figure in a forward-thinking movement to expose the futility of statecraft in addressing protracted conflicts. In "Reconciliation as *Realpolitik*: Facing the Burdens of History in Political Conflict Resolution" (Chapter 14), he privileges the psychodynamics of protracted conflict for strategies for lasting change. Echoing a major theme of the current volume, such an understanding suggests the importance of the *Moralpolitik* for conflict resolution. Montville cites Justice Richard Goldstone, who is chief prosecutor at the International Criminal Tribunal in the Hague, for his efforts to promote reconciliation in post-conflict settings. Montville's chapter offers insight into the depths of identity-conflict, and the moral necessity of reconciliation.

For advocates of a realist perspective on international relations, a study of threats would seem superficial in relation to analysis of the causes of war. But the notion of causation needs to be broadened to include cognitive factors of protagonists, and indeed, this book can be read as a study in the major sources of violence. As threat narratives seep into a group's deeply held beliefs, they become inseparable from a collective axiology of identity and difference, and can be manifested in violent conflict. The consequences of embedding notions of the threatening Other into an ingroup worldview can be extremely lethal. In a way, the processes of demonizing the Other and glorifying the ingroup are the most powerful sources of violent conflict.

Notes

1. Such a study is rife with controversy. For Plato values are reified in the "true realm" of abstract forms. However, Nietzsche found in such lofty declarations the elements of a con-job, ideas of value exploited for the purposes of domination over the weak.
2. "This is how our ethical stances are dictated. Your democratically elected governments perpetuate atrocities against my people and your support of them makes you responsible. . . . Until we feel security, you'll be our target. Until you stop the bombing, gassing, imprisonment and torture of my people, we'll not stop this fight. We are at war and I am a soldier." (Mohammad Sidique Khan, *Guardian Weekly*, September 9-15, 2005, p. 12.)
3. As Suzanne Langer writes, some of the greatest human achievements are found in the symbols that govern general orientation in nature, on the earth, and in society (Langer 1942, 287).

References

Arendt, H. 1958. *The Human Condition.* Chicago: University of Chicago Press.

_____. 1994. "Understanding and Politics," in *Essays in Understanding: 1930-1954.* New York: Schocken Books, pp. 307-327.

Buber, M. 1989. *I and Thou.* Translated by Ronald Gregor Smith. New York: Scribner Classics.

Emirbayer, M and Mische, A. 1998. "What is Agency?" *American Journal of Sociology*, vol., 103, no 4, pp. 962-1023.

Esses, V. M., Haddock, G., & Zanna, M. P. 1993. "Values, stereotypes, and emotion as determinants of intergroup attitudes." In D. M.

Mackie & D. L. Hamilton (Eds.), *Affect, cognition, and stereotyping: Interactive processes in group perception.* New York: Academic Press, pp. 137-166.

Harré, R. and Langenhove, L. V. eds., 1999. *Positioning theory: moral contexts of intentional action.* Oxford: Blackwell.

Khan, M. "We are at war. . . . I am a soldier" Friday September 2, 2005. *Guardian Weekly,* p. 12.

Korostelina, K. 2006. *Social identity: Structure, dynamics and implications for conflict.* Forthcoming.

Langer, S. 1942. *Philosophy in a New Key: Study in the Symbolism of Reason, Rite and Art.* Cambridge, Massachusetts: Harvard University Press.

Mackie, D. M. & Hamilton, D. L. eds., 1993. *Affect, cognition, and stereotyping: Interactive processes in group perception.* New York: Academic Press.

Pitkin, H. F. 1972. *Wittgenstein and Justice.* Berkeley, California: University of California Press.

Thucydides. 1989. *The Peloponnesian War: The Complete Hobbes Translation.* With Notes and a New Introduction by David Grene. Chicago: The University of Chicago Press.

Part I: Threat Narratives and Collective Axiology

Chapter 2

The Texture of Threat

Rom Harré

Introduction

We can begin the investigation of the concept of "threat" with a true story. For many years I have been coming to Georgetown University to teach in the Spring Semester. Sometimes my ID card has survived unscathed, sometimes it has expired—quite capriciously it seems. One January, some years ago, I went into the library to get a book I needed for the preparation of a lecture for a class meeting the next day. I handed over the card to the librarian who said, with a slightly triumphant air, "It has expired." So I said "I am going to go over to security", the office where ID cards are dealt with. To my amazement the librarian said, "Are you threatening me?" I still wonder what he meant. As a student of the psychological quirks of my fellow humans I should have said "Why do you say that?" Of course, it must have been that the librarian suffered something like the feeling of menace that the mention of "security" conjured up. Perhaps it might have been his sense that I might be an important person, whose complaint at his officiousness would go to the highest quarters.

Here is one fragment of the grammar of "threat", "threatening", and related terms. Threats are directed towards someone or sometimes even some thing, and they imply that something painful, unpleasant or destructive is likely to happen to the being threatened. So far this story describes threat, even though it was quite imaginary. There was no harmful intention on my part, so the key was his belief in my hostility. However, had it been a "real threat" then my intentions in mentioning "security"' would have been germane, as well as my willingness to complain, thus setting in motion a harm. Notice too, the implicit conditionality of implicit content ascribed to the remark by the librarian. "If you do not check out the book, some harm will ensure!"

We can also say that the environment is threatened by indiscriminate drilling for oil, and the economy is threatened by unrealistic wage demands or the dam by the rising water. The relation between conditionality and harm is quite clear in these contexts too. If the water continues to rise the dam will burst.

The concept of 'empty threat' is related. A threat may be empty if the threatener does not have the power or the means to carry out the threat by doing the harm. It may also be empty if the means exist but the threatener does not have the will to carry through the harmful action if the condition for neutralizing or suspending the harm is not met.

What the Dictionaries Have to Say

Remembering that psychological phenomena are identified in the first instance by the uses of the vernacular, it will prove useful to begin with some dictionary entries. For 'threat' Webster's Dictionary gives the following:

1. an expression of intention to inflict, injury or damage.
2. one that threatens
3. an indication of something impending "the sky held a threat of rain."

This does not seem very illuminating, since the conditionality aspect is omitted. However, it does include the idea of something impending, which may or may not be tied to conditionality. It might be tied to probability. Oxford English Dictionary more or less echoes this:

1. a stated intention to inflict injury, damage or other hostile action on someone.
2. a person or thing likely to cause damage or danger.
3. the possibility of trouble or danger.

Again the *if* component of the concept is implicit. A stated intention is only a threat if there is some contingent condition that has to be satisfied before the blow will fall, such as non-compliance with a command.

Some Nodes in the Field of Family Resemblances

"There is a threat of rain", "There is a threat of famine", "There are black clouds about and the drought has gone on for many weeks." The threats and the realization of the threats conveyed by these sentences are both material states of the world and they are more or less causally linked. At least the conditions that embody the threat are, or will be parts of, the cause of its realization. The harm is to human beings, and is more or less explicit, such as ruin of the harvest or starvation. Here we have non-conditional (but not unconditional) assertion of something impending that is probable but not certain.

We could equally talk sensibly of the promise of rain, though hardly of the promise of famine. Whether black clouds are a threat or a promise depends on whether rain is a blessing or a disaster. So whether a causal relation between two states constitutes the groundwork of a threat or of a promise depends on the larger context in which the discussion is going on. If, in the case of the famine, the outcome is dire and there are no reasonable circumstances in which it would be welcomed (though by a great stretch of the imagination it might be possible to think of one; say as said by the commander of an army besieging town), then drought does threaten famine rather than promise it.

In human affairs we may wish to substitute intentions for causes to set up a parallel grammar for 'threats' between persons. If you read my raised fist as a threat, you are presuming that I have at least some intention of bringing it down (on you) resulting in your pain and humiliation. If you are one of those strange creatures who enjoy being beaten, then my raised fist can hardly be a threat. In sado-masochistic circles it may even be seen as a promise. The link rests on the likelihood of fulfilling intentions rather than causing effects. However, in general, and setting aside psychological quirks, the effects must be seen as undesirable, should they come about. Of course, unless my raised fist when brought down did indeed cause you pain, neither threat nor promise would be appropriate.

Could I properly be said to threaten to kiss you? Could there be a threat of a desirable outcome? Again, circumstances matter. If my kiss were known to you to be a signal to a hostile onlooker, then indeed an act that would normally be thought to have pleasant consequences might be threatening. Kisses in horseplay among eight year olds might also be conceived as threats—soppy. A mild form of sexual harassment might be described as someone sensing a threat of being kissed. So only in the rare instances of the kiss bringing harm could the evident immanence of osculation be described as threatening.

Threats can be verbally formulated, and take the form of speech-acts. A speech-act has three components: locutionary, the uttering of some words; illocutionary, the effective meanings ascribed to those words; perlocutionary, the consequences of many sorts that ensue from the utterance of the words stood as having a certain illocutionary force.

However, threats need not be verbal. One might wordlessly threaten someone with a raised club or even with a narrow smile. But the threat depends on what the victim believes to be the likely consequence of non-compliance with the implicit 'if' clause. The non-verbal performance could be analyzed in a way parallel to the above analysis of the verbal threat. Only if a hostile intention can be ascribed to the one who threatens is the one who believes him or herself to be threatened is drawing a defensible conclusion. I was not threatening the librarian since I had no hostile intention, no matter what he may have thought.

Logically, threat statements are conditionals, with an implicit qualifying clause.

The initiating conditions are not sufficient to necessitate the unwelcome outcome. If rain was certain, the black clouds could not be cited as the grounds for the *threat* of rain. If the falling of the fist were a condign punishment from which there is no appeal, the raised fist is not a threat.

In the human case the implicit clause runs something like this: 'unless you comply with . . . , or cease to do . . . and so on, the fist will fall'. The point of the threatening gesture would be lost of the fist were necessitated to fall. Threats are intended to enforce compliance. But how? By the anticipation of pain, humiliation or some other aversive personal state coming about if the escape condition is not met and the threat is realized. Of course, it is important that the target person believe that compliance will avert the threat. This ties in threats with the grammar of expectations, but not with that of hoping, wishing[1] and wanting. These words are used in situations in which the fulfillment is desirable and the realization of the consequence what one wants. 'Expecting' can be used of both pleasant and unpleasant consequences.

"Threatening" goes with "fearing", "dreading" and so on. "Anticipating" has a similar grammar to "expecting". We can be anticipating winning and anticipating losing; anticipating pleasure when invited to a wine tasting and anticipating pain on the way to the dentist.

Threatening situations often rely on the concept of "danger." The existence of a threat makes the situation dangerous. "Danger" is like the other concepts we have been studying in that it is necessarily unfulfilled. "Danger! High Voltage" is a dire warning. The current cannot be said to be dangerous to the victim when he or she is being fried by it, just as dynamite cannot be said to be explosive when it is exploding.

Two more related concepts need to be examined—"menacing" and "warning." We could have said that raising a fist is a warning, rather than glossing it as a threat. We could have said that a raised fist is menacing rather than threatening. Are there any differences here? In English law we have "threatening behaviour" as a misdemeanor and "demanding money with menaces" as a crime. Could we imagine "demanding money with felicitations"? Yes, Dick Turpin was ascribed this particularly courtly habit. Yet, in the end he was hanged just the same.

However, considered as a speech act or as a gesture subject to the 'grammar' of speech acts, a warning and a threat are rather close to one another. Dire consequences will follow if one ignores a warning, just as dire consequences will follow if one does not do what is required to neutralize the threat. However, though natural forces can sometimes be talked of as threats, generally we use the word 'warning' for a speech act that alerts one to a dangerous natural situation. The German word "Steinschlag" on a mountain road alerts one to the possibility that rocks may fall. "Danger: Weir" alerts the boatman to a dangerous water fall ahead. Of course, intrepid white water rafters take such a notice more as an invitation than as a warning. They thrive on danger. The conditionality of the realization of the danger in actual harm is just what keeps the adrenalin flowing. So, it is the desirability or undesirability of the consequences rather than physical effects that matter conceptually.

However, "warning" too is used in a field of family resemblances. A threat may be delivered by saying "I am warning you or I'll . . ." in a slow and ominous way. This raises a further semantic question. Must a threat be delivered in such a way that the danger/harm component is explicit and detailed? A cheeky child might respond to the above with

"You and who else?" The raised fist is an icon of a specific harmful consequence, being struck. Would it still count as a threat if the promised harm were unspecified?

Finally, we must note the use of the word "threat" to refer to the threatening entity itself. The raised fist is not only the bearer of a threat, but it is a threat. The continuing existence of a witness to a crime is a threat to the perpetrator and so is him or herself a threat, who perhaps ought to be eliminated.

The Krieglandschaft

Kurt Lewin coined this expression for the power of a war landscape to structure the movements of people within it. Danger was believed to emanate from certain points in the landscape with a certain range of directions and menaces. For example, a machine gun emplacement on the brow of a hill would fill the territory under the sweep of the gun with danger. Such an entity is a threat. Certain other points and areas are endowed with reciprocal properties of safety and comfort. In generalizing this insight, Lewin drew on the mathematical theory of topology to set out the kinds of relations that can obtain between 'regions' in a personal and/or social space. Thus, we can look for boundaries, and ask whether they are permeable or impermeable, and by which people and in what circumstances. The psychology of people in prison or otherwise physically constrained can be illuminated by attention to how the basic topological structure of the perceived environment is represented in the beliefs of the prisoners and displayed in the patterns of their movements (Lewin 1936, Ch. IV).

This leads us to a further level of the semantic field of threat. Structural linguistics inform us that the meaning of a concept is determined as much or more by which its use excludes than by what it positively affirms. To understand "threat" fully we must attend to what using the concept routinely excludes, such as comfort and safety.

Erving Goffman (1971, Ch. 6) developed Lewin's insight in two directions relevant to our exploration. He pointed out the importance of sustaining normal appearances in allowing life to proceed without anxiety and continual scrutiny of the environment. However, commonplace urban city layouts may offer the wherewithal for a 'texture of threat' to develop. He describes the pattern of anxiety and alertness that rises and falls as a person approaches a road junction late at night in a part of the city notorious for street crimes. The cross street slowly opens up to scrutiny as the walker approaches the junction, and more and more of the street becomes visible. Goffman summarizes the geometry of this layout with the idea of 'lurk lines' boundaries of the field of vision in which something dangerous might lurk (Goffman 1971, 294–299). Behind one's back, around sharp corners and in the dark are cited by Goffman as regions where a threat may lurk. There is nothing special about an urban landscape in this regard since dangerous bulls, territorially aggressive dogs and hungry lions may be lurking in the shadows and behind the trees.

Goffman emphasized the importance for the unfolding of strips of life that the world displays something like normal appearances. For a cityscape to be threatening the people who feel this must believe or know that there are dangers, that is possibilities of harm. Goffman's study of how the layout of streets contributes to the "texture of threat" was based on urban experiences. But landscapes, forests, deserts, the sea and so on are also contexts in which danger can be felt to be present. What are the normal appearances of cityscape or a stretch of jungle, or a reach of the sea (recall the devices used in the movie *Jaws*) may be entirely local.

Threat is perceived as a condition of the environment, but it is made up of two components. There is the furniture of the world that includes the people in and around the scene, and there is the requirement that the person who "feels a threat" has begun to be suspicious that these are not really normal appearances nor are some of the people going about their own personal business. Goffman calls the former "the furnished frame." It has an outside and an inside. It is taken for granted that the 'walls' are secure, and that what furnishes the frame is safe and/or manageable. Fragility of the frame coupled with suspicion as to the attributes of the material furnishings and the intentions of the human occupants of the frame are the material for generating a local texture of threat.

The right word to use is "threat" because in this case, as in the situation of threat as an illocutionary act, the two components that are prominent in the grammar of the concept are danger, meaning the possibility of harm, and conditionality, meaning that if certain conditions are fulfilled the harm will ensue.

Rom Harré

Positioning and Threat

A brief sketch of positioning theory will be needed to test out the idea that uttering threats and behaving in a meaningful way is, at the same time, to position oneself in relation to the person or persons who are subject to the threat (Moghaddam & Harré 2004).

Positioning theory is an analytical method for revealing the structure of small-scale episodes, in which rights and duties to perform certain kinds of actions interpreted as the performances of acts, are distributed and sometimes redistributed among the actors. When someone threatens someone else, questions of the positioning of the actors are bound to arise. Does the one who threatens have the right (or duty) to threaten the other? The theory relates three aspects of an encounter to one another. Each can be seen as mutually determining both of the others.

a. A position, defined as a cluster of rights and duties to speak and act in certain ways is related to the acts available to an actor so positioned.
b. The acts someone so positioned with the others in an episode seen as realizing a certain story line according to local narrative conventions.
c. Story lines can be analyzed according to one or more of the standard narratological frames, such as the "functions" of Vladimir Propp (1968) or the actants of Algirdas Griemas (1971).

To adopt a threatening posture or to utter threatening words is to be declaring, displaying or claiming a power to harm, and a willingness to do that harm. Furthermore, it is to position oneself as one who has the right (or the duty) to make such a threat and to impose the harmful consequence on the person who fails to comply with the escape condition. Threats are intentional, that is directed to someone or, rarely, something. This becomes tied to a position, since the actor is asserting a conditional right (and sometimes a duty) to commit that harmful act, the content of the threat. The right is conditional on the person threatened failing to conform to the demand made by the actor.

This analysis provides the dynamic link between an action/act analysis of threatening words and gestures and the moral status of the threatener relative to the one who is threatened. Only as the teacher can one threaten a recalcitrant pupil with a detention. Only as an agent of the Inquisition can one threaten a distinguished astronomer with the instruments of torture.

Threats in the Law

The material in this section is taken from the UK Larceny Act of 1916. The section in which the concept of threat plays a major role is headed "Demanding money etc. with menaces". The first subsection deals with someone who 'makes a demand in writing for some valuable property *with menaces'* [my italics], whatever they may be. The next section deals with blackmail, in which someone writes a letter "accusing or threatening any other person (whether living or dead) of any crime to which this section applies with intent to extort or gain thereby any property or valuable thing from that person." In the next clause the offence is widened to include the case of someone who "accuses or threatens to accuse any . . . person . . . of any such crime. . . ." The scope of the threat is also extended to cover "the use of unlawful violence to or restraint of the person of another" compels someone to make over various kinds of goods to the threatener. The Act includes the qualification that "it is immaterial whether any menaces or threats be of violence, injury or accusation. . . ."

Implicit in all this are two principles:

1. What is threatened will cause pain, humiliation or injury to the person threatened, that is some sort of harm.
2. Fear of these outcomes is likely to influence the person to succumb to the threat.

"Demanding with menaces with intent to steal" covers cases in which someone with "menaces or by force demands of any person anything capable of being stolen." Threatening to publish a libel gets by as a mere misdemeanor.

Conclusion

The conceptual structure of the concept of threat turns out to be quite complex. It not only involves the likelihood of harm, but also context relative relationships between threatener and threatened which the source of the threat is human. This necessarily invokes positioning theory, since in almost all kinds of human relations that are "up close and personal" the rights and duties of the actors are involved.

Notes

1. The full horror of W. W. Jacobs' story of the Monkeys Paw is forged by the grammatical contrast between the normal welcome one gives to the arrival of what one wishes for and the terrible things that actually fulfilled the old people's generic wishes.

References

Goffman, E. 1971. *Relations in Public*. New York: Basic Books.

Griemas, A. J. 1971. "The Interpretation of Myth." In P. *Structural Analysis of Oral Tradition,* edited by Maranda & E. Maranda,. Philadelphia: University of Pennsylvania Press.

Lewin, K. 1936. *Principles of Topological Psychology*. New York: McGraw-Hill.

Moghaddam, F. M. & Harré, R. 2004. *Self and Others*. New York: Freeman

Propp, V. 1968. *The Morphology of the Folk Tale*. Austin TX: University of Texas Press.

Chapter 3

Moral Denigration of the Other

Daniel Rothbart and Karina V. Korostelina

Why violence? Why do some communities find in their heritage values that promote reconciliation and peace, while others fail to foster such values? Why do some communities interpret innocent interactions with members of outside groups as fraternizing with the enemy and a deep affront to their sense of personal survival? In the eternal quest for understanding human existence, kings and slaves, generals and foot soldiers, poets and scientists alike have pondered these questions. Part of the mystery arises from the interconnected repercussions that violence engenders. All violent acts have consequences—positive and negative, foreseen and unexpected, subtle for some and fatal for others. Violence sets in motion an unending sequence of occurrences that can never be fully anticipated. Violence holds mysteries even for those committing the act. An agent of violence initiates, and in turn is potentially influenced by, the action, becoming both a "doer" and a "sufferer." To act violently and to suffer violence are like opposite sides of the same coin, and the story that an act starts is composed of its consequent deed and sufferings (Arendt 1958, 190). Some suffering is caused by denigration, hatred, and stigmatization. Projections of the evil, destructive, and malicious Other are essentialized, acquiring a cognitive force in the minds, and lives, of ingroup participants.

To determine why communities develop such different responses to conflict, some with violence and others with dialogue, this chapter examines the ways in which threat narratives shape ingroup responses to the Other. In threat narratives, blame quickly shifts from negative, individual attribution to collective denigration. "Who committed this crime, this injustice?" "Who aided the work of the criminals?" "Who supported their cause in word or deed?" The answers to these questions foster collective devaluation and in turn prove the immoral, uncivilized, or subhuman character of the Other.

How exactly do threat narratives lead to essentializing the Other-as-enemy? In this chapter, we develop the following themes: *(1) in the context of protracted social conflict the transition from polimodal identities to a single, dominant identity establishes a seemingly fixed opposition between "We" and "They"; (2) such an opposition is defined by categories of virtues and vices, conferring on group identities an axiology of difference; (3) a major source of retaliation and revenge rests on the influence of axiological difference on ingroup identity.* Without rehearsing the well-worn theme of the flagrant lies of propagandists and demagogues, we examine how the threatening Other is defined through an axiology that is distilled cognitively from stories of violence, victimization, and criminality and how that axiology is positively correlated to act violently.

The Dynamic of Identity and Conflict

Communities living in peace with their neighbors exhibit a multiplicity of identities, such as religious, national, regional, city, local community, and/or professional union. Some identities are more salient than others. Some identities are interconnected and mutually strengthened.

Even peaceful communities live with negativities of outsiders, as conveyed through derision, degradation, or accusations of immorality. For example, each nation in Europe possesses negative stereotypes and anecdotes about the other nations, even those with whom they have enjoyed centuries of peace. In Italy, inhabitants of the South and North attribute negative stereotypes to one another; Catalans and Andalusians in Spain perceive each other in derisive terms (Ros *et. al.* 2000).

Several factors influence the unfavorable perception of outgroups. First, the human need for differentiation can be inadequately satisfied in homogenous societies with negligible cultural diversity (Brewer 2000, 2001). In such cases people tend to develop ingroup loyalties to a community, city, or ethnic minority, stressing minor differences to outsiders within the wider society (Volkan 1997). Second, since positive social identity is formed on the basis of favorable social comparisons (Tajfel 1986; Turner 1994), members of any ingroup tend to denigrate the outgroup. Thus, certain stereotypes, biases and prejudices shape ingroup identity. Third, even in situations of economic and social equality, operating ingroup/outgroup comparisons lead inevitably to an underestimation of the economic and social powers of the ingroup, as well as to perceptions of relative deprivation, thus fueling further negativities (Davis 1959; Gurr 1993; Runciman 1966).

Asymmetrical status or inequality is the fourth factor in the negative estimation of outgroups. In stratified societies with economic and political inequality, minority groups and groups with low status experience a stronger sense of collective self and more ingroup homogeneity (Brewer 2000; Ellemers, Kortekaas & Ouwerkerk 1999; Simon 1992; Simon & Hamilton 1994). Their concerns about social identity, self-esteem, and dignity, combined with the perceived insecurity attendant upon their lower status, lead to stronger ingroup bias and negative projections (Gerard & Hoyt 1974; Mullen 1992; Sachdev & Bourhis 1984). For those communities with a history of intergroup violence, ingroup identity solidarity tends to supersede other kinds of identities.

Inequality and a history of conflictual relations can exaggerate unfavorable images. Nevertheless, cross-cutting practices, such as intermarriages, can maintain stability and balance within the larger identity system.

For communities engaged in generations of hostility, the multiplicity of group identities converges to a single dominant category, possibility retaining the symbols of a nationality, ethnicity, or religion. This unified, privileged identity is then juxtaposed against that of the dangerous Other. Members of different groups with multiple identities seek in their primary social identity a sense of security and moral legitimacy. Reliance on ideological myth becomes a powerful instrument for shaping ingroup identity, demonizing the Other, and providing cohesion in dangerous world.

For example, in Bosnia, conflicts over employment, social welfare and political influence were framed in religious terms, rather than regional or class terms. Despite closer relations between ethnic groups than between regional groups in pre-war Bosnia, a new powerful categorization of religious and ethnic differences emerged, defining boundaries among Serbs, Slovaks and Bosniyaks. This differentiation immediately provoked the perception of other groups as evil and stressed moral authority of the ingroup.

Characterizing the Threatening Other

The "true purpose" of violence often confounds its victims. For survivors of genocide, or relatives of torture victims, simple questions about the purpose of their ordeal quickly escalate to complexities. Uncertainties about the perpetrators feed the panic that follows an attack. Who committed this crime? Will it happen again? What will they do next? And what is our standing in the world? Such questions provoke an inspection into the intentions, motives, purposes, and character of the unknown Other. Victims form stories about the Other that convert the threat from private episodes confronting individuals to a shared public danger. The evolving public discourse makes sense of the violence by conveying the "truth" about the perpetrators.

Storytellers infuse the narratives with moralisms about the criminal's reprehensible actions. Many threat narratives address at least one of the following three themes: normative agency, predictability, and global positioning. First, storytellers progress easily from outlining behaviors of criminals to their depraved character. Never limited to the empirical "facts" about the criminal's behaviors, threat narratives are infused with moral indictment. The notion of criminal responsibility implies both causal efficacy and moral culpability. Threat narratives seek to explain the criminals' normative agency—their comprehensive culpability—as it were. Within the threat narratives, the violent act reveals agents' motives, intentions, plans, projections, and future actions. The familiar duality between pure description and moralistic judgment is abandoned in threat narratives. The truth about an agent's capacity to exert influence merges with normative denunciation. As victims of torture, rape, and brutality recount their personal suffering, axiological differences emerge. A threat exhibits a vice, and a vice tends to be associated with a calamity, tragedy, or severe hardship. The virtues (kindness, sincerity, honesty, or personal sacrifice) are contrasted with vices (unkindness, insincerity, dishonesty, or brutality). Both virtues and vices are manifested in very different behaviors (MacIntyre 1981, 205).

A second question addressed through threat narratives centers on the predictability of additional crimes. "Will they strike again?" "Will we (the good people) be victimized by their criminality?" "What will happen as we confront enemies at our gate, or possibly within our midst?" The fear of the unknown, of the unknowable consequences of future violence, is one of the most disturbing aspects of threats, whether real or fabricated. Pivotal elements about past encounters are distilled, and future possibilities are anticipated. The meaning of violence goes beyond the immediacy of a physical episode—it can alter the social landscape of a community.[1] In recounting such horror, storytellers strive towards, but rarely attain, a single coherent framework for explaining and predicting violence, and for charting a path from past to future. However, the veracity of such narratives can never be demonstrated through scientific methods associated with empirical testing of hypotheses. Predictions about the long-range actions of remote groups of individuals based on a few stories of past behavior are at best highly speculative, and at worse purely fabricated. Typically, the inherently dangerous character of remote, or even familiar, groups is immune to standard methods of scientific testing. Phenomenological methods are needed to assess those characterizations that are encased in normative terms.

A third question addressed, at least implicitly, through threat narratives concerns the normative standing of the ingroup in relation to the threatening Other. Psychological studies of religious-based terrorism show how terrorists committed to a divine authority acquire feelings of absolution and adornment. Such feelings rest on the belief in a sacred covenant with a higher authority. The devotee feels cleansed of feelings of badness, self-loathing, inferiority, and insignificance (Piven 2002, 120), ironically through acts of violence that would generally engender those feelings in the first place. In recounting the morally reprehensible actions of members of the outgroup, storytellers offer the faithful ingroup a scenario for establishing a moral separation from criminals. The faithful ally themselves with those who exemplify civility, morality, and virtue. By reassuring their own sense of virtue, the faithful reestablish their moral privilege and reassure themselves of their existential orientation in a world of violence and evil. The "good people" secure their "higher" standing in a dangerous world, rewarding the faithful and comforting the "innocent."

Threat narratives shape value commitments that intensify group differences. Listeners are carried, as it were, across an analytical boundary between what is true about the act to what is wrong with the criminals. The capacity of the threatening Other to act becomes inseparable from their degenerate character. To its victims, the enemy is definable by two essential traits—their agency and immorality.

Underpinning the threat narrative is a system of normative positioning of groups. Normative positioning captures one aspect of social encounters (Harré and Van Langenhove 1999). More than simply a distillation of prescriptions and injunctions, a normative position encapsulates a set of moral obligations, rights, duties, and expectations that guide individuals in their interactions. A positioning system comprises a set of rules and resources that are deployed for acting and thinking, for doing and reflecting, or for living and understanding. In relation to a normative order, individuals can adopt, locate themselves within, be pushed into, be displaced from, or be refused access to the home or outside group (Harré and Van Langenhove 1999, 5-6). The normative order legitimizes group decisions and actions.

The comprehensive adherence to a particular religious faith can provide a strict normative order. For devout followers of a religious tradition, a covenant with God includes embracing "His" understanding of the normative order. A religious order can be particularly intransigent, since such an order originates in the mythic origins of a sacred past and extends into an indefinite future. Additionally, normative ordering is always responsive to modulation from accounts of new occurrences (Moghaddam 1999, 77). Moral positioning reflects a tension between stability and change, between fixed identities and social border crossings. New experiences pose a risk to the stability of a moral order.

To illustrate the three themes of threat narratives—normative agency, predictability, and global positioning—we turn to the case of the

1994 genocide in Rwanda. Before the Rwandan genocide, the country's radio stations delivered intense expressions of hatred and fears to a wide audience (Chrétien 1995, 68). Who are the Tutsi? What will they do? What is our moral relationship to them? Listeners heard that Tutsi were foreigners, committed to stealing power from Hutus by changing their identities and acquiring the outward expressions of Hutu—the genuine Rwandans (Klinghoffer 1998, 37). The Tutsi were, presumably, deviously infiltrating powerful positions of the state, economy, and religious institutions, positions that rightfully belonged to Hutus.

As the Hutu demonize the Tutsi, the Hutu must also fear future attacks (the second question). From the radio broadcasts, the Tutsi were depicted as "the enemy," as seeking to kill Hutu on a massive scale, hoping to conquer lands of the genuine Rwandans (Hutus).[2] These messages demanded Hutu vigilance against the Tutsi manipulations, exposing their lies, condemning their declarations, and unveiling their evil plans. Fear was intensified by the uncertainty of where and when they would strike. Such messages condemned Hutus for their naivety in the face of such machinations, of failing to understand the depth of Tutsi commitment (Klinghoffer 1998, 37).

This combination of immorality and unpredictability in the actions of the Other leads to a sense of instability in the world. Illustrating the third question answered by threat narratives, the apparent threat to Hutu survival promoted an existential need to reaffirm their own moral status in such a world. The Hutus needed to regain their sense of relative moral superiority over the Tutsi. The faithful need to feel absolved for the past indiscretions, and justified in the sacrifices that lay ahead.

Axiological Difference

What are the sources of ethnic violence?[3] Reflection on the three themes presented above suggests the importance—indeed the centrality—of an axiology of difference (AD) in the conversion of private hatreds to public devaluations. One example of axiological differentiation is the practice and process of stigmatization.

Global devaluation of the Other creates a kind of security that remedies the fears brought about by chaos and violence. By externalizing an evil to a stigmatized group, one is "saved," living in a state of grace, purified in one's dealings with the "unclean" Other, regardless of what those dealings might entail.[4] One finds one's place in the world of virtuous figures by projecting responsibility for evil deeds to a stigmatized group. As an added bonus, the moral sanctity of the "untainted" ingroup is solidified. Stigmatization, the practice of marking certain individuals or groups as tainted, diminishes the moral worth, political autonomy, or social status of those groups and individuals. Character traits of individuals are converted to negativities of the stigmatized group. The group is viewed as unjust, immoral, uncivilized, or possibly inhuman simply because of their membership, their assigned social identity. Stigmatized groups are marginalized, viewed as threatening, and often reassigned to a separate social space.[5] Over time, the stigmatized group can become the scapegoat, responsible for assorted crimes, injustices, or even a general state of disorder. Even cases of an involuntary stigma, such as a physical handicap, can lead to attribution of a vicious character.

The conversion of private hatreds to public devaluations, whether through the process of stigmatization or the nurturing of threat narratives, becomes a major source of protracted conflicts. As previously mentioned, such conversion is underpinned by an axiology of difference that defines social divisions in normative terms.

Of course, AD has no physical existence *per se*. It "exists" only as constructions used for addressing the three themes of agency, predictability, and normative order mentioned above. Stories of violence and victims, dangers and safety, enemies and heroes, foster construction of normative boundaries. As storytellers ascribe blame and condemn the evil-doings of the Other, ingroup virtues are solidified. The institutions and policies of the faithful are glorified—indeed almost purified—when contrasted with those of the vilified Other. AD emboldens the ingroup to create, maintain, and reinforce certain social relations, as well as prohibit, close off, and denigrate other kinds of social relationships. Yet, axiological differences are dynamic, continually being reconfigured as a result of shifting boundaries of Self and Other. Such constructions defy explanation through the familiar scientific categories of true/false, rational/irrational, and real/unreal. Appeal to empirical data, coherent scientific theories, and corroborated causal hypotheses alone cannot demonstrate the negativities of the dangerous Other.

Some may object that the notion of axiological difference is undermined by the fundamentalist attribution error. According to this error, people tend to explain negative behaviors of others by overemphasizing their character traits, while underemphasizing circumstantial factors that influenced behaviors. Based on this error, explanations of outgroup violence would be found in negative dispositions of the Others, but the similar behaviors of ingroup members are rationalized by the circumstances of the social environment.

But this apparent polarity in thinking between character traits and circumstantial influences is misleading. Our study of threat narratives shows that the rationale for ingroup actions relies not only on circumstances surrounding ingroup actions but also on deeply embedded dispositional characterizations. To protect the homeland, and those born within its borders, actions are rationalized through categories of virtues and vices. Responding to the enemies lurking at a nation's borders, the "good citizens" demand security, and may demand destruction of potential invaders. In so doing, they find solace in their sense of moral superiority to the Other, often associated with the need to preserve "mankind," "civilization," or "social order." The exploits of heroes, the strength of the leaders, and the sacrifices of the population promote moral distancing from evildoers. As hostilities continue over time, the "necessity of circumstance" is inseparable from perceived axiological differences.

The dynamism of AD is revealed in three kinds of constructed forms: mythic narrative, sacred icons, and normative orders.

Mythic narrative

Stories of the threatening Other gain potency through dissemination of shocking images, harrowing anecdotes, and accounts of violence. Over time, such stories solidify perceptions of the Other through seemingly fixed negativities that are grounded, presumably, in a common place of origin, a shared ancestry, or common flaws. Through the power of such images, certain particularities of places, times, and actors become sacred to both storytellers and listeners.[6]

Axiological differences are shaped by episodes occurring in a mythic past and that exude the sacred. Mythic events do not occur in chronological time. On the contrary, mythic history conveys its own time.[7] An episode that becomes sacred is venerated in a way that lifts it outside the tide of sequential events, as if it reigns over almost the whole experiential world.[8] The sacred episodes acquire archetypical meanings that shape group consciousness and contribute to the mythic narratives that color their perceptions of the Other. A sacred episode becomes a prototype of a normative order. The sacred/profane duality at work in the process of axiological differentiation defines momentary gods, acquiring mythic form as "victims," "criminals," or "heroes."

Children's stories highlight positive and negative prototypes of behaviors. Parents and teachers shape children's persona by recounting the exploits of heroes and villains. Children identify with the positive traits of certain figures in the story, linking their own identity to that of the hero, generating a collective sense of pride and self-esteem that comes from virtue, goodness, and achievement. The threatening, aggressive, and vicious character of the villains they encounter in the stories is associated with members of their society's outgroup. The negative consequences of the villains' actions are conveyed in terms of shame, loss, and failure. Ingroup identity is developed and reformulated by the process of intergroup interaction, i.e., during the process of raising children (Barth 1969).

Mythic narratives often relay on prototypes of positive or negative personalities (Turner 1994). The need for clarity and coherence in such an evaluation promotes agreement among other members of the ingroup. Members of the ingroup that conform to the positive prototypes are estimated as having positive morality, while members of the outgroup that exhibit characteristics similar to the negative prototypes are estimated as having aberrant or even no morality. Such a sense of instilled morality enables children to socialize in their group and to interact harmoniously among members of their group as they develop.

Thus, this social self-concept includes bequeathed memories of the ingroup and serves as a basis for negative estimation of other groups.

Iconic Order

In protracted violent conflict, enemy images have stunning effects on the "righteous" tribes, marking a major stage in characterizing others as dangerous. Enemy images are lifted above the immediacy and locality of a particular encounter, exceeding the conditions of their empirical origins. (Consider, for example, the photograph of U.S. soldiers raising the American flag on Iwo Jima—this image, initially bound to a particular place and time, has become a powerful icon.) Emerging from specific storylines about localized episodes, icons function as the graphic expressions of negativities. A particular episode, event, action, or encounter is privileged, venerated, and almost sanctified in this transition in the minds of the faithful. Certain impressions produce demonic images, adding to the religious significance of profane episodes.[9] Viewed through such images, a stranger's actions function as *prototypes* of their unjust, immoral, uncivilized, or possibly inhuman character.

Icons appear frequently in eschatological stories of religious traditions. The motif (symbolic content) of such an order is idealized and other-worldly. By linking sensory images to cognitive content, the iconic order exhibits a projective capability, opening avenues to a charged realm, typically inhabited by figures, whether imaginary or real, of a scared past. Through the use of icons, uncertainties and doubts about the Other are suppressed. Complexities about their character are replaced by emotionally-charged images. This icon-making contributes to global denigration of the Other.

Each icon converts (individual) images of a particular action, experience, episode, encounter, or event, into (collective) symbols intelligible to group. For example, during military training, both the enemy's demonic character and the warrior virtues are depicted through iconic projections. Such virtues center on a sacred home, and link nativeness to a territory, grounding ingroup identity in the geographic roots of a land.

A close association between people and place, between group identity and a territory, are included in the "natural" order of things. A nationality seems to be forever linked to a homeland. Liisa Malkki argues that the territorial icons associated with terms like "native," "indigenous" and "nature" foster essentialist notions of social identity, rooted in the soil of a territory. Territorization becomes a metaphor for a nation's people, as in "the land rose in rebellion." Such a reliance on territoriality suggests a static ontology as the "natural" condition, as if the borders between nations are rooted in nature itself (Malkki 1995).[10] The rigidity provided by this perceived ontology can fuel mutual hatreds among protagonists of protracted conflict.

The threatening Other is often dehumanized through bestial images. For example, Hutu propagandists resorted to species-attribution, portraying Tutsi through stunning images of insects, reptiles, and predators. They depicted the Tutsi as groups of cockroaches preparing inconspicuously for unspeakable crimes against Hutu society. Hutu propagandists also portrayed the Tutsi as snakes posing as "real" Hutus. The snake imagery here reinforces characteristics of secrecy, malice, and predation. The Tutsi men coerce their women to seduce Hutus for purposes of conquering Rwanda (Klinghoffer 1998, 10).[11] Because the Tutsi were tainted as dangerous foreigners, Hutus were implored to exterminate them. Hutus were told to "get to work," "clear the bush," and "clean around their houses," euphemisms for killing Tutsi (Klinghoffer 1998, 45).

Consider the conflict in Senegal over Casamance. Casamance is separated almost entirely from the rest of Senegal (which is administered by French) by the Gambia, which was colonized by the British Empire. Casamance also differs from the rest of Senegal by climate; Senegal has a dry climate with a rainy season of only three months, while Casamance is green and has sufficient rain. Many historians stress that Casamance had been part of Senegal long before the colonial era and peacefully co-existed with the rest of the Senegalese nation and people. Other scholars show that until the early years of the 20th century, Casamance was involved in many insurgencies and forms of resistance against French control, while most of the Senegalese nation was relatively peaceful. Because of these perceived "rebellious" stories and icons of the

Casamance populations, many Senegalese, explaining the cause of the current crisis in Casamance, label the province a "rebellious" one. The Senegalese stress ethnic and cultural differences that may cause potential conflict and label any "Diola" a "rebel", regardless of whether she or he is a member or supporter of the secessionist movement. Such global denigration of all "Diolas", bolstered by threat narratives and iconic depictions, exemplifies the axiological differentiation we have been outlining. In reality, the same distinctness could be applied to all other ethnic groups in the region, which evolved as separate political entities before merging into one Senegalese nation—the Bassari in the extreme southeast, the Pulaar in the north, and the Wolof in the west central part of the country. These ethnic differences influenced each group's negative view of the others, but did not produce violence before the Casamance conflict. The attribution of icons and political labels like "rebellious" resulted in over-emphasizing of the distinctness of the Casamance and Diola identities and played important role in developing of ethnic and regional identity and causes violent conflict in the region.

Normative Order

A third element underpinning the process of axiological difference centers on the formation of a normative order that is defined through dualities of sacred/profane, good/evil, or virtuous/vicious. To accept "who we are," it becomes necessary to define "who we are not," that is, "who are the Others." Such divisions are often contested and emotionally-charged. For example, consider the charged meanings of such terms as "Israeli," "Arab," "Hamas," "Palestinian" (Rouhana 1997). At the same time, the formation of salient identity fosters stereotypes, prejudice, and discrimination, while avoiding direct interactions with its members. By contrast, people with non-salient ethnic identity tend to perceive ingroup and outgroup as neighbors in a common society (Korostelina 2003, 2004).

Any duality of ingroup/outgroup identities rests on value judgments about how the world should be organized. Such judgments in turn promote a kind of prototype modeling. A prototype provides an idealized model *of* particular experiences or occurrences, offering the symbolic content of salient identity features, categories, or processes. But in its projective function, the prototype emerges as a model *for* later generations of storytellers in their efforts to grasp and express the meanings of new occurrences. In this latter respect, the model guides storytellers in ways of speaking and thinking about subsequent encounters.

In particular, the construction of teliomorphic models underpins the salience of ingroup/outgroup identities. By definition, a teliomorphic model provides an idealized redepiction of a subject matter in a more perfect form. Teliomorphic models of group identities are constructed in binary form, lending an aura of eternal truth to in-group virtues and out-group vices. The model's properties improve upon those of the narrative's subject matter, re-envisioning an idealized totality of the past. Of course, such a model has no real-world existence *per se* apart from the mythic constructions that are distilled from a repository of beliefs.

Every nation-state presupposes a normative order—a community of individuals bound by reciprocal moral obligations. This arose from the formation of a system of nation-states. Following the Treaty of Westphalia of 1648, a bargain arose between the state and its subjects: the state would protect its subjects from the ravages of war in exchange for the subjects offering their material and human resources necessary to fight. Over time, the state became authorized by international law to take action under certain conditions against those who violate such obligations. Because of the way the nation-sate has developed, the realism of the political order is inseparable from a specific normative commitment to keep dangers out (Mansbach, R. W. and F. Wilmer 2001, 74).

Consider for example how the military blends political realities with normative commitments. Military training, in particular reinforces a value-system of ingroup virtues and outgroup vices. In conferring a new person on young recruits, the normative differences between the ingroup virtues and outgroup vices correspond to the differences between the sacred homeland and the profane foreign land. To prepare recruits for combat, pain, and extreme sacrifices, the nationalism of military training relies on mythic dualities of scared/profane, good/evil, and virtuous/vicious. The homeland becomes a sacred realm that offers a bounty of riches for her people (as well as for potential conquerors). The homeland as defined in military training is threatened, subject to danger, and vulnerable to an enemy's attacks. An embattled form of nationalism thus sanctifies the soldier's mission. Those born in the homeland are virtuous, just as those born in the enemy region possess an immoral character. The distinction that seems to be rationalized by geographical separations offers justification for "good violence," which stands in stark contrast to the enemy's "bad violence." The values of the "faithful" enable them to act from a place of moral superiority over the enemy.

For an example of normative commitments at work in situations of violence, consider the savagery exhibited by the Japanese Imperial Army during the massacre at Nanking. The brutality inflicted on the Chinese was unthinkable up to that time. Men were forced to rape their own children or mothers at gunpoint for the amusement of the Japanese soldiers. Over 20,000 women from the ages 7-77 were raped, and then murdered or turned into sex slaves. Living victims were used as bayonet practice; some were doused with gasoline and burned; some buried alive or were forced to bury their friends and family alive; and many were decapitated. At the end of six weeks of savagery, the Japanese Imperial Army had murdered 300,000 people in Nanking. For Japanese soldiers, the Chinese were seen as subhuman, in part because of their "cowardly" retreat and surrender following the Japanese invasion. With this characterization, the Japanese felt justified in treating them as animals. The current Japanese government refuses to admit or apologize for the atrocities committed by Japanese soldiers during World War II. (In the light of this refusal, the nomination of Japan to the United Nations Security Council has provoked a rapid growth of anti-Japanese sentiment among Chinese people.)

Accusations of immoral behavior, such as human rights abuses, can pose threats to the ingroup sense of virtue. In many cases, such recognition provokes strong resistance. For example, relations between Armenia and Turkey have been strained since the period spanning 1915-1923, when Turkish soldiers killed more than 1.5 million Armenians. Today, Armenians insist that this calamity constitutes genocide, but the Turkish government denies the characterization of genocide, declaring that Armenians died in a civil war that broke out during the First World War. Recently, scholars planned a conference in Istanbul in the summer of 2005 to analyze these varying conceptions of the events from 1915-1923. The very notion of such a conference provoked strong negative reactions from political leaders in Turkey. The Minister of Justice stressed in his speech to Parliament that conference represented to Turkey a stab in the back.

Identity Justice

So, in cases of protracted conflict, threat narratives reaffirm images of a dominant group in ways that suppress individualistic values, lifestyles, and actions. Such constructions are tied to fabricated notions of historical inevitability, rationalizing national policies by appeal to the course of world events. Framed in terms of virtues and vices, such notions can be totally captivating, fostering a need for unquestioned obedience of the ingroup members.

In protracted social conflict every protagonist group carries the banner of justice into battle. How "justice" is defined in such campaigns rests on the group's perceptions of a dangerous Other. Consider, for example, the connection between nationalism and a notion of international justice. Nationalism rests on a demand for equity (justice) in relations among other nation-states, suggesting the need to stability of the system of nation-states. The demand for equity among nations has the effect of promoting intra-national homogeneity, suppressing axiological differences among a nation's social groups, and disregarding the political claims of the disenfranchised within each nation.

The kind of justice tied to nationalism contrasts sharply with the justice associated with demands of indigenous groups. Such demands privilege the historical originality of the "first peoples" who of course deserve a special set of political rights[12] (Rothbart forthcoming). In narratives about the plight of indigenous groups, the very notion of indigenous identity is infused with a demand for "justice" to redress past crimes, eliminate the instruments of oppression, and reduce the conditions of structural violence against these original inhabitants.

Those within the indigenous group find unity in their shared experiences, and solidarity in their struggles against the nation's "high power" groups.

The justice narratives of nationalism and those of indigenous identity share the following feature: both types of narratives function cognitively as second-order structures that organize stories of violence and victims, dangers and purity, evil and virtue. This organization fosters a sense of ingroup/outgroup positioning in a dangerous world and offers a rationale for actions.

The sense of ingroup justice rises from, and is in continual dialogue with, the myth-making powers of storytelling. How should this contrast be defined? From a scientific perspective, historical events occur *in* chronological time. But for groups traumatized by past violence, events acquire a mythic quality, defined by categories of the sacred and the profane. By "reliving" its traumas through narrative, the group finds meaning in mythic past. Both kinds of justice narratives prioritize a mythic history, enabling its members to visualize the future by knowing the sacred past. Through such storytelling practices, axiological divisions are solidified. This relation between the mythic past and axiological differences is depicted in the following figure:

Teliomorphic Model

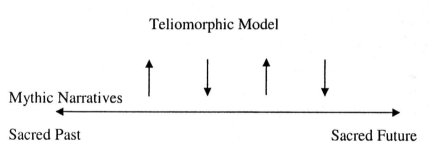

Figure 3.1
Mythic Time

In Figure 3.1 a teliomorphic model of the social world is a second-order idealization of first-order narratives. This model is not static. It continually changes from the infusion of new, potentially sacred, episodes. In turn, the application of the teliomorphic model to new circumstances rests on the process of narrative exemplification. In this figure the symbol '↑' represents a sacred episode that is recounted through generations of storytelling. The process of narrative exemplification is represented as ↓, which depicts the transition from second-level teliomorphic model to first-level determinations of right and wrong, good and bad. The application of AD to present or future scenarios thus confers a sense of stability to ingroup identity, and consistency (even fairness) in the implementation norms associated with an AD. The virtue of justice demands uniform application of the axiological order, establishing a moral requirement for consistency, that is, always doing the right thing under similar conditions. Exactly what those circumstances are rests on the nuances of ingroup value-commitments.

Modeling Axiological Difference

Again, protagonists of violent conflict often legitimize their struggle through stories of "real" differences among nations, ethnic groups, or races. Yet, such stories are infused with normative judgments. All race-talk, for example, is inescapably axiological, and is never completely reducible to physically real distinctions among groups. Over time, the ingroup both fears and needs an "enemy." They act from an embedded sense of normative commitment that includes ideas of group (axiological) differences. AD is a set of constructions that are used to validate, vindicate, rationalize, or legitimize actions, decisions, and policies. Such constructions serve to solidify the ingroup members, and assist them in making sense of their hardships and struggles. Yet, group differences are always vulnerable to shifting circumstances from life's encounters and from evolving ways of thinking about what is right and wrong.

We recommend that each AD associated with protagonist groups can be studied with respect to two variables: the degree of collective generality and the degree of axiological balance.

1. Collective generality. One significant factor in the analysis of AD is the degree of collective generality. This refers to the ways in which

ingroup members categorize the Other, how they simplify, or not, their essential character. Specifically, we offer the following four criteria for determining the collective generality for a particular ingroup:

1. homogeneity of perceptions and behaviors of outgroup members,
2. long-term stability of their beliefs, attitudes, and actions,
3. resistance to change in their ideas about the Other,
4. the scope or range of category of the Other.

A high level of collective generality reflects a notion of the outgroup as homogeneous, exhibiting unchanging behaviors, committed to long-term fixed beliefs and values, and projecting a wide-ranging, possibly global, scope. A low degree of collective generality leads to the perception of the outgroup as differentiated, subject to change, manifesting various kinds of behaviors, and relatively limited in scope. For example, adherents of so-called fundamentalist religions tend to rely on a high level of collective generality. This is evident in the narratives associated with some traditions of an apocalyptic struggle with the cosmic forces of evil. In other conflict settings the protagonist groups adopt a low degree of collective generality, which represents a complex and nuanced understanding of the Other.

But the degree of generality is always subject to change. For example, escalation of hostilities can prompt protagonists to broaden their target from a local group to an entire race, ethnic group, nationality, or culture. This has the effect of globalizing the conflict. Such an expansion can be represented analytically as a transformation from low generality to high generality of AD. In initial stages of a conflict, the outgroup tends to be perceived in its diversity, as evident in rival political parties, social movements, and value commitments. As hostilities escalate, the degree of collective generality increases. The outgroup is perceived as a monolithic unit, acting as a single "entity," speaking with one voice usually through a glorified leader. In such cases the ingroup tends to expand the category of the outgroup to include more and more nationalities, religious and ethnic groups, or races.

High Degree of Generality

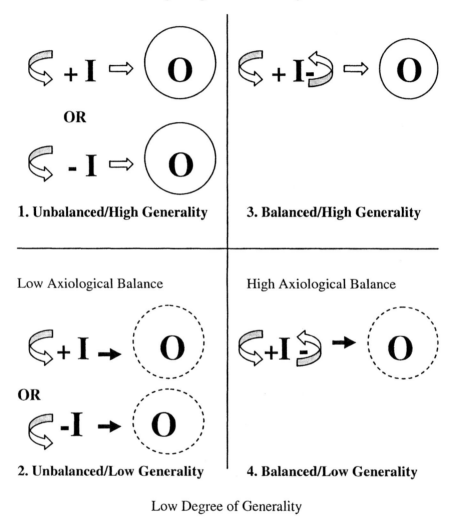

Low Degree of Generality

Figure 3.2

Four Types of Axiological Difference

2. Axiological Balance. A second factor in defining axiological difference centers on the notion of balance. Axiological balance refers to a kind of parallelism of virtues and vices attributed to groups. When applied to stories about the Other, a balanced axiology fosters positive and negative characterizations. Under some conditions, the members of the group act virtuously; under other conditions they act viciously. With a balanced axiology the faithful adopt a stance of judicious recognition in the "goodness" and "badness" of the Other. Groups with high degree of axiological balance recognize their own moral failings.

In contrast, a low degree of axiological balance corresponds to a monolithic depiction of both ingroup and outgroup identities. This tends to promote a "tunnel consciousness," and a diminished capacity for independent thought. In its extreme form, a low axiological balance is correlated to exaggeration, inflation, and fabrication of outgroup vices and ingroup glories. The "Them/Us" duality seems fixed in the timeless social order. With a fabricated sense of its collective virtues, the ingroup promotes a sense of moral supremacy over the outgroup. Such an unbalanced depiction of group differences provides a ground for a struggle against criminal elements of the world.

The range of axiological balance and collective generality can be depicted in Figure 3.2 above. In this figure +I and -I represent positive and negative ingroup identities, respectively. The symbol ⟹ refers to a projection of characteristics to an outgroup. A "dotted" circle refers to low degree of collective generality.

Two variables—axiological balance and collective generality—define collective axiology for each identity group. To repeat from Chapter 1, a collective axiology is a system of value-commitments that offers moral guidance in relations with those within, and outside of, the group. It provides a sense of life and world, serves as criteria for understanding actions and events, and regulates ingroup behaviors. With these criteria, individuals clarify group membership. Armed with its collective axiology, a group traces its path from a sacred past and transcends the finitude of individual life. A collective axiology extends retrospectively from the salient episodes of the past to a vision of the uncertain future. An individual's identity and values that are acquired at birth and left behind at death exist before that birth and behind that death.

Quadrant 1 represents the pattern of *low* axiological balance and *high* collective generality. Such a pattern is familiar to analysts of protracted conflict. The sacred ingroup requires loyalty and obedience. This kind of identity is often associated with extreme forms of nationalism, fascism, racism, and sectarianism.

As this unbalance axiology becomes embedded in group identities, the negativities can be blinding. Over time, the ingroup loses its ability to see any virtues in the Other, to understand their complexities, and to evaluate their decisions. In the totalizing effect of protracted conflict, visions of evil tend to overpower visions of goodness. The retributive justice of "an eye for an eye" can blind protagonists to exactly what a just world would look like. The vices of the Other tend to dominate the social landscape. In many conflict settings, the symbols of negativities— the images of evil-doings of the Other— are far more mesmerizing than images of ingroup virtues. The cries for vengeance can galvanize the "faithful" and motivate them in collective violence. The freedoms to shape one's own individual identity, to retrieve the sacred stories of the past, and to envision a promising future are undermined.

When carrying out violent actions against a perceived enemy and enduring enormous sacrifices, combatants often recount the enemy's criminality, hear the cries of innocent victims, recite the words of the inspiring leader, the sufferings of the helpful and weak, and the malice of the enemy. Such stories can quickly become fairy tales of horror and grief. The enemy might be likened to witches who devour the helpless. Their evil-deeds are believed to continue unless heroes from the sacred tribe intervene with presumably special powers. In religious conflict, retribution can be justified and tied to promises of adornment by a transcendent Being. In such situations, faithful defenders of the ingroup believe that their actions will lead to spiritual glory, and will allow them entrance to the holiest regions that are reserved for sacred figures. Similarly, in protecting the nation from potential invaders, the young military recruit is prepared to offer his/her life in exchange for eternal glory, seeking to walk in the path of the nation's sacred figures. (See Chapter 10 by Alpher and Rothbart in this Volume.)

Quadrant 2 represents cases of *low* axiological balance in which group differences are *not* generalizable. With respect to low axiological balance, the ingroup views itself as morally pure, sacred, glorified, while the outgroup is characterized as exhibiting mixed values and virtues. This kind of mixed attribution of values can be found in the patriotic sentiments of a nation's powerful social classes. For example, East Timoreans continue to struggle for ethnic identity, as they seek to overcome the "totalizing" effects of Indonesian nationalism. (See Chapter 8 below by Lena Tan, "From Incorporation to Disengagement: East Timor and Indonesian Identities, 1975-1999").

Quadrant 3 portrays a high degree of axiological balance and a high degree of collective generality. The ingroup identity associated with this quadrant are characterized by positive and negative values. Individuals are relatively free to criticize the ingroup. The characteristics of groups in Quadrant 3 are also evident in Sandra Cheldelin's study of gender stereotyping as a major source of violence against women (See Chapter 11 in this volume by Sandra Cheldelin, "Gender and Violence: Redefining the Moral Ground.")

Quadrant 4 represents groups with a balanced axiology and low projectability. In such cases, both the ingroup and the outgroup identities portray a balanced axiology of virtues and vices. With such a balance, individuals are able to openly criticize ingroup and outgroup characteristics. Nevertheless, the support and loyalty to ingroup values in this quadrant are important and ingroup identity is relatively salient. This collective axiology is found in liberal and humanistic movements, peacebuilders, and human right advocates. This is illustrated in the humanitarian ideals in the field of international relations. (See Chapter 6 below "Humanitarianism and Intolerance: Two Contemporary approaches to the Other" by Peter N. Stearns).

Conclusion

The analysis above leads to the following six conclusions:

- The prolongation of social conflicts finds its source in the value-commitments of protagonist groups.

- In protracted conflicts, axiological differences have a unifying effect on members of the ingroup, compensating for fears and uncertainties brought on by hostilities.
- Axiological differences promote a mythic ordering of episodes based on dualities of sacred/profane, good/evil, and virtuous/vicious.
- The agency of the threatening Other is both causal and normative.
- During periods of crisis, a core axiology tends to dominate the national, religious, or ethnic identities.
- Identity-justice functions cognitively as a second-order instrument for understanding and responding to perceived threats.

Reflection on AD invites attention to certain strategies for peacebuilding. Conflict resolution practitioners can deploy specific techniques for productive partnerships, based on peaceful concepts of the ingroup and centering on possible positive icons of the Other. Rather than transforming, suppressing, denigrating, or circumventing a community's collective axiology, conflict practitioners should exploit overlapping values embedded in the religious/cultural heritage of each group (Gopin 2000). The legacy of a religious tradition reveals both contributions to violence and the prospects for peacemaking. In recognition of this, analysts must be prepared to explore the particular value-commitments of adherents of relevant religious traditions.

Lasting peace requires transforming the collective consciousness of the ingroup, reversing the role as victim in relation to the "demonic" character of the Other. By asking "What can we do together to make our future better?", practitioners will change the emphasis of group narratives from opposition to mutual recognition of human rights. It is important to facilitate this transformation with narratives of pride and self-esteem. Practitioners can change the protagonists' scope of moral responsibility to include the well being of those outside of their home community. A spiral of retribution and retaliation can be reversed when protagonist groups expand their normative commitments associated with responsibilities, rights, and duties afforded to ingroup members. Such strategies are intended to undermine the polarity of Self and Other that seems to perpetuate conflictual relationships.

Notes

1. In committing a violent act, an agent is anticipating possibilities, imagining alternative scenarios in hypothetical pathways to the future (Emirbayer and Mische 1998).

2. Threat narratives in such broadcasts perpetuated the myth of Tutsi as invaders. The follow is an excerpt from such a broadcast (Klinghoffer 1998, 45):

> These people are not Rwandans, they are vengeful Ugandans. We hate them, we are disgusted with them, and nobody will accept that they take power. These people do not deserve to live in Rwanda or to represent Rwanda.

3. The levels-of-analysis framework seeks answers to this question through various levels of a social/political system. For a summary of the levels-of-analysis model, see (Levy 1998). Underpinning the levels-of-analysis framework are multiple meanings of the notion of a source of conflict, drawing attention to the poly-semantic character of "causation." In some contexts, "causation" refers to a causal mechanism of entities and forces that are responsible for patterns of behaviors. In another context, a cause refers to empirical regularity of observable events, as evident in casualty reports of battles. A third notion of causation is appropriate for revealing the psycho-dynamics of particularly powerful political leaders, exhibiting for example characteristics of abnormality or possibly insanity.

4. Edward Tiryakian, Chapter 13, *infra.*

5. Erving Goffman identified three kinds of stigmas. First, a stigma can be conferred on individuals with physical deformities, disabilities, and chronic diseases, precipitating an avoidance reaction from members of the wider community, or even acts of open hostility. Second, stigma can be conferred on individuals based on knowledge of their socially deviant behavior. Information about former criminals, political radicals, or religious heretics in a fundamentalist society can be a source of stigmatization. Third, stigma can be attributed to individuals because of their race, national origin, or religious heritage. A stigmatized person is separated, avoided, or occasionally even removed from society (Goffman 1974, Ch. 4).

6. The mythic elements of ethnic identity are well documented by anthropologists. The relative positions of groups emerge from jointly

6 The mythic elements of ethnic identity are well documented by anthropologists. The relative positions of groups emerge from jointly constructed storylines in which the groups play parts. According to Anthony Smith, an ethnic community is a named human population (1) with a myth of common ancestry (2), shared memories and historical experiences (3), and cultural elements (4), a link with a historic territory or homeland (5), and a measure of solidarity, that is, as sense of common ethnicity (6). (Smith 1996, 6).

7 To adherents of a strict religious tradition, sacred events become protophenomena, transcending the accidental circumstances of their empirical grounding (Cassirer 1947, 18-20).

8 E. Cassirer offers an excellent analysis of the differences between discursive thought, associated with scientific inquiry, and mythic thought associated with religious traditions (1955, 56).

9 E. Cassirer writes: "In stark uniqueness, the momentary god confronts us, not as part of some force, which may manifest itself everywhere, but as something that exists only here and now, in one indivisible moment of experience, and for only one subject whom it overwhelms and holds in thrall." (Cassirer 1947, 18-19).

10 Not all group identities rely on territorial icons. Malkki illustrates a de-territorialized identity in the displacement of Hutu refugees in Burundi. The Hutus refused to become naturalized, to put down roots in a place in which they did not belong. Their "true nation" was formed centrally by the "natives" in exile (1995, 66). In such cases, the problems of refugees, the homeless, and their wanderers, create pathological behavior, seen in other terms as a form of stigmatization. A de-territoriality epistemology of identities gives priority to shifting border conditions, potentially shaped, and reshaped, through the evolving borders, which are the markings of sameness and difference.

11 Before such ethnic hatreds conveyed by Hutu propagandists, Belgian colonial authorities exploited Hutu/Tutsi divisions for political purposes. The Tutsi were thought to have "nobler," more "naturally" aristocratic features in contrast to the "coarse" Hutus. Such racial fabrications rationalized, to the Belgians, the domination of the Tutsi over the Hutus throughout Rwanda. Belgians placed Hutus in forced labor camps, road construction, and forestry crews, while Tutsis were their taskmasters (Gourevitch 1998, 57-58).

12 The recognition of indigenous people is clearly documented in the proceedings of the Indian Assembly presiding over the Commission on the Right of Indigenous Peoples in Venezuela. See Villalón (2002).

References

Arendt, H. 1958. *The Human Condition.* Chicago: University of Chicago Press.

Barth, F. ed. 1969. *Ethnic groups and boundaries: The social organization of culture difference.* Boston: Little, Brown.

Brewer, M. B. 2001. "The Many Faces of Social Identity: Implications for Political Psychology." *Political Psychology,* no. 22, 115-126.

Brewer, M. B. 2000. "Superordinate Goals Versus Superordinate Identity as Bases of Intergroup Cooperation." Pp.117-132, in *Social Identity Processes,* edited by D. Capozza and R. Brown. London: Sage.

Cassirer, E. 1947. *Language and Myth.* New York. Dover Publications.

Cassirer, E. 1955. *The Philosophy of Symbolic Forms: Mythical Thought.* New Haven: Yale University Press.

Chrétien, J. P. 1995. *Rwanda: Les medias du genocide.* Paris: Karthala.

Davis, J.A. 1959 "A formal Interpretation of the Theory of Relative Deprivation," *Sociometry,* no. 22, 280-96.

Ellemers, N., Kortekaas, P. and Ouwerkerk, J. W. 1999. "Perceived Intragroup Variability as a Function of Group Status and Identification." *Journal of Experimental Social Psychology,* no. 31, 410-436.

Emirbayer, M. and Mische, A. 1998. "What is Agency?" *American Journal of Sociology,* vol. 103, no. 4, 962-1023.

Gerard, H., and Hoyt, M. F. 1974. "Distinctiveness of Social Categorization and Attitude toward Ingroup Members." *Journal of Personality and Social Psychology,* no. 29, 836-842.

Goffman, E. 1974. *Frame Analysis: An Essay on the Organization of Experience.* Cambridge: Harvard University Press.

Gopin, M. 2000. *Between Eden and Armageddon: the Future of World Religions, Violence, and Peacemaking.* Oxford; New York: Oxford University Press.

Gourevitch, P. 1998. *We Wish to Inform You that Tomorrow We Will Be Killed with Our Families: Stories from Rwanda.* New York: Picador.

Gurr, T. R. 1993. *Minorities at Risk: A Global View of Ethnopolitical Conflict.* Washington, D.C.: United States Institute of Peace.

Harré, R. and Van Langenhove, L. eds. 1999. *Positioning Theory: Moral Contexts of Intentional Action.* Oxford: Blackwell.

Klinghoffer, A. J. 1998. *The International Dimension of Genocide in Rwanda.* New York, N.Y.: New York University Press.

Korostelina, K. 2003. "The Multiethnic State-Building Dilemma: National and Ethnic Minorities' Identities in the Crimea." *National Identities*, no. 2, 141-159.

————. 2004. "The Impact of National Identity on Conflict Behavior: Comparative Analysis of Two Ethnic Minorities in Crimea." *International Journal of Comparative Sociology,* no. 3-4, 213-230.

Levy, J. S. 1998. "The Causes of War and the Conditions of Peace," *Annual Review of Political Science,* no. 1, 139-166.

Mansbach, R. W. and F. Wilmer 2001. "Borders and (Dis)orders: The Role of Moral Authority in Global Politics," Pp. 73-90, in *Identities, Borders, Orders: Rethinking International Relations Theory*, edited by M. Albert, D. Jacobson, and Y. Lapid., Minneapolis: University of Minnesota Press.

Malkki, L. 1995. "Refugees and Exile: From 'Refugee Studies' to the National Order of Things." *Annual Review of Anthropology*, no. 24, 495-523.

MacIntyre, A. C. 1981. *After virtue : a study in moral theory.* Notre Dame, Indiana: University of Notre Dame Press.

Moghaddam, F. A. 1999. "Culture and Private Discourse," Pp. 74-86, in *Positioning Theory: Moral Contexts of Intentional Action*, edited by R. Harré and L. Van Langenhove. Oxford: Blackwell.

Mullen, B., Brown, R., & Smith. 1992. "Ingroup Bias as a Function of Salience, Relevance, and Status: An Integration." *European Journal of Social Psychology*, no. 22, 103-122.

Piven, J. 2002. "On the Psychosis (Religion) of Terrorists," Pp. 119-148, in *The Psychology of Terrorism: Theoretical Understandings and Perspectives*, edited by C. Stout. London: Praeger.

Ros M., Huici C., Gomez A. 2000. "Comparative Identity, Category Salience and Intergroup Relations." Pp.81-95, in *Social Identity Processes*, edited by D. Capozza and R. Brown. London: Sage.

Rothbart, D. Forthcoming. "Social Justice and Indigenous Identities." *Social Justice*, no. 6.

Rouhana, N. 1997. *Palestinian Citizens in an Ethnic Jewish State: Identities in Conflict.* New Haven: Yale University Press.

Runciman, W.G. 1966. *Relative Deprivation and Social Justice.* London: Routledge and Kegan Paul.

Sachdev, I., and Bourhis, R.Y. 1984. "Minimal Majorities and Minorities." *European Journal of Social psychology*, no. 14, 35-52.

Simon, B. 1992. "The Perception of Ingroup and Outgroup Homogeneity: Re–Introducing the Intergroup Context." Pp. 1-30, in *European Review of Social Psychology* 3, edited by W. Stroebe and M. Hewstone, Chichester, UK: Wiley.

Simon, B. and Hamilton, D. 1994. "Self-Stereotyping and Social Context: The Effects of Relative Ingroup Size and Ingroup Status." *Journal of Personality and Social psychology*, no. 66, 699-711.

Smith, A. 1996. "Ethnic Identity." Chapter 2, in *Ethnic Conflict and International Security*, edited by J. Hutchinson and A. Smith, New York: Oxford University Press.

Tajfel, H. 1986. "The Social Identity Theory of Intergroup Behavior." Pp.7-24, in *Psychology of Intergroup Relations*, edited by S. Worshel and W. Austin. Chicago: Nelson–Hall.

Turner, J. C., Oakes, P. J., Haslam, S. A., & McGarty, C. 1994. "Self and Collective: Cognition and Social Context." *Personality and Psychology Bulletin,* no. 20, 454-463.

Villalón, M. E. 2002. "Do Differences Engender Rights? Indian and *Criollo* Discourses Over Minority Rights at the Venezuelan National Constituent Assembly." *Social Justice*, vol. 3, no. 1-2, 8-42.

Volkan, V. 1997. *Bloodlines: From Ethnic Pride to Ethnic Terrorism.* New York: Farrar, Straus, and Giroux.

Chapter 4

Identity Under Siege: Injustice, Historical Grievance, Rage, and the 'New' Terrorism [1]

Dennis J. D. Sandole

Introduction

Veteran *New York Times* columnist and Middle East observer Thomas Friedman has remarked that the London bombings of July 2005 were:

> not about the poverty of money [but] about the poverty of *dignity* and the *rage* it can trigger. One of the London bombers was married, with a young child and another on the way. I can understand, but never accept, suicide bombing in Iraq or Israel as part of a nationalist struggle. But when a British Muslim citizen, nurtured by that society, just indiscriminately blows up his neighbors and leaves behind a baby and pregnant wife, to me he has to be in the grip of a dangerous cult or preacher–dangerous to his faith community and to the world (emphasis added) (Friedman 2005).

So, why would a British-born and educated citizen blow himself up in order to kill anonymous others in the morning rush hour of one of the world's great cities? Many, including Londoners, would be unable to provide an adequate answer to this question other than, "He was brainwashed," "a fanatic," "crazy," or all of the above.

But any of these responses would miss a more nuanced explanation that falls between the cracks of discrete *identities*: Pakistani, Muslim,

British, European, minority, male. Indeed, one can hear young men in Leeds, Bradford, Birmingham, London, and elsewhere in Britain asking themselves, "Who [or *what*] am I?"

Whoever and whatever they tentatively conclude they might be, the National Front and other agents of the right wing in Britain and elsewhere have been calling them "WOGS," "niggers," and other epithets for years, even engaging every now and then in "Paki-bashing" to drive home the point that they are not wanted anywhere in the UK. The upshot is that they do not feel particularly "British" or whatever their parents originally were before coming to Britain.

In the midst of their identity ambiguity, discrimination, and marginalization, along comes a persuasive *Salafist* imam, friend, book, or video that reveals to them details of The Prophet, Islamic history, the Caliphate, the Crusades, lost glory, and how the *Crusaders*–Americans, British, Israelis, Russians, and others–are *still* perpetrating injustices against Muslims in Iraq, Afghanistan, Palestine, Chechnya, and elsewhere; in effect, continuing a genocidal strategy launched nearly a 1000 years ago by Christian Europeans to obliterate Islam.

They will also learn that the *Holy Qur'an* calls upon all Muslims worldwide to defend the *Umma* (the global Islamic community), if necessary even with their own bodies as delivery systems of death and destruction against non-Islamic infidels and Islamic apostates still attacking and oppressing Islam.

We have in these and other elements a toxic, combustible brew that can cohere into a compelling philosophy and strategy for filling the void of the impoverished Self with a sense of heroic meaning and purpose to rectify the injustices visited upon Muslims for centuries, including by their own governments, by attacking symbols and persons of the "double standards"-based world they live in.

The purpose of this chapter is to explore the complex etiology of the "new" terrorism by examining how *identity* and other factors may be playing a role in motivating Muslims (especially young males), including those born, raised, and educated in the West, to kill themselves in order to kill others, including their fellow countrymen and women and even co-religionists.

The "New" Terrorism

Although terrorism is as old as humankind itself (see Wheeler 1991; Friedman 2002), the attacks of 9/11, among others, are *"new"* for the following reasons:

1. They are "catastrophic" (see Hamburg 2002), causing the death and injury of hundreds or thousands of "soft targets" (i.e., innocent civilians).
2. They are launched from within the territory and/or against the civilian populations of major developed, former or current imperialist countries.
3. They tend to be carried out by young Muslims, usually males, prepared to give up their lives in the execution of their acts of violence (see *The 9/11 Commission Report* 2004).

Clearly, most "sensible" people throughout the world would define the "new" terrorism as unacceptable and demand that it be stopped. But in order to at least "manage" it to an acceptable degree, we must first study it to know what makes it "tick." We would then be able, in the long run, to deal effectively with its underlying causes and conditions, in addition to employing, in the short term, law enforcement and military resources to deal with its overt symptoms.

Origins of Violent Conflict

As the thinkers and practitioners of conflict resolution and peacebuilding attempt to prevent, among other things, future Yugoslavias, Rwandas, Columbine High Schools, *and* 9/11-type terrorist attacks, they may need to pay attention to a level of analysis that tends to be avoided for conceptual as well as ideological and emotional reasons: the *intra-psychic* level. If, as John Burton (1984) and Robert North (1990) have argued, the *individual is the basic unit of explanation at all levels*, then we had better not only pay attention to the individual, but also to all that she or he (but probably mostly *he* [see Wrangham and Peterson 1996]) brings to those other levels: interpersonal, intergroup, interorganizational, international, interregional, etc.

Quite simply, conflicts may be raging or suppressed by the Self, or repressed by Others and, therefore, merely "contained" as the ethnic conflicts of the 1990s were during the Cold War. Alternatively, conflicts may be latent at the *intra-actor level*–either intra*psychic*, intra*group*, intra*organizational*, intra*national*, intra*regional*. In either case, the conflicts may–either on their own (via *transference*), and/or through outside manipulation (via the *functions-of-conflict thesis* [see Sandole 1999])–spill over to the external domain.

Hence, as I have argued elsewhere (Sandole 1987), unless conflicts at the *intra*-actor level are dealt with first, then conflicts at the *inter*-actor level–good intentions to the contrary–may only worsen. To deal effectively with conflicts at the "second [or subsequent]-order of manifestation," therefore, we may have to deal with them first at their "first-order of manifestation."

The question arises, of course, how do we, the "Concerned International Community," do that with *complex* conflicts where something that happened in 1389 for Serbs, 1453 for Greeks, 1690 for the Irish, 1915 for Armenians, has helped shape the *identity*, worldviews, and definitions of conflicts of present-day Serbs, Greeks, Irish, and Armenians? [2] For until they deal effectively with such complexity, the Serbs, Greeks, Irish, and Armenians, among many others, are consigned to "forever fighting the last war."

This is clearly the case with the Irish, as indicated by the ominous "Marching Season" every summer in Northern Ireland, when thousands of marches take place in commemoration of historical events, such as the Battle of the Boyne of 12 July 1690. For such events, time is *nonlinear*, even "compressed" (see Volkan 1997). Paralleling "post-traumatic stress syndrome," the same "pivotal event"–the *"chosen trauma"* (ibid.)–is played out ("re-enacted") time and time again, almost as if, each time, for the first time. Richard Rose (1971, 354–355) eloquently captures this phenomenon in the Irish context as follows:

Londonderry on August 12, 1969, aptly illustrates how time past and time present can fuse together in an explosive way. Protestants there that day were commemorating the 280th anniversary of the liberation of the besieged Protestant bastion within the old walled city from Catholic hordes surrounding it. As they looked over Derry's walls, the marchers could see that Catholics, as in Jacobite times, were present in great numbers in the Bogside just below their fortifications. Catholics did not have to turn their minds further back than the previous twelve months to anticipate what might happen next. In that period, the Royal Ulster Constabulary several times entered the Bogside in large numbers, assaulting Catholics on the streets and in their homes in ways that official enquiries could later amnesty but not excuse. The Catholics began to build barricades to prevent a recurrence of this. This recalled Protestants from ancient history to the present. The barricades were interpreted as the beginning of yet another Catholic insurrection. The approach of the police to the barricades was seen by the Catholics behind the lines as yet another instance in which Protestants sought, in the words of an eighteenth-century Irish song, to make "Croppies lie down." In such circumstances, *it hardly matters whether an individual interpreted events in seventeenth, eighteenth or twentieth-century terms.* In Northern Ireland, the conclusions drawn–for or against the regime–are much the same in one century as in the next (emphasis added).

Muzafer Sherif's (1967, 29) discussion of the "heavy hand of the past" is relevant here:

each child in time acquires from his cultural heritage a past in human relationships that becomes his own, in the sense that he experiences its facets as his personal tastes, preferences, likes and dislikes....

Hence, "myths, traditions, and symbols of national pride handed down from one generation to another are among the factors conducive to 'modern wars between nations and groups of nations'" (Cantril 1950, 18; cited in Sherif 1967, 26). They help to keep *"conflicts-as-process"* in an ongoing or resurrectable state (Sandole 1999, 129–131).

One particular proposition becomes salient here: The "last frontier" may not be "outer space," but "inner space." Moreover, we may have more knowledge about "outer" than we do of "inner space." Well-intentioned third parties, each with 15-45 hours of workshop training, may be quite content to walk into–perhaps "emotionally trespass"–the wretched, ravaged conflict space of, e.g., ethnic Albanians and Serbs or a divorcing husband and wife, to help them see "reason," without any awareness that Heisenberg's *Uncertainty Principle* is alive and well in the social as well as physical domain: our "mere presence" in the parties' *turbulent*, dynamic, constantly shifting space may be enough to exacerbate further an already precarious situation (see Benjamin 1990). But adherence to the "theology" of the *primacy of the single factor* precludes us from seeing that.

Accordingly, I have argued that there is a need for a comprehensive, *multilevel* approach (Sandole 1993, 1998, 1999, 2003), not only for understanding, but also for dealing with *complex* conflicts where everything is related to everything else (see Waldrop 1992). The narrative of the three blind men and the elephant just will not do anymore (if it ever did!). To "capture the totality of the beast," we must put Humpty Dumpty back together again (see Waltz 1959; Wilson 1998).

"Inner space," as a *complex* problem area, comprises at least three possibilities:

1. *Individual*: a set of experiences and/or a physiological problem that affects one particular person's behavior in adverse ways (e.g., one of the Columbine High School shooters, Eric Harris, was on medication for a problem, and was rejected for enlistment in the U.S. Marine Corps a week before the shootings);

2. *Group*: experiences that affect an entire group of people in their relations with others (e.g., how the ethnic Albanians of Kosovo envisage relations with Serbs); and/or

3. *Universal*: something about "human nature" that may predispose *all of us* to act in certain ways under certain circumstances (e.g., "looting" during natural or human-made disasters). This is, of course, a reference to the *"nature/nurture"* debate that has engaged social thinkers and practitioners for years. It is also part of the overall recognition that whichever of these possibilities applies in a given conflict situation, will (or should) affect the type of third party intervention selected.

Ethnicity

Part of the "nurture" that interacts with "nature" is *ethnicity*: a sense of shared culture, race, language, worldview, history, traditions. Ethnicity is a component of *identity* shared with, in each case, members of an *identity group* (see Burton 1979, 1990, 1997). Although identity can be constructed, expressed and otherwise experienced in terms of other criteria (not all of which are mutually exclusive)–such as gender, religion, class, nationality–the felt expression, satisfaction, and violation of one's (*"inner-core"*) need for identity through ethnicity can border on primordial intensity (see Boulding 1962, 312).

In this regard, the *need* for identity (but not its culturally-based *construction*) seems to be, like other needs (e.g., for recognition and security), a *basic human need* common to all individuals (see Burton ibid.). As such, ethnicity is a fundamental criterion in terms of which to express, satisfy, and experience violation of one's need for identity. Especially in the *Realpolitik* world, it is often in terms of ethnicity (and related criteria such as religion and nationality) that fairly rigid, *ethnocentric* distinctions are made between *ingroups* ("us") and *outgroups* ("them"). Indeed, violent conflict and war are often played-out between such groups, leading to the construction and recording of their ethno-national histories in terms of great battles, victories and defeats, military leaders, and the like.

Accordingly, members of identity groups tend to be socialized not only in terms of who they are, but also who they are *not*: who has been out to "get them!" In this regard, the results of interviews I conducted of senior CSCE/OSCE negotiators in Vienna in 1993, 1997, and 1999 indicate that historical memories of atrocities committed by members of certain ethnic groups against members of other ethnic groups are among the *perceived* primary causes of the Balkan wars of the 1990s (see Sandole 2001; forthcoming).

So, it is not just the historically-based "chosen traumas"–the collective memories of profound assault and loss associated with 28 June 1389 for Serbs; 29 May 1453 for Greeks; 12 July 1690 for Irish Catholics; 24 April 1915 for Armenians–that are significant, continuing to be experienced emotionally on a regular basis in *"collapsed time"* as part of a post-traumatic stress syndrome (see Volkan 1997, Chs. 3–4), but also each successive, "real world" replay of the traumatic event which builds upon and reinforces the original sense of assault, loss and, therefore, grievance.

This is what makes *identity*-based conflicts so intractable. Unless these particular examples of *"conflict-as-startup conditions"*– deep-rooted historical memories of assault and loss among different identity groups–are dealt with effectively, then *"conflict-as-process"* is never far from the surface, always ready to be re-ignited under certain conditions, as is painfully clear in the Middle East, Northern Ireland, Balkans and elsewhere (see Sandole 1999, 129–131).

Hence, the ultimate challenge for conflict resolutionists and peacebuilders in each case is to discover or invent ways to deal with the past as a *necessary* (but clearly not *sufficient*) condition for the parties to "let go" of the "heavy hand of the past" and collaboratively develop a constructive future based on *common* security: not an insignificant task given that the parties' identities are based, in part, on their historical memories of victimhood and reinforced *virulent* ethnocentrisms.

This challenge is especially acute with regard to *apocalyptic terrorism*.

Apocalyptic Terrorism

Discussions about definitions of *terrorism*, including ours earlier in this chapter, typically suggest the playing of a "name game" worthy of Foucault's claim that discourses are "constructed" in historically contingent time and privileged at the expense of other voices (e.g., Foucault 1981). For example, why are the U.S. nuclear bombings of Hiroshima and Nagasaki or the U.S./British firebombing of Dresden during World War II *not* acts of terrorism, while the attacks on the World Trade Center and Pentagon are? Why is what Mel Gibson's character did to the British and what the British did to his forces in the film, "Patriot," not acts of terrorism, but of guerrilla warfare and warfare, respectively?

Given that terrorists, guerrilla fighters, and soldiers all kill people, including innocent civilians ("collateral damage")–with soldiers killing more combatants and noncombatants than are killed by guerrillas and terrorists combined–what can possibly be the difference between them?

Is it the case that "terrorists" are people whose acts of violence we do not approve of, while guerrilla fighters and soldiers (especially our own) are people whose acts of violence we *do* approve of? Just witness the carnage in Israel and Occupied Palestine: from the perspective of President George W. Bush and Prime Minister Ariel Sharon, U.S.-supplied Apache helicopter gunship and F-16 jet fighter attacks by Israeli forces on a Palestinian refugee camp, in which civilians are killed in a crowded market place, are acceptable acts of *national defense*, whereas a Palestinian teenager who blows herself up to kill the maximum number of Israelis on a crowded rush hour bus is a criminal, worse, a terrorist.

So, are there really meaningful differences between terrorists, guerrilla fighters, and military personnel? The short answer is, yes! Although there are significant exceptions–certainly during recent and current U.S.-led military operations in Afghanistan and Iraq–uniformed soldiers "aim" to kill other uniformed soldiers, guerrillas, and any one else who might be trying to kill them; guerrillas intend to kill political leaders and uniformed police and soldiers; and terrorists intend to kill anybody, especially easily accessed civilians ("soft targets").

Despite these differences, it is possible to have fighters from all three categories in the same "theatre of operations," with some activities clearly blurring the distinctions. For example, to revisit the discussion above, was the Holocaust an act of terrorism or an act of War against European Jewry? Does it matter? Or in Iraq, was the U.S.-led targeting of Baghdad and other parts of the "Cradle of Civilization" during March/April 2003, by 20,000 cruise missiles and other precision guided munitions, warfare or terrorism? For the surviving kin and neighbors of the estimated 20,000-100,000 Iraqi dead, do the differences between "terrorism" and "war" matter?[3] Although U.S., British, and other "coalition" soldiers fought and "won" the three-week war against Iraqi troops, they are still involved in conducting military operations–and are still dying in the process–but against whom? Former Iraqi soldiers, Baathists, disgruntled civilians, "holy warriors," guerrillas, insurgents, "foreign fighters," and/or terrorists?

So yes, there do appear to be differences, but once these fighters enter into the *"fog of war,"* those differences may cease to exist in any meaningful sense.

Where does this leave us with regard to *apocalyptic terrorism*? "Apocalyptic" connotes religion, the last book of the New Testament (i.e., the Book of Revelation), a final battle on Earth between [Christian] Good and [Satanic] Evil ("Armageddon"). One implication of "apocalyptic terrorism" is that acts of violence are expressed in a messianic struggle waged on a wide scale. Acts of "apocalyptic terrorism," therefore, are not necessarily confined *within* state boundaries. Benjamin Barber's "Jihad Versus McWorld" (1992), Samuel Huntington's "Clash of Civilizations" (1993, 1996), and Mark Juergenmeyer's (2000) "Cosmic Warfare" come to mind here.

Accordingly, the "apocalyptic terrorist" would tend to be a non-state actor using, within the Westphalian system of international law, "illegal" means against symbolic and human representations of an enemy (e.g., the West in general, especially the U.S. and UK), in order to defend his or her *identity*–and *"identity group"* (see Burton 1990, 1997)–in global, religious, "civilizational," and/or ideological terms. As such, "apocalyptic terrorism" would seem to be qualitatively different from, say, the terrorism of the IRA to end the British presence in Northern Ireland; the terrorism of the African National Congress (ANC) to end *apartheid* in South Africa; and the hijackings of the Palestine Liberation Organization (PLO) during the 1970s and the suicide bombings by, among others, Hamas and Islamic Jihad during the second *intifada* to end Israeli occupation of Palestine.

Apocalyptic terrorism need not necessarily be "catastrophic" or involve the voluntary death of the terrorist; but more and more, with the increased availability of chemical, biological, and nuclear weapons of mass destruction (see Warrick 2003), apocalyptic terrorism is likely to become more catastrophic and to involve the voluntary deaths of its perpetrators.

A question arising at this point, is: what determines whether a person—willing to commit acts of violence to achieve his or her goals—becomes an apocalyptic terrorist willing to destroy him or herself in the execution of acts of catastrophic violence?

One answer is suggested by one interpretation of the great Abrahamic religion, Islam. It is clear that for many Arabs and Muslims worldwide, Islam is under siege by U.S.-directed globalization undergirded by a neo-"Crusader" mentality. This, plus U.S. policy in the Middle East, has encouraged some Arabs and Muslims to define Americans, the British, Israelis, Jews, Christians, and others as "the Enemy" and, therefore, as targets of *rage*-based acts of violent defense of Islamic values.

A case in point is revealed by the 19 young men who committed the catastrophic acts of 11 September 2001, giving up their lives in the process. All 19 were male, Arab, and *Wahhabist* (i.e., *Salafi*) Muslims. *Wahhabism*—a more traditional, and for some, more "pure" form of Islam—is the brand of Islam practiced in Saudi Arabia since the establishment in the 18th century of an alliance between the House of Saud and religious reformer Muhammad ibn Abd al-Wahhab. It is an indelible part of the Saudi state and of Saudi consciousness. (Fifteen of the 19 terrorists were Saudi citizens.) More significantly, *Wahhabism* is also exported worldwide by the oil-rich state, with the Taliban in Afghanistan and Pakistan being among the most Wahhabist of all.

The primary inspiration for the 11 September attacks, Osama bin Laden, is not only a very wealthy Saudi and founder of the global terrorist group, *al Qaeda*, but also a *Wahhabist*. Bin Laden has issued, since 1996, *fatwa*–edicts in effect declaring war–against the U.S. and Americans in general for committing blasphemy against Islam by stationing, since the Gulf War of 1990–1991, in excess of 5,000 U.S. military personnel in Saudi Arabia, site of the two holiest shrines in Islam: Mecca where The Prophet was born and Medina where The Prophet established the first Islamic state.[4]

Osama bin Laden and others like him have additional grievances against the West: Allowing Orthodox Christian Serbs to slaughter Bosnian Muslims with impunity during the genocidal implosion of former Yugoslavia during the 1990s; *carte blanche* U.S. support for nearly everything that Israel does to the Palestinians; U.S. support for corrupt regimes in the Arab world (e.g., in Egypt and Saudi Arabia); and the U.S.-led wars and military occupations in Afghanistan and Iraq.

Until recently, there was not too much knowledge on the "Western street" about religion or the impact of religion in Saudi Arabia. What many people knew–and still only know–is that Saudi Arabia is a major source of oil for, and major ally of, the West, especially the U.S. People did not know, and still do not know, too much about *Wahhabism*. And only recently have we learned that, in Saudi Arabia (Harris 2003):

> the demonizing of Christians, Jews and the West is pervasive in official books used throughout the government-controlled school system.... A study, co-sponsored by the American Jewish Committee, of the Saudi Arabia Ministry of Education books used in grades 1 through 10 reveals that Saudi children are taught intolerance and contempt for the West, Christians and Jews in subjects ranging from literature to math.

> Children in the eighth grade learn in a geography book that "Islam replaced the former religions that preceded it" and that "a malicious *Crusader-Jewish alliance* is striving to eliminate Islam from all the continents." Christians and Jews are denounced as

"infidels" and are presented as enemies of Islam and Muslims. Saudi schoolbooks implore Muslims not to befriend Christians or Jews, as in a ninth-grade jurisprudence schoolbook that states: "Emulation of the infidel leads to loving them, glorifying them and raising their status in the eyes of the Muslim, and that is forbidden."

Even grammar and math books are full of phrases *exalting war, jihad and martyrdom.* Saudi youth are educated to *reject all notions of western democracy.* Saudis are instructed that the West is a "decaying society" on its way to extinction (emphasis added) (Also see PBS 2001).

Powerful stuff, and we know the impact of our earliest learned "lessons," especially beliefs concerning those who have oppressed our *identity groups* for centuries. Into such an emotionally charged historical and *identity*-based setting has entered an Islamic cleric whose *fatwa* may have had catastrophic consequences in the UK and elsewhere:

Intelligence officials are trying to gauge the reach and power of a cleric who has spent most of his time in London or "Londistan," as [U.S. officials] call the area around the Finsbury Park Mosque. A London imam, Abu Qatada, appears to European authorities to have had a role, possibly more inspirational than organizational, in any number of planned and accomplished catastrophes. According to a British dossier ... as far back as the mid-'90s, Abu Qatada issued a *fatwa* for the slaughter of women and children in Algeria by a radical organization called the Armed Islamic Group (GIA). Jordanian authorities implicated Abu Qatada in the planned (but thwarted) Millennium attacks on American tourists. The imam was said by the French to have provided "spiritual advice" for terrorist plots in Strasbourg and Paris in 2000

and 2001, and 18 tapes of his sermons were found in the
Hamburg apartment of Muhammad Atta, the lead
hijacker on 9-11 (Isikoff et. al., 2003, 28 & 30).

It is not only religious identity and historical memory that may stir the
passions, however. According to Shireen Hunter (1998), "Most Muslim
societies have remained largely rural and traditional and hence more
religion minded":

> From a cultural perspective, most of the Islamic
> world is at the preindustrial, even feudal, stage of
> development, when religion has a great hold on the
> society and the people (ibid. 166).

As such, there might be a greater tendency for people at this level of
development–and those who *identify* with them–to feel empowered by the
simplicity, clarity, and "purity" of *Wahhabism*, and therefore to comply
with *fatwa*, even those issued by nonclerics such as Osama bin Laden,
designed to enhance their sense of empowerment toward the hegemonic
Western world.

As is clear from Stanley Milgram's (1974) experiments, it does not
take too much for obedience to be elicited by calls to violence, even in
highly ad hoc, secular, Western settings. And if such calls to violence are
made to dispossessed, disempowered, marginalized people–Frantz
Fanon's (1968) *Wretched of the Earth*–with an accompanying plea to
voluntarily forfeit their lives in the process of striking back, such persons
might be more likely to perpetrate acts of catastrophic, apocalyptic
terrorism because of the profound sense of *meaning* associated with
voluntarily giving up their lives to change the world, as the 19 young men
so clearly did on 11 September 2001.[5]

How do Muslim clerics view such "life-forfeiting" actions? According to Joyce Davis (2003a), who has conducted interviews in the Middle
East on this issue:

> While Islam prohibits suicide, it is one's duty as a
> Muslim to fight evil and to defend the Islamic community
> [the *Umma*] and if all one has as a weapon in that struggle
> is one's body, then martyrdom is acceptable.

So, if one elects to die in the defense of one's identity group, instead
of because one is "merely depressed," that is acceptable. And there are
apparently many Muslims who at least support such selfless acts on behalf
of the larger Islamic community. For example, according to the 2003
survey conducted by the Pew Global Attitudes Project:

> The [U.S.] is losing a propaganda war for the hearts
> and minds of millions of Arabs spurred by the Sept. 11,
> 2001, terrorist attacks on New York and the Pentagon,
> according to a survey released [on 3 June 2003].

> The survey suggests that al Qaeda leader Osama bin
> Laden inspires more confidence than President Bush
> across much of the Arab and Muslim world. It also shows
> a further slump in public perceptions of the [U.S.] over
> the past year around the globe, with favorable ratings
> down to as low as 1 percent in Jordan and the Palestinian
> territories.

> "We have gone from bad to worse over the past year,"
> said Andrew Kohut, director of the Pew Research Center,
> noting that hostility toward the [U.S.] has increased as a
> result of the invasion of Iraq. "We have been unable to
> make the case against bin Laden with Muslims because
> they see the [U.S.] as a threat" (Dobbs 2003). [6]

In the Pew report for 2002:

> Perhaps the most alarming finding is that a majority
> of respondents in Lebanon and Ivory Coast, and sizable
> minorities in Nigeria, Bangladesh, Jordan, Pakistan, and

> at least five other countries, say *they believe that suicide*
> *bombing in defense of Islam is justifiable* (emphasis
> added) (AM 2003).[7]

Accordingly, many in the Arab and Muslim worlds seem to despise the West, particularly the perceived primary driving force of Western culture and influence, the U.S. For those among them willing to commit catastrophic attacks against the U.S., if all they have in response to their *rage* are their own bodies as weapons in defense of Islam, then:

> The war on terror will never be neat or clear-cut. Nor
> will it be short. "These people have a different sense of
> time," says a senior intelligence official. *"They hark*
> *back to the Crusades.* For them, the jihad is
> never-ending" (emphasis added) (Isikoff et al. 2003, 31).

Hence, Joyce Davis' (2003a) characterization of the "apocalyptic" nature of this struggle as *"a world war."* Such a conceptualization of the fight against the "new" terrorism follows in part from the universalism inherent in Islam, plus the global nature of the perceived onslaught on traditionalism and, therefore, Islam. The *Umma* is now global!

So, when Muslims in Malaysia and Indonesia express their concern for their *"Muslim brothers"* in Palestine and question the *"double standards"* implicit in the U.S. role in the Middle East, this is not a mere expression of ethnocentrism at the intergroup level, but an expression of the "civilizational rallying" that plays a major role in the "clash of civilizations" (Huntington 1993, 1996). Nevertheless, involved here is a "writ large" version of what we normally find in ethnocentric discourse and experience: a keen sense of "ingroup-outgroup" differences with a minority ingroup, in this case Muslims worldwide, who feel that the Christian (now Judaic/Christian) Western outgroup is pursuing a Crusade against them that goes back nearly a thousand years.

By implication, Western attacks on Muslims anywhere in the world are perceived by particular Muslims (e.g., in Malaysia and Indonesia) as attacks on *them*: a global, civilizational expression of the "circling of the wagons" phenomenon usually associated with the integrative functions of conflict at the intergroup level (see Simmel, 1955; Coser 1956). This was clearly the gist of a videotape of one of the London bombers, Mohammed Sidique Khan, shown on *al Jazeera* in early September 2005, who expressed the view that he was a "soldier" in a war against those who were killing *his* people (see Hosenball 2005).

When "God" explicitly enters the picture, we should not be too surprised at the consequences. One Saudi, who uses a bit more than his body to commit *catastrophic* violence at the interpersonal level, justifies it as follows:

> Saudi Arabia's leading executioner, Muhammad Saad Al-Bashi, will behead up to seven people in a day. "It doesn't matter to me: Two, four, ten. As long as I'm doing *God's will*, it doesn't matter how many people I execute," he told [the Arabic-language] *Okaz* newspaper in an interview....
>
> He says he is calm at work because he is doing *God's work*....
>
> He has executed numerous women without hesitation, he explains. "Despite the fact that I hate violence against women, when it comes to *God's will*, I have to carry it out" (emphasis added) (Grove 2003).

If Milgram's (1974) subjects felt that their "Obedience to Authority" was embedded in the ad hoc authority structure of the experimenter and if the Nazi perpetrators of the Holocaust felt that their genocidal behaviors were legitimized by the deeply rooted military tradition of "following orders," then what can we possibly say or do about people who feel they are being called upon by God to commit acts of catastrophic, apocalyptic, "cosmic" violence against those who are perceived to be assaulting God's Word and Domain?

"Why do they hate us?" is the question that motivated Joyce Davis (2003b) to write her book, *Martyrs: Innocence, Vengeance and Despair in the Middle East.* One answer is, quite simply, because the same types of people–in terms of race, culture, and religion–who launched the Crusades against Islam nearly a thousand years ago, are still perceived by Arabs and Muslims to be oppressing, marginalizing, and humiliating Islam: the U.S.-led wars and occupations of Afghanistan and Iraq being merely the two most recent examples of "Crusader" efforts to keep Islam in a backward state of development.

It is important to bear in mind, however, that "Crusader" symbolism does not inhere only in Muslim historical experience. In part because of the "chosen trauma" phenomenon (Volkan 1997) experienced regularly by Serb Orthodox Christians:

> In July 1995, Bosnian Serb forces overran the predominately Muslim town [of Srebrenica], which had been declared a United Nations "safe area" under the protection of Dutch peacekeeping troops, and went on to kill up to 8,000 Muslims (IHT 2003, 2).

Ensuring that this event of 11 July 1995–"Europe's worst atrocity since World War II"–would become a reinforced "chosen trauma" for Bosnia's Muslims (*and Muslims worldwide*), a "report by a Bosnian Serb government committee sparked outrage [in 2002] by suggesting that Muslims imagined or fabricated the massacre in Srebrenica" (ibid.).

Perhaps in response, "for the first time, a Bosnian Serb government delegation attended" the eighth anniversary of the 1995 Srebrenica massacre:

> "I came here because I regard it to be my moral duty," said the Bosnian Serb prime minister, Dragan Mikerevic....
>
> Mikerevic said his government was preparing a new report [on the massacre] but stopped short of saying the previous one was wrong (ibid.).

Ten years after the slaughter at Srebrenica:

Fewer than half of Serbs polled... believed the Srebrenica massacre took place.... Instead of coming to terms with its past, Serbia has circumvented the issue with the narrative skills of a psychopath. For example, a debate on Srebrenica at the Belgrade Law Faculty earlier this year was initially titled "10 Years After the *Liberation* of Srebrenica" (emphasis added) (Brkic 2005).

Accordingly, "chosen traumas," indelibly etched into the *identities* of Christians, Jews and Muslims–the three Abrahamic "People of the Book" –continue to be painfully experienced in "collapsed time" as a collective form of *post-traumatic stress syndrome*. There are profound implications here for conflicts in the Middle East, Southeast Asia, Chechnya, and elsewhere, plus the global war on terrorism, the perceived "clash of civilizations" and "cosmic warfare"–the level at which apocalyptic terrorists are more and more likely to give up their own lives in the commission of acts of catastrophic violence, and in the process, perhaps even see themselves (and be seen by others) to be doing *"God's work."*

Dealing with Identity Conflicts

Armenian-Turkish/ Azerbaijani Relations

Clearly, "chosen traumas" (as well as "chosen glories") can become part of the "heavy hand of the past" determining one's *identity* which, together with a hypothesized *"need for an enemy"* (Volkan, 1985, 1988), bifurcate the world into *ingroups* ("us") and *outgroups* ("them"), with "them" being the ones who violated "us" at some point in time, or at frequent points in time, the likelihood being that they will do so again (see Montville 1993).

On the assumption that the *need for identity*, like the *needs for recognition and security*, are *basic human needs* (Burton 1997), once identity based on certain traumas reflects this us-them bifurcation, it is very difficult to change. Moreover, the successive re-experience of the chosen trauma–either indirectly through recalled painful memories or directly through "repeat performances"–further reinforces the original sense of loss and the us-them distinction, increasing the likelihood that, via transference, *current* experiences of loss will be interpreted in the light, and as reflections, of the *historical* ones. What this means is that conflicting parties, for example, Armenians, Azerbaijanis, and Turks, may be consigned to living forever "in history" (see Fukuyama 1989, 1992), unable to break loose from the past to develop their common futures.

Hence, as argued earlier, a major challenge for peacebuilders is to discover or invent innovative ways for aggrieved parties to "let go" of the past–of their chosen traumas–so that they can *reframe* their definitions of the "Other" as being part of a collaborative *common security system*, instead of continuing to be the "Enemy" which is out to destroy them and which, therefore, must be destroyed itself.

As Turkey begins the historical process of negotiating entry into the pre-eminent *peacebuilding* entity of our time, the European Union (EU), it is tempting to ask, "What is the relevance of these theoretical insights for the Armenian-Azerbaijani conflict over Nagorno-Karabakh (an Armenian enclave in Azerbaijan)?" Let me respond initially through a personal story. In June 1992, while a war between Armenia and Azerbaijan over Nagorno-Karabakh was ongoing, I visited Armenia for the first time as part of my Institute's development of its Caucasus Working Group (see Sandole 1997a, 1997b). The trip included visits to Yerevan State University–our partner in Armenia–to meet with Prof. Dr. Lyudmila Harutyunyan, chair of the Department of Sociology, plus the Rector, Vice Rector for International Affairs, and other officers of the University. We also visited Echevan, located along the border with Kazakh on the Azerbaijani side, to meet with the provincial governor Ms. Jema Ananian, and Armenian refugees of the conflict.

During the brief visit to Echevan, an Azerbaijani offensive occurred at that point on the border, with my colleagues and I within earshot of heavy weapons fire. What impressed me the most–other than being in a country at war during a time (and at the site) of a major offensive against it–was that Armenians defined Azerbaijanis as *"Turks"*! Moreover, they saw themselves as roughly 3 million Armenians in Armenia, with some 4 million in the diaspora, juxtaposed to some 7 million "Turks" in Azerbaijan and 63 million Turks in Turkey, for a total of 70 million Turks surrounding 3 million Armenians. The fact that both Turkey and Azerbaijan had imposed blockades on landlocked Armenia reinforced this sense of massive encirclement, plus the sense that the "Turks" were intent on completing a process they started in 1915.[8]

The Armenian chosen trauma–the deep-rooted historical memory of outrage–that seems to be at work here, as an example of the heavy hand of the past, is the 24th of April. That is the day in 1915 when, for Armenians worldwide, the first *genocide* of the 20th Century began in Istanbul and lasted until 1923. Via transference from the past to the present, Armenians view the conflict over Nagorno-Karabakh as an effort by *"Turks"* to finish off the *"final solution"* they started in 1915.

Officially, Turks say yes, many Armenians (but also Turks) died in Eastern Anatolia during World War 1, but nowhere near the 1.5 million claimed by Armenians and certainly not because of an official Turkish governmental plan to exterminate all Armenians, like Nazi Germany nearly did to European Jewry during the Holocaust of World War II.

As evidence to support their view, Turks claim that, in Eastern Turkey, many Armenians–in fact, tens of thousands–were killed because Armenians joined Russians (and their Armenian kin from the Russian Empire) in waging warfare against the collapsing Ottoman Empire to carve out an Armenian homeland–a period in which total chaos reigned. It was this chaos and reciprocal fratricide, and not an ordered plan associated with official Turkish governmental edict that resulted in, from the Turkish point of view, the deaths of 500,000 Armenians, mostly from disease. In addition, Turks point to the fact that Armenians in Western Turkey were not subjected to atrocities and that the Ottoman ambassador to Britain was an Armenian. Surely, they argue, if Turkey was conducting a genocide against Armenians, its main emissary to the British Empire would not be an Armenian. As a Turkish ambassador put it to me, "can you imagine Hitler having a Jew as his ambassador to Britain?"

How do Armenians view this Turkish interpretation of events? On the one hand, Armenians see a massive Turkish coverup of a genocide that took place nearly 100 years ago, assisted by intense lobbying of governments abroad. On the other hand, they are outraged that, all these years later, Turks cannot even acknowledge what members of an older generation did.

This absence of acknowledgement of a major defining event in Armenian history, corresponding to a dominant component of Armenian *identity*, constitutes, for Armenians, a major assault to that identity–to their sense of who they are. Contrariwise, for many Turks, although the accusations of genocide are not against them but an earlier generation, the accusations nevertheless constitute an assault on *their* identity as Turks.

Accordingly, we can hypothesize that, for the *present* conflict between Armenia and Azerbaijan to be effectively addressed, the still existing, *historical* conflict between Armenia and Turkey must be effectively addressed, if not prior to dealing with the current conflict, then certainly at some later point in time (see Lederach 2001; Montville 1993).

So, even though the Karabakh conflict has, since May 1994, been characterized by a fairly stable ceasefire, and the Armenian and Azerbaijani presidents have had occasional meetings ever since former U.S. Secretary of State Madeleine Albright brought them together in April 1999, at some point in time, the Armenian-Turkish conflict will have to be addressed as a necessary (but not sufficient) condition for whatever Armenian-Azerbaijani agreement does emerge, if it is to have prospects for developing into a long-term, self-sustaining peace on the Karabakh issue.

Hence, during their future meetings, which may eventually result in a breakthrough, the Armenian and Azerbaijani presidents, with the assistance of their American, French, and Russian colleagues from the OSCE's Minsk Group Process (see *OSCE Handbook* 2000, 62-67), should concentrate on developing further:

1. the nature of the land exchange and other significant compromises they will have to make, plus
2. how they will "sell" the agreement to their respective constituents, and agree that
3. a significant next step should be to encourage Turkey and Armenia to set up a *joint historical commission* to finally lay to rest the

nature of their common past.

Once a major impediment to resolving the Armenian-Turkish conflict, this last point has become more thinkable in recent years:

> With world opinion turning against the Turkish position, some ex-government officials in Turkey are advocating a new approach: *convening a panel of scholars from around the world, including Turkey and Armenia, and giving them full access to all archives to look at the historical record.* This would benefit Turkey by taking the issue of the Armenian genocide out of the political realm, at least for awhile. The idea also appeals to Western diplomats and politicians who, more than anything else, want the issue to go away....
> Ending this long-standing dispute will help Turkey achieve its primary national goal: *winning entry into the European Union.* Not ending it will put Turkey on a collision course with any number of nations that might pass Armenian genocide resolutions in the future, including the United States (emphasis added) (Glastris 2001, B4).

One historic, albeit unsuccessful, step in this direction was the creation of the Turkish-Armenian Reconciliation Commission (TARC) (see Mooradian 2003):

> On July 9, 2001, in Geneva, news outlets announced that the Turkish-Armenian Reconciliation Commission (TARC) had been formed "to promote mutual understanding and good will between Turks and Armenians and to encourage improved relations between Armenia and Turkey." The Commission accepted the task of "reconciling" a host of conflicts. These conflicts include those that exist between the Armenian nation and

the RoT and conflicts exclusively between the RoA and Turkey's government.

> TARC arrived on the scene as an *unofficial* ["track-2"] group to reconcile the entrenched differences. [Holocaust survivor and Nobel laureate] Elie Wiesel said, "I see this event as a miracle. *If Turks and Armenians can meet and talk, that means others can do it, too"* Six months later [however], in December 2001, TARC teetered on the brink of collapse (emphasis added) (Mooradian 2005).

The reasons for TARC's failure had a lot to do with the partisan, activist nature of the Turkish and Armenian participants and their lack of appropriate conflict resolution skills training, which resulted in their inability to get beyond their *emotionally based positions* to develop trust in the process and each other. These factors, however, could be dealt with through careful selection of new participants who have a keen sense of will and purpose, plus appropriate training, perhaps conducted by the Conflict Analysis and Resolution Program at Sabanci University in Istanbul, Turkey,[9] together with the Conflict Resolution Program in the Department of Sociology at Yerevan State University in Yerevan, Armenia (see Sandole 2005d).

An upgraded, post-TARC effort at Turkish-Armenian reconciliation could (and should), therefore, be undertaken. Unless efforts are made to address the deep-rooted, historical conflict between Armenia and Turkey–the primary *conflict-as-startup condition* in Turkish-Armenian relations–efforts to deal only with the current Armenian-Azerbaijani conflict will be superficial, perpetually at risk of breakdown into the ordered chaos of ethnic bloodletting: renewed *conflict-as-process*.

We have only to look at events of the 1990s in the Balkans to see the consequences of earlier applications of "band-aids" to complex, deep wounds, as seems to have occurred during the Tito years in former Yugoslavia. Under the circumstances, all the Caspian Sea oil flowing from the Baku-Tblisi-Ceyhan and other pipelines may not be enough to withstand the gravitational pull of Armenians' unresolved chosen trauma of the past.

Accordingly, to facilitate long overdue economic development of the South Caucasus (Armenia, Azerbaijan, and Georgia), as well as Turkey's entry into the European Union–with profound developmental and security implications for the North Caucasus and Central Asia–the time has surely come to lay to rest, once and for all, the matter of the Armenian genocide! *Cognitively* and *evaluatively*, a rational plea; but *affectively*, perhaps a nonstarter (see Boulding 1956).

Theory-Based Practice

Imagine a post-TARC problemsolving taskforce comprised of Turkish, Armenian, Israeli, American, and European scholars,[10] facilitated by *appropriately trained* and experienced professionals (see Mitchell and Banks 1996), the objective being to finally deal with the issue of the Armenian genocide, as a necessary condition for dealing with the Armenian-Azerbaijani conflict over Nagorno-Karabakh. Let's also imagine that all members of the taskforce have had access to *all* archives– e.g., Armenian, Turkish/Ottoman, German, American–dealing with events in eastern Anatolia during 1915–1923.

Using the *"Four-Worlds Model of the Perceptual-Behavioral Process"* (see Sandole 1987; Popper 1972) as a point of departure, the facilitator, operating at the "cognitive" level, would be helping the parties to "experience" perceptions at various levels, e.g.:

1. *Bare sensation*: an *ambiguous* sense of *what* may be in one's perceptual field (Y).
2. *Recognition and identification*: a *clear* sense of *what* is in one's perceptual field (Y).
3. *Analysis and explanation*: a sense of *why* what is in one's perceptual field may be there (X). And
4. *Interpretation*:
   a. The meaning of the *"what"-"why"* (Y-X) relationship (e.g., acts of frustration [X] and aggression [Y]) within a more

comprehensive frame (frustration-aggression theory). And
b. An exploration of alternative responses to the *what*.

Confounding the otherwise nice, neat progression from "bare sensation" to "recognition and identification" are some bases for resistance to perception which operate at the *unconscious* level of the perceiving actor:

1. *Cognitive blindness*: the condition of not being able to perceive something in, for instance, either *World 1 (nature)* or *World 3 (human-made)* because of the absence of a corresponding concept, model, theory and/or paradigm in the perceiving actor's *World 2 (mental)* (e.g., the initial nonperception of *reversed* colors and shapes in the famous Bruner-Postman [1949] playing-card experiment).
2. *Cognitive resistance*: the condition of not being able to perceive the anomalous thing *over time*, presumably because the existing concepts, models, theories, and/or paradigms in the perceiving actor's *World 2 (mental)* fail to shift in order to accommodate it (e.g., the successive nonperception of anomalous cards in the playing-card experiment).
3. *Evaluative-affective resistance (EAR) 1*: the perceiving actor's experience of *cognitive dissonance* (Festinger 1962) the longer the anomalous thing remains in his/her perceptual field, suggesting to the actor that something is not quite right with "what is going on" around her or him but which, like in "bare sensation," he or she cannot quite grasp the nature of. What seems to be going on here is that the actor experiences dissonance *affectively* as anxiety but then, *defence mechanisms* are activated, protecting the actor from recognizing the nature of the anomalous thing and, in the process, protecting the status quo concepts, models, theories, and/or paradigms in his/her *World 2 (mental)* (e.g., when some participants in the playing-card experiment indicated their confusion over what they were "seeing": red [*black*] hearts or black [*red*] spades).

Again, these three bases of resistance to the detection of anomalies operate at the unconscious level of perceiving actors. In the move from "bare sensation" to "recognition and identification," a *well-trained*, experienced, and effective third-party facilitator might be able to guide conflicting parties to shift from "cognitive blindness" to "evaluative-affective resistance [EAR] 1."

But then an ethical dilemma presents itself: should the third-party facilitator actively generate further dissonance to the point that it overrides internalized defense mechanisms, in the process causing a "Kuhnian" *and* personal crisis on the part of perceiving actors (see Kuhn 1970)?

Suppose Turkish and some Israeli members of the taskforce persist in arguing that, yes, thousands of Armenians were killed during 1915–1923, but that this was not due to an official, Turkish governmental policy. By contrast, Armenian, American, European, and other Israeli/Jewish members argue that all the data indicate that, while the deaths may have been confined to Armenians living in the eastern part of the country, it was certainly Turkish officials who ordered the massacres. Should the facilitator then "push" the unconsciously/consciously resisting actors to experience even more "acute personal distress"–in the process moving from EAR 1 (unconscious resistance) to EAR 2 (conscious, often hostile resistance) –to the point that they undergo a *"paradigmatic shift"* to a *relational empathy-based "third culture"*(see Broome 1993) and collectively experience the anomalous thing as the "same" thing?[11]

Let's put this into the context of the protracted Israeli-Palestinian conflict, with Israelis embedded in, and reliving and responding symbolically to the fears and horrors of the Holocaust and Palestinians locked in the grip of captivity, humiliation, persistent displacement from their land and marginalization by the international community.

Imagine, following the Israeli withdrawal from Gaza, a taskforce comprised of Palestinians and Israelis facilitated by American and European friends of the Middle East. Imagine also that the facilitators–nongovernmental conflict resolution professionals as well as governmental diplomats and other specialists–are encouraging the Israeli and Palestinian participants to shift from "cognitive blindness/resistance" to EAR 1, by presenting "objective data", such as: Israeli deaths as a proportion of the Israeli population; Palestinian deaths as a proportion of the occupied Palestinian population; elements of Israeli firepower (planes, helicopters, and tanks); elements of Palestinian firepower (small arms, homemade rockets and their own bodies attached to explosives); who surrounds and occupies whom?; who is surrounded and occupied by whom?; who controls whom?; who is controlled by whom? Indeed, who has the power to build a fence around whom?

Suppose that, after such data have been presented, the facilitators surface the view that Israeli Prime Minister Ariel Sharon's earlier declaration of war on the Palestinians–resulting in U.S.-equipped Israeli F-16 fighter aircraft, Apache helicopter gunships and tanks invading Palestinian refugee camps and townships to inflict sufficient pain and punishment on the Palestinians until they begged for peace–amounted to, at minimum, a counter-productive, self-defeating policy, and at worst, a series of steps toward *genocide*. In other words, suppose the facilitators moved the more powerful party, the Israelis, from EAR 1 (unconscious resistance) to EAR 2 (conscious, hostile resistance). Would an *ethical* line have been crossed? Does it matter if the Israelis back up, pause, and reflect on their behavior and in the process, recognize that *they will never have security unless the Palestinians have security (and vice versa)*? (See Sandole 2005a.)

Again, lots of questions, and few answers. But one thing is clear. The horrible acts of violence being committed against Israelis in cafes, pizzerias, discotheques and elsewhere have produced diverse responses. On the one hand, there are Israelis who say, "We have to kill them all, all the Arabs. Why does half the world tell us not to go to war? If we want, we could kill them in one hour" and "Let's really let them understand what the implication of their actions is.... Very simply, wipe them out. Level them." By contrast, there are the 300-plus Israeli reservists who feel that their country's "35-year occupation ... has corrupted the nation," who refuse any longer to "dominate, expel, starve, and humiliate" the Palestinians (see Hockstader 2002a, A17; 2002b). There is also the young Israeli journalist, Ilan Goren (2002, B2), who talks about what his generation has been going through:

> confusion, loss of belief, a quiet despair born of the realization that *we kill them and they kill us and nobody is*

any better off.... Can anyone in the government see that wrecking Palestinian houses, invading homes, killing hundreds and degrading another nation is not only an inefficient way to fight terror, but also is immoral (emphasis added)? (Also see Sandole 2005a.)

So, there may be hope for the future of the Israeli-Palestinian conflict, a conflict which plays a pivotal role in driving global terrorism. This optimism has been reinforced in the wake of Palestinian leader Yassir Arafat's death by the resurrection of the Israeli-Palestinian peace process and Israeli withdrawal from Gaza.

Conclusion

As we conclude, let's return to where we began: the London bombings of July 2005. Islam, like Judaism and Christianity before it, must make the journey to a "third culture," so that one can be a Muslim–of Pakistani, Afghan, Turkic, Azerbaijani, Iranian, Arabic, Malay, or any other heritage–*and*, at the same time, a British, American, Dutch, French or any other citizen pursuing the "dream" of the new homeland.

This chapter has revealed some basic knowledge for achieving that goal. Nevertheless, significant challenges remain, as expressed poignantly by Ms. Sabaa Saleem (2005), a Muslim Pakistani-American and foreign editor for *The Washington Post*:

Why do young people who are supposed to be my brothers or sisters in faith terrorize innocent civilians to make a point I can scarcely fathom? I reject everything extremists say, every excuse they make, and I see only my reality and their misguided outlook.

But there is some inner voice nagging at me, reminding me that when I speak with peaceful Muslims from America, Australia, England, Pakistan and Scotland, I become aware of their reality, which *conflicts* on some very deep levels with my own. With fresh eyes, I begin to see *their point of view*. And I realize that *their voices* have been adopted and warped by Islamic radicals.

I feel that the *concerns of moderate Muslims are legitimate* when I read this: According to two British organizations, *at least* 25,000 Iraqi civilians have died so far in the war, more than one-third of them killed by U.S. troops and their allies and more than 1,000 of them children. *Killed in a war that the Muslims I have spoken with found difficult to justify.*

And when I read this: Nearly 8,000 Muslim men and boys were massacred by Bosnian Serb forces in Srebrenica in July 1995, and callously tossed into mass graves in the surrounding area. They were murdered with U.N. troops standing by, unable to act. Murdered after the world had vowed that genocide would never taint Europe again. And while some implicated in the atrocity have been tried, its two main architects [Radovan Karadjic and General Ratko Mladic] remain at large.

And when I read this: Muslim men, who had not been tried or charged with a crime, were subjected to sickening acts of torture and humiliation. Acts that came at the hands of soldiers from our home, the United States, one of the foremost proponents–at least publicly–of human rights and the Geneva Convention.

And when I read this: U.S. citizens and permanent residents with Middle Eastern ties have been arrested and held without charge or access to lawyers for months at a time, while their families have struggled against an officially imposed wall of silence.

Ms. Saleem (ibid.) suggests, with regard to the etiology of suicide bombing and other acts of apocalyptic/catastrophic terrorism, an interesting array of conflict/conflict resolution theory, which overlaps with our earlier discussion of "origins of violent conflict" and what I call the *dissonance theories* (Sandole 1999, 117–121):

> The Muslims I have spoken with, and many others I know, have stressed that [the above] events contribute to their formulation of history, their sense of what is right with this world, and of what is horribly wrong. It is these incidents, however, that are taken up by extremists and used to justify acts of violence that, by their very nature, are unjustifiable. And thus, the *worldview* and *anxieties* of mainstream Muslims are painted with the black brush of extremism.

> As a Pakistani relative in Australia said, mainstream Muslims "do not support bloodshed. What they do support is a *representation of their concerns.*"

> But representation is often difficult to find, he said, expressing what is becoming a familiar sense of *frustration.*

> As I continued talking to Muslim friends and relatives in Britain after the first London bombing, ..., person after person expressed moral repugnance at the attacks in London and Egypt, but still showed concern and *frustration* about what is happening to Muslims daily.

> "Those bombers ... hear about Muslims dying in Bosnia, Chechnya, Iraq, Afghanistan, and *emotion* takes over." The bombers ... wanted *revenge.*

> "Any moderate Muslim would be horrified [by the

bombings]. I could never imagine myself, in the name of my religion and what my religion stands for, killing another innocent human being, never.... [W]e feel so outraged and traumatized by this, *even though* there are people out there who have been living with this, day in and day out, their whole families wiped out, and *where is the shock and horror for them?"*

To conclude on an optimistic yet somber note, Ms. Saleem (*op. cit.*) still has high hopes that the "third culture" will be achieved for her and others:

I have come to understand that my belief in the United States and all it stands for has been shaken, and I am afraid to look at what lies underneath.... All my life, I have felt *torn between my Pakistani-Muslim heritage and my American upbringing.* Often, I would grow *frustrated* with the constant balancing act. Now, I believe this turmoil was preparation for the difficult times ahead, when my *dual perspective* would coalesce to form an *outlook* that can *bridge two worlds.*

I stand with a *foot in both of these worlds,* not a relativist, not an apologist, but a *Muslim American woman* hoping that one day Americans and moderate Muslims around the globe will emerge from the ominous shadow of violence, and try to understand each other (emphasis added).

Needless to say, achieving, maintaining, and developing further a "third culture" among otherwise *competing identities,* especially those involved in what some see as global warfare and a "clash of civilizations" (see, e.g., Huntington 1993, 1996; Merry 2005; Sandole 2005b), requires much more than the efforts of conflict resolutionists. But conflict resolution is an appropriate point to start if we really want to turn all this around into the ultimate expression of the "third culture": a "dialogue of civilizations"!

In the meantime, let me close with a letter to the editor I had published in the *International Herald Tribune* about the conflict that Malay Muslims in southern Thailand are having with the central government in Bangkok (Sandole 2005c):

> Philip Bowring makes a strong case, based upon a recent report by the International Crisis Group, that violence in southern Thailand is a result, not of an international jihad, but of *historical grievances* compounded by repressive measures taken by the Thai government against ethnic Malay Muslims for more than 100 years ("Southern Thailand's homegrown ills," Views, May 27).
>
> Until now this seems to have been the case, but longterm conflicts over *identity* tend to be messy. The more that Thailand's Malay Muslims feel that they are *under siege* by the government, with *forced assimilation* Bangkok's preferred option, the more likely they would welcome support from fellow Muslims in the region and *worldwide*.
>
> Hence, Bowring's reference to the ICG report's "worry that radical outside forces could gain influence if the region's *sense of victimization* is not reversed." Rocket science is not required here, but should the Thai government continue *exacerbating Thai Malay Muslims' historical grievances with further repression*, then the conflict dynamic and level could shift catastrophically. While "civilizational jihad" may not have caused the unrest in southern Thailand, it may become one of its results (emphasis added).

Notes

1. This chapter builds on sections of Sandole (2002) and Sandole, Ruff, and Vasili (2004).

2. Interestingly, with the exception of the Irish case, the "Other" for the Serbs, Greeks, and Armenians is the same: Ottoman Turkey. Hence, although the Ottoman Empire no longer exists, it remains an integral part of the *identities* of, among others, Serbs, Greeks, and Armenians, whose ancestors are perceived to have been assaulted and oppressed by it. That Serbs continue to refer to Bosnian Muslims (Bosniaks) as "Turks," as do Armenians of Azerbaijanis, is further testament to the power of past events on the present and future.

3. For various estimates of Iraqi civilian casualties, see Conetta, 2003; Thomas & Brant, 2003, p. 27; WP, 2005; and www.washingtonpost.com/nation.

4. Most of these troops have since been withdrawn.

5. On "man's search for meaning," see Frankl (1985). Also see Hedges (2002).

6. For the Pew 2003 report, see:
<http://people-press.org/reports/pdf/185.pdf>

7. For the Pew 2002 report, see:
<http://people-press.org/reports/display.php3?ReportID=165>

8. Interestingly, although they are *"Turkic""* Azerbaijanis are not, according to Turkish Law 2510 of 1934, viewed as *"Turkish."* In contrast to, say, Albanian and Bosnian Muslims, they are not viewed as being of "Turkish descent and culture," and hence, there has been a "conspicuous absence of [Azerbaijani] immigration to Turkey" (see Kirisci, 2000). Nevertheless, Turkey has consistently been supportive of Azerbaijan in the conflict over Nagorno-Karabakh.

9. www.sabanciuniv.edu/fass/conflict/

10. Israeli scholars would be included for at least three reasons: (1) Israel is the national homeland of, among others, Jewish descendants of victims of the Nazi Holocaust who, more than nationals of other countries, could sympathize with Armenians regarding genocide; yet, perhaps paradoxically, (2) the Israeli Government, which has enjoyed a positive (even military) relationship with Turkey since the mid–1990s, tends to side with the official Turkish view that a genocide did *not* occur against Armenians during 1915–1923 (see Sandole, 2005d); nevertheless (3) Israeli and Jewish academics in general are prominent

amongst scholars of genocide.

11. For insights on the role and value of *emotion* in third party interventions, see Jones and Bodtker (2001).

References

AM 2003. "The Next 'Special Relationship'?" *Atlantic Monthly*: 39.

Barber, Benjamin R. 1992. "Jihad Vs. McWorld." *The Atlantic Monthly* 269, no. 3: 53–65.

Benjamin, Robert D. 1990. "The Physics of Mediation: Reflections of Scientific Theory in Professional Mediation Practice." *Mediation Quarterly* 8, no. 2: 91–113.

Boulding, Kenneth E. 1956. *The Image: Knowledge in Life and Society.* Ann Arbor: University of Michigan Press.

———. 1962. *Conflict and Defense: A General Theory.* New York: Harper Torchbooks (Harper and Row).

Bowring, Philip 2005, "Thailand's Homegrown Ills," *International Herald Tribune*, 27 May: 8.

Brkic, Courtney Angela 2005. "The Wages of Denial." *New York Times*, 11 July, <www.nytimes.com/2005/07/11/opinion/11Brkic.html>.

Broome, Benjamin J. (1993). "Managing Differences in Conflict Resolution: The Role of Relational Empathy." In *Conflict Resolution Theory and Practice: Integration and Application,* Dennis J.D. Sandole and Hugo van der Merwe (eds.). Manchester (UK): Manchester University Press and New York: St. Martin's Press.

Bruner, J.S. and Leo Postman (1949). "On the Perception of Incongruity: A Paradigm," *Journal of Personality*, vol. XVIII: 206-223.

Burton, John W. 1979. *Deviance, Terrorism, and War: The Process of Solving Unsolved Social and Political Problems.* New York: St. Martin's Press and Oxford (England): Martin Robertson.

———. 1984. *Global Conflict: The Domestic Sources of International Crisis.* Brighton (England): Wheatsheaf Books.

———. 1990. *Conflict: Resolution and Provention.* London: Macmillan and New York: St. Martin's Press.

―――――. 1997. *Violence Explained: The Sources of Conflict, Violence and Crime and their Prevention.* Manchester: Manchester University Press.

Cantril, Hadley, ed. 1950. *Tensions That Cause Wars.* Urbana: University of Illinois Press.

Conetta, Carl. 2003. "The Wages of War: Iraqi Combatant and Noncombatant Fatalities in the 2003 Conflict." Project on Defense Alternatives *Research Monograph #8*, 20 October <www.comw.org/pda/0310rm8.html>.

Coser, Lewis A. 1956. *The Functions of Social Conflict.* New York: Free Press and London: Collier-Macmillan.

Davis, Joyce M. 2003a. Interview on "Evening Exchange" with Kojo Nnamdi (Howard University PBS, Channel 32), 6 June.

―――――. 2003b. *Martyrs: Innocence, Vengeance and Despair in the Middle East.* New York: Palgrave Macmillan.

Dobbs, Michael. 2003. "Arab Hostility toward U.S. Growing, Poll Finds." *Washington Post*, 4 June: A18.

Fanon, Frantz. 1968. *The Wretched of the Earth* (translated by Constance Farrington). New York: Grove Press.

Festinger, Leon 1962. *A Theory of Cognitive Dissonance.* Stanford: Stanford University Press.

Foucault, Michel 1981. *Power/Knowledge: Selected Interviews and Other Writings 1972-1977* (edited by Colin Gordon). New York: Random House.

Frankl, Viktor E. 1985. *Man's Search for Meaning.* Revised and Updated. New York and London: Washington Square Press (Simon & Schuster).

Friedman, Adina 2002. "Terrorism in Context." In *Terrorism: Concepts, Causes, and Conflict Resolution*, edited by R. Scott Moore. A Publication of the Working Group on War, Violence and Terrorism, Institute for Conflict Analysis and Resolution (ICAR), George Mason University, Fairfax, Virginia: Fort Belvoir (Virginia); U.S. Defense Threat Reduction Agency.

Friedman, Thomas L. 2005. "A Poverty of Dignity and a Wealth of Rage." *New York Times*, 15 July. <www.nytimes.com/2005/07/15/opinion/15friedman.html>.

Fukuyama, Francis. 1989. "The End of History?" *The National Interest*, Summer: 3–18.

———.1992. *The End of History and the Last Man*. New York: Free Press.

Glastris, Paul. 2001. "Armenia's History, Turkey's Dilemma." *Washington Post*, 10 March: B1 and B4.

Goren, Ilan (2002). "My Generation Never Had Innocence to Lose." *The Washington Post*, 17 March: B1-B2.

Grove, Lloyd (2003). "The Reliable Source." *The Washington Post*, 6 June: C3.

Hamburg, David A. 2002. *No More Killing Fields: Preventing Deadly Conflict*. Lanham (Maryland), Boulder, New York, and Oxford: Rowman & Littlefield.

Harris, David A. 2003. "Seeds of Hate in Saudi Arabia." *Washington Post*, 7 June: A23.

Hedges, Chris 2002. *War is a Force That Gives Us Meaning*. New York: Public Affairs (Perseus Books).

Hockstader, Lee. 2002a. "Blast Hits Central Jerusalem: Palestinian Woman Triggers 2nd Attack at Site in Six Days." *Washington Post*, 28 January: A1 and A17.

———. 2002b. "No Consensus Among Israelis As Palestinian Fight Rages On." *Washington Post*, 2 March, A16.

Hosenball, Mark. 2005. "Al Qaeda: A Link to London?" *Newsweek*, 12 September: 11.

Hunter, Shireen T. 1998. *The Future of Islam and the West: Clash of Civilizations or Peaceful Coexistence?* Westport (Connecticut) and London: Praeger.

Huntington, Samuel P. 1993. "The Clash of Civilizations?" *Foreign Affairs* 72, no. 3, Summer: 22–49.

———. 1996. *The Clash of Civilizations and the Remaking of World Order*. New York: Simon & Schuster.

IHT. 2003. "Muslims in Bosnia Remember Massacre: Anniversary of Killings in Srebrenica is Marked by Thousands of Mourners." *International Herald Tribune*, 12–13 July: 2.

Isikoff, Michael, Daniel Klaidman and Evan Thomas. 2003. "Al Qaeda's Summer Plans." *Newsweek*, 2 June: 24–31.

Jones, Tricia S., and Andrea Bodtker. 2001. "Mediating with Heart in Mind: Addressing Emotion in Mediation Practice." *Negotiation Journal* 17, no. 3, July: 217–244.

Juergensmeyer, Mark. 2000. *Terror in the Mind of God: The Global Rise of Religious Violence*. Berkeley: University of California Press.

Kirisci, Kemal. 2000. "Disaggregating Turkish Citizenship and Immigration Practices." *Middle Eastern Studies* 36, no. 3, July: 1–22.

Kuhn, Thomas S. 1970. *The Structure of Scientific Revolutions*, Second Edition. Chicago and London: University of Chicago Press.

Lederach, John Paul. 2001. "Fostering Authentic Reconciliation Processes." *Report* of The Joan B. Kroc Institute for International Peace Studies (Notre Dame, Indiana: University of Notre Dame). Issue no. 20, Spring: 1–4.

Merry, Robert W. 2005. *Sands of Empire: Missionary Zeal, American Foreign Policy, and the Hazards of Global Ambition*. New York: Simon & Schuster.

Milgram, Stanley. 1974. *Obedience to Authority: An Experimental View*. New York, Evanston (Illinois), San Francisco, and London: Harper & Row.

Mitchell, Christopher R. and Michael Banks. 1996. *Handbook of Conflict Resolution: The Analytical Problem-solving Approach*. London: Pinter.

Montville, Joseph V. 1993. "The Healing Function in Political Conflict Resolution." In *Conflict Resolution Theory and Practice: Integration and Application*, edited by Dennis J.D. Sandole and Hugo van der Merwe. Manchester: Manchester University Press and New York: St. Martin's Press.

Mooradian, Moorad. 2003. "Reconciliation: A Case Study of the Turkish Armenian Reconciliation Commission," *Working Paper No. 24*,

Institute for Conflict Analysis and Resolution (ICAR), George Mason University (www.gmu.edu/departments/icar).

Mooradian, Moorad. 2005. *A New Look at TARC*. Watertown (Massachusetts): Tekeyan.

OSCE Handbook. 2000. Third edition, second impression, June. (Edited by Walter Kemp, Michal Olejarnik, Victor-Yves Ghebali, Andrei Androsov, and Keith Jinks.) Vienna, Austria: Organization for Security and Cooperation in Europe.

North, Robert C. 1990. *War, Peace, Survival: Global Politics and Conceptual Synthesis*. Boulder: Westview Press. PBS. 2001. "Saudi Time Bomb?" *Frontline*, 15 November, <www.pbs.org/wgbh/pages/frontline/shows/saudi>.

Popper, Karl R. 1972. *Objective Knowledge: An Evolutionary Approach*. Oxford: Oxford University Press.

Rose, Richard 1971. *Governing Without Consensus: An Irish Perspective*. London: Faber and Faber.

Saleem, Sabaa U. 2005. "Being Muslim in a Mad, Sad World: There's Right, There's Wrong, and More Than One Way to See Things." *Washington Post*, 31 July: B3.

Sandole, Dennis J.D. 1987. "Conflict Management: Elements of Generic Theory and Practice." In *Conflict Management and Problem Solving: Interpersonal to International Applications*, edited by Dennis J.D. Sandole and Ingrid Sandole-Staroste. London: Frances Pinter and New York: New York University Press.

———. 1993. "Paradigms, Theories, and Metaphors in Conflict and Conflict Resolution: Coherence or Confusion?" In *Conflict Resolution Theory and Practice: Integration and Application*, edited by Dennis J.D. Sandole and Hugo van der Merwe. Manchester: Manchester University Press and New York: St. Martin's Press.

———. 1997a. "Developing Conflict Resolution in Transcaucasia: A University-Based Approach." In "Strengthening Transitional Democracies Through Conflict Resolution," Special issue of *THE ANNALS* of the American Academy of Political and Social Science, edited by Raymond Shonholtz and Ilana Shapiro. vol. 552, July:

125–138.

————. 1997b. "Institutionalizing Conflict Resolution in Transcaucasia: A Progress Report." In "Conflict Management Within Transitioning Societies," Special issue of *NIDR News* (National Institute for Dispute Resolution, Washington, DC), edited by Raymond Shonholtz and Juliette Linzer. vol. IV, no. 4, September/October: 7, 11–12.

————. 1998. "A Comprehensive Mapping of Conflict and Conflict Resolution: A Three Pillar Approach," *Peace and Conflict Studies*, vol. 5, no. 2, December: 1–30 <www.gmu.edu/academic/pcs/sandole>.

————. 1999. *Capturing the Complexity of Conflict: Dealing with Violent Ethnic Conflicts of the Post-Cold War Era*. London and New York: Pinter/Cassell (Continuum International).

————. 2001. "'Clashes of Civilization' and Other Possible Influences on Ethnic Warfare in Former Yugoslavia: The Views of CSCE/OSCE Negotiators, 1993 and 1997." Paper presented at the 42nd Annual Convention of the International Studies Association (ISA), Chicago, Illinois, 20–24 February.

————. 2002. "Virulent Ethnocentrism: A Major Challenge for Transformational Conflict Resolution and Peacebuilding in the Post-Cold War Era." *Global Review of Ethnopolitics*, vol. 1, no. 4: 4–27 <www.ethnopolitics.org>.

————. 2003. "A Typology." In *Conflict: From Analysis to Intervention*, edited by Sandra Cheldelin, Daniel Druckman, and Larissa Fast . London and New York: Continuum International.

————. 2005a. "Hurting Stalemate in the Middle East: Opportunities for Conflict Resolution?" *ICAR News* (Institute for Conflict Analysis and Resolution, George Mason University), Spring: 1, 6-9 <www.gmu.edu/departments/icar>.

————. 2005b. "The Western-Islamic 'Clash of Civilizations': The Inadvertent Contribution of the Bush Presidency." Presented at the Annual Convention of the International Studies Association (ISA), Honolulu, Hawaii, 1-5 March 2005 <www.isanet.org>. Published in *Peace and Change*, vol. 12, no. 2, Fall: 54-68.

————. 2005c. "Thailand's Muslims" (Letter to the Editor). *International Herald Tribune*, 7 June: 9.

————. 2005d. "Turkey's Unique Role in Nipping in the Bud the 'Clash of Civilizations'." Paper presented at the first World International Studies Conference (WISC), Bilgi University, Istanbul, Turkey, 24–27 August.

————. forthcoming. *Peace and Security in the Postmodern World: The OSCE and Conflict Resolution*. London and New York: Routledge (Taylor & Francis).

Sandole, Dennis J.D., Kimberly Dannels Ruff, and Evis Vasili. 2004. "Identity and Apocalyptic Terrorism." In *Apocalyptic Terrorism: Understanding the Unfathomable*, edited by R. Scott Moore. A Publication of the Working Group on War, Violence, and Terrorism, Institute for Conflict Analysis and Resolution (ICAR), George Mason University, Fairfax, Virginia. Fort Belvoir, Virginia: U.S. Defense Threat Reduction Agency (DTRA), April.

Sherif, Muzafer. 1967. *Group Conflict and Cooperation: Their Social Psychology*. London: Routledge and Kegan Paul.

Simmel, Georg. 1955. *Conflict and the Web of Group-Affiliations*, translated by Kurt H. Wolff and Reinhard Bendix. New York: Free Press and London: Collier-Macmillan.

The 9/11 Commission Report: Final Report of the National Commission on Terrorist Attacks Upon the United States 2004. New York and London: W.W. Norton.

Thomas, Evan and Martha Brant. 2003. "Victory in Iraq." *Newsweek*, 21 April: 24–32.

Volkan, Vamik D. 1985. "The Need to Have Enemies and Allies: A Developmental Approach." *Political Psychology* 6, no. 2, June: 219–245.

————. 1988. *The Need to Have Enemies and Allies: From Clinical Practice to International Relationships*. Northvale (New Jersey) and London: Jason Aronson.

————. 1997. *Bloodlines: From Ethnic Pride to Ethnic Terrorism*. New York: Farrar, Straus and Giroux.

Waldrop, M. Mitchell. 1992. *Complexity: The Emerging Science at the Edge of Order and Chaos*. New York and London: Simon & Schuster.

Waltz, Kenneth N. 1959. *Man, the State, and War: A Theoretical Analysis*. New York: Columbia University Press.

Warrick, Joby (2003). "Dirty Bomb Warheads Disappear: Stocks of Soviet-Era Arms for Sale on Black Market." *The Washington Post*, 7 December: A1 and A28.

Wheeler, Everett L. 1991. "Terrorism and Military Theory: An Historical Perspective." In *Terrorism Research and Public Policy*, edited by Clark McCauley. London: Frank Cass.

Wilson, Edward O. 1998. *Consilience: The Unity of Knowledge*. New York: Knopf.

WP. 2005. "The Week in Iraq," *The Washington Post*, 10 September: A19.

Wrangham, Richard and Dale Peterson (1996). *Demonic Males: Apes and the Origins of Human Violence*. New York and Boston: Mariner Books (Houghton Mifflin).

Chapter 5

Identity Salience as a Determinant of the Perceptions of the Other

Karina V. Korostelina

A social group often achieves solidarity among its members by demonizing the Other. (See chapter 3 in this Volume.) Research confirms the role of identity salience in amplifying conflict intentions toward members of other groups. But it is not enough to note that salient identity advances negative attitudes and dispositions toward others and leads to violence. It is important to determine why this occurs. Why does salient identity influence conflict behavior and negative attitudes toward other groups?

This chapter begins by analyzing current studies of the impact of social identity on negative perceptions and hostilities toward the Other. Identity salience is considered unstable and can be increased by such factors as the existence of a majority or significant outgroup, threat, or negative attitude toward the ingroup, change in a person's goals and values, and change in the social situation of an individual or ingroup. When identity becomes highly salient, it can displace all other identities and dominate attitudes and behavior. This chapter provides a research example that shows the impact of identity salience on the willingness to defend ingroup goals and fight against outgroup goals.

The following four studies aim to explore the mechanism of the influence of identity salience on conflictual behaviors. Since the ingroup primacy—the feeling of supremacy of ingroup goals and values over personal goals and values—is derived from identity salience, the first study proposes that for ingroup members with less salient social identity, ingroup primacy has a stronger impact on the readiness for conflict behavior. The second study analyzes the structure of narratives about the Other in light of the view that salient identity influenced the construction and content of these narratives. The third study examines the structure of consciousness of people with salient and non-salient ethnic identity and reveals differences in the perception of other groups and the world as a whole. The fourth and final study explores the structure of the value systems of the individual or group, proposing that salient ethnic identities lead to a high level of similarity between ingroup and personal values and to the significance of values of ingroup primacy and interdependence.

Identity Salience

Salient identity can be defined as the most important identity for the individual, and it can be influenced by such factors as permeable/impermeable group boundaries, positive or negative inter-group comparisons, identity distinctiveness issues, and the socialization processes (Berry, Kim, Power, Young, & Bujaki 1989; Brewer 1991, 2001; Tajfel & Turner 1979). Salience can vary on a continuum from strong to weak: each identity can be very salient, salient or non salient. As Phinney (1991) shows, persons with strong ethnic identity salience have strong feelings for their group memberships, evaluate their group positively, prefer or are comfortable with their group membership, and are interested in the group, its culture, and its history.

Striker (1969) has argued that various identities exist in a hierarchy of salience, and one identity can be invoked over others not only because of its salience, but also because of the level of commitment to that identity. One highly salient identity can prevail over another. Due to the hierarchy of salience, these identities may exhibit stable or situational characteristics. Striker noted that if one identity has salience for a long period, it becomes a central identity and has a strong influence on behavior. At the same time, Ting-Toomey (2000) notes that for some individuals ethnic identity becomes more salient when its members are confronted with interpersonal problems, such as stereotypes, prejudice, and discrimination.

Several findings confirm the importance of social categories on one's choice of group identification. For example, McGuire and colleagues found that children representing ethnic minorities in their classes tend to describe themselves in terms of ethnic groups, while children in families with a prevalence of the other gender (such as being the only girl in a family of five brothers) stress their gender identity in self-description (McGuire, McGuire, Child, & Fujioka 1978). The study of Ellemers, Spears, and Doosje (1997) show that people with salient identity find more in common with other members of their ingroup and do not want to leave the ingroup even in situations of threat. Salient social identity influences the level of satisfaction in ingroup activities (Wann and Branscombe 1990). Identity theory also indicates that numerous, authoritarian, and powerful outgroups influence the development of salient identity. When this is institutionalized in a social system, this asymmetrical mix of different influences on salient identity leads to development and change within an individual's structure of identities. Research has shown that even disproportion between groups can increase salience of identity. As the research of Kinket and Verkuyten (1997) demonstrates, situational salience (percentage of Dutch and Turkish students in the classroom) affects weak rather than strong identity.

According to Oakes' functional approach to salience (Oakes 1987), the use of the category in a given context depends on the accessibility of the category and the fit between the category and reality. As Huddy (2001) argued, four factors influence the acquisition of identity: the valence of group membership, the defining social characteristics of typical group members, the core values associated with membership, and the characteristics of common outgroups who help to define what the ingroup is not. Gerson (2001) maintains that the development and salience of identity is influenced by practices: "what people do and how they conceptualize or represent what they constitute membership in various groups" (2001, p. 183).

Any salient identity—central or situational, old or new—can influence personal attitudes, emotions, and values. In specific situations, this salient identity determines an individual's entire worldview and perceptions. Below, I discuss three factors that lead to an increase in the salience of social identity. The first factor is the existence of a majority or prevalence of people relating to a specific social category, such as gender or class. Group categories relevant to this group must be a part of the person's system of social identities. For example, if class identity is not very important for a person, but is a part of her or his system of identities, her or his class identity can become salient and even dominant. If a person's national identity is not a significant identity while they are living in their own country, it can become salient once these individuals are exposed to a foreign country in which they become a minority. Interestingly, even identities that go unnoticed by a person can develop into salient identities. For example, a social psychologist colleague went to Crimea, Ukraine to conduct conflict resolution training. For several days, she lived in a situation in which everyone spoke Russian and Ukrainian, but no English. During this time she realized that her "English speaking" identity become very salient for her, in spite of the fact that she had not previously thought about herself in terms of this category.

The second factor that affects social identity salience is threatening or negative attitudes toward the ingroup. If an individual listens to negative remarks about the ingroup or faces negative attitudes toward the ingroup, their corresponding social identity becomes salient and significant. Usually, this identity has a secondary position in a person's hierarchy prior to their exposure to anti-ingroup sentiments. But following that exposure, those negative sentiments can promote enhanced ingroup solidarity, loyalty, and subsequent negative attitudes toward the outgroup. For example, a regional (city) identity can be insignificant for a person, but if this person experiences negative remarks about their territory from inhabitants of other regions, they tend to defend their ingroup identity, its values and characteristics actively, and ally themselves strongly with the ingroup. The more often an individual faces such situations, the more salient his or her regional identity becomes. For example, a friend who was born in one American state and moved to another state told me that he never identified himself in relation to his native state. But in his new environment, he faced jokes and remarks about his native place which activated a feeling of affliction prompting him to defend his ingroup. He realized after moving that his ingroup identity was very important for him, and his story is an example of an identity becoming salient.

The third factor affecting social identity salience is a change in personal goals and values. Any type of activity can become significant for a person when she or he attaches a social identity to the activity, making it salient. For example, if a person begins to care for an ill parent and this activity becomes an important part of the person's life, their social identity as a son or daughter become salient and takes the dominant place in their identity system. Another example is when one's professional goals or career develops into an individual's main activity. In this case, their professional identity comes becomes salient and therefore the dominant over individual identity.

Although these three aforementioned factors affect the salience of social identities, any change in the social situation of an individual or ingroup will lead to the ascension of another identity's salience, creating the necessity of restructuring within the system of identities. If one of the core, leading identities becomes salient, changes are less considerable, because interconnections between core identities are more stable and strong. But if one of the short-term identities becomes salient, a significant imbalance grows and there must be restructuring efforts to return to a stable position. There is a possibility for an inverse process, whereby a core identity can become a situational or short-term identity. For example, if a person resides in the surroundings of ingroup members for a long time, the need for individuation can weaken the individual's ingroup identity. Changes in the system of person's goals and values can also decrease the importance of a goal as a result of the individuals' loss of interest. In this case, the social identity connected with this goal or value can become less salient and move to the subsystem of situational and short-term identities. For example, one of my students told me that his sports team membership was very important to him and that his identity as a team member was salient. But when he took a great interest in the field of conflict resolution, he lost many connections with his sport team. He still met with this teammates from time to time, but his sports team identity become situational and then disappeared altogether.

The Impact of Identity Salience on Attitudes and Readiness for Conflict

The majority of studies of social identity provide evidence *of* the relationship between the salience of social identities and attitudes toward outgroups. The theory of social identity suggests that the need to acquire high social status and a positive identity through membership in socially prestigious groups is the basis for the formation of intergroup prejudice (Brown 2000; Huddy & Virtanen 1995; Jackson, Sullivan, Harnish & Hodge 1996; Tajfel & Turner 1979; Taylor, Moghaddam, Gamble & Zellerer 1987; Wright, Taylor & Moghaddam 1990). This basic need leads to the formation of positive auto-stereotypes to compensate for the low social status of one's own ingroup (Lalonde 1992; Mummendey and Otten 1998; Van Knippenberg 1978; Van Knippenberg & Van Oers

1984). In fact, research has demonstrated that strong identification with racial and ethnic groups among South Africans influences their desire for group solidarity, their antipathy toward outgroups, their fear of threat, and their feelings of intolerance (Gibson and Gouwa 1999). There is also an echo effect: the intention of a national minority to become autonomous or independent will provoke a nationalistic reaction among the indigenous majority (Hagendoorn, Csepeli, Dekker & Farnen 2000). Other research results confirm the role of subjective group membership in shaping political attitudes and behavior (Conover, 1988; Miller, Gurin, Gurrin, &Malanchuk 1981); and yet more research revealed strong correlations between ingroup identification and outgroup hostility (Branscombe & Wann 1994; Grant & Brown 1995). The studies show that negative stereotypes can be reinforced not only by ingroup members attributing antagonistic goals to outgroup members, but by ingroup members attributing goals to themselves based on the assumption that outgroups may become hostile to these shared goals (Hagendoorn, Linssen, Rotman, &Tumanov 1996). Experimental research conducted on the impact of personal and national identity on prejudice against immigrants in Holland demonstrated an insignificant effect (Hagendoorn, Linssen, Rotman, & Tumanov 1996). However, it was shown that participants with less salient national identity [in condition of stressing of Holland identity demonstrated an increase in anxiety regarding new immigrants.

I propose that the salience of social identity is connected with the *primacy of the ingroup,* with respect supremacy of ingroup goals and values over personal goals and values. The primacy of the ingroup identity contains several components: (1) predominance of ingroup goals over personal goals, (2) the readiness to forget all internal ingroup conflicts in situations of threat to the ingroup, and (3) the readiness to unite against outgroups. The higher the level of ingroup primacy for ingroup members, the higher their willingness will be to disregard their own goals and values and follow the modes of behavior required by the ingroup.

Ingroup primacy can increase or decrease the influence of identity salience on conflict behaviors of ingroup members. Some groups require a high level of ingroup primacy as a condition of group membership, while other groups provide opportunities for maintaining a balance between personal and ingroup values and goals. If high ingroup primacy is obligatory to membership, a salient ingroup identity will lead directly to inter-group prejudice and conflict behavior. If high ingroup primacy is not required for membership, ingroup members with salient identities can rethink and revise their attitudes toward the outgroup and their readiness for conflict behavior based on their personal experience. This freedom to rethink will reduce the impact of identity salience on intergroup prejudice.

My research confirms the strong impact of identity salience on the readiness for conflict with another group as a part of a connotative component of prejudice. The readiness for conflict with the outgroup is an extreme consequence of intergroup prejudice, and aims to increase as the group seeks to dominate, or defends itself against, the outgroup. The readiness for conflict with the outgroup reflects the willingness to defend one's own group in situations of real or perceived threat from other groups, to control and prevent actions of the members of other groups that can be potentially dangerous or unpleasant for one's own group (or can increase status of other group), or to punish or take revenge on members of the other group. People with a high level of readiness for conflict engage in harassment and fighting with members of other groups more often than with members of their own group. The readiness for conflict with the outgroup is a function of inter-group bias and inter-group discrimination, and depends on calculations of possible risks to vested interests and the possibility of strong opposition from outgroups.

My research on the impact of identity salience shows that group members who identify strongly with their group show higher readiness for conflict behavior than those who identify less, or they support the ingroup goals and oppose the outgroup goals. The study was conducted in Crimea in different towns and villages after the events of September 11, 2001. The sample was stratified by location, number of resettlements, and rural-urban status. Respondents were provided with a questionnaire and selected answers from the list. Participation was voluntary. Participants included 505 Russians and 578 Crimean Tatars distributed across these locations in equal proportions. Participation was voluntary. Of the participants, 42% were male and 58% female; 39% were between ages 20 and 30; 31% were between ages 30 and 45; 20% were between ages 45 and 60; 10% were above 60; 55% were residents of towns; and 45% were residents of villages.

The hypothesis that salient ingroup identity leads to increased endorsement of ingroup goals and stronger opposition to outgroup goals was tested in two ways. Participants were divided into two groups: those with weak and strong salient ethnic identity. Subsequently, half of the participants answered the questions from their personal standpoint (personal identity), while the other half answered the questions as ingroup members (social identity).

The results showed that highly salient ethnic identity reinforced the support of ingroup goals and that this same salient social identity led to more opposition toward outgroup members. In particular, strongly identifying Crimean Tatars endorsed Crimean Tatar cultural autonomy. Thus, salient social identity leads to the readiness to defend ingroup values.

The next step was to define the factors that determine this influence. As I mentioned above, the primacy of the ingroup, or the belief in the supremacy of ingroup goals and values over personal goals and values, can increase or decrease the influence of identity salience on conflict behavior patterns of ingroup members. My research confirmed that the primacy of an ingroup has a higher influence on the readiness to defend norms, values, and the safety of the ingroup if the ingroup identity is less salient and has smaller impact on this readiness.

Feelings of ingroup primacy were measured by several questions regarding (1) the predominance of ingroup goals over personal goals, (2) the readiness to forget all internal ingroup conflicts in a situation of threat, and (3) the readiness to unite against the outgroup. The higher the level of feeling of ingroup primacy for members, the higher the individuals' willingness to disregard their own goals and values and follow ways of behavior required by a collective ingroup identity.

I propose that feelings of ingroup primacy play a less important role if social identities are salient and have a strong impact on the readiness for conflict behavior. If social identity is less salient and has less influence on the readiness for conflict behavior, feelings of ingroup primacy contribute to the increase in the readiness to fight.

A partially saturated General Linear Model was used to test this proposition for two groups simultaneously: one with a low level of social identity salience (211 respondents) and the other with a high level of social identity salience (203 respondents). For the first group (with low salient ethnic and religious identity), feelings of ingroup primacy had strong effects on the readiness to defend the safety of the ethnic group, on the readiness to defend the safety of the religious group, on the readiness to defend the norms and values of the ethnic group, and on the readiness to defend the norms and values of the religious group. Religious identity had a significant impact only on the readiness to defend the safety of the religious group.

For the second group (with strong salient social identity), ethnic and religious identities both had significant effects on the readiness to defend the safety of the ethnic group, on the readiness to defend the safety of the religious group, on the readiness to defend the norms and values of the ethnic group, and on the readiness to defend the norms and values of the religious group. The feeling of ingroup primacy had a significant impact only on the readiness to defend the norms and values of the religious group.

Therefore, for ingroup members with a low level of social identity salience, feelings of ingroup primacy had an impact on the readiness to defend the safety, values, and norms of the ethnic and religious groups. Only religious identity influenced the readiness to defend the safety of the religious group. For ingroup members with a high level of social identity salience, the readiness to defend the safety, values, and norms of the ethnic and religious groups were influenced by the ethnic and religious identities. Feeling of ingroup primacy only impacted the readiness to defend the norms and values of the religious group. Ingroup members with salient social identity had stronger feelings of ingroup primacy; however, feelings of ingroup primacy didn't play an important role in the formation of the readiness for conflict behavior. It was the salient social identity that led to the readiness for conflict. For ingroup members with less salient social identity, ingroup primacy had a stronger impact on the readiness for conflict behavior. In other words, people with a low level of social identity salience showed the readiness for conflict behavior only when they felt that the ingroup goals and values were more important than personal goals and values, and believed that the existence of an enemy could unite the ingroup against the outgroup. For people with salient ethnic identity, readiness for conflict was the result of identity salience; ingroup primacy was derived from social identity salience and did not have a direct impact on the readiness for conflict behavior.

Identity Salience and Perception of the Outgroup

Understanding the impact of identity salience on the readiness for conflictual behavior requires an analysis of the influence of identity salience on the perception of other groups. My study compared the perceptions of the ethnic outgroup by people with and without salient social (ethnic) identities, for the purpose of discovering the effects of identity salience on the assessment of characteristics and interaction with outgroup members. I propose that a salient social identity influences the perception and understanding of social situations reflected in stories about members of the outgroup, their behavior, and their characteristics. Such narratives reveal the knowledge, attitudes, and opinions of people that are socially determined and depend on the specificity of intergroup relations.

During this study, 100 Russians were asked to tell stories about interactions with one other ethnic group, the Crimean Tatars. They also answered a short questionnaire on ethnic identity salience. Respondents were distributed into two groups of salient (43 persons) and non-salient (57 persons) ethnic identity. All stories were examined using the discourse analysis method (van Dijk, 2001).

Analysis of the stories from people with salient ethnic identity showed the following structure of discourse:

Time: not used

Place of Encounter: public transportation – 40%, market – 40%, school – 10%, neighborhood – 10%.

Conditions: riding public transportation, meetings with friends, shopping

Outgroup:
➤ Are rude, cruel, aggressive – 60%
➤ Steal – 30%
➤ Destroy, ruin – 27%
➤ Use cunning – 25%
➤ Are a bother – 23%
➤ Are insincere – 20%
➤ Are hidebound – 15%

➤ Are hospitable – 13%
➤ Are ready to help – 7%

Ingroup:
➤ Offended
➤ Defended ethnic group
➤ Provoked by other group

Interaction:
➤ Aggression – 45%
➤ Deception, fraud – 32%
➤ Harassment – 30%
➤ Theft – 15%

Consequences: negative attitudes, spite, resentment

The analysis of stories from people with non-salient ethnic identity showed the following structure of discourse:

Time: usual

Place of Encounter:
➤ Neighborhood – 35%
➤ Work, study – 25%
➤ Family, friends – 25%
➤ Shopping – 10%
➤ Street, transportation – 5%

Conditions: connected with work or community

Outgroup:
➤ Are hospitable – 33%
➤ Are ready to help – 30%
➤ Are ready to understand – 27%
➤ Steal – 15%
➤ Use cunning – 12%
➤ Destroy, ruin – 10%
➤ Are a bother – 10%
➤ Are hidebound – 5%

Ingroup:
➤ Good
➤ Tolerant
➤ Fair
➤ Victims
➤ Suffering

Interaction:
➤ Friendship – 35%
➤ Cooperation – 35%
➤ Help – 20%
➤ Harassment – 15%
➤ Aggression – 12%
➤ Theft – 10%
➤ Deception, fraud – 5%

Consequences: positive or negative attitudes, readiness for cooperation, spite

The comparative analysis of stories of people with salient and non-salient ethnic identities about cases of interaction with the representatives other ethnos reveals the following cognitive models of inter-ethnic interaction for both groups:

    1)   Stories from people with salient ethnic identity were characterized by high similarity and connected only with situations of interaction with the strangers in public places. The stories of people with non-salient ethnic identity were more diverse and connected with the situations of everyday contacts with neighbors, in the community and at the workplace.

    2)   All the stories from people with salient ethnic identity were negative, while by contrast 60% of the stories from people with non-salient ethnic identity viewed the outgroup positively.

    3)   People with salient ethnic identities emphasized situations of insults in public places, while people with non-salient ethnic identity described the positive and negative acts of interaction in everyday conditions.

    4)   People with salient ethnic identity tended to generalize about the character of the Other. In 45% of cases, there were

statements like "all the Tatars." The stories from people with non-salient ethnic identities had individual character.

5)   In the stories from people with salient ethnic identity, social actions connected with negative emotional conditions involving rejection, intensity, and antagonism prevailed. They did not use positive emotions or describe out-groups or themselves negatively. The behavior of outgroup members in these stories was perceived as aggressive and antagonistic; the situations of inter-group interactions were described as depressing and tense. The attitudes of people with non-salient ethnic identity were more diverse; they attributed and expected both negative and positive actions from Tatars. In the situations described by the people with non-salient ethnic identity, the Crimean Tatars quite often acted as the initiators of interactions, providing offers, help, etc.

6)   People with salient ethnic identity attributed only negative emotions to members of the outgroup, with a prevalence of anger and disgust. People with non-salient ethnic identity described various emotions, including interest, pleasure, and pleasant surprise.

7)   The people with salient ethnic identity perceived the outgroup as an absolutely strange group of people with minimal interaction. The people with non-salient ethnic identities described Crimean Tatars as neighbors in society.

Salience of Identity and Structure of Consciousness

This study aimed to analyze the structure of consciousness of people with salient and non-salient ethnic identity by examining the constructs of consciousness reflected in the perception and estimation of the other ethnic group. To study personal constructs, Kelly's repertory grid test (1955) was used. Kelly suggests that people develop a set of personal constructs that they use to understand the world and the people in it. These constructs are bipolar (i.e. they have two ends), or are dichotomous, and vary from one person to another. To study a person's constructed system, Kelly developed a repertory grid. This idea originated when a therapist asked clients to think about people they knew and find words to describe them, providing the therapist with the main constructs. In its modified version, respondents receive the list of constructs arranged in a grid. Respondents are then asked to assess significant people or events by noting them on the grid. Certain constructs cluster together that show distinctive ways of understanding the world.

For the repertory grid in this study, I used matrix 15*7. Seven different roles were listed in columns; each proposed the social position of people from other ethnic groups: neighbors of other ethnicities, co-workers of other ethnicities, community leaders of other ethnicities, etc. There were 100 respondents (50 Russians and 50 Crimean Tatars), ranging from 20 to 40 years old. Crimean Tatars were asked to assess Russians and Russians were asked to assess Crimean Tatars. Respondents were asked to identify the exact person for each social role and assess him or her using 15 pairs of characteristics (constructs for evaluation of roles) presented in rows. Respondents assessed each person by each characteristic using a five-point scale. The grid offered for Crimean Tatars is presented in the Table 5.1.

Table 5.1. Repertory grid

	My Russian neighbor	My Russian co-worker	Russian teacher	Etc.
Moral – immoral				
Wise – shortsighted				
Responsible – irresponsible				
Interested – indifferent				
Etc.				

The results of individual grids were summarized in two group grids by calculating means. The data *were* analyzed by correlation and factor analyses by groups with salient and non-salient ethnic identity. This analysis provided an opportunity to find the structure of interconnections between different criteria of estimations (constructs of consciousness) for people with salient and non-salient ethnic identity. Results showed that representatives of both ethnic groups with salient ethnic identity had strongly interconnected constructs of consciousness. Analysis revealed 67 significant correlations among the constructs, which means that the characteristics of people with salient ethnic identity used to assess representatives of other ethnic groups are interrelated. People with a salient ethnic identity based their conclusions about the characteristics of persons of other ethnicity on very firm assumptions that logically follow one another. While attributing one characteristic to the person of another ethnicity, people with salient ethnic identity automatically attributed him or her with a set of other characteristics. For example, if a person with a salient ethnic identity considered people of another ethnicity cruel, they immediately attributed them with shortsightedness and irresponsibility.

Figure 5.1 presents an example of the connections between constructs of consciousness for people with salient ethnic identity. All lines represent significant correlations.

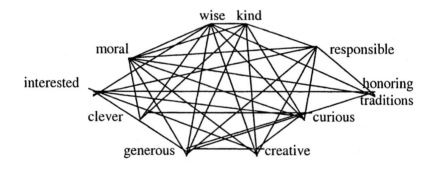

Figure 5.1

Factor analysis found two main factors in the structure of consciousness of people with salient ethnic identity. The first factor included such characteristics as clever, kind, wise, generous, and morally inquisitive. The second factor included such characteristics as generous, inquisitive, honoring traditions, moral, and responsible. By attributing the person of another ethnicity with such characteristics as 'malicious,' people with salient ethnic identity simultaneously regarded this individual as silly, thoughtless, stingy, and adaptive. Having decided the person of the other ethnicity was careless, they automatically attributed them with characteristics of nonsense, unscrupulousness, levity, cowardice, and rage.

Correlation analysis of constructs of consciousness of people with non-salient ethnic identities revealed only 15 correlations among the criteria of assessment. This means that the characteristics people with non-salient ethnic identity used to assess representatives of other ethnic groups are independent and represent complex judgments. People with non-salient ethnic identity consider persons of another ethnicity as possessing different characteristics and having unique personalities. They used the set of criteria to assess people of other ethnicities and took each characteristic into separate consideration. While characterizing people of another ethnicity, people with non-salient ethnic identity tend to avoid overgeneralizations and stereotypes. For example, having decided that the person is clever, such people separately assess his or her kindness, creativity, wisdom, etc.

Figure 5.2 presents an example of the connections between constructs of consciousness for people with non-salient ethnic identity. All lines represent significant correlations.

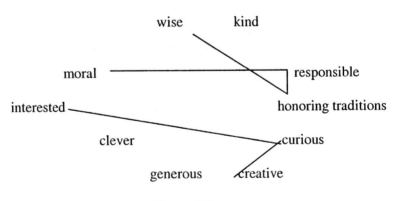

Figure 5.2

Thus, salient identity leads to the perception of the world as rigidly connected and determined. Salient identity reduces the ability to understand the world by various criteria and by using polymodal measures of assessment; it leads "tunnel consciousness" in their understanding of other groups, situations, and activities involving ethnic/religious/national identity. People with non-salient social identity have a multi-dimensional approach to the assessment of the world, use different criteria, and consider both positive and negative sides of people and events. Using the metaphor of a color palette, one could say that people with salient social identity perceive the world in one color while people with non-salient identity use multiple colors to paint reality.

Salience of Identity and Values

Value commitments are deeply embedded their sense of ingroup identity. I propose that the values of individuals with salient ethnic identity will be more strongly connected to the values of their ethnic group than the values of individuals with non-salient ethnic identity. I also propose that individuals with salient ethnic identity will assess another ethnic group by attributing them with values opposite to those of their own ethnic group. In other words, people with salient ethnic identity will deny the existence of their most important values among the representatives of a different ethnic group.

To verify these propositions, I conducted a study of values attached to two ethnic identities—Russians and Crimean Tatars. Research was conducted using the Rokeach Value Survey (RVS; Rokeach 1973), designed to measure an individual's perception of the relative weight attached to certain values as guiding principles in his or her life. It consists of two alphabetically ordered lists of 18 values. One list consists of terminal values, such as freedom, happiness, and a world at peace, which concern the "end state of existence." The second list contains instrumental values, such as ambitious, helpful, and polite, which deal with "modes of conduct." Each value is followed by a short defining phrase. I asked respondents to rank the terminal and instrumental values separately in terms of importance to themselves, to their ethnic group, and to the other ethnic group (in their opinion). The most important value receives a rank of 1, the second most important value receives a rank of 2, and so forth. Finally, I calculated group medians of ranks for groups with salient and non-salient ethnic identity.

Karina V. Korostelina

To verify the first proposition, I compared the ranks of personal and group values for people with salient and non-salient ethnic identities from both ethnic groups (Tables 5.2 and 5.3).

The analysis shows that people with salient ethnic identity from both ethnic groups perceive their values as very close to ingroup values. Many values in the "group list" have the same rank as values in the "personal list." People with salient ethnic identity also display a high level of consistency in their answers (or, a low dispersal of answers).

Table 5.2. Ranks of personal and group instrumental values

Instrumental Values	Crimean Tatars			Russians		
	Both groups	Salient ident.	Non-salient ident.	Both groups	Salient ident.	Non-salient ident.
Polite	1. 5	1	3	4	4	2
Ambitious	8.5	9	7	16.5	17	15
Cheerful	4.5	5	8	7.5	7	10
Obedient	7.5	8	10	14	13.5	16
Independent	7	7	5	7	8	5
Clean	14.5	14.5	13	14.5	14	13.5
Intellectual	9	10	11	7	8	5.5
Responsible	6.5	6	5	5.5	5	4
Logical	14	14	12.5	13	13	11
Self-control	10	10	9	7.5	8	6
Courageous	11.5	12	14	9	9	7
Imaginative	11	10.5	11	7	7.5	6
Forgiving	11	12	8.5	8.5	9	4.5
Broad-minded	11	11	9	12	13	10.5
Honest	4.5	4.5	5	2	2	4
Capable	12.5	12	10	11	12	14
Loving	6	6	5	2.5	2	1.5
Helpful	2	2	3	6	6	6.5

This finding means that people with salient ethnic identities attribute the same significance to group values as they do to personal values. Independently of ethnic background, they consider group and personal values very similar and comparable; the structure of their value system depends on and is based on the group values structure. People with non-salient ethnic identity place different importance on group values and personal values: some of their personal values are more essential than group values and some have less significance. Moreover, they display a high dispersal of answers, varying different ranks for values within the group. They possess their own value structure independently from the group value system.

The correlation analysis of interrelations between group values and personal values confirms this finding. It shows significantly higher interrelation between group and personal values for people with salient ethnic identity than for people with non-salient ethnic identity.

Table 5.3. Ranks of personal and group terminal values

	Crimean Tatars			Russians		
Terminal Values	Both groups	Salient ident.	Non-salient ident.	Both groups	Salient ident.	Non-salient ident.
An exciting life	11	12	10	12	12	9
Wisdom	10.5	10	10	10	10.5	10
Happiness	1.5	3	1	2	2	1.5
Accomplishment	8	8	7	6.5	7	4
Inner harmony	15	15.5	12	11	11	9
Mature love	4	4	3	4	4	4.5
Comfortable life	4,5	5	4	10	10	8
True friendship	6.5	6	7	6	6	5.5
Soc. recognition	12	12	15	15	15.5	17
Self-Respect	12	13	8	11	10.5	6.5
National security	12	11	13	13.5	13	13
Salvation	13,5	14	15	10.5	10	12
Pleasure	10.5	10	9	16	16	14
Freedom	9	9	7	9	9	6
Family security	4,5	4	6	3	2	5
Equality	12.5	12	9	12	12	8
A world at peace	16	16	11	13	13.5	10

The results also show that some values hold significant differences between group and individual ranks for both ethnic groups. Instrumental values such as obedient, forgiving, broad-minded, and such terminal values as inner harmony, social recognition, self-respect, freedom, equality, and world in peace have significantly different ranks for people with salient and non-salient ethnic identity. Analysis revealed several groups of divergent values:

1)   Values connected with ingroup primacy: obedient, social recognition.

2)   Values connected with personal independence (social and cognitive): inner harmony, self-respect, broad-minded, freedom.

3)   Values connected with relations: forgiving, equality, world in peace.

Individuals with salient ethnic identity in this study consider obedience and social recognition as more important values than do people with non-salient ethnic identity. Loyalty to the ingroup, primacy of ingroup norms, and following the rules and goals of the ingroup are important in interrelations with the ingroup. People with salient ethnic identity also expect social recognition and support from their group, which is one of the main functions of social identity. For people with non-salient ethnic identity, loyalty to ingroup and reciprocal ingroup recognition are less important values.

Values associated with personal independence are given greater priority for those with non-salient ethnic identity. They value inner harmony, self-respect, personal freedom, and open-minded thinking in their relations with others. Therefore, people with non-salient ethnic identities possess personal worldviews and ways of life. In contrast, individuals with salient ethnic identity subordinate personal values to those of the group. It is interesting that self-respect is more important for people with non-salient ethnic identity than for people with salient ethnic identity. The former believe that self-esteem leads to self-respect and inner harmony, while the latter stresses that self-esteem is provided by social identity and close relations with the ethnic group.

For people with non-salient ethnic identity in this study, values of forgiveness, equity, and peace were more significant than for people with salient ethnic identity. One possible explanation of this finding is that people with salient ethnic identity concentrate more on the happiness and well-being of their ethnic group than on that of other groups. As previous research shows, they have more negative stereotypes and attitudes toward other groups and perceive a larger social distance between ingroup and outgroups. These patterns of behavior and consciousness lead to the perception that their ethnic group occupies a special position in society—an ethnocentric view that assumes the dominance of ingroup goals and status.

Overall, this study revealed that individuals with salient ethnic identities maintain similar values with their ingroups and consider the values of ingroup primacy and interdependence as significant. Individuals with non-salient ethnic identities tend to rely on a value system that privileges one's personal worldview, style of life, and sense of equality in relations with others. They are more prone to forgive others and to foster relationships with those of other groups.

The analysis of values associated with other groups show that people with salient ethnic identities use their own most important values as a basis for the negative evaluation of other ethnic groups. The perception of "others" is not based on objective assessment of the others' values. People with salient ethnic identity perceive members of other ethnic groups in terms of their own most important values, and see them negatively. Thus, the main instrumental values for Crimean Tatars are civility (being polite) and helpfulness; they deny the existence of these values among Russians and believe them to be among the least important values for Russians, even though Russians perceive themselves also as polite and helpful. The main important instrumental values for Russians are honesty and loving kindness; Russians perceive Crimean Tatars as people who do not value honesty and love while these values are among significant for Crimean Tatars.

The analysis of stories about the ethnic groups in this chapter demonstrates that Crimean Tatars with a salient ethnic identity stress the perceived cruelty and non-politeness of Russians because these characteristics contradict the main values of Crimean Tatars. Russians with salient ethnic identity accuse Crimean Tatars of dishonesty since their main value is honesty. Therefore, my research shows that people with salient ethnic identity have strongly interconnected personal and ingroup values and use their most important values as the lens through which to blame and denigrate people from other ethnic groups. The subordination of individual values to ingroup values together with salient ethnic identity leads to distorted perceptions of outgroup members and the tendency to discredit their value commitments. This devaluation can provoke extremely negative attitudes and even violence toward outgroup members who, presumably, neither regard nor respect the most important values of the ingroup.

Conclusion

Our research presented shows that salient ethnic identities lead to greater endorsement of ingroup goals and opposition to outgroup goals than non-salient ethnic identities. People with salient ethnic identity see other ethnic groups as opponents, rivals, and even enemies and are ready to defend and engage them in violence. Why does salient identity influence conflict behavior and negative attitudes toward other groups? Why does it lead to a readiness to violence against the Other?

One of the factors identified in this chapter was the feeling of ingroup primacy. People with salient ethnic identity showed readiness for conflict with the outgroup independent of the level of ingroup privacy: ingroup supremacy is derived from identity salience. People with non-salient social identity were ready to fight with others only if they felt that ingroup goals and values were more important than personal goals and values, or if they believed that the existence of an enemy would unite the ingroup against the outgroup. Thus, the ingroup must be extremely important for people with non-salient social identities to influence their readiness to fight.

A second factor emerging from the research is the structure of narratives about the Other. As the study showed, salient identity influenced the construction of stories about other ethnic groups. Storytellers resorted to over-generalizations, stereotypes, and negative characterizations. People with salient ethnic identity perceive the outgroup as absolutely alien, in spite of minimal interaction. The stories told by people with non-salient ethnic identity were diverse, positive, and possessed individual character. People with non-salient ethnic identity described other ethnic groups as neighbors in society.

The third factor arising from the research was the structure of consciousness. Salient identities lead to the perception of the world as rigidly connected, determined, and cut off from various interpretations; these patterns of perception produce the "tunnel consciousness" that causes people to perceive representatives of other groups, situations, and activities within the narrow perspective. Non-salient social identity is connected with a multi-dimensional approach to the assessment of the world, committed to the use of different criteria, and cognizant of both the positive and negative characteristics of people and events.

The fourth factor identified in this chapter was the structure of value systems. Non-salient ethnic identity contributed to the development of a personal, independent system of values connected to a personal worldview, to an individual style of life and to the equality of people. Salient ethnic identity led to a high level of similarity between ingroup and personal values and to the privileging of values of ingroup primacy and interdependence. People with salient ethnic identity used their most important values as a lens through which to denigrate people from other ethnic groups, devaluing them, and denying them the virtues of the ingroup.

Thus, salient ethnic identity changes (1) the balance of relations between person and ingroup, leading to ingroup primacy; (2) the content and composition of narratives about the Other; (3) the structure of consciousness and creation of tunnel perception; and (4) the structure of value systems and its subsequent affect on the evaluation of Other. Consequently, salient social identity leads to the perception of the Other only in negative terms, to the rising of social distance, to the devaluation of others, and to a readiness for conflict and violent action.

References

Berry, J., Kim, U., Power, S., Young, M., & Bujaki, M. Acculturation attitudes in plural societies. 1989. *Applied Psychology*, no. *38,* 185-206.

Branscombe, N., & Wann, D. 1994. Collective self–esteem consequences of outgroup derogation when a valued social identity is on trial. *European Journal of Social psychology,* no. 24, 641-657.

Brewer, M. B. 2001. The many faces of social identity: implications for political psychology. *Political Psychology,* no. 22, 115-126.

Brewer, M. B. 1991. The social self: being same and different at the same time. *Personality and Social Psychology Bulletin,* no. 17, 475-482.

Brown, R. 2000. Social identity theory: past achievements, current problems and future challenges, *European Journal of Social Psychology*, no. 30, 746-778.

Conover, P.J., 1988. The role of social groups in political thinking. *British Journal of Political Science,* no. 18, 51-76.

Ellemers, N., Spears, R. and Doosje, B. 1997. Sticking together or falling apart: ingroup identification as a psychological determinant of group commitment versus individual mobility. *Journal of Personality and Social Psychology*, no. 72, 617-626.

Gerson J. M. 2001. In between states: national identity practices among German Jewish immigrants. *Political Psychology*, no. 1, 179-198.

Gibson, J.L., & Gouwa, A. 1998. *Social identity theory and political intolerance in South Africa.* Unpublished manuscript, University of Houston.

Grant, P., & Brown, P. 1995. From ethnocentrism to collective protest: Responses to relative deprivation and threats to social identity. *Social Psychology Quarterly*, no. 58, 195-211.

Hagendoorn, L., Linssen, H. and Tumanov, S. 2001. *Inter-group Relations in States of the Former Soviet Union, the Perception of Russians.* Hove: Psychology Press.

Hagendoorn, L., Csepeli, G., Dekker, H., & Farnen, R. 2000. European Nations and Nationalism: Theoretical and historical perspectives. Aldershot: Ashgate.

Horowitz, D. 1975. Ethnic identity. In N. Glazer and D. Moynihan, *Ethnicity, theory and experience.* Cambridge: Harvard University Press.

Huddy, L. 2001 From social to political identity: A critical examination of Social Identity Theory. *Political Psychology*, no. 1, 127-156.

Huddy, L. and Virtanen, S. 1995. Subgroup differentiation and subgroup bias among Latinos as a function of familiarity and positive distinctiveness. *Journal of Personality and Social Psychology*, no. 68, 97-108.

Jackson, L. A., Sullivan, L. A., Harnish, R., and Hodge, C.N. 1996. Achieving positive social identity: social mobility, social creativity, and permeability of group boundaries. *Journal of Personality and Social Psychology*, no. 70, 241-252.

Kinket, B., & Verkuyten, M. 1997. Levels of ethnic self-identification and social context. *Social Psychology Quarterly*, no. 60, 338-354.

Lalonde, R. N. 1992. The dynamics of group differentiation in the face of   defeat. *Personality and Social Psychology Bulletin*, no. 18, 336-342.

McGuire, W.J., McGuire, C. V., Child, P., & Fujioka, T. 1978. Salience of ethnicity in the spontaneous self-concept as a function of one's ethnic distinctiveness in the social environment. *Journal of Personality and Social Psychology*, no. 36, 511-520.

Miller, A.H., Gurin, P., Gurin, G., & Malanchuk, O. 1981. Group consciousness and political participation. *American Journal of Political Science,* no. 25, 495-511.

Mummendey, A., and Otten, S. 1998. Positive-negative asymmetry in social discrimination. In: W. Stroebe & M. Hewstone: *European Review of Social Psychology*, vol. 9, 107-143.

Oakes, P. 1987. The salience of social categories. In J.C. Turner, M. A. Hogg, P. J. Oakes, S. D. Reicher, & M. S. Watherell. (Eds.) 1987, *Rediscovering the social group: A self-categorization theory.* Oxford: Blackwell.

Phinney, J. 1991. Ethnic identity and self- esteem: a review and integration. *Hispanic Journal of Behavioral Science*, no. 13, 193-208.

Striker, S. 1969. Identity salience and role performance: the relevance of symbolic interaction theory for family research. *Journal of Marriage and the family,* no. 30, 558-564.

Striker, S. 1969. Identity salience and role performance: the relevance of symbolic interaction theory for family research. *Journal of Marriage and the family,* no. 30, 558-564.

Taylor, D., Moghaddam, F., Gamble, I. and Zellerer, E. 1987. Disadvantaged group responses to perceived inequality: From passive acceptance to collective action. *Journal of Social Psychology*, no. 127, 259-272.

Tajfel, H., and Turner, J.C. 1979 An integrative theory of intergroup conflict. In W. G. Austin & S. Worchel eds., *The social psychology of intergroup relations.* pp. 33-48. Monterey, CA: Brooks/Cole.

Ting -Toomey, S., Yee-Jung, K.K., Shapiro, R., Garcia, W., Wright, T.J., and Oetzel J.G. 2000. Ethnic/ cultural identity salience and conflict styles in four US ethnic groups. *International Journal of Intercultural* Relations, no. 24, 47-81.

Van Knippenberg, A. 1978. Status differences, comparative relevance and intergroup differentiation. In: H. Tajfel (Ed.) *Differentiation between social groups: Studies in the social psychology of intergroup relations*, 171-199. London: Academic Press.

Van Knippenberg, A. and Van Oers, H. 1984. Social identity and equity concerns in intergroup perceptions. *British Journal of Social Psychology*, no. 23, 351-361.

Wann, D.L. and Branscombe, N. 1990. Die hard and fair- weather fans: effects of identification on BIRGing and CORFing tendencies. *Journal of Sport and Social Issues*, no. 14, 103-117.

Wright, S., Taylor, D. and Moghaddam, E. 1990. Responding to membership in a disadvantaged group: From acceptance to collective protest. *Journal of Personality and Social Psychology*, no. 58, 994-1003.

Part II: Multiple Value-Systems

Chapter 6

Humanitarianism and Intolerance: Two Contemporary Approaches to the Other

Peter N. Stearns

Two dialogues have developed in many parts of the world over the past century, each showing signs of growing intensity over the past thirty years. One, the most novel, emphasizes the importance of certain rights for all people, featuring an active sense of moral responsibility for other human beings with whom there is no national or religious link. The second, hardly new in contemporary history but gaining further significance amid a growing mixture of peoples, emphasizes a particular national, ethnic or religious identity asserted in terms of hostility and intolerance toward others. This essay sketches this intriguing dualism, including ways in which each approach can contribute to the other. Obviously, the tension between the two currents overlaps the even larger debate between globalization (of some sort) and clash of civilizations as models for a global future (Huntington 1998). Following the basic sketch, we turn to some comments on how the tension plays out in the United States, where distinctive features not only of the national role, first as a leading Cold Warrior and now as "only superpower", but also of key aspects of recent emotional dynamics, have generated divided reactions to the two approaches to the Other.

Hostile identification of Others goes well back in the human experience, of course. When Socrates urged that Greeks only enslave non-Greeks (a bit of advice his colleagues ignored), or Islamic law did the same concerning nonMuslims (again with mixed results), they clearly displayed an early capacity to use national or religious distinctions as a means of stigmatizing others. Concern about racial differences, during the Aryan invasions of India, undoubtedly contributed to the formation of the caste system, as a means of creating hierarchies based on Otherness. Attacks on Jews, through traditional European anti-semitism, or the early racist condemnations of Native Americans, on the basis of which so many attacks could be justified, provide other familiar examples.

With all this, however, modern approaches offer two novel components, both of which potentially led to more systematic and also more significant conflicts. The rise of nationalism was the principal contributor to the more systematic quality of many identity issues, while increasing movement of peoples made the same issues more frequent and important.

Nationalism could, in principle, embrace the Other, arguing only that each nation had its own identity that should be cherished but with openness and tolerance for other, equally valid nationalisms. This was, in principle, the vision of liberal nationalists like the Italian Mazzini, and later of Woodrow Wilson and of course of Gandhi (Baily 1970; Mosse 1975). In practice, however, and almost inevitably, most nationalism drifted into negative identification both of other, external nationalities and of internal subgroups that did not easily fit nationalism's integrated vision of culture and politics (Anderson 1983). New forms of anti-Semitism, often more virulent than the traditional version, were one result of this latter impulse in Western Europe (Pulzer 1964). Intolerant nationalism could also give traditionally open religions a more hostile tone. Thus, while Gandhi's vision of Indian nationalism pointedly embraced both Hindu and Muslim, the more militant approach of leaders like Vinayak Savarkar identified Indian interests more narrowly with Hinduism, and proved virulently anti-Muslim (and indeed, murderously hostile to Gandhi himself). Savarkar did, like Gandhi, urge an end to the caste system – nationalism in this sense could reduce some traditional identities in favor of national unity and strength – but his combination of nationalist fervor with Hinduism imported an unusual degree of intolerance into what had typically been a more open religion, and in ways that would inform the subsequent rise of Hindu nationalism directly. Sometimes, of course, nationalism provided new language for older ethnic and religious antagonisms, as in the Balkans, though again with some intensification in the process. More generally, however, the encouragement nationalism provided for almost every conceivable people and territory to think in terms of exclusive identity contributed greatly to a mentality of clash and conflict, even in regions that had traditionally experienced normally peaceful coexistence. This flavor of exclusive nationalism progressively informed non-nationalist movements as well, as in regional loyalties that defied larger national unities but with the same language of us-and-them, and in renewed efforts to use wider religious banners to form identities that might transcend nationalism – as, most notably, in the use of Islamic fundamentalism to capture a larger geography, but with a nationalist-like intolerance for others that countered more traditional Islamic practice.

Imperialism surely encouraged the intolerant version of nationalism as well. Struggles for national independence inevitably cast Western colonialists in terms of the Other (though this might be qualified by a desire to imitate selective aspects of Western culture, like science). Groups seen as collaborationist drew attack as well, whether under nationalist banners – Britain's divide and rule policy in India encouraged intolerant nationalisms both among Muslims and among Hindus – or more purely ethnic labels, as with Hutu attacks on the colonially-more-favored Tutsis. Again, there is no basis for blaming all modern identifications of a degenerate Other as rooted in nationalism, given some comparable conflicts in the past, but the exclusionary language of nationalism unquestionably encouraged more systematic divisions. "Ethnic cleansing" was not unprecedented, but its contemporary spread, from the late 19th century onward, owed much to the cultural-political language of nationalism.

Nationalism was complicated finally – and this obviously related to imperialism – by the strong current of racist thinking that emanated from the West during the 19th and early 20th centuries. Racism enhanced nationalist beliefs in certain groups – both foreign and domestic – as inher-

ently inferior, dangerous, even unhygienic, creating new attention to
dangerous others particularly within one's own borders. Immigrant and
racially segregated slums in major cities literally around the world by the
early 20th century highlighted the extent to which new ideas, intermin-
gled with new migration streams, were creating new designations for
groups regarded as other.

Whether nationalist- or racist-inspired or more traditional, hostility
toward an identified other began to matter more deeply when, with modern patterns of migration, travel and communication, different peoples
began to encounter "others" more frequently. Indeed, the rise of nationalism itself fed on the need to find new identities when in contact with
strangers. Notoriously, for example, Italian immigrants to the United
States, previously associated with peasant village loyalties, discovered
that they were Italians, and different from (and probably better than)
other national ethnicities only when they reached their new home (Bodnar 1985); the same had been true earlier of the Irish, who were often
more militantly self-identified from across the Atlantic, during the 19th
century, than were their brethren who had stayed at home under British
rule. The movement of peoples could offer other encouragements toward
intolerant identities: virtually all immigrant groups to the United States,
and also native Americans, learned that hostility to African Americans
was a near-necessity in the hierarchies of American life. Slovak immigrants quickly became anti-Black, as part of the same impulse that fed
their own ethnic identity, while Indian nations like the Cherokee, eager
for greater acceptance among the white majority, clearly identified even
free Blacks as an inferior other, incapable of admission to tribal citizenship (Yarbrough 2005; Zecker 2005). Still more familiar were the reactions of groups claiming majority status to the arrival of strangers, in the
form of efforts at racial exclusion or other limitations on immigration or
at least citizenship as well as outright violence, whether visited on Asian
immigrants to the 19th-century United States or Turkish "guest workers"
in contemporary Germany. A vicious circle could be established through
which majority intolerance toward immigrant others bred retaliatory hostilities on the part of immigrants and immigrant-sending populations.
Welcome exceptions to the characteristic results of population mixing,

such as the relatively tolerant racial situation in Hawaii, tended to high-light the more troubled standard outcomes.

New thinking, inspired by nationalist identities, and new patterns of population contact created a tightly connected combination, powerfully generating new distinctions between in-groups and others, accelerating the incidence of conflict and, often, the levels of violence involved.

Intriguingly, however, the same period saw an efflorescence of a new kind of moral thinking, explicitly focused on basic human rights of peoples regardless of location or identity. The new thinking – which one historian has designated as the humanitarian sentiment (Haskell 1985) – first surfaced explicitly in the anti-slavery campaign of the late 18th/early 19th centuries. Anti-slavery advocates urgently argued that opposition to the institution–one of the older arrangements in the history of human civilization–was an ethical imperative precisely because, where such fundamental violations of human freedom and dignity were concerned, there was no Other; noone, however distant or racially or culturally for-eign, should be treated as mere property (Drescher 1989).

The roots of this new humanitarianism, cresting first in places like Britain, France, and the Netherlands, lay in an interesting juxtaposition of new Protestant sects, notably Methodism and Quakerism, and the broader surge of Enlightenment thinking. While it is tempting to contrast this cosmopolitan embrace with the passions of Romanticism, which so often informed nationalist sentiments, the new moral advocate's fre-quently important Romantic enthusiasm for the oppressed into their own dialogues. The capacity not just to advocate human rights as a matter of Enlightenment reason, but also to resonate to dramatic tales of injustice on a personal level, was a vital characteristic of inclusive world opinion. Dramatizations such as Harriet Beecher Stowe's, very much in a broadly Romantic vein, were at least as important in fueling human rights attacks on slavery as were discourses about common humanity.

The novelty of this thinking deserves clear emphasis. While earlier discussions of natural law provided some basis for considering a com-mon humanity, before the 18th century it was the world religions that provided the most extensive framework for considering obligations across conventional political and cultural lines. Christians, as the cru-sades demonstrated, could be roused on behalf of co-religionists and religious sites in distant places. Muslims had opportunities to consider the fates of fellow Muslims, and the annual international experience of the Hadj provided direct occasions to discuss shared issues and concerns with co-religionists from Morocco to Indonesia. But this range was predicated on religious affiliations, not shared humanity, and they included a very clear notion of others outside these affiliations. The new commitment to basic human rights, wherever abuses such as slavery might be found, was quite different: preventing the worst forms of mistreatment applied without distinction; there was no Other involved.

Slavery and the slave trade, in this new way of thinking, were simply wrong, regardless of how distant and unfamiliar the victims. The focus, admittedly, was on assuring protection against worst abuses, not in more elaborate concerns about victims' lives. Thus the end of slavery did not always usher in as much improvement as might have been imagined, and there were limits to the information and concern involved. Still, the passionate devotion to ending wrongdoing to strangers was major development, and obviously, in the case of the most literal slave systems, it gradually paid off. Pressures by this new human rights thinking moved European governments, first, to address the systems under their control, and it played a major role in American thinking (and also Russian, about the similar situation with serfs). Brazilians later cited the same kinds of pressures from human rights advocates, and the movement easily extended into the 20th century with the final formal renunciations of slavery by Middle Eastern regimes (Stearns 2005).

Once launched, furthermore, the new thinking readily adopted additional targets (Boli & Thomas 1999). Anti-slavery sentiment itself helped frame a potent, British-organized program against forced labor in the Belgian Congo. A major campaign against real or imagined white slavery in the late 19th century was slightly less altruistic, in that there was genuine fear of seizure of one's own women and corruption by foreign pimps and exploiters.

Here too, however, there was a deep commitment to protecting otherwise unknown individuals. Similar compassion stirred the massive European reaction to Ottoman atrocities against Bulgarians, in the 1870s, and then Armenians thereafter (Saab 1991). Again, a shade of Otherness might creep in: advocates were at pains to note that Bulgarians were

Europeans and Christians and indeed quite civilized; Armenians, more distant, won less attention.

New rights movements quickly picked up the new cosmopolitanism (Berkovitch 1999). Three major international women's rights groups formed in the 1880s all bent on identifying and redressing wrongs to women anywhere around the world. Particular attention went to places like China, where the new thinking, combined with direct missionary activity and Chinese reform sentiment, steadily eroded the practice of footbinding. Western feminist advocacy could be somewhat patronizing, particularly after the suffrage began to be won in the West itself, but there was little question that the interest in women as women, regardless of race, place or religion, was sincerely intended.

Rights watchers also agitated on lynching issues in the United States, from the 1890s onward, contrasting American claims of civilization to the reports of barbaric practice. Interestingly, this was one of the first global issues on which Japanese public opinion extensively engaged, roused by sincere indignation and also a sensitivity to signs of Western racism (Sakashita 2004).

Cosmopolitan human rights efforts obviously faded during the inter-war period, the direct victim of strident nationalism and the erosion of any unified front against the abuses that surged in Ethiopia, Spain and elsewhere – not to mention the Holocaust itself.

The catastrophic failures of the World Wars era themselves help explain the massive new surge in cosmopolitan thinking after 1945. It seemed vital to many groups to prevent any repetition of the barely-challenged crimes of the 1930s and 1940s. Other factors combined as well. The decline of Europe's power gave a new impetus to the use of human rights thinking as a means of retaining some voice in world affairs, sometimes with, sometimes without the United States; there could be no small echo of white man's burden, as well, in some of the Western strictures directed against rights abuses in newly-independent states. But decolonization itself, removing one of the constraints on earlier human rights approaches, produced additional voices for some major international campaigns. The conversion of the Papacy, during the 1960s, to a role as world opinion, and not just sectarian, leader was another huge step (Hanson 1987). Even the Cold War contributed in a way, making both sides eager to score human rights points off the other; the United States, for example, was encouraged toward greater racial equality by its concern for human rights sentiments in other parts of the world.

The result, most certainly, was an unprecedented flurry of cosmopolitan concerns. Amnesty International, formed in 1961, was devoted to the protection of human rights regardless of person or place. It carefully formulated a triangulated attack – one "third world" case, one Western case like the British in Northern Ireland, and one communist case – to demonstrate its firm nonpartisanship. With a host of regional and other international groups, including Human Rights, adding to the list of relevant NGOs, rights concerns steadily broadened, to include not only overt political repression, but also torture, the death penalty in any form, and most recently rape and domestic abuse of women (Korey 1998; Clark 2001).

The campaigns were not idle. International human rights sentiment, distributed toward a wide array of cases, carried off a set of victories in the 1980s and 1990s, along with fierce local efforts: the removal of many brutal regimes in Central America and a realignment of United States policy in the region was one case in point, the successful attack on apartheid another. Activity slowed somewhat in the later 1990s, but humanitarian sentiment played some role in action against the ethnic atrocities in the Balkans and the liberation of East Timor. It also encouraged Israeli concessions during the decade. New campaigns, particularly against labor abuses in places like Indonesia, Vietnam and Africa, added significantly to the range of action and to the criteria now applied to the decent treatment of people regardless of origins (Stearns 2005). These labor campaigns often provided only individual, sometimes brief successes, but they did begin to rally some of the multinational corporations to more regular monitoring and publicity. Never before had distant opinion had such impact on the policies of individual states, like South Africa, or giant economic combines.

Human rights concerns, as well as a variety of foreign policy resentments against the United States, also prompted the most massive single manifestation of opinion ever recorded in the more than 25 million people who demonstrated on a single Sunday in February, 2003, against imminent American attack on Iraq (Stearns 2005). While concern included resentment against American arrogance, it focused mainly on protecting prospective Iraqi victims and on disputing the moral premises of preemptive war. Obviously the effort failed in the short run, but it served as measure of the surges of cosmopolitan moral responsibility that had clearly become a standard part of the international landscape.

The central dilemma is obvious. New particularist intensities, racist, ethicist, and nationalist, competes with a willingness to embrace humanity, and the tension has sharpened in recent decades with new centers of conflict but also a new boldness on the part of cosmopolitan advocates.

Weaknesses in the humanitarian approach compound the dilemma and contribute to its lack of resolution. While the emergence of cosmopolitan concern, and the real passion behind it, is genuinely significant, consistency has not always been forthcoming. Even during the long campaign against slavery, there were brief surges of intense concern, rather than sustained pressure. The distraction of more immediate problems and the dependence of humanitarian outrage on the selections of the media, themselves fickle in playing up to a public thirst for novelty, help explain the frequent ebbs and flow in cosmopolitan campaigns. Then there are also blindspots. The contrast between intense interest in the Balkans atrocities, and the almost total neglect of the genocide in Rwanda, was too gaping to ignore. While cosmopolitanism is genuine, it still may favor more recognizable people over more distant ones, and tends to get more involved when there seems to be some Western responsibility (even for apartheid) than in areas where conflict may begin to seem simply endemic. French intellectuals, urging action in the Balkans, noted with dismay that this was happening "just two hours from Paris" – i.e., to Europeans – whereas implicitly Rwanda was well beyond the pale. Small wonder that local military leaders, in the hotspots of Africa or Southeast Asia, feel free to ignore the occasional manifestations of indignation – humanitarian outrage means little to them in any event, and it is unlikely to be sustained.

Humanitarianism may also seem tainted by undue Westernism, not surprisingly given its association with the Enlightenment and the long period of Western world power. Whether in women's rights or the protection of political dissent, the thrust of most global humanitarianism has embodied values initially articulated in the West, at least in modern form. A flurry of Southeast Asian protest in the mid–1990s against the individualism of the human rights campaigns, toward communitarian values more appropriate to an emphasis on orderliness, showed some of the issues involved, though the flurry itself died down and drew rejection from many Asian advocacy groups. The gap between cosmopolitan campaigns and many of the traditions of Islam is more troubling currently. Western-based world opinion has often been biased against Islam; the campaigns against Ottoman atrocities had some genuine base, but also a widespread belief in Turkish corruption and inherent violence. Other targets, like veiling for women, expressed deep outrage against what may be viewed as fairly inconsequential targets. Winning Muslim participation in humanitarian thinking, beyond defense of Islam itself, is an obvious current challenge, and it may require some significant mutual adjustments for which the particular history of Western humanitarianism is not well prepared. There have been cases of significant addition to support for humanitarianism: Japanese and Korean participation is now routinely high, as is Latin American; international Jewish groups joined in as early as the first decades of the 20th century; and the rethinking of papal involvement was revealing. But there is still a road to travel in separating cosmopolitanism from a sometimes patronizing Westernism (Stearns 2005).

World opinion, whatever its target, often rouses righteous resistance against outside interference–as in the recent case of the United States in Iraq, or the equally American defiance (until recently) of international, including papal, attacks on the death penalty. Or it encourages a scattered gesture, like the Chinese release of a political prisoner or two, rather than real redress.

Most important of all, perhaps, humanitarian sentiment varies greatly in effectiveness. Occasionally, moral outrage itself, when pressed against relevant policymakers, does the trick, as was ultimately the case with the slave trade; massive petitions can work. More often it is combined with attempts at boycott (crucial against apartheid) or the mobilization of military force, as in the Balkans. But sometimes it is essentially weaponless, as in the demonstrations against the war in Iraq or the considerable support for basic Palestinian demands against Israel. And one of cosmopolitanism's crucial limitations in the struggle against narrower identities lies precisely in this uncertain capacity to implement. There have been some exceptions– apartheid was one–but too often a determined, identity-focused opponent can stare down the humanitarian sentiment.

Two conclusions follow. First, there is no end in sight to the ongoing juxtaposition of narrow identities and the new cosmopolitanism. Even convinced cosmopolitans can find themselves easily caught up in hostilities to Others, when the issues hit home – the level of British nationalism, surprising even to participants, in the Falklands war was a case in point, when humanitarian objectivity immediately went out the window. Issues that spur identity conflict show no sign of slackening, and indeed growing inequalities in the global economy may press them further. Yet humanitarian sentiment, despite its collapse in the interwar decades and its continued inconsistency, persists strongly as well. It simply does not, to its partisans, advance adequately.

But second, a clearer and more systematic approach to the humanitarian sentiment might produce some modest gains in effectiveness. There is, by definition, no leader of the sentiment; it comes in response to a combination of pressing issues, media selections, and the effectiveness of advocacy groups. Clear advantages in the ability to communicate abuses and rouse quick support, notably through use of the Internet, have not been matched by careful considerations of strategy or of shedding some of the neo-imperialist baggage rights campaigns sometimes bring in their wake. Other than through communications technologies, the greatest advances have involved enlisting support on an increasingly, though not yet literally, global basis. The ability to prioritize projects and think through available implementation devices, the ability even to develop greater consistency in campaigns once launched, has not necessarily improved since anti-slavery – still one of the approach's great triumphs. Without claiming that more careful planning would change the balance between humanitarianism and narrow identity conflicts, some new strategic imagination is conceivable on the humanitarian side that might make it a more effective force in superseding some of the conflicts (Gould 2004).

Perspectives on humanitarianism offers interesting insights into a set of current American dilemmas, during one of the country's recurrent tests of nationalist assertiveness against a commitment to a broader humanity. Here, we deal with a common misperception, and yet another endemic tension.

The misperception involves frequent American belief that the nation has long been the leader in global humanitarian sentiment. In fact, this is not the case. American initiative has been crucial in a few campaigns, against apartheid most notably. And Americans have participated valiantly in other crusades, including of course anti-slavery. But the geographic base of humanitarian sentiment has historically resided in Western Europe, where even today more human rights NGOs are based and where participatory membership is larger than in the United States. And, not surprisingly, humanitarian sentiment has not infrequently targeted the United States, rather than simply welcoming it as an ally. Racial issues – slavery itself, then lynching and discrimination – most commonly drew cosmopolitan outrage. But by the 1950s sentiment against undue American power supplemented this concern, placing the United States frequently in a global opinion crosshairs. Not surprisingly, in turn, Americans have often reacted to cosmopolitan preachments as a foreign force, as for example in the dismissive stance toward outside protests against the death penalty. The relationship between the United States and humanitarianism, as eager participant and yet also as target, is inherently complicated, and this complication will only increase to the extent that American power does not seem open to curtailment by normal diplomatic and military methods.

Yet, as Senator Ted Kennedy pointed out during the 2004 Democratic National Convention, the United States was literally born with an openness to global scrutiny. The Declaration of Independence proclaimed its "decent respect to the opinions of mankind." And many Americans, from that time forward, have been most comfortable in assuming their congruence with international views and standards; indeed, an American desire for global approval has sometimes constituted a characteristic – whether endearing or naïve – of American public reactions and even diplomatic maneuverings. At the same time, however, the United States, at least as much as its global counterparts, developed a fierce, assertive nationalism, ready to preach its distinctiveness and superiority in school programs and to trumpet them in the press. Reactions to massive immigration – though liberal by most comparative standards – were conditioned by a belief in the possibility of converting these strangers through Americanization, so that identities would adequately fuse; this could also affect outlooks to Others who had not undergone this process. Long isolation reduced the direct conflict between this narrower sense of the nation and larger cosmopolitanism; and some Americans fondly believed that, since American standards had global applicability, there was no real conflict in the first place.

Conflict there was, however, and it has been increasing in recent decades for several interrelated reasons. First was the growing divergence between many American values and policies and those of counterparts in Western Europe and the Pacific Rim, from the 1970s onward. Americans' increasingly open and policy-focused religiosity contrasted with secularism. The nation's commitment to militarism contrasted with a more civilian-centered spending policy. Gaps became blatant in the 1990s, with the striking distinction between the European Union's insistence on abolition of the death penalty as condition of membership, and the growing enthusiasm for the same penalty in the United States. It became harder for many Americans and key traditional allies, who were also central players in the humanitarian sentiment, to understand where each was coming from. One result was a growing American sense that world opinion was out of whack, even aside from specific attacks on American policies.

More important still was the United States' forced introduction into worlds filled with Others, first in World War II, with its demonization of military opponents, then with the Cold War – this latter heightened of course by more intense fears of possible outright attack. Many Americans became more familiar with thinking about the world in binaries – us and them – than in terms of a common humanity. The proof of the pudding came with the Cold War's end, which was greeted not just with relief but with a surprisingly eager quest for a new Other to replace the old. The facile equation of Saddam Hussein with Hitler, as a prelude to the first Gulf War, was a clear sign of a certain metallic nostalgia for the pleasure of having a hostile Other. Some of the dependence, of course, was purely military: lots of personnel and contractors had a big stake in encouraging a sense of potential attack. But more may have been involved, reflecting a habituation to an us-them distinction and also some broader features of an evolving emotional environment. The trauma of the attacks of 9/11 in this sense fed into, and greatly promoted, an established frame of mind.

It was in the broader emotional environment that a third set of factors clustered... During the 20th century Americans had been progressively schooled to resist unduly strong emotion. Emotional intensity was seen as both irrational, damaging both to workplace and to personal relationships, and dangerous for the health (Stearns 1994). Hostility to jealousy increased, for example, prompting Americans, when jealous in fact, to check carefully with friends to make sure they were concealing properly (Salovey & Rodin 1988). This contrasted markedly with characteristic reactions in France, where jealousy prompted anger, or Holland, where it spurred sadness; only Americans rushed to camouflage. Wider comparative surveys in the 1980s, against groups as diverse as Greeks, Chinese, and Jamaicans, again showed Americans particularly interested in concealing intense emotions (Sommers 1984). Demonstrations of anger, in particular, became a sign of weakness, a lesson that was drubbed into workplace supervisors from the 1920s and 1930s onward. Politicians learned that public displays of anger constituted a crucial sign of vulnerability and inadequacy (Reich 1997), and a host of tests, including political debates, were staged to demonstrate the ability to rise above the emotion. At the same time, by the 1960s, some of the traditional targets of emotional release in American society, such as racial minorities or women, became less appropriate for attack. Without claiming magic harmony, political correctness did force changes in snide references and relieving humor–another constraint on traditional emotional outlets for many Americans. Of course there were alternative forms of release. A national predilection for violent sports and violent films clearly helped Americans come to terms with their own, usually restrained, emotional lives. But this dependence on surrogate emotional performance merely confirmed the rather restrictive emotional norms many Americans accepted in their own daily activities.

But there was also the release of the foreign enemy, against whom emotions could range unrestrained (Greven 1991). The same politicians who bobbed and smiled at domestic opposition could wax fierce in their condemnations of communists or terrorists, and the equation, in context, made good emotional sense. Many Americans shared the pleasure in venting on an Other enemy, all the more in that there was some legitimate reason to fear the same opponent.

Yet here was another barrier between many Americans, who rather perversely enjoyed a sense of fear-aggression against an outside Other, and the less satisfying openness to wider cosmopolitan sentiment. Moralistic fervor could as readily be directed against foreign threat, and foreigners who seemed to coddle aggression, as against humanitarian abuses. The nation divided, on this issue as on others. The division was complex. In advance of the war against Iraq, about a third of the nation stood for conflict regardless, another third opposed, and a middle third favorable but only if backed by international opinion. Even today, despite the success of 2004 campaign slogans criticizing the idea of running American policy options through Paris, it is not clear how comfortable the United States will remain amid international resentment, how satisfying a sense of embattlement against others will prove to be.

What is clear is that the tension between modern humanitarian sentiment and a delight in identifying the other is not just a global issue, but a contemporary American one as well. Given United States influence, its internal tension can project outward, to encourage others also to think more fully in terms of us and them; one of the hazards of this aspect of the American approach is its encouragement to clash-of-civilization reactions based not just on policy differences but emotional antipathies, in which the United States helps to create its own Other. Or, alternatively, other leaders can seek to exploit the American distinctions by applying similar dualisms to their own policy situations, as in the case of current Israeli policy and elements of Russian as well. Distinguishing between American national identity and a distinct opponent, in other words, can have wider consequences at the superpower level. For the American dilemma is no mere intellectual abstraction. It results from old divisions compounded by recent diplomatic experiences and a too-often-unacknowledged sense of emotional constraint in daily life. Here, as with the wider issues of humanitarianism and nationalism, those who would wish to tip the balance toward the more altruistic view would do well to consider the varied, though not intractable, roots of the current American divide.

Reference

Anderson, Benedict. 1983. *Imagined Communities: Reflections on the Origins and Spread of Nationalism*. London: Verso.

Baily, Samuel ed. 1970. *Nationalism in Latin America*. New York: Knopf.

Berkovitch, Natja. 1999. *From Motherhood to Citizenship: Women's Rights and International Organizations*. Baltimore: Johns Hopkins.

Bodnar, John. 1985. *Transplanted: a History of Immigrants in Urban America*. Bloomington: Indiana University Press.

Boli, John and G. Thomas, eds. 1999. *Constructing World Culture: International Nongovernmental Organizations since 1875*. Stanford: Stanford University Press.

Clark, Ann Marie. 2001. *Diplomacy of Conscience: Amnesty International and Changing Human Rights Norms*. Princeton: Princeton University Press.

Drescher, Seymour. 1999. *From Slavery to Freedom*. New York: New York University Press.

Gould, Carol. 2004. *Globalizing Democracy and Human Rights*. New York: Cambridge University Press.

Greven, Philip. 1991. *Spare the Child: the Religious Roots of Punishment*. New York: Knopf.

Haskell, Thomas. 1985. "Capitalism and the Origins of Humanitarian Sensibility." *American Historical Review* 90: 339–61, 547–66.

Hanson, Eric. 1987. *The Catholic Church in World Politics*. Princeton: Princeton University Press.

Huntington, Samuel. 1998. *Clash of Civilizations and the Remaking of the World Order*. New York: Simon and Schuster.

Korey, William. 1998. *NGOS and the Universal Declaration of Human Rights*. New York: St. Martin's.

Mosse, George. 1975. *Nationalization of the Masses*. New York: Fertig.

Pulzer, Peter. 1964. *The Rise of Political Anti-Semitism*. New York: Wiley.

Reich, Robert. 1997. *Locked in the Cabinet*. New York: Knopf.

Ross, Andrew, ed. 1997. *No Sweat: Fashion, Free Trade and the Rights of Garment Workers*. London: Verso.

Saab, Ann. 1991. *Gladstone, Bulgaria and the Working Classes*. Cambridge: Harvard University Press.

Sakashita, Fumito. 2004. "Lynching across the Pacific". Paper presented to the *Organization of American Historians*, Boston, Mar. 26.

Salovey, Peter and Judith Rodin. 1988. "Coping with Jealousy and Envy," *Journal of Social and Clinical Psychology*, 7: 15–33.

Sommers, Shula. 1984. "Adults Evaluating Their Emotions: a Crosscultural Perspective," in *Emotions in Adult Development*, edited by Carol Malatesta and Caroll Izard. Beverly Hills: Sage.

Stearns, Peter N. 1994. *American Cool: Constructing a Twentieth-Century Emotional Style*. New York: New York University Press.

Stearns, Peter N. 2005. *Global Outrage: the Orgins, Evolution and Impact of World Opinion*. London: Oneworld.

Yarbrough, Fay A. 2005. "Legislating Women's Sexuality: Cherokee Marriage Laws in the Nineteenth Century." *Journal of Social History 38*.

Zecker, Robert. 2005. "Where Everyone Goes to Meet Everyone Else: The Translocal Creation of a Slovak Immigrant Community." *Journal of Social History 38*.

Chapter 7

Cultural Differences of Perceptions of the Other

Karina V. Korostelina

People live in a complex system of relationships with their social environments. Cultural differences go beyond the sphere of communication processes and encompass such areas as traditional values and beliefs, standards and rituals of behavior, norms of interpersonal relations, and social structure and hierarchy. These cultural differences also significantly impact the formation of social and individual identity. This chapter uses the analysis of *culture* to examine how threat narratives shape ingroup responses to the Other, and how blame quickly shifts from individual attribution to collective denigration. Two types of cultures—collectivistic and individualistic—are examined. Each culture type influences perceptions and social interactions within groups and towards other groups. These two culture types are described in detail in order to determine the psychological elements that must be considered when seeking to understand how both (collectivist and individualist) dimensions influence the degree of a person's dependence on the group, orientation toward personal or group values and goals, and readiness for interaction with the Other. Two processes, individuation and social identification, compete with one another in *identity-formation*: the less developed the process of individuation, the more salient the process of social identification, and vice versa. I propose that social identity prevails in collectivistic cultures and its members are more disposed towards discrimination against representatives of other groups.

In order to understand the impact of cultural dimensions on identity, it is important to distinguish between belonging to a category *and* internalizing the category's meaning, or the difference between categorical groups and groups of membership. The first study in this chapter aims to identify the main themes in the narratives of people from collectivistic and individualistic cultures, with the proposition that collectivistic cultures with predominant social identity prioritize topics of group relationship and support (topics which play an important role in the perception, understanding, and interpretation of social reality), while individualistic cultures prioritize personal relationships and achievements. The second study examines changes in the causal relationship between social identity and attitudes in the transition from polymodal, individual identities to a single, dominant, group identity which employs a fixed opposition between 'We' and 'They.' In this chapter I explore different models of relations between identity, attitudes, and conflict behavior based on uniquely tailored survey.

Cultural Dimensions as a Determinative Factor of Interconnection Between Social and Personal Identity

Individuals live in a complexity of interrelationships. As one person influences another, they in turn are influenced by the relationship they have with that person. Over time, cultures form around values, beliefs, and attitudes. A culture can be defined through ten features: national character/basic individuality, perception, conception of time, conception of space, thinking, language, non-verbal communication, values, behavior, and social groups and relations.

Changes in one feature can lead to changes in all the features. These features can be characterized as parts, processes, and results of three main categories of culture. This classification reflects a model of culture proposed by Trompenaars and Hempden-Turner (1997). The authors suggest that culture is a set of three circles, including (1) main attitudes and views, (2) norms and values, and (3) products.

Sociologists describe two main types of relations to the notion of public good: one type based on the group priority (collectivistic orientation) and the other type based on the priority of individual. These early ideas of Durkheim (1969) were further developed in the research of

Hofstede (1980, 2001), Marcus and Kitayama (1991), and Triandis and Gelfand (1988). Collectivistic orientation characterizes societies where the group is primary and the person is secondary. Individualistic orientation characterizes societies in which the person is at the center of the society.

The "collectivism-individualism" duality depicts the dichotomy between the cultures of East and West. For example, Hofstede (1980) shows that most individualistic cultures flourish in English-speaking countries, beginning with the U.S. and Great Britain, whereas most collectivistic cultures can be found in Asia and South America (Taiwan, Hong Kong, Singapore, Japan, Peru, and Columbia). Of course, collectivism can be realized in different forms. For example, "contextual collectivism" thrives in Japan, and "simple collectivism" thrives in Korea (Triandis' 1988).

The sociocultural dimensions have been studied in sociology as culturally determined dichotomies that serve as bounds for the development of personal choice; in social psychology, they have been studied as the systems of value orientations; in cross-cultural psychology, they have been studied as a universal psychological phenomenon. In all these conceptual schemas, sociocultural dimensions create specific continuum of cultural variation and lead to the study of culturally and socially determined communications and interrelations among groups.

In his groundbreaking research, Triandis (1988, 1995) shows that cultural characteristics change with environmental transformations, forming what he calls specific cultural syndromes. A cultural syndrome is the explicit set of values, attitudes, beliefs, norms, and models of behavior that distinguish one group or culture from another. Triandis describes individualistic and collectivistic cultures as idiocentric and allocentric. The normative structure of groups in allocentric cultures significantly differs from the structure of groups in idiocentric cultures. Marcus and Kitayama (1991) also assess the connections between these two orientations and psychological functioning.

The principle of group profit is a collectivistic norm; the principle of individual benefit is typical to individualistic norms, though this principle also includes recognizing the interests of others and the norms of exchange. The norms of exchange have two different interpretations: one is based on the principle of justice, while the other takes the survival of the most adopted individuals as its reference point. These two interpretations of the norms of exchange create different foundations for the attitudes toward public welfare: the first one exhorts 'play honestly,' the second advocates rational behavior. The differences between allocentric and idiocentric cultures are also reflected in other normative rules, including justice, law, and distribution of power, rights, responsibilities, and resources.

In collectivistic cultures power is perceived as an attribute of the group; the will of the group can be expressed in different ways such as by a majority of votes, via the opinion of elders (or the elite), or from the mouth of a charismatic leader. The belief that power is used for the interest of the group attaches legality to the authority, a belief which is more important than the prescribed procedures of decision making and voting. When the connection among individuals is interpreted as following the principle of survival, the notion of legitimacy answers to another criteria. The power is considered as legitimate if it based on the will and agreement of the parties and depends on procedural criteria of the establishment and use of power.

A collectivistic paradigm implies a common responsibility for the well-being and morality of each group member, as well as a sense of cooperation, share holding, support, help, and intimate contact among group members. An individualistic paradigm assumes that each person is responsible for his or her own destiny, and that all social responsibilities rest on an implicit social contract. The differences between individualism and collectivism are shown in Table 7.1 (based on ideas of Triandis (1988, 1998), Trumbull, Rothstein-Fisch, and Greenfield (2000)).

Demographic characteristics and social class have a strong impact on these cultural dimensions. As research shows, Poles with high education have more individualistic values and behavior than their compatriots with lower levels of education; the inhabitants of towns and cities are more individualistic than people who live in the countryside; men show more individualistic behavior than women; younger people are more individualistic than elders (Daab 1991). Noricks (1987) shows that Americans after the age of 56 are inclined to consider their social context and other people in their decision making more than their earlier years of life. People who have lived in other countries and study in foreign institutions also can change their attitudes.

Table7.1
The differences between individualism and collectivism

Differences	Individualism	Collectivism
Content of Self	Individual differences	Social categories
Way for Self-Actualization	«I do that I want»	«I am not a burden for my group »
Values	Independence and achievement	Interdependence and group success
Norms	Self-expression, individual thinking, personal choice	Adherence to norms, respect, group consensus
Regulation of Behavior	Personal attitudes and estimation of profit	Ingroup norms
Roles	Egalitarian relationships and flexibility in roles	Stable, hierarchical roles (dependent on gender, family, age)
Goals	Personal goals more important than group goals	Group goals more important than personal goals
Differences Between Groups	Not salient	Salient
Understanding the Physical World	Knowable apart from its meaning for human life	Understandable in the context of its meaning for life
Property	Private property, individual ownership	Shared property, group ownership
Type of Relations	Horizontal	Vertical

The 'individualism-collectivism' dimension is not a-political and can be characterized by several parameters. Triandis (1998) described two types of cultural dimensions: horizontal and vertical. Horizontal collectivism is characterized by the perception of the person as a part of a group in which all members are equal. Vertical collectivism also suggests the attachment of a person to a group, but disclaims the equality of members. Horizontal individualism connects the conceptions of autonomy and equality. Vertical individualism implies autonomy of individuals, but denies equal rights and opportunities for all.

The 'individualism-collectivism' dimension also includes other parameters. For example, Parsons (1951) proposes the existence of a parameter that characterizes "self-oriented behavior based on personal interests" and "group-oriented behavior based on common interests of a group." Another parameter—uncertainty avoidance—was proposed by Hofstede (2001). Cultures with low tolerance for uncertainty and ambiguity tend to create a rule-oriented society that institutes laws, rules, regulations, and controls in order to reduce the amount of uncertainty. High tolerance for uncertainty is reflected in a society that is less rule-oriented, more readily open to change, comfortable with more and greater risks, and is more tolerant; consequently, such societies are more individualistic. As research shows, cultures with a low tolerance for uncertainty are characterized by a strong tendency for group agreement and a low tolerance toward new or different people. These tendencies lead to a high level of anxiety, connected with a fear of disapproval from the group, to the search for an absolute truth, a need for a formal rules and norms, and low motivation of achievement (Oberg 1960; Taft 1977).

Individuation and Social Identification

Psychological analyses of group dynamics and group mentality show that individualism and collectivism are ingrained in the psyches of individuals, and connected with the identification of the collectivity. The processes of individuation and social identification lead to identity-formation. The development of self-conception also includes cognitive differences between 'Me' and 'Not Me' (as differentiation from other people) and identification with the subjects of the social world (acknowledgment of similarity with other people and connections with groups). Individuation leads to the perception of the social world as composed of the set of varied objects (individuals) and thus, this process creates the differential system 'Me/Others.' Identification, on the contrary, eliminates the distinction between objects and forms the conception of 'self' as identical or similar with others. If the notion of group becomes the leading cognitive category, the social world is divided into ingroups and outgroups, and this process forms the differential system 'We/They.'

J. Reykowski (1997) suggests that the process of forming group identity (and collectivistic orientation) depends on the type of socialization a child receives, such as an education that accents obedience, conformity toward groups norms, and respect for group values, as well as traditions and symbols that lead to the development of collectivistic orientation.

In this chapter I consider how two processes—individuation and social identification—'compete' with each other in the formation of identity: the less developed the process of individuation, the more salient the process of social identification, and vice versa. Collectivistic culture, to a significantly greater extent than individualistic culture, contributes to the development of group identity and creates more possibilities for the manifestation of this identity among members of the society. Among representatives of individualistic cultures, individual identity is developed as initial and basic, and usually dominates in the dyad of social and individual identity. In this context a person perceives and estimates the world from an individual point of view and takes an individual approach to situations. In collectivistic cultures, group identity is formed before individual identity and becomes a leading one throughout a person's whole life. Social identity impacts the system of stereotypes and attitudes shared with other members of a group. In these cases, individual identity can only become independent if a person changes his or her social environment, switching to one with a dominant individualistic culture.

Much of the research on cultural dimensions confirms that members of collectivistic cultures are more likely to discriminate against representatives of other groups. Thus, Polynesians show more discriminatory behavior than do the Greeks in their discrimination against the French (Triandis 1977). Hinkle and Brown (1990) stressed that the interrelations between social identity and intergroup comparison are stronger in collectivistic cultures than in individualistic cultures. Results show that the outcome of comparison between the groups is important only for members of groups in collectivistic cultures. Other studies demonstrate that representatives of both individualistic and collectivistic cultures discriminate against outgroups in the minimal intergroup situation, but representatives of individualistic cultures show less discriminatory behavior (Morales, Lopez, Vega 1998). Croker and Luhtanen (1990) found that intergroup discrimination is connected with group esteem but not with self-esteem: people with high group esteem demonstrated stronger discrimination against members of the outgroup.

I believe this phenomenon can be explained through identity theory. In collectivistic cultures, group identity is dominant and determines positive attitudes toward members of the ingroup as well as aloof, negative attitudes toward outgroup members. Thus, a high level of differentiation between "us" and "others" leads to the differentiation of behavior: positive toward the ingroup and negative toward other groups. The more salient social identity is, the more impenetrable the intergroup boundaries become, and the more difficult contact with representatives of outgroups becomes. In individualistic cultures where individual identity prevails, members do not distinguish people using categories of "us" and "others"; rather, they communicate with everyone following the single formula "Me" and "They." Therefore negative attitudes toward outgroup members are not salient in individualistic cultures. Consequently, salient group identity suppresses the positive relationships with representatives of other groups.

Clearly therefore, types of culture impact the process of identity formation. Such dimensions as individualism—collectivism influence the degree of a person's dependence on their group, their orientation around personal or group values and goals, and their readiness for interaction with representatives of other cultures. The cultural dimension has significant effect on interrelations between social and individual identity in the system of identities, and on the leading role of one of these identities in the life of a person and his or her social interactions.

Categorical Groups and a Group of Membership

To gain a deeper understanding of the impact of culture on the structure of an identity system, it is important to distinguish between belonging to a category and internalizing its meaning. Barth (1981) considers the differences between nominal identity (or "membership"), which is based on name, and virtual membership, which is based on experience. In other research, this dyad was analyzed as a difference between (a) category, which unites people based on common characteristics evident for others, and (b) group, members of which know about their sameness and describe themselves based on this similarity (Jenkins 1996). Young (1997) understands this dyad as representing differences between association, in which a person is associated with a group but maintains a sense and understanding of individual identity, and membership, in which the group constitutes a part of the personality of its members. Scholars consider that an association is the equivalent to an addition of an adjective to a person's self-description and does not constitute a common experience or worldview whereas membership in a group influences the very identity of a person. Turner (1987, 1994) describes these two different experiences using the terms 'membership' group, which does not have a significant impact on identity, and 'reference' group, which does significantly impact and alter individual identity.

I see this difference as a differentiation between a categorical group and a group of membership. A group can be described as categorical if a person only describes himself or herself with this category: I am a father, I am a doctor, or I am a woman. This group satisfies all main criteria of the group: the person realizes the features of a prototype or typical member of this group, shares common characteristics of members of this category, and can understand the differences with members of other categories. For example, a woman who characterizes herself as a mother knows what it means to be a good mother, which features she has as a mother, and how women who do not have children are different from her. But despite these categorical similarities, she does not necessarily share the values and goals of all people in this category (mothers), does not have close contact with a "group of mothers", and is not interrelated with them. She can stay at home or go to work but in either case she may not necessarily have any contact with other mothers. In the categorical group, a person characterizes himself or herself as an individual and interacts with other people from this individual position.

In a membership group a person has continual, intimate contact with other members of the group, shares their values, beliefs, and feelings, and participates in efforts to reach the common goals of the group. He or she interacts with other people not as an individual but as a member of the ingroup dealing with members of either ingroups or outgroups, and orienting primarily around the stereotypical features of those members. In a membership group, a person characterizes himself or herself as a member of the group, stressing his or her similarity and closeness with other ingroup members. Thus, to extend our previous example, a woman can become a member of the local mothers club, meet with them every week, and work together with others to improve (for example) the ecological situation or state of education in their community. A woman aligning herself in membership terms will share values, goals, and beliefs and experience group commonality.

The prevalence of categorical groups or membership groups is one of the main characteristics of individualistic or collectivistic cultures and is one of the most important influences on the process of identity formation. Categorical groups prevail in individualistic cultures, influencing personal orientation and supremacy of individual identity. Collectivistic cultures are characterized by the prevalence of membership groups, which influence the formation of group orientation and social identity. The same group can operate as both a collective and a group of members, depending on the orientation of its members. For example, a member of an ethnic group can draw his or her goals and values from the group, share his or her destiny with the group, and actively fight for the rights of the ingroup and/or discriminate against members of other groups. In this case, the ethnic group is operating as a group of membership. But if a person only ascribes to an ethnic group, characterizing himself or herself by ethnicity, and does not share group goals and beliefs, does not participate as an active member of the group, and does not perceive the world in terms of ingroups and outgroups, the ethnic group is operating as a categorical group. Categorical and membership groups are identified in the field of social categorization theory, but authors do not analyze the differences between them as well as the outcomes of affiliation with each of those group types. I suggest that categorical groups can be described in terms of a role theory of identity and membership groups in terms of a group theory of identity.

In individualistic cultures, the development of a person is based on a reflection of their own behavioral and personal characteristics; the process of self-representation reflects an understanding of the differences between the person and others, and is mostly conscious. In collectivistic cultures, groups and intergroup relations have significant impact on personal development. A person perceives the group and intergroup processes as primal and seldom analyzes them; the process of self-representation, based on group characteristics, therefore contains many unconscious components. The prevalence of conscious and unconscious elements in self-representation and worldview is one of the most important characteristics of individualistic and collectivistic cultures. The identity of representatives of individualistic cultures is a product of personal reflection and is realized. The identity of representatives of collectivistic cultures contains groups beliefs and values that are adopted unscrutinized and therefore not well-realized and mostly unconscious.

The Structure of Narratives in Collectivistic and Individualistic Cultures

The findings above concerning collectivist and individualistic cultures suggest the following proposal: in collectivistic cultures with predominant social identity, such concepts as close relationships with family and the greater ethnic group, social recognition, and group support determine the character of individual perceptions, understandings, and interpretations of the social reality; in individualistic cultures with predominant individual identity, the most important concepts reflect personal growth, individual achievements, and close relationships with one's partner. To verify this proposition, we created the following unfinished "fairy tale."*

> A father of two brothers died and left land and a house to the older brother. The younger brother, smart and brave, went on a journey to find his destiny. After encountering different troubles and adventures, he found a sacred cave. In the middle of the cave, he saw a patterned trunk. He opened the trunk and . . . .

Our respondents—representatives of a collectivistic culture (Crimean Tatars) and an individualistic culture (Russians)—were asked to complete the fairy tale. Their stories were analyzed using a special system of codes that identified six main and 14 auxiliary themes. The main themes included the following: (1) own people, motherland; (2) returning to family, family reunion, union with relatives; (3) loss of the sense of life, loss of life; (4) self-realization, understanding of own personality, personal growth; (5) love, new partner, new family; and (6) professional realization, work, job. The list of auxiliary themes included: (1) social recognition, (2) help, (3) involvement, (4) achievements, (5) self-affirmation, (6) close relationships, (7) returning, (8) separation, (9) endless search, (10) deception, (11) ordeal, (12) struggle, (13) gain, and (14) defeat.

Each main and auxiliary theme was measured by its intensity on a five-point scale outlined as follows: (1) leading; (2) one of the leading; (3) salient, repeating; (4) mentioned several times; and (5) mentioned one time.

The findings show that the main themes for Crimean Tatars involve returning to family, family reunion, motherland and ethnic group. Their auxiliary themes stressed help, involvement, social recognition, and close relationships. Such main themes as self-realization, understanding of own personality, personal growth; love, new partner, new family; and professional realization, work, job prevailed in the narratives of Russians. The most important auxiliary themes for them include self-affirmation, achievements, close relationship, and social recognition. The results were examined using factor analyses of main themes and auxiliary themes for each ethnic group—Russians and Crimean Tatars.

Analysis revealed three factors among the main themes of the Crimean Tatars' narratives.

Factor one includes two main themes: (a) returning to family, family reunion, union with relatives (with weight 0.65) and (b) professional realization, job (with weight -0.82). Interpretation: The most important theme in the narratives of the Crimean Tatars is that of returning to the family and uniting with it once again. This theme far outweighed the values of professional career, interesting job, etc.

Factor two takes in two main themes: (a) people, motherland (with weight 0.56) and (b) lost of self (lost of the sense of life, lost of life) (with weight -0.87). Interpretation: In the Crimean Tatars' narratives, the connection with one's ethnic group, land, and motherland is the most important condition of life, of understanding the self. A person can feel fulfilled only in living within one's ethnic group, and in one's Homeland.

Factor three contains two main themes: (a) love, new partner, new family (with weight 0.72) and (b) self-realization, understanding of own personality, personal growth (with weight -0.83). Interpretation: Love and relationship with one's partner are more important than self-realization. Family values prevail over the values of personal growth and development.

Analysis revealed five factors among the auxiliary themes of Crimean Tatars' narratives.

Factor four encloses three auxiliary themes: (a) social recognition (with weight 0.83), (b) achievements (with weight 0.77), and (c) help (with weight 0.66). Interpretation: Social recognition can be attained only through providing help to the ingroup. This represents a person's most important achievement.

Factor five contains four auxiliary themes: (a) involvement (with weight 0.40), (b) endless search (with weight -0.80), (c) separation (with weight -0.75), and (d) self- affirmation (with weight -0.33). Interpretation: Involvement in the ingroup is perceived as the happy end of the quest for a meaningful life. Self-affirmation leads to separation from the group and an endless quest for fulfillment. People can be happy only through their connections with others and their identification with the group.

Factor six encloses three auxiliary themes: (a) involvement (with weight 0.47), (b) returning (with weight 0.40), and (c) deception (with weight -0.86). Interpretation: If a person is connected with the ingroup, the social environment becomes trustworthy, stable, and a defense from any threats. Deception is the result of solitude and absence of fellowship.

Factor seven includes three auxiliary themes: (a) ordeal (with weight 0.85), (b) self- affirmation (with weight 0.64), and (c) returning (with weight -0.33). Interpretation: Individuals experience a sense of inner peace upon returning home. People who seek self-affirmation must endure suffering and struggles in life. The only way to overcome such ordeals is to return home.

Factor eight contains three auxiliary themes: (a) returning (with weight 0.48), (b) defeat (with weight -0.90), and (c) separation (with weight -0.47). Interpretation: Returning home (to the ethnic group, the motherland) is perceived as a gain through unity with the family and ingroup. Separation from the group and the attainment of personal autonomy seemed to be a major hardship.

Additional factor analysis included such variables as the salience of ethnic identity in addition to both main and auxiliary themes. This further analysis revealed one main factor that includes five components: (a) salient ethnic identity (with weight 0.81), (b) ethnic group, motherland, people (with weight 0.79), (c) social recognition (with weight 0.33), (d) deception (with weight -0.40), and (e) separation(with weight -0.34). Interpretation: Ethnic identity is associated with unity with the ethnic group, the motherland, and land as well as with social recognition by the ethnic group. Separation from the ethnic group is considered an act of deception.

Consequently, analysis shows the following features present in the narratives of Crimean Tatars:

1. Separation, self-affirmation as an independent person, personal development, and growth are perceived as negative, faithless, connected with defeats, deceptions, and ordeals. The search for personal autonomy is seen as endless and fruitless, the results of which extend beyond the boundaries of the narrative. Thus, the concept of personal development does not retain adequate models in collectivistic cultures.

2. Enhancing one's professional career and achievements in work are viewed as an act of separation from the ingroup, as interests subdominant to family and ethnic group values. Social recognition can be achieved only through unity with the ingroup, providing help to the ingroup, and participation in the ingroup.

3. The most acceptable, wise, and successful choice a person can make is the choice to return to the ingroup, to achieve reunion with the family, ethnic group, and motherland. This choice is perceived as the safest for the psychological health of the person, defending from external threats, providing confidence and trust. Returning to the ethnic group terminates all ordeals and defeats, as well as all attempts for self-realization, which is not viewed as important or desirable. The most significant goal for a person in collectivistic culture therefore becomes social recognition.

4. The most esteemed way of life in collectivistic culture is immersion within a unified group. Ethnic identity serves as a guarantor

of personal security and stability in the social environment. Group values and perceptions dominate over personal opinions and attitudes.

Analysis revealed three factors among main themes of Russians' narratives.

Factor one includes three main themes: (a) love, new partner, new family (with weight 0.82), (b) professional realization, job (with weight 0.68), and (c) lost of the sense of life, lost of life (with weight -0.52). Interpretation: The presence of a loving partner (or nuclear family) and a successful professional career enables one to achieve a fulfilling life.

Factor two contains two main themes: (a) self-realization, understanding of own personality, personal growth (with weight 0.89) and (b) lost of the sense of life, lost of life (with weight -0.58). Interpretation: Another important factor of personal integrity is self-realization, which promotes an understanding of one's personality.

Factor three includes three main themes: (a) lost of the sense of life, lost of life (with weight 0.36), (b) returning to family, family reunion, union with relatives (with weight -0.78), and (c) own people, motherland (with weight -0.68). Interpretation, Factor Three: The good life is also rooted in family, one's ethnic group, and the motherland. They are important sources for stability and general sense of life. All three main factors are connected with self-realization, a sense of personal life, and personal development.

Analysis revealed three factors among auxiliary themes of Russians' narratives.

Factor four comprises of five auxiliary themes: (a) struggle (with weight 0.78), (b) ordeal (with weight 0.75), (c) gain (with weight 0.63), (d) achievements (with weight 0.62), and (e) self- affirmation (with weight 0.60). Interpretation: Self-affirmation is a result of gains and achievements attained through life's struggles.

Factor five contains four auxiliary themes: (a) returning (with weight 0.85), (b) close relationship (with weight 0.65), (c) gain (with weight 0.43), and (d) ordeal (with weight 0.35). Interpretation: Returning from travel to family and home and developing close relationships with loved ones represents a gain in the struggle with life's ordeals.

Factor six encloses three auxiliary themes: (a) social recognition (with weight 0.78), (b) self- affirmation (with weight 0.50), and (c) achievements (with weight 0.38). Interpretation: Social recognition is perceived as a result of successful self-affirmation and achievements. Thus, social recognition is connected with personal development and the acknowledgement of personal achievements.

Additional factor analysis of the Russians' narratives included such variables as the salience of ethnic identity in addition to both main and auxiliary themes. This analysis revealed one main factor that includes five components: (a) social recognition (with weight 0.80), (b) salient ethnic identity (with weight 0.66), (c) achievements (with weight 0.35), (d) self-affirmation (with weight 0.35), and (e) professional carrier, work, job (with weight 0.34). Interpretation: For the Russians, ethnic identity was one component in a complexity of social recognition and personal achievement.

Consequently, our analysis showed the following five tendencies in the narratives of the Russians:

1. The integrity of self is the most important concept. The loss of self is avoided only through professional self-realization and happiness in one's nuclear family (defined as one's spouse and children, not connected with previous generations). Having achieved these two goals, a person can stop his or her search for self-affirmation. The ethnic group and the motherland also contribute to one's personal integrity, but their role is less significant than the role of professional career and nuclear family.
2. The most appropriate and successful means for attaining personal integrity is individualistic self-affirmation, connected with personal development. Additionally, a person must endure struggles to attain self-awareness.
3. The narratives are characterized by marginality: the search for personal integrity is described both through (a) separation, personal development, and autonomy and (b) returning to the ingroup and reconnecting with the ethnic group and the motherland.
4. Social recognition considered results from personal growth and professional achievements. The respect from the society and ingroup is based more on independency and personal accomplishments than on help and participation in ingroup.

5. Ethnic identity is part a complexity of achievements, centering on pride in one's Russian identity and self-realization as a professional, spouse, and parent. Personal attitudes and worldview are more important than group norms and perceptions.

Study of Social Identity, Attitudes, and Readiness for Conflict Behavior in Individualistic and Collectivistic Cultures

The transition from polimodal individual and social identities to a single, dominant group identity, with a fixed We/They duality, reflects the infraction between attitudes and identity. Two main theories of intergroup relations, social identity theory and realistic conflict theory, give contradictory explanations for the interconnection between identity and attitudes. Realistic conflict theory prioritizes conflicts of interest between groups and negative attitudes toward members of outgroups for defining ingroup identity. Social identity theory suggests that strong identification with the ingroup leads to the development of intergroup prejudice, negative attitudes, and conflict behavior.

To examine the causal relationship between social identity and attitudes, I conducted a study of the interconnections between social identity, attitudes, and readiness for conflict behavior. I hypothesize that this relationship can be described by a basic model (Figure 1).

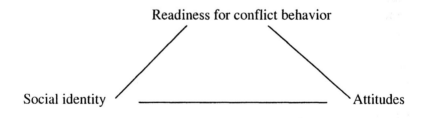

Figure 7.1
Basic model of interconnections between social identity, attitudes, and readiness for conflict behavior

Residents of select towns and villages in Crimea were interviewed during September 2001, soon after the events of September 11. The sample was stratified by location, number of resettlements, and rural/urban status.

Participants were Russians (257) and Crimean Tatars (257), and were equally distributed across these locations. Of the participants, 41 percent were male and 59 percent were female; 38 percent were between 20 and 30 years old, 32 percent between 30 and 45, 18 percent between 45 and 60, and 12 percent above 60; 58 percent were residents of towns and 43 percent are residents of villages. Participation was voluntary. Respondents were provided with a questionnaire and selected answers from a list.

Respondents were also tested using Triandis' INDCOL scale (Triandis 1995) for collectivistic/individualistic cultures. The scale includes the following questions: The decision of where to work should be made jointly with one's spouse, if one is married, and it is reasonable for a son to continue his father's business. Results show that Russians perceive their ethnic group as collectivistic on the parameter of orientation to the group, and individualistic on the parameters of openness to change, orientation to interaction with other groups, and weak social control. Crimean Tatars estimate their group as highly collectivistic based on all parameters.

Table 7.2.
Parameters of individualism/collectivism in %

Ethnic group	1A	1B	2A	2B	3A	3B	4A	4B
Russians	62	38	58	42	79	21	43	57
Crimean Tatars	100	0	8	92	41	59	55	45

Notes: Group orientation (1A) – self-orientation (1B)
Openness to change (2A) – resistance to change (2B)
Openness to interaction (3A) – denial of interaction (3B)
Strong social control (4A) – weak social control (4B)

The study of readiness to defend ethnic and religious groups shows that Crimean Tatars are more prone to defend the norms and values of their ethnic group than Russians, who are more prone to defend the safety of their ethnic group (see Table 7.3).

Table 7.3
The readiness to defend ethnic and religious groups among
Russians and Crimean Tatars

Readiness to defend	Ethnic group		Religious group	
	Safety	Norms and values	Safety	Norms and values
Crimean Tatars: Individual Group	2.2163 2.3541	2.2974 2.3840	2.2305 2.3008	2.2555 2.3758
Russians: Individual Group	2.3268 2.3125	2.1868 2.2568	2.0039 2.1137	2.0118 2.1490

The differences between the two ethnic groups are significant with respect to the willingness to defend the ethnic group. Interestingly, Crimean Tatars show a higher readiness to defend the safety, norms, and values of the religious group than the Russians.

I conducted regression analyses of the interrelations between national, ethnic, religious, and regional identities, attitudes, and readiness to defend ethnic and religious groups. The analysis showed that the national identity of the Crimean Tatars is connected with individual and group readiness to defend the values and norms of their religious group. These findings confirm the results of previous research (Korostelina 2001, 2002) which showed that national identity motivates Crimean Tatars to preserve the cultural independence of their group. The ethnic identity of Crimean Tatars is connected with individual and group readiness to defend safety of ethnic group and individual and group readiness to defend values and norms of the ethnic group.

The religious identity of the Russians is connected with individual and groups' readiness to protect the religious group and individual readiness to defend the values and ideas of the ethnic group. The religious identity of Crimean Tatars is connected with all factors except individual readiness to defend the safety of the ethnic group. The most significant interconnection was found in the individual and group readiness to defend the safety of the religious group and individual readiness to defend the norms and values of the religious group.

The ethnic and regional identity of Russians and the regional identity of Crimean Tatars were not closely connected with the readiness to defend ethnic and religious groups through violent means. Interestingly, religious identity is connected with the readiness to defend the ethnic group, especially its norms and values by any methods and actions. Religious identity is connected with the readiness for conflictual behavior for both representatives of both ethnic groups.

Consequently, the readiness to defend ethnic and religious groups using violent methods is connected with religious identity. For Crimean Tatars, Muslims with highly salient ethnic and religious identity, religious identity is significantly connected with 7 of 8 possible indexes that confirm the importance of this identity for representatives of collectivistic cultures.

The results of analyses of interrelations between types of social identity and attitudes show that the national identity of Crimean Tatars is connected with ideas about opposition between religions, the split within the Muslim world, and the support for Jihad. Belonging to the Ukrainian nation weakens opinions about unity and the tolerance of Muslims. The national identity of Russians is connected with attitudes about opposition between religions.

The ethnic identity of Russians is connected with attitudes that Talibs are terrorists and the perceived relation between terrorism and the Muslim religion.

The religious identity of Crimean Tatars is connected with the belief that Muslims support Jihad (which carries negative connections), that Talibs are terrorists, and that it is important to be vigilant against terrorists. The religious identity of Russians is connected with the concept of opposition between religions and the perceived relation between terrorism and the Muslim religion.

The regional identity of Crimean Tatars is connected with beliefs that war in Afghanistan is just. The regional identity of Russians also is connected to the support of the war in Afghanistan, as well as with attitudes about the split between the Muslim and Western worlds.

Thus, the social identity of Crimean Tatars is more strongly connected with particular attitudes toward terrorism than is the social identity of Russians. Each of the ethnic, national, and religious identities of Crimean Tatars exhibits 3 of 8 possible interconnections with attitudes; regional identity is connected with only one attitude. For Russians, more significant interconnections were found for regional identity (3 connections out of 8); each of the religious and ethnic identities had two interconnections; only one interconnection was found for national identity.

The strongest connection with social identity was found for the following attitudes of Crimean Tatars: the opposition of the Muslim and Western worlds, the belief that Talibs are terrorists, and the idea that a split within the Muslim world is exacerbating the war on terrorism. For Russians, attitudes about the opposition of the Muslim and Western worlds have the most significant interconnections with social identity.

The analysis of interconnections between attitudes and individual readiness to defend the ingroup shows that for Russians, the readiness to defend the safety of one's ethnic group is connected with attitudes regarding the link between terrorism and the Muslim religion, the concept of opposition between religions, the support for Jihad by Muslims, the perception that Talibs are terrorists, and the importance of the unity of the world in war on terrorism. Individual readiness to defend the norms and values of their ethnic group is connected with attitudes about the association between terrorism and the Muslim religion, the concept of opposition between religions, the split within the Western world, the support for Jihad by Muslims, the belief that Talibs are terrorists, support for war in Afghanistan, and the importance of the unity of the world in the war on terrorism.

Individual readiness to defend the safety of the religious group among Russians was connected with attitudes about support for Jihad by Muslims and support for the war in Afghanistan. Individual readiness to defend the norms and values of the religious group is connected with attitudes about the association between terrorism and the Muslim religion, support for Jihad by Muslims, the belief that Talibs are terrorists, and the importance of the unity of the world in war on terrorism.

For Crimean Tatars, the readiness to defend the safety of the ethnic group is connected with attitudes about the split within the Western world, support for Jihad by Muslims, and vigilance in the war on terrorism. Individual readiness to defend the norms and values of the ethnic group was connected with attitudes about opposition between religions, the split within Muslim world, and support for Jihad by Muslims. Individual readiness to defend the safety of the religious group among Crimean Tatars was connected with attitudes about support for Jihad by Muslims. Individual readiness to defend the norms and values of the religious group was connected with negative attitudes toward the war in Afghanistan.

Thus, the attitudes of Russians were more significantly connected with individual readiness to defend the ingroup than the attitudes of Crimean Tatars. For Russians, our study shows 19 significant interconnections (12 on the level $p < .001$), while for Crimean Tatars only 8 interconnections were found (3 on the level $p < .001$). Individual readiness to defend the norms and values of the ethnic group for Russians revealed the highest number of significant interconnections with attitudes (7 out of a possible 8 connections). Significant interconnections with attitudes were also found for the individual readiness to defend the safety of the ethnic group (5 interconnections). For Crimean Tatars, more significant interconnections with attitudes were found for the readiness to defend the safety, as well as the values and norms of the ethnic group (3 connections for each).

The analysis of interconnections between perceived group readiness to defend the ingroup and attitudes shows that group readiness to defend the safety, as well as the values and norms of the ethnic group among Crimean Tatars is not connected with any attitudes. Perceived group readiness to defend the safety of the religious group among Crimean Tatars is connected with an attitude that Muslims support Jihad, and a perceived group readiness to defend the values and norms of the religious group is connected with attitudes about the split within the Western world.

For Russians the group readiness to defend the safety of the ethnic group was connected with attitudes about support for Jihad by Muslims, the belief that Talibs are terrorists, and the importance of the unity of the world in the war on terrorism. Group readiness to defend the norms and values of the ethnic group was connected with attitudes about the association between terrorism and the Muslim religion, the concept of opposition between religions, the split within the Western world, support for Jihad by Muslims, the belief that Talibs are terrorists, and the importance of the unity of the world in the war on terrorism.

Group readiness to defend the safety of the religious group among Russians was connected with attitudes about support for Jihad by Muslims. Group readiness to defend the norms and values of the religious group was also connected with attitudes about support for Jihad by Muslims.

Thus, perceived group readiness to defend the ingroup is less strongly connected to attitudes than to individual readiness. The tendency for the prevalence of interconnections between readiness and attitudes among Russians was confirmed for group readiness to defend the ingroup. Group readiness to defend the norms and values of the ethnic group among Russians had more significant interconnection with attitudes (6 connections out of 8 possible connections); 3 significant interconnections were found for group readiness to defend the safety of the ethnic group. For Crimean Tatars, group readiness to defend the safety, norms, and values of the ethnic group did not have any significant interconnection with attitudes.

Consequently, the social identity of Crimean Tatars was more strongly connected with the readiness to defend the ingroup than was the social identity of Russians. The religious identity of Crimean Tatars displayed a higher number of interconnections with attitudes (7 significant connections out of 8). The study reveals four significant connections with attitudes for ethnic identity and two connections with attitudes for the national identity of Crimean Tatars. No interconnections were found for regional identity. For Russians, connections with attitudes were found only for religious identity (3 significant interconnections). The national identity of Crimean Tatars was connected with individual and group readiness to defend the norms and values of the religious group. The ethnic identity of Crimean Tatars was connected with individual and group readiness to defend the safety of the ethnic group, and with individual readiness to defend the norms and values of the ethnic group. The religious identity of Russians was connected with individual and group readiness to defend the safety of the religious group, and with individual readiness to defend the norms and values of the ethnic group. Therefore, readiness to defend the ingroup was connected with religious identity for both groups, and with ethnic identity for Crimean Tatars. No connection with readiness to defend the ingroup was found for regional identity.

The social identity of Crimean Tatars was more strongly connected with attitudes toward terrorism than was the social identity of Russians. Each of the social identities of Crimean Tatars (ethnic, national, and religious) displayed three significant interconnections with attitudes; for regional identity, only one significant interconnection was found. For Russians, regional identity exhibited three significant interconnections with attitudes; religious and ethnic identities exhibited two significant interconnections with attitudes; and only one interconnection was found for national identity.

The social identity of Crimean Tatars was more connected with the readiness to defend ingroups than with attitudes. Indeed, 13 interconnections were found between social identity and the readiness to defend the ingroup (6 on the level $p < .001$), while 10 interconnections were revealed between social identity and attitudes (only 1 on the level $p < .001$). The social identity of Russians was more strongly connected with attitudes than with the readiness to defend ingroups. Accordingly, 8 interconnections were revealed between social identity and attitudes (4 on the level $p < .001$), while 3 interconnections were found between social identity and the readiness to defend the ingroup (2 on the level $p < .001$).

The attitudes of Russians were more strongly interconnected with individual readiness to defend the ingroup than the attitudes of Crimean Tatars. Thus for Russians, the study revealed 19 significant interconnections (12 on the level $p < .001$), while for Crimean Tatars only 8 significant interconnections were found (3 on the level $p < .001$). Among Russians, individual readiness to defend the norms and values of the ethnic group had the highest number of interconnections with attitudes (7 out of 8 possible interconnections). Significant interconnections with attitudes also were found for individual readiness to defend the safety of the ethnic group (5 interconnections), as well as for individual readiness to defend the norms and values of the religious group. For Crimean Tatars, individual readiness to defend the safety, norms, and values of the ethnic group had 3 interconnections with attitudes. Only one significant interconnection with attitudes was found for individual readiness to defend the religious group.

This study reveals fewer interconnections between attitudes for perceived group readiness to defend the ingroup than attitudes for individual readiness, while it confirms the tendency for a prevalence of interconnections between readiness and attitudes among Russians. Group readiness to defend the norms and values of the ethnic group among Russians had more significant interconnections with attitudes (6 connections out of a possible 8); 3 significant interconnections were found for group readiness to defend safety of ethnic group. For Crimean Tatars, group readiness to defend the safety, norms, and values of the ethnic group does not have any significant interconnection with attitudes.

My research findings imply the necessity of revising the basic model of interrelations between attitudes, readiness to defend the ingroup, and social identity (Figure 7.1). Figure 7.2 shows the basic model with data for the Crimean Tatars gathered during our study (interconnections at p < .001 level are shown in brackets):

Readiness to defend ingroup

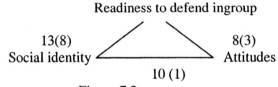

13(8)   8(3)
Social identity   Attitudes
10 (1)

Figure 7.2
Interrelations between attitudes, readiness to defend the ingroup, and social identity for Crimean Tatars

Consequently, for Crimean Tatars, social identity is the initial factor in the formation of conflicted behavior. The readiness for conflict behavior strongly influences attitudes; social identity also has an impact on attitudes. The basic model therefore takes the following form:

Figure 7.3
Model of interrelations between attitudes, readiness to defend the ingroup, and social identity for Crimean Tatars

Figure 7.4 shows the basic model with data for the Russians gathered during our study (interconnections at p<.001 level are shown in brackets):

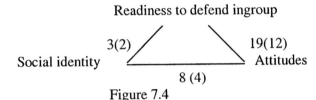

Readiness to defend ingroup

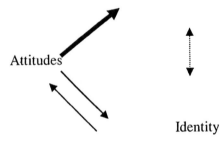

Figure 7.4
Interrelations between attitudes, readiness to defend the ingroup, and social identity for Russians

Consequently, for Russians attitudes are the initial factor in the formation of conflict behavior and the development of social identity, and have a strong influence on the readiness for conflict behavior. The basic model therefore takes the following form (Figure 7.5):

Readiness for conflict behavior

Attitudes

Identity

Figure 7.5
Model of interrelations between attitudes, readiness to defend the ingroup, and social identity for Russians

For representatives of collectivistic cultures, salient social identity plays a determinant role in the formation of conflict behavior. The ideas of connection with the ingroup, subordination to the ingroup, and unity with its members are more important than personal autonomy. Social recognition and respect are the results of help for and involvement in the ingroup. Salient social identity impacts attitudes and perception of the situation: group values and perceptions dominate personal opinions and attitudes. People are ready to defend and fight for ethnic identity to insure personal security and social stability. Salient social identity influences the readiness to defend the safety as well as the ideals and values of the ingroup using any methods including violence. Attitudes and readiness for conflict behavior are interconnected; however, readiness for conflict behavior occupies the primary position.

For representatives of individualistic cultures, personal development and achievements are more important than involvement and connections with the ingroup. Social recognition and respect are the result of personal success, professional accomplishments, and self-realization. The personal perception and estimation of the situation (attitudes) precedes and determines the readiness for conflict behavior. Attitudes have a strong impact on social identity. Salient social identity also influences readiness for conflict behavior; nevertheless, attitudes can increase or decrease this influence. For representatives of collectivistic cultures, strong belonging to an ingroup determinates the readiness for conflict behavior, whereas for representatives of individualistic cultures, individual estimation of a situation carries the strongest impact on the readiness for conflict behavior.

In cases of protracted conflict, collectivistic cultures are prone to threats and have a great tendency towards violence in their relations with the Other. The close connection with the ingroup leads to shaping ingroup responses to the Other; individual attitudes and perceptions are subordinate to the process of collective devaluation and dehumanization. In individualistic cultures, personal views and attitudes can contradict group perceptions, but the strong negative narratives of others shift from negative individual attribution to collective denigration.

Notes

* This study was conducted together with O. Dzhuzha

Chapter 7

References

Barth, F. 1981. *Process and form in social life*. London: Routledge & Kegan Paul.

Crocker, J., and Luhtanen, R. 1990. Collective self-esteem and ingroup bias. *Journal of Personality and Social Psychology*, no. 58, 323-338.

Durkheim, É. 1969. Individualism and the Intellectuals. *Political Studies*, no. 17, 14-30. Translation of 1898c.

Hofstede, G. 1980. *Culture's consequences: International differences in work- related values*. Beverly Hills, CA: Sage.

Hofstede, G. 2001. *Culture's Consequences: Comparing Values, Behaviors, Institutions, and Organizations Across Nations*. Thousand Oaks CA: Sage Publications.

Hinkle, S., Brown, R. 1990. "Intergroup comparisons and social identity: Some links and lacunae." In D. Abrams & M. A. Hogg (eds), *Social identity theory: Constructive and critical advances*. New York, Harvester/Wheatsheaf.

Jenkins, R. 1996. *Social identity*. London: Routledge.

Markus, H., & Kitayama, S. 1991. Culture and the self: Implications for cognition, emotion, and motivation. *Psychological Review*, no. 98, 224-253.

Morales, J.F., López-Sáez, M. and Vega, L., 1998, *Discrimination and Beliefs on Discrimination in Individualists and Collectivists*, In S. Worchel, J.F. Morales, D. Páez and J.C. Deschamps (eds.), *Social Identity: International Perspectives*, Londres, SAGE, Pp. 199-210.

Oberg, K. 1960. Culture shock. Adjustment to new cultural environments. *Practical Anthropology*, no. 7.

Parsons, T. 1951. *The Social System*. Glencoe, IL: Free Press.

Reykowski, J. 1997. "Patriotism and collective system of meanings." In D. Bar-Tal and E. Staub (eds.) *Patriotism in global age*. Chicago: Nelson Hall.

Taft, R. 1977. Coping with unfamiliar cultures. In N. Warren (Ed.). *Studies in cross-cultural psychology*, vol. 1, Pp. 125-153. London, England: Academic Press.

Triandis, S.H. & Gelfand, M.J. 1998. Converging measurement of horizontal and vertical collectivism and individualism. *Journal of Personality and Social Psychology.* no. 74, Pp. 118-128.

Triandis, H.C., Bontempo, R., Villareal, M.J., Asai, M. ,and Lucca, N. 1988. Individualism and collectivism: cross-cultural perspectives on self-ingroup relationships. *Journal of Personality and Social Psychology*, no. 54, Pp.323-338.

Trompenaars, F. and Hampden-Turner, C. 1997. *Riding the Waves of Culture: Understanding Diversity in Global Business*, McGraw-Hill.

Trumbull. E., Rothstein-Fisch, C., and Greenfield, P. M. 2000. *Bridging Cultures in Our Schools: New Approaches That Work. Publisher?*

Turner, J. C., Oakes, P. J., Haslam, S. A., and McGarty, C. 1994. Self and collective: Cognition and social context. *Personality and Psychology Bulletin,* no. 20, 454-463.

Turner, J. C., Hogg, M. A., Oakes, P. J., Reicher, S. D., and Watherell, M. S. 1987. *Rediscovering the social group: A self-categorization theory*. Oxford and New York: Basil Blackwell.

Young, I. M. 1997. *Interesting voices: Dilemmas of gender, political philosophy, and policy*. Princeton, NJ: Princeton University Press.

Chapter 8

From Incorporation to Disengagement: East Timor and Indonesian Identities, 1975-1999

Lena Tan

Introduction

For twenty-four years, Indonesia steadfastly defended its 1975 annexation of East Timor which had been prompted by the belief of Suharto's New Order regime that the latter's independence would be a great threat to the archipelago's national interest (Schwarz 2000; Taylor 1999). Between 1998 and 1999 however, East Timor was discussed in a radically different way by the new team that had taken over the running of the country after President Suharto had been forced to resign. East Timor's political status as the archipelago's twenty-seventh province was no longer a non-negotiable issue in Indonesian politics. Headed by B.J. Habibie, the team concluded that Indonesia's national interests were not inextricably linked to the retention of East Timor. In fact, Indonesia's national interests laid crucially with changing its approach to East Timor and resolving this issue even if it meant withdrawing from a territory that they had forcefully tried to integrate at great cost to Indonesia's international reputation and to the hundreds of thousands of East Timorese who had lost their lives.

What explains the dramatic reversal in policy which had been considered *fait accompli* by many within Indonesia for almost a quarter of a century? How did East Timor, once considered an integral part of the national interest and national security, become 'historical baggage' and an obstruction to the fulfillment of its goals in the post-Suharto period?

How and why was East Timor framed and represented in discussions regarding Indonesia's national interests in such different terms by Suharto and the New Order elites on the one hand, and Habibie and his advisers on the other?

Realpolitik explanations focusing on economic or strategic reasons are inadequate. Economically, East Timor was neither an asset nor a prize—Indonesia had nothing to gain from annexing it (Leifer 1983) and in fact recognized that it "would almost certainly be a liability."[1] In 1998, worsening economic conditions arising from the 1997 Asian financial crisis and the need for international economic support were certainly present when President Habibie came into power but they were not new to the Indonesian government. International pressure had existed since the early 1990s and the difficult economic conditions often cited began in 1997.[2] Yet there had been no contemplation of change in their East Timor policy before June 1998.

Others have argued that Habibie's actions were entirely self-interested. A technocrat and Suharto protégé who had ascended to the office of the president by virtue of the fact that he was the vice-president of Indonesia when Suharto resigned, Habibie's need to widen his political base may have led to the change. However, Habibie's decision did not increase the size of his domestic constituency. First, the *reformasi* remained unconvinced that he was at heart, a democrat. Furthermore, most Indonesians did not have basic and accurate information about Indonesia's involvement in East Timor due to censorship and a news blackout, and believed that East Timor's incorporation had been at the latter's own request. Unlike the rest of the world, they did not see their East Timor policy as an act of colonization (Anwar 2000). Finally, Habibie's offer of independence as an option for the East Timorese also alienated important sections of the military, a pivotal centre of power in Indonesian politics whose support was necessary for him to maintain his presidency (Lloyd 2000).

A third possible explanation that draws on theoretical insights from International Relations focuses on the role of transnational networks in diffusing norms and ideas of anti-colonialism, self-determination, sovereignty, democracy and human rights to Indonesia and exerting pressure on western governments and international organizations as the critical factors in paving the road to its disengagement from East Timor (Smith and Muetzelfeldt 2000). While transnational networks, East Timorese freedom fighters as well as liberal and progressive NGOs in Indonesia emphasizing human rights and democracy were indeed part of the story, they were not, as we shall see later, the full story.

In order to account for these puzzling differences, this chapter examines how two very different conceptions of Indonesia's identity by two very different groups of elite policymakers led to radically different perceptions of East Timor policy in 1975 and 1998-1999. In particular, this chapter illustrates how an official Indonesian identity promulgated by the elites of Suharto's New Order's produced perceptions of East Timor as a dangerous threat and led to its brutal annexation and occupation. The resolution of this conflict in 1999 on the other hand is a reflection of how a transformation in identity converted these threat narratives of East Timor into issues of human rights, democracy and morality for Indonesia.

Indonesian Diversity and Contentious Political Identities

The idea of 'Indonesia' as a common political space is a recent invention. Historically, the islands of the Indonesian archipelago were inhabited by people of great ethnic and religious diversity who developed and evolved under different social, political and economic conditions. It was Dutch colonialism and intervention over centuries which initiated a process that eventually led to the political integration of these islands as the Dutch East Indies and eventually, Indonesia (Anderson 1991). Later, resistance against a common enemy, their Dutch colonizer, strengthened the acceptance of the idea of an Indonesian nation.

This emergence of a national consciousness has, from its inception till today, been marked by fundamental differences over visions of Indonesian identity (Bertrand 2004; see also Brown 2002). Reflecting competing political objectives and projects on the country's true mission as well as the means of achieving them, these differences can be found along two important dimensions (Brown 2002). First, there have been disagreements over who may constitute legitimate citizens of the Indonesian nation-state—should this decision be based on a claim to common ethnic ancestry, similar ethno-cultural and religious attributes of the majority or common political and civic ideals? The second dimension is based on differences in ideas and principles of governance such as proposals for specific institutions, political constitutions, legal systems, and rules of property (Brown 2002).

From the 1920s to the 1940s, political elites debated and struggled to define the meaning of the Indonesian nation, its character and political goals which were represented by varied political agendas (Bertrand 2004). The nationalists focused on independence and envisioned "a nation based on the modern, European principles of self-determination, democracy and modern political institutions" (Bertrand 2004, 30). A second group, the Islamists, called for the people of this diverse archipelago to unite into one nation based on Islam as the common characteristic (ibid). The third main group had socialist ideals and argued for a communist program (ibid.). A fourth group, the integralists, envisaged an Indonesia based on the idea of "the state as a large family in which members of the society were integrated as whole" (Schwarz, 2000, 8; see also Bertrand 2004; Bourchier and Hadiz 2001).

As they prepared for independence in 1945, the political elite did agree on one extremely important matter—the necessity of territorial and national unity. Extremely conscious of the fragility and vulnerability of a state with a diverse population spread across an archipelago, the critical question for them centered on how unity in the midst of such great diversity and geographical separation was to be achieved (Kingsbury 2002). During discussions at the Constituent assembly of 1945, it was agreed that "matters such as state organization, religion, class, estate, regional language and culture, local and regional history and economy, as well as party politics, were not allowed to disturb national unity" (Holtzappel 1997, 72). For committee members, it was clear that "something new had to be invented that could unite and guide the minds of the Indonesians and substitute for the loss of local culture, religion and local history as sources of Indonesian nationalism" especially in the "absence of a homogeneous and uniform Indonesian cultural heritage that could serve as the source of the new state and nation" (Holtzappel 1997, 72–3).

Specific national objectives and values first came together on 1 June 1945 when Sukarno enunciated Pancasila, consisting of five principles – nationalism or Indonesian unity, humanitarianism, Indonesian democracy through consultation and consensus, social justice, and belief in God – as the formal ideological and philosophical basis of the Indonesian nation and state. Belief in God, the first principle, "recognizes that the state will be based on religious belief and that every Indonesian should believe in God" (Ramage 1997, 12). While implying "belief in a monotheistic religion, a concession to Muslim concerns," it also "stipulates that Indonesians should respect their fellow citizens even if they have different religious beliefs" (ibid.). The second principle is humanitarianism or in Indonesian, *kemanusiaan yang adil dan beradab*. Literally meaning 'a just and civilized humanity', this principle "represents the ideal of humanitarian behavior between all peoples" and "emphasizes tolerance and respect between all Indonesians" (Ramage 1997, 13). Indonesian national unity (*persatuan Indonesia*), the third principle, focuses on the importance of "maintaining the unity and integrity of Indonesia as a single state" (ibid.). The fourth principle emphasizes Indonesian-style democracy where the decision-making process is one dominated by *musyawarah* (consultation) and *mufakat* (consensus), and other idealized concepts of traditional village governance. Social justice (*keadilan social*), the fifth and final principle, "posits a goal of economic and social egalitarianism and prosperity for Indonesia" (Ramage 1997, 14).

These Pancasila principles were the means to *consciously* construct and unify at one level, "groups of different ethnicity, size, contact with the modern world, and experience with colonial rule" (Bertrand 2004, 28) into a single Indonesian nation-state through civic ideals. It was also a way of bridging the differences in visions of Indonesian nationhood among the political elite. The inauguration of Pancasila as the official ideological and philosophical basis of the Indonesian nation was however, only just the beginning of a long and self-consciously aware process to negotiate, construct, unify, secure and consolidate the archipelago's diversity into one united 'Indonesia' (Anderson 1991). Differences between the political elite remained unresolved throughout the 1950s and the first part of the 1960s (Aspinall and Berger 2001). The provisional 1950 constitution, based on liberal democratic principle reflected the vision of secular nationalists while sidelining those of the Islamists and communists (Bertrand 2004). Within the space of a few years, the unresolved tension between the Islamists on the one hand, and the nationalists and other secularists who continued to favor a more inclusionary and Pancasila-based Indonesian nation came once again to the fore (ibid.). With his eyes focused on securing the unity of the nation and the stability of the state, President Sukarno suppressed the demands of the Islamists with presidential decrees and military force (ibid.).

Suharto's New Order and an Official Indonesian Identity, 1966–1998

Sukarno's rule however, had disastrous consequences for Indonesia. Economically, his grandiose developments projects and mismanagement left the country deeply in debt. Politically, his aggressive policy of confronting neighbors like Malaysia and his growing alliance with the Indonesian Communist Party left the staunchly anti-communist military extremely nervous. After he was deposed, Suharto and the military who had replaced him at the helm identified three factors as the cause of Indonesia's problems. The first was the lack of a consensus among post-independence elite regarding the state structure and political system for Indonesia as it emerged from colonial rule (Anwar 1998). The second factor was in the different *aliran* or streams of political orientations present such as Islam, secular nationalism, traditional Javanism, socialism and communism which each "had its own ideals of what the Indonesian state should be and its own notion of the most serious threats to that ideal" (Anwar 1998, 490). These differences had resulted in considerable tensions among the national elite. The third factor could be found in the growing differences between the central government and the regions in Indonesia.

Out of this analysis emerged a consensus among elite politicians and the military that Indonesian national interests laid with the preservation of sovereignty, unity and territorial integrity, political stability and economic development. The sovereignty of the Indonesian state, and relatedly, the country's national unity and territorial integrity, were regarded

as sacred and non-negotiable (Anwar 1998). Political stability was a necessary pillar for the successful fulfillment of the first goal and this was to
be achieved through preventing the emergence of domestic anti-
government forces or the infiltration of hostile foreign interests which
could threaten the country's national unity. Last but not least was economic development, seen "not only as an end in itself to increase prosperity and social welfare – a key aim of the independence struggle – but,
equally important, as a prerequisite for political stability" (Anwar 1998,
487). These interests were laid out clearly in their comprehensive security doctrine known as *Ketahanan Nasional* or National Resilience,
which it is critically important to note, was directed, unlike most countries, inwardly rather than outwardly. This doctrine states that:

> the ideal of the national struggle is to realize a unitary
> Republic of Indonesia that is independent, united, sover-
> eign, just and prosperous based on Pancasila and the
> 1945 Constitution (Anwar 1998, 484).

In order to attain the objectives of the New Order's political project
and its vision for Indonesia, the elites in Suharto's regime called for
building and developing a dynamic, tenacious, sturdy and tough nation
with the national strength to cope with internal and external threats and
challenges to Indonesian life and its national objectives (Anwar 1998).
The core building blocks for such a project were to be all-encompassing,
including military capability, economic development as well as the construction and maintenance of a cohesive and united society with a strong
national identity (ibid.).

Constructing the New Order's Indonesia:
Pancasila and an Official National Identity

In the New Order's political project, the construction of a common and
hegemonic Indonesian identity based on Pancasila was particularly important because its civic principles and ideals were seen as the means of
tying all Indonesians together in order to prevent the chaos and divisions

of the first two decades of the country's independence (Bourchier and Hadiz 2001). However, its principles of tolerance, social justice and unity in the entire archipelago's diversity were increasingly mixed with integralism, one of four prominent competing political projects for Indonesia that had been present in 1945.

Rooted partly in the traditions, practices and beliefs of the Javanese aristocracy as well as in anti-Enlightenment European thought, integralism "conceived the state and society as an organic totality" (Ramage 1997, 18). The primary emphasis was on social obligations rather than individual rights or constraints on the powers of government (Ramage 1997). More importantly, the authority structure of the Indonesian state should parallel the patterns found within traditional families and orderly village societies (Bourchier and Hadiz 2001). These integralist elements enabled the presentation of Suharto and the New Order government as the guardian and head of the family of Indonesia in which its members behaved according to culturally authentic 'village' values of *musyawarah* and *mufakat* (consultation and consensus) (ibid.). Indonesians and Indonesian society were thus supposedly characterized by unity, harmony, co-operation, consensus and the rights of the collective over the individual.

Critically, key members of the New Order elite like Suharto, Adam Malik, and General Ali Murtopo incorporated Pancasila into integralism by arguing that the former was the "product of Indonesia's indigenous culture, and value system" (ibid.). For them, Pancasila was an "ideological expression of indigenous political culture" and "Indonesian personality, and therefore, the only appropriate basis of state for Indonesia" (Ramage 1997, 18). Hence, Indonesia's political and constitutional life should be based on the principles and ideals of Pancasila and embody what they claimed was the country's rural and communitarian culture (Bourchier and Hadiz 2001). Alternative political projects based on the ideas and principles of Islam, liberalism and communism were regarded as divisive and "alien and unsuited to the Indonesian 'national character'" (Bourchier and Hadiz 2001, 29).

In the mid-1980s, the Suharto regime pushed through the law on Mass Organizations where "all social organizations and political parties were legally required to make Pancasila their sole principle, or *asas tunggal"* (Vatikiotis 1998, 95). Through a comprehensive program aimed at government employees and students, Pancasila was presented as part of the cultural and historical traditions of Indonesia and therefore, "the 'sole basis' of Indonesian national identity" (Berger 1997, 344). Over the course of Suharto's thirty-three year rule, the New Order and *its* Pancasila vision of Indonesian identity became synonymous with the national character and national tradition (ibid.). However, it was also one that had become increasingly imposed on society. The stress on the communitarian elements of Pancasila as an integral part of who Indonesians are provided the regime, like other states in Southeast Asia, with an ideational and identity-based argument for rejecting ideas and concepts like human rights and democracy as mostly western in origin, and pronounce them inappropriate and irrelevant for an Indonesian social, economic and political context, and dangerous for its long-term aspirations of economic development. In overshadowing and overwhelming its civic and tolerant dimensions, Indonesia's official identity became increasingly narrow, exclusionary and linked to authoritarian political practices (Aspinall and Berger 2001; Bertrand 2004).

While the Suharto regime did use this conception of Indonesian identity as a means of silencing dissent, it does not negate the fact that its central importance to the New Order went beyond self-interest on the part of its ruling elite (Bourchier and Hadiz 2001). Suharto considered the *asas tunggal* policy "as a great, even an epoch-making, achievement of his administration. Uniting all political forces under Pancasila, he believed, enabled Indonesia to put behind it the ideological and religious conflict that had torn at its fabric in the past" (Bourchier and Hadiz 2001). For Suharto, Pancasila and his regime's conscious efforts to forge and maintain a single Indonesian identity was an integral and essential part of Indonesia's national interest. In other words, having an Indonesian identity, albeit a specific one imposed by the New Order, was necessary for the survival of the state and nation. It was itself part of the national interest.

East Timor: the New Order and Indonesian National Interests

In 1975, East Timor was an under-developed half-island which had been under Portuguese rule for more than four hundred years with very little in terms of military capability or economic wealth. Yet, Indonesia, indisputably far more powerful than East Timor, was convinced that its independence would be a significant threat to the country's national interests (Crouch 2000). The key players in Indonesia's campaign to annex East Timor—Ali Murtopo, Benny Murdani, Yoga Sugama, Suharto, members of his 'Palace Advisory' group, Harry Tjan, Liem Bian Kie, and the Department of Defense—were focused on a particular sequence of events which they were convinced would unfold with East Timor's independence.

First, they were certain that an independent Portuguese Timor would be economically poor, militarily weak and thus, unable to survive on its own (Taylor 1999). Crucially, they saw a direct relationship between East Timor's assumed lack of viability as a sovereign state and Indonesia' security and national interests. In particular, they were convinced that East Timor would fall into the hands of communism, either through leftist-leaning domestic political parties or external influence. More importantly, communism in East Timor would seep into Indonesia, infiltrate it and threaten its security, national unity and territorial integrity.[3]

In a conversation with R.A. Woolcott, the Australian Ambassador to Indonesia, the head of Indonesia's intelligence services and regular chairman of the Special Committee on Portuguese Timor, Yoga Sugama expressed this fear of communism and its threat to Indonesia's unity and security. In this conversation, reported at length and almost verbatim by Woolcott in a cablegram to Canberra, Sugama was quoted as saying:

> there is 'too much at stake for us.' We cannot permit an Angola situation on our doorstep...If the Soviet Union involved itself in the issue Indonesia would also be in a position not unlike that which Kennedy had found himself at the time of the Cuba crisis.[4]

When questioned on this analogy by Woolcott, Sugama clarified that "the reference to Cuba was that the Soviet subversive and political activities in Timor could be almost as dangerous to Indonesia in the political field as Soviet missiles in Cuba had been seen to the United States in the military field."[5] There was a real fear of communist subversion on the part of the key Indonesian players and their conviction that it was necessary to combat it.[6]

Hence, it is quite clear, as Michael Leifer argues, that "the augury of political change in East Timor after April 1974 conjured up a variety of worst possible cases, including the prospect of a point of entry for hostile forces being opened up into the soft exterior of the Republic and encouragement being provided for separatism within the archipelago" (Leifer 1983, 155). While this explanation is supported by primary sources documenting conversations of Australian diplomats and government officials with Suharto and members of the Special Committee, it raises the very important question of whether the particular sequence of events predicted by the Indonesians was even warranted.

In the period after Portugal declared its intention to begin decolonization processes for the remnants of its empire in 1974, East Timor, in anticipation of its independence, began to formulate and implement nationwide development plans in areas like education, health and politics where indigenous society and culture had central roles (Taylor 1999). It was thus a society with newly established institutions, nationalist ideologies and aspirations for independence. The political, economic and social structures that had been put in place also augured well for its development and survival as a sovereign state (ibid.).

Despite the lack of supporting evidence showing that an independent East Timor would be a real threat to Indonesia, these fears, documented in meetings between the Indonesian elite who were responsible for the campaign to annex East Timor and Australian as well as American government officials, were very real to Suharto and his advisers. As Ambassador Woolcott astutely pointed out:

> Whether or not these fears are justified the fact is that they exist and are held by President Soeharto and by other Indonesian leaders, particularly in the powerful

military and intelligence communities. Except for the Foreign Minister, Mr. Malik, and the Information Minister, Mr. Mashuri, senior civilians in the government have no role in policy-making on the issue.[7]

How then did the prospect of an independent but weak East Timor and by many accounts, a viable state with the ability to resist foreign incursions, result in Indonesia's interpretation of it as a threat and a potential enemy that had to be eliminated?

Suharto's conversations with Prime Minister Gough Whitlam of Australia, a person whom he trusted and considered a friend, as well as those he had with U.S. President Gerald Ford provide important insight into these processes. In his meetings with them, Suharto elaborated at great length about the dangers and threats of communism which he said laid not in their military strength but principally in their fanaticism and ideology.[8] This, according to Suharto, was a lesson that Indonesia had learned from the problems it had encountered in its "struggles for independence against Communism."[9] Here, Suharto was referring to an event that had been seared into the collective and institutional memory of the Indonesian military—the Madiun uprising of 1948 in East Java when communists staged an internal revolt by declaring a Soviet republic just as the Dutch were returning to reclaim Indonesia as their colony after the end of World War II. Taking place when Indonesia's independence was clearly at stake, this revolt could have provided the Dutch with the means of dividing and re-conquering Indonesia. While the military (ABRI) was able to 'save Indonesia' from the possible catastrophe of falling back into Dutch control by extinguishing what they have labeled an "unforgiveable act of treachery," communists and communism have since been objects of deep distrust because of their supposed and continued ability to divide and destroy Indonesia's unity. This fear was compounded by the "abiding sense of territorial vulnerability arising from geographic fragmentation and social diversity"[10] in Indonesia. Critically, Suharto and the other members of the Special Committee on Portuguese Timor remained absolutely convinced that "communists remained intent on subverting and overthrowing governments, such as the Indonesian one" (Leifer 1983, 155).

In East Timor, the popularity of the leftist-leaning political party Freitlin (*Frente Revolucionara de Timor Leste Independente*) and its rise as the party of choice for many East Timorese was enough to spark off fears that the New Order's conscious efforts to build and forge a strong, sovereign and united Indonesia with a single national identity based on the principles of Pancasila was at tremendous risk from the potential presence of an alternative in the form of communism. Suharto, while discussing the dangers of communism with Whitlam and Ford, also spoke at length about the importance of Pancasila as the basis of national life and identity in Indonesia's strategy to unify and nationalize "the people to prepare to fight the threats which eventually will be made against our independence."[11]

Ensuring the dominance and hegemony of the official Indonesian national identity played a significant part in their strategy to preserve the national and territorial unity of Indonesia, "a concern deeply ingrained not only in the military but in the wider Indonesian psyche" (Fukuda, 2000, 22; and see also Leifer 1983). Thus, East Timor had to be incorporated despite the cost to Indonesia's image and economy in order to prevent what they were sure was the greater problem[12] – the threat to the New Order's political project of forging a conception of an Indonesia that was based solely on the ideals and principles of Pancasila.

Reframing East Timor: Habibie and a New Indonesia

One of the first things that B.J. Habibie initiated as President of Indonesia was a suggestion to ameliorate and eventually resolve the East Timor issue in May 1998. This was surprising as East Timor was not high on the agenda of the *reformasi* movement at the height of their demonstrations and protests against the Suharto regime. *Reformasi* activists as well as those who had been part of the movement to grant self-determination to East Timor did not anticipate or expect Habibie's initial June 1998 announcement regarding special autonomy for the region. Domestic actors were mostly concerned with political reforms within Indonesia and solving its massive economic problems. International actors like Japan and the EU were hardly pressing Indonesia on this issue as they were

more concerned about Indonesia's stability and by extension, that of
Southeast Asia. How then did the changes come about?

Dewi Fortuna Anwar, senior foreign policy adviser and many say,
the 'real' Foreign Minister during Habibie's time in office, has stated that
Indonesia's national interests were "the consolidation of democracy,
strengthening of national unity, and economic progress"(Anwar, personal
interview, 21 July 2004). East Timor was to play a crucial role in the
achievement of these interests for Habibie and his advisers. During this
period of reform and fundamental change to its political system, retaining East Timor would have been inconsistent with the true intent of Indonesia or "the vision of itself as a country stressing human rights, independence and self-determination" (ibid.). Thus, letting East Timor go, for
President Habibie and his advisers, "was a very rational and logical step
to take." (U. Juoro, personal interview, 29 July 2004). In fact, it would be
"very irrational of Indonesia to do otherwise for it would be against the
constitution" (D.F. Anwar, personal interview, 21 July 2004). For these
policymakers, resolving the East Timor issue was intertwined with
achieving their political project of building a new and just Indonesia
where democracy and human rights would have a central place. They had
turned the Suharto regime's understanding of Indonesia's national interests vis-à-vis East Timor on its head.

In order to understand how East Timor was reconsidered and reframed by Indonesia, it is important to embed these changes within the
challenges to the New Order's conception of Indonesia posed by activists
and intellectuals over a long gestation period. The latter proposed an alternative vision of Indonesia where norms of human rights and democracy had a central place. Important pieces of this process to renew Indonesia were changes to Indonesia's policies in East Timor. When Habibie
and his advisers arrived on the scene, they were to incorporate the ideational and identitarian links from the arguments and insight of these activists and intellectuals.

Challenging the New Order's Conception of Indonesian Identity: The Re-Emergence of Norms of Human Rights and Democracy

Challenges to the New Order's particular construction of Indonesian identity took place slowly over the course of two decades. In that time, human rights violations and increasingly authoritarian practices and policies, excused on the basis of communitarianism and the greater good, became a serious problem in Indonesia. Concurrently, norms of human rights and democracy began to seep into the country as a result of these practices. A nascent Indonesian human rights network began to take root with the 1975 establishment of the *Lembaga Bantuan Hukum* (LBH), one of the first and most important NGOs in Indonesia which sought to change the foundations of social, economic and political inequality through legal aid (Uhlin 1997).[13]

At about the same time, a second human rights network was emerging out of the Indonesian invasion of East Timor. Together with the resistance movement in East Timor, this network, comprising NGOs from Australia, groups linked to the Roman Catholic Church, parts of the Dutch government, Portugal and Brazil, worked to provide information about the repression of political dissent in Indonesia and the loss of lives in East Timor (Jetschke 1999). These two networks however, developed independently of each other in the beginning. The Indonesian network focused initially on economic development, social justice and popular participation as activists faced imprisonment for any criticism of the New Order government (ibid.) Moreover, co-operation with the East Timor network was blocked by the underlying nationalism of many Indonesian NGOs (ibid.).

In the mid-1980s, Indonesian NGOs began to challenge the government's emphasis on economic growth and the rosy portrayal of its economic performance by highlighting negative consequences like the growing income inequality in the country (ibid.). More importantly, these critics highlighted how these economic disparities in Indonesia and the arbitrary actions of state agencies contravened Pancasila's principles of social justice, and consultation and consensus respectively (ibid.). In doing so, they were beginning to challenge the regime's own policies and behavior using the principles underlying the official and hegemonic conception of Indonesian identity. Since most NGOs had at least rhetorically accepted Pancasila through the *asas tunggal* policy, it was far more difficult for the government to denounce them as anti-Pancasila and thus, anti-Indonesian (ibid.). In this way, they started to contest, challenge and slowly chip away at the New Order's definition of Indonesian-ness as well as its practices to consolidate it.

In the late 1980s and 1990s, the erosion of the New Order's Indonesian identity accelerated with the emergence of viable alternatives. During this period, conceptions of the nation were articulated in democratic-pluralist ways by critics of the regime. *Demokrasi* ('democracy'), *keterbukaan* (openness) and *hak asasi manusia* (human rights) emerged not only at the centre of the agenda of these groups but as "key themes in public debate, [that were] discussed and promoted by the media, academics, a wide range of semi-oppositional political groups, and elements from within the government itself" (Aspinall 1996, 228). Unlike the New Order which argued that human rights and democracy were concepts only suitable in the west and therefore, non- as well as un-Indonesian, these critics, who were later to agitate for *reformasi* (reform) in the last months of Suharto's rule, explicitly rejected such a vision of Indonesia. Presenting a vision that was markedly different from that of the New Order, their conception of Indonesian nationhood, while by no means monolithic, was based on the ideals of democracy and inclusionary interpretations of Pancasila.

While the New Order argued that Indonesia's period of democracy from 1950 to about 1957 was chaotic, inefficient and ultimately unsuitable for Indonesia's *kepribadian bangsa* (national personality), many pro-democracy activists questioned such a judgment of that period (Uhlin 1997). Instead of a failure, they pointed to the period as one where there was a mostly independent judiciary, fair and peaceful elections, a free press, politicians committed to democratic values, and a respect of human rights (ibid.). As part of their argument, they also pointed to the "recognition of the rights accorded to Indonesian citizens by the 1945 constitution, particularly the right to organize and to freedom of expression" (Uhlin 1997, 146). By drawing on this period, pro-democracy activists were able to show that "there has been a long contest in Indonesia between democratic and authoritarian politics" (Nasution quoted in Uhlin

1997, 146-7). Democracy and human rights, contrary to the New Order's claims, were therefore shown to be concepts, principles and norms that were not alien to Indonesian history and tradition (Uhlin 1997). In doing so, these regime critics challenged the hegemony of the New Order's official Indonesian identity and the exclusionary and authoritarian political practices that had become associated with it.

Making the Links between Indonesian Democracy and East Timor

In November 1991, video footage smuggled out of East Timor showed the indiscriminate massacre of civilians who were gathered at the Santa Cruz cemetery in Dili to commemorate the death of a pro-independence supporter (Cotton 2000). This video documentation of the Santa Cruz events was particularly important in opening the eyes of the world *and* Indonesians to the East Timor issue because it captured the brutal nature of Indonesian rule in a way that previous reports trickling out of East Timor never could.

These events had an important outcome – the emergence of young Indonesian pro-democracy and human rights activists from groups like SPRIM (*Solidaritas Perjuangan Rakyat Indonesia untuk Maubere*) who began to work with activists from East Timor and speak out against Indonesian policies for the first time (Uhlin 1997). The two previously weakly connected network structures of East Timor and Indonesia were finally coming together (Jetschke 1999). Particularly important were the ideational links that were being made between the democratization of Indonesia and the support for East Timorese opposition against Indonesian occupation and its self-determination by sections of what was to become the *reformasi* movement in the 1990s. These links were later to play a significant part in the unfolding of events and final decisions that eventually converged in the offer of an indirect referendum to the people of East Timor in January 1999.

East Timor, for these activists, functioned on both strategic and symbolic levels. In their examination of other authoritarian regimes like Portugal in the 1970s, these pro-democracy activists realized that the struggle for independence in East Timor could be instrumental in hastening the breakdown of the New Order regime.

> We remember that the Vietnam war was not only fought in the battlefields of Vietnam but also in the streets of Washington, New York, or Ohio. In the same spirit, we have to inform the Indonesian people about the unjust war in East Timor. The colonial war in Mozambique and Angola hastened the fall of the fascist regime in Lisbon. We believe that the struggle of the East Timorese can also accelerate the process of democratization in Indonesia.[14]

The lessons learned from these observations were responsible for directing the attention and support of some groups of activists to the struggle against the Indonesian colonial occupation of East Timor and its self-determination (Uhlin 1997).

Activists in the pro-democracy and pro-East Timor independence movements believed that Indonesia's East Timor policy exposed the true nature of the Indonesian state and symbolized all that was wrong with the country (Rachland Nashidik, personal interview, 21 July 2004; Wilson, personal interview, 27 July 2004). The brutality and impunity of the military in East Timor was repeated in other parts of Indonesia where dissenters of the regime were "subjected to the same techniques of harassment, intimidation, and torture, along with tight controls on freedom of assembly, association, and expression" (Fukuda 2000, 24). Just as significant was the fact that the occupation of East Timor was understood not only as a breach but a betrayal of "Indonesia's founding principles specifically of the 1945 constitutional preamble, which states that 'independence is the right of all peoples'." (Rachland Nashidik, personal interview, 21 July 2004; Wilson, personal interview, 27 July 2004; and Munir, personal interview, 21 July 2004). Thus, "Indonesians campaigning for democratic reform in Indonesia saw 'self in the other' and sided with the East Timorese, realizing that they were fighting against the same repressive force" (Fukuda 2000, 24).

Some Indonesian activists insisted that "without resolving the East Timor conflict Indonesia's democratization could not be complete" (Fukuda 2000, 29). In a 1994 speech, Rachland Nashidik, a student leader in the 1980s and activist of the organization, PIJAR said:[15]

> [A] true democracy in Indonesia is impossible without a solution for the East Timor issue. The struggle for democracy in Indonesia goes hand in hand with the anticolonial struggle in East Timor. That is why the democratic movement in Indonesia has put East Timor firmly on their political agenda.[16]

In the work of students and other activists, challenging the hegemony of the regime's interpretation of Pancasila and its construction of Indonesia nationalism was also a critical component. Activists like Munir consciously deconstructed the nationalism propounded by Suharto and the New Order in order "to focus or frame nationalism as one that was against colonialism and imperialism and for justice" (Munir, personal interview, 21 July 2004). Instead of the integralist and nativist elements which had taken on increasingly authoritarian features, these activists were consciously expounding a new interpretation of Indonesian nationalism different from the military and state. They were determined to present a vision of and for Indonesia that was "related to justice, humanitarian issues, to Indonesia's principles at independence and Indonesia's history" (ibid.).

For many of these Indonesian-East Timorese solidarity groups, "the objective was to create pressure from within Indonesia, to internalize international principles of democracy and human rights, and thereby to redefine Indonesian national identity" (Goodman 1999). These strategies and actions were thus important in eroding the New Order's ideational and identitarian foundations, and in placing new alternatives with their attendant norms and discourses in the political sphere.

Normative Changes at the State Level

Critically, the official levels of the Indonesian government were not deaf to proclamations for the protection of human rights by non-governmental organizations in and outside the country. Official Indonesia was in fact, listening. In the past, the Suharto government responded to criticism of its human rights record by arguing that it was a western concept and therefore, irrelevant for Indonesia. Their invocations of the principle of non-interference and their questioning of the legitimacy of international jurisdiction would however, slowly give way to changes at the behavioral, rhetorical and communicative level (Jetschke 1999).

The establishment of a National Commission on Human Rights in 1993 was one such change. As Anja Jetschke (1999) points out, this was a highly significant concession on the part of the Indonesian government for it was institutionalizing human rights within the Indonesian state, a clear illustration of its growing receptiveness and acceptance of these norms in its domestic context. Similarly, there were changes at the rhetorical and communicative levels. After years of making culture-specific counter-arguments, Indonesia began to openly acknowledge that it had a human rights problem in international foras like the United Nations. After the Dili massacre in 1991 for example, members of the Commission on Human Rights (CHR) and Indonesian delegates arrived at a common description of the human rights situation in Indonesia and developed ways to address it (ibid.). In 1992, the Indonesian human rights delegate at the UN Human Rights Commission stated that their motivation was "to learn and benefit from such a visit in order to minimize, if not eradicate, the practice of torture in Indonesia" (Jetschke 1999, 159). This statement was significant for two reasons. Firstly, it was the Indonesian government's first public acceptance of allegations of torture in the country (ibid.). Secondly, it was an acknowledgment of the validity of the international norm.

Hence, there was an important and discernible shift in the parameters of the debate between the Indonesian government and its domestic and international critics. Earlier periods saw Indonesia contest norms of self-determination and human rights advocated by critics with the principle of non-interference in domestic affairs. This was transformed, as illustrated above, to a situation where discussions were conducted on the basis of the consensual norm of human rights and consequently, to matters of norm compliance and implementation. Thus, the Indonesian government was exhibiting both behavioral and rhetorical changes toward allegations of human rights violations by the 1990s (ibid.). Alone however, all these developments were insufficient for supplanting the New Order, its hegemonic conception of Indonesia and its East Timor policy. It would take the fateful convergence of several developments in the 1990s and an economic catastrophe to do this.

Economic Crisis, the Fall of Suharto and a New Indonesia

In the 1990s, changing internal and external political, social and economic conditions created ever visible and growing discrepancies between the principles underlying the New Order's Indonesian identity, its stated mission, and its actual political and economic record and practices. Politically, the fall of the Berlin wall, the collapse of the Soviet Union and the restoration of its diplomatic ties with China in the 1990s called into question the claims that communism still posed a real threat to Indonesia. Relatedly, the government and the military's insistence over the past twenty-five years that a constant state of vigilance was required to prevent Indonesia from falling into anarchy and disorder was also questioned by some sections of society (Vatikiotis 1998a). These momentous changes in the international system also challenged the regime's obsessive concern and fear of threats to Indonesian identity and unity posed by the values espoused by communists, radical Muslims, and westernized liberals.

Domestically, the rise of Sukarno's daughter, Megawati Sukarnoputri in the PDI (Indonesian Democratic Party) in the mid-1990s was a significant development. Unlike Suharto and the increasingly corrupt and nepotistic conditions of his rule, Megawati was perceived as devoted to and part of the masses, someone who would never use her position to enrich herself or her family (Eklof 1999). When there were suggestions that Megawati should be nominated for President of Indonesia, the regime reacted by engineering her overthrow as head of the PDI, a position to which she had been popularly elected. Her unjust removal was conceived "as symbolic of a general pattern of injustice in society" by her supporters (ibid.). Moreover, the regime's efforts to portray itself as one that was based on 'Indonesian-style' democracy and the principles of consensus and consultation was also debunked in a highly visible manner by these events.

University students, activists, lawyers, academics, non-governmental organizations, public intellectuals, liberal Muslims and to some extent, peasants, formed a growing though not united movement calling for reform which was based on the democratic-pluralist vision of and for Indonesia. Spreading out beyond highly populated areas like the island of Java to other parts of the archipelago, this movement and its alternative conception of Indonesia became increasingly visible on the political stage.

Economically, the regime's oligarchic and patrimonial elements also became far more pronounced as Suharto's cronies and children began to treat Indonesia as their own private economic fiefdom (Aspinall and Berger 2001). For example, they were involved in almost every single infrastructure project that was awarded in the country. Typically, Suharto's children, acting as the local agent, would enjoy a 10-15 percent stake in these projects without paying for them. By the time of the crisis, they had connections with hundreds of companies (Schwarz 2000). Their actions, Suharto's unwillingness to rein them in, and the growing inequality between the rich and the poor called into question the regime's insistence that Indonesia was an integrated family where everyone worked together towards common goals of social justice and equality.

While these new developments posed considerable challenges to the credibility and integrity of the regime's stated mission and political objectives, Suharto had been able to draw strength from the fact that Indonesians had enjoyed steady economic growth and improvements in living standards under his leadership, a sharp contrast to the Sukarno period (Schwarz 2000). Politically, the New Order government had restored order and purpose to what had previously been a chaotic and ineffective system. Socially, there was a greater sense of nationhood which had strengthened national unity. According to Adam Schwarz, many Indonesians "would say that an extended period of restricted political activity and circumscribed press freedom – in which public expressions of ethnic and religious animosities are not welcome – has helped lower the temperature in sensitive areas" (Schwarz 2000, 41). Hence, a great many Indonesians had been willing to pay the price of less political freedom in exchange for economic growth, political stability and order.

Thus, the rumblings of the 1990s may have remained rumblings if not for the Asian financial crisis of 1997-98 which eventually created unsustainable conditions for Suharto to remain in power. During the last months of 1997, Indonesian society began to feel the acute effects of the crisis. When the Indonesian rupiah lost 58 percent of its value within a six-month period, poverty levels escalated (Eklof 1999). In the beginning, the economic crisis did not appear insurmountable as the Indonesian government had taken measures in August and September that were widely praised internationally. This was short-lived as Suharto's unwillingness to take concrete actions against the corruption and nepotism of his regime led to a gradual but continuous erosion of public and market confidence. Despite rising unemployment and poverty rates, Suharto put up fierce resistance against the dismantling of the business empires of his family and cronies (Aspinall and Berger 2001). This only served to underscore the ever-widening gap between the New Order's practices and policies, and the principles underlying its stated political project and vision of Indonesia. The massive disjunctures arising out of this confluence of events provided the political space for the *reformasi* movement to gather strength and to persuade others that their alternative vision of Indonesia was not only right but the only game left in town (Berger 1997). After a tumultuous period in May, Suharto resigned and was replaced, following the constitution, by his vice-president, B.J. Habibie, a German-trained aerospace engineer who had served as Indonesia's Minister of State for Technology since the 1970s. Within the first weeks of his presidency, Habibie made his rather surprising remark in a BBC interview that autonomy or special status for East Timor was an option. It was the first sign of change in Indonesia's position after twenty-four years of resisting the East Timorese independence movement and enduring international condemnation.

Disengaging From East Timor, 1998–1999

By the time Habibie came into power, he was much more aware of the significance of the East Timor issue. During his time as vice-president of the country, he was placed in charge of global affairs and East Timor was always raised whenever he met foreign leaders (D. F. Anwar, personal interview, 21 July 2004). Moreover, his chief advisers while he was vice-president were Dewi Fortuna Anwar, Indria Samego and Umar Juoro, academics and intellectuals he had known from their connections with ICMI and its think-tank, CIDES (Centre for Information and Development Studies).[17]

Anwar and Samego in particular, had already been critical of Indonesia's East Timor policy in their private capacity as academics before Habibie's rise to power. Samego had been personally critical and skeptical of the government's reasons and justification for the integration of East Timor into Indonesia. While many in the New Order saw East Timor as Indonesia's twenty-seventh province, Samego understood East Timor to be "culturally, historically and from the perspective of international law, not related to Indonesia" (Indria Samego, personal interview, 19 July 2004). In an op-ed, Samego wrote:

> In order that the decolonization of East Timor is considered suitable for universal standards and Indonesia's intervention can be met well, it will be advisable to weigh East Timor's wish to decide its own fate. Maybe this will be better for us.[18]

Anwar, a political scientist and an influential member of Habibie's inner circle, who later became the Assistant Minister/State Secretary for Foreign Affairs, and spokesperson on foreign affairs, had already conducted research on East Timor and other conflict areas in Indonesia while she was with the Center for Regional and Political Studies at LIPI (D.F. Anwar, personal interview, 21 July 2004). There, the researchers had concluded that the root causes of the conflict in East Timor arose from the fact that historically, East Timor had never been part of Indonesia but had been incorporated into the republic through what Anwar described as a problematic military intervention that had never been internationally condoned. Moreover, they recognized that the continuing East Timorese resistance only resulted in greater military domination and repression. It had evolved into an increasingly violent, untenable and cyclical situation where resistance led to military repression and human rights abuses which in turn invoked more resistance as well as international criticism and so on (ibid.). At LIPI, Anwar and her colleagues had already concluded that it was essential to end the cycle of violence. Self-determination had also been discussed (ibid.).

At CIDES, they were also coming to similar conclusions. Various studies conducted on East Timor showed that the situation was unsustainable and "a solution that would be just to East Timor and just to Indonesia" was needed (ibid.). Hence, Habibie's advisers, coming from the liberal wing of ICMI, which he chaired from its founding until he became president, had already thought of the East Timor issue in ways fundamentally different from the military and Suharto.

Besides the instrumental role played by these advisers and in particular, Dewi Fortuna Anwar, in articulating a different understanding of the East Timor issue[19], the Habibie administration was also articulating a new political identity for Indonesia. In place of the New Order's widely discredited project, Habibie and his team proposed to reorient and reorder Indonesian life as a "nation and state to pursue its original course, as mandated by the Preamble to the 1945 Constitution" (Singh 2000, 295). In other words, they wanted to restore the principles that were important in both Indonesia's fight for independence and its 1945 constitution as the key guiding principles in the renewal and restoration of their country. For Habibie and his advisers, democracy and human rights were significant pieces of this larger process to ensure that Indonesia became what its founding fathers originally intended where independence did not only mean getting rid of the colonial system but replacing it with one that was democratic and just (Anwar, personal interview, 21 July 2004).

The attempt to resolve the fate of East Timor was an important part of this agenda to put in place a new Indonesia where human rights, independence and self-determination were primary. In this matter, East Timor had taken on a symbolic and strategic significance for Habibie and his advisers, reflecting the arguments that had been made by Indonesian

NGOs and activists in the past. This was based on the realization on the part of Anwar and other close aides of Habibie that Indonesia's image in the international arena had suffered greatly because of the East Timor issue. Habibie himself chose to justify the highly unpopular policy transformation that he had initiated and eventually implemented by arguing that "Indonesia's position in the international community has always been compromised because of the East Timor issue" during his very important accountability speech to the People's Consultative Assembly when he was fighting for his political life (Singh 2000, 321). Moreover, Indonesia had to "face the fact that in order *to restore Indonesia's image*, we had no other choice but to try and solve the East Timor problem in a manner acceptable to the international community" (Singh 2000, 322).

In addition, Habibie also noted in his accountability speech that "no less than 8 resolutions of the UN General Assembly and 7 resolutions of the UN Security Council on East Timor have been adopted, which demonstrate that the international community has not all recognized East Timor as part of the Unitary State of the Republic of Indonesia" (Singh 2000, 321). Also, the "end of the Cold War and the increasingly great attention of the world to the issues of democracy and human rights have made the East Timor question as one of the unavoidable international agendas, and Indonesia's claim that the East Timor issue has already been solved could not hold ground" (Singh 2000, 322). Finally, he added that:

> In the midst of global openness and interdependence, it would be extremely difficult for us to maintain the conventional pretext that since the status of East Timor was constitutionally sanctioned by the People's Consultative Assembly in 1978, we could decline the international community's demand without possibly risking the isolation by the rest of the world.[20]

These statements point to the acceptance of the validity of international norms of human rights and democracy and more importantly, a need to abide by them in order to be part of such a community.

In the steps leading to the August 1999 referendum in East Timor, it was a letter from the Australian Prime Minister John Howard which was to play a singularly important role. This letter suggested that Indonesia consider France's Matignon Accords with New Caledonia as a model (Anwar, personal interview, 21 July 2004; Umar Juoro personal interview, 29 July 2004; Dr Muladi, personal interview, July 30 2004). These accords gave New Caledonia autonomy with the possibility of a referendum some time down the road. If Indonesia adopted and successfully implemented such a model, it would, Howard added, "allow time to convince the East Timorese of the benefits of autonomy within the Indonesian Republic." [21] It was hoped that this would address "the East Timorese desire for an act of self-determination in a manner which avoids an early and final decision on the future status of the province."[22] Since Australia had been the only western country to acknowledge Indonesia's sovereignty over East Timor and therefore, its closest supporter of the issue in the past, the shift in Australia's position was considered significant by Indonesia.

Just as important however was the parallel Howard drew in his letter between Indonesia's situation with East Timor and France's policy on New Caledonia. For Habibie, the reference to the latter implied that Indonesia was a colonial power and this was a catalytic eye-opener. It became extremely clear then that the rest of the world was viewing Indonesia as a colonial power. In the eyes of Habibie and the other cabinet members, Indonesia, with its revolutionary history of fighting Dutch colonialism, was resolutely anti-colonial (Muladi, personal interview, 30 July 2004). Indonesia's entry into East Timor, they came to fully comprehend at that time, had "violated Indonesia's commitment to oppose all forms of colonialism" (Anwar 2000, 20). There was sadness and irony in their realization that

> Indonesia, which prided itself on being a country born our of post-colonialism, as a country that came out of an anti-colonial revolution and has in fact specifically stated in its preamble to the Constitution that Indonesia opposed all sorts of colonialism, that it was accused of doing exactly the same thing in East Timor (ibid.).

President Habibie himself is quoted at this cabinet meeting as saying: "What are we doing in East Timor, because this is actually violating our own commitment to our constitution to oppose colonialism" (ibid.). At the crucial January 1999 cabinet meeting prompted by Howard's letter, Indonesia took these suggestions in a direction that even the Australians had not anticipated – the decision to allow the 2-ballot option where independence would be granted should the East Timorese reject special autonomy within the Republic of Indonesia. It was "one of the most dramatic manifestations of Habibie's claims to be manufacturing a culture of democracy in Indonesia" (Greenlees and Garran 2002, 99).

Thus, one of the most important causes of this fundamental change in Indonesia policy was its transition from an authoritarian regime to a democracy with a major emphasis on human rights. By then, East Timor was not just a human rights issue. It had also become an important part of who or what Indonesia was as a nation and as a people. When confronted by the issue of colonial or territorial possessions, old policies were no longer be compelling or logical for Habibie and his advisers with their new political identity for Indonesia. This new identity framed the issue in a different way and led to a reconstitution of the country's national interests, paving the path for disengaging from East Timor.

Conclusion

Identity, as the chapter illustrates, is neither singular nor uncontested. Challenges to a dominant identity may arise when there are disjunctures between its stated mission and vision for the state, and its ability to fulfill them. These disjunctures create openings for other political actors to contest and propose alternatives to a previously essentialized construction of the self. Through such processes of challenge and destabilization, a new political identity may emerge and become dominant, radically affecting previously calcified understandings of the other and dislodging the form and substance of what had been conflictual situations in the past.

Notes

1. Memorandum to Canberra, 28 June 1974, "Portuguese Timor". NAA: A10463, 801/13/11/1, ii]. Doc no. 11 in Way (ed).

2. Moreover, difficult economic conditions need not always result in capitulation to the demands of international organizations and foreign governments. Malaysia, for example, handled the same financial crisis by implementing policies that were very different from those recommended by the IMF.

3. Record of Meeting With Tjan. 21 August 1974 [NAA: A1838, 49/2/1/1, iii] in Way (ed), Doc 22. Brief for Whitlam, 2 September 1974 [NAA: A10463, 801/13/11/1, iii], in Way (ed), Doc 24; and Background paper, Canberra, 11 September 1974, "The Future of Portuguese Timor." [NAA: A1838, 3034/10/11/24, iii] Doc. no. 28 in Way (ed).

4. Cablegram to Canberra. 14 August 1975. "Portuguese Timor" [NAA: A10463, 801/13/11/1, xi], Doc 166 in Way (ed)

5. Cablegram to Canberra. 14 August 1975. "Portuguese Timor" [NAA: A10463, 801/13/11/1, xi], Doc 166 in Way (ed)

6. Besides communism, there was also fear that an independent East Timor could threaten Indonesia's national unity and territorial integrity by acting as a catalyst for separatism within the archipelago. See Dispatch to Willesee, 2 June 1975, "The Portuguese Timor Problem as seen from Jakarta" [NAA: A1838, 3034/10/6/9, i] Doc 137, in Way (ed).

7. Dispatch to Willesee, 2 June 1975, "The Portuguese Timor Problem as seen from Jakarta" [NAA: A1838, 3034/10/6/9, i] Doc 137, in Way (ed).

8. Memorandum of Conversation Between Presidents Ford and Suharto, 5 July 1975. Gerald R. Ford Library, National Security Adviser Memoranda of Conversations, Box 13, July 5, 1965 – Ford, Kissinger, Indonesian President Suharto. Downloaded from http://www.gwu.edu/~nsarchiv/NSAEBB/NSAEBB62

9. Ibid.

10. Dispatch to Willesee, 2 June 1975, "The Portuguese Timor Problem as seen from Jakarta" [NAA: A1838, 3034/10/6/9, i] Doc 137, in Way (ed).

11. Ibid.

12. Memorandum to Canberra, 28 June 1974, "Portuguese Timor". NAA: A10463, 801/13/11/1, ii]. Doc no. 11 in Way (ed).

13. However, the establishment of an Indonesian human rights network was partially interrupted after 1975 when the government cracked down on domestic opposition.

14. Abdullah cited in Uhlin, 1997, p.197-8.

15. An organization that was one of several outspoken new pro-democracy and human rights groups which had the courage to deal with the East Timor issue in the early 1990s.

16. Rachland Nashidik at a conference on East Timor at Porto, Portugal in October 1994.

17. Anwar was Assistant to the Vice-President for Global Affairs while Indria Samego was Assistant to the Vice-President in the area of Politics and Security. See Crouch (2001), Greenlees and Garran (2002); and Tapol Bulletin who also point to their influence on Habibie.

18. *Republika,* 29 November 1996.

19. See also Tapol Bulletin, no. 151 (March 1999: 3).

20. Singh , 2000, p.325.

21. Text of Prime Minister Howard's letter to President Habibie, 19 December 1998 in *East Timor in Transition 1998-2000: An Australian Policy Challenge* (Canberra: Dept of Foreign Affairs and Trade, 2001), p. 182.

22. Ibid.

References

Anderson, B. 2001. "Imagining East Timor." *Lusotopie* 2001: 233-239
———. 1991. Imagined Communities: Reflections on the Origins and Spread of Nationalism. London: Verso.
Anwar, D.F. 2000. "The East Timor Crisis: an Indonesian View." In *East Timor- the Consequences,* edited by Bruce Brown. Wellington: The New Zealand Institute of International Affairs.
———. 1998. "Indonesia: Domestic Priorities Define National Security." In *Asian Security Practice. Material and Ideational Influences,* edited by Muthiah Alagappa. Stanford, CA: Stanford University Press.
Aspinall, E. and M.T. Berger. 2001. "The Break-up of Indonesia? Nationalisms after Decolonisation and the Limits of the Nation-state in Post-Cold War Southeast Asia." *Third World Quarterly,* 22,1003–1024.

Aspinall, E. 1996. "The Broadening Base of Political Opposition in Indonesia. In *Political Oppositions in Industrialising Asia,* edited by Garry Rodan. London: Routledge.

Berger, M.T. 1997. "Old State and New Empire in Indonesia: Debating the Rise and Decline of Suharto's New Order." *Third World Quarterly,* 18(2), 321–361.

Bertrand, J. 2004. *Nationalism and Ethnic Conflict in Indonesia.* Cambridge: Cambridge University Press.

Bourchier, D. and V. R. Hadiz, eds. 2001. *Indonesian Politics and Society. A Reader.* London: Routledge Curzon.

Brown, D. 2002. "Why Might Constructed Nationalist and Ethnic Ideologies Come into Confrontation With Each Other?" *The Pacific Review,* 15(4), 555–570.

Crouch, H. 2000. "The TNI and East Timor Policy," in *Out of the Ashes: Destruction and Reconstruction of East Timor,* edited by James J. Fox and Dionisio Bebe Soares. Adelaide: Crawford House Publishing.

Eklof, S. 1999. *Indonesian Politics in Crisis. The Long Fall of Suharto, 1996-98.* Copenhagen: NIAS.

Fukuda, C. M. 2000. "Peace Through Non-Violent Action: The East Timorese Resistance Movement's Strategy for Engagement." *Pacifica Review,* 12(1), 17–30.

Goodman, J. 1999. "Indonesians for East Timor." *Inside Indonesia,* no. 59 (July-September 1999).

Greenlees, D. and R. Garran, 2002. *Deliverance. The Inside Story of East Timor's Fight for Freedom.* NSW, Australia: Allen and Unwin.

Holtzappel. C. 1997. "Nationalism and Cultural Identity." In *Images of Malay-Indonesian Identity,* edited by Michael Hitchcock and Victor T. King. Kuala Lumpur: Oxford University Press.

Jetschke, A. 1999. "Linking the Unlinkable? International Norms and Nationalism in Indonesia and Philippines." In *The Power of Human Rights: International Norms and Domestic Change,* edited by Thomas Risse, Stephen C. Ropp and Kathryn Sikkink. Cambridge, UK: Cambridge University Press.

Kingsbury, D. 2002. *The Politics of Indonesia.* Melbourne: Oxford University Press.

Leifer, M. 1983. *Indonesia's Foreign Policy.* London: GeorgeAllen & Unwin.

Lloyd, G. J. 2000. "The Diplomacy on East Timor: Indonesia, the United Nations and the International Community." In *Out of the Ashes. Destruction and Reconstruction of East Timor,* edited by James J. Fox and Dionisio Babo Soares. Adelaide: Crawford House Publishing.

McDonald, H. et al, 2002. *Masters of Terror. Indonesia's Military and Violence in East Timor in 1999.* Canberra: Australian National University.

Naipospos, C. 2000. "East Timor in the Dynamics of Indonesian Politics." *Bulletin of Concerned Asian Scholars,* 32(1 and 2), 87–90.

Ramage, D. E. 1997. *Politics in Indonesia. Democracy, Islam and the Ideology of Tolerance.* London: Routledge.

Schwarz, A. 2000. "Introduction: The Politics of Post-Suharto Indonesia." In *The Politics of Post-Suharto Indonesia.* edited by Adam Schwarz and Jonathan Paris, NY: Council of Foreign Relations Press.

Singh, B. 2000. *Habibie and the Democratization of Indonesia.* Sydney: Book House.

Smith, G. and M. Muetzelfeldt. 2000. "Global Governance and Strategies for Civil Society." *Pacific Review,* 12(3), 265–279.

Taylor, J. 1999. *East Timor. The Price of Freedom.* London: Zed Books.

Uhlin, A. 1997. *Indonesia and the Third Wave of Democratization. The Indonesian pro-Democracy Movement in a Changing World.* NY: St Martin's Press.

Vatikiotis, M. R.J. 1998. *Indonesian Politics Under Suharto. The Rise and Fall of the New Order.* New York: Routledge.

———. 1998a. "The Military and Democracy in Indonesia." In *The Military and Democracy in Asia and the Pacific,* edited by R .J. May and V. Selochan. Adelaide: Crawford House Publishing.

Way, Wendy. ed. 2000. *Australia and the Indonesian Incorporation of Portuguese Timor, 1974–1976. Documents on Australian Foreign Policy.* Victoria, Australia: Melbourne University Press.

Chapter 9

Islamic Tradition of Nonviolence: A Hermeneutical Approach

S. Ayse Kadayifci-Orellana

Go, my dread lord, to your great-grandsire's tomb,
From whom you claim; invoke his warlike spirit.

...

O, let their bodies follow, my liege,
With blood and sword and fire to win your right;
In aid whereof we of the spirituality
Will raise your highness such a mighty sum
As never did the clergy at one time
Bring in to any of your ancestors.

Archbishop of Canterbury, in the Life of King Henry the Fifth, Act I, by
William Shakespeare

The unique power of religion to mobilize the population to kill and be killed has often been used by political and religious leaders to justify their constructed ends. Especially in conflicts where religion plays a critical role in defining the identities of the parties, religious myths and symbols are often used to justify violence and to depict negative enemy images of the *other*. Shakespeare elegantly conveys this uncanny relationship between religion and war in the first act of the Life of King Henry the Fifth through a dialogue between the King, who is about to launch a war against France, and the Archbishop of Canterbury. In this dialogue the King asks the Archbishop as a "Christian King" whether this war is justifiable. The Archbishop not only responds affirmatively but also encourages him actively by stating that, to support the King the clergy will raise him "such a mighty sum as never did the clergy at one time bring in to any of your ancestors."

The field of conflict resolution, which attempts to analyze conflict dynamics and explain the causes of conflict in social life, is a product of the Western social sciences influenced by the philosophical, epistemological, and methodological traditions rooted in the Enlightenment. Enlightenment worldview had us believe that the secular sciences based on reason and rationality would triumph over the reign of religious myth and symbolism and that the time of religious wars was over. Thus, positivist-oriented conflict resolution theories,[1] informed by the experiences of First and Second World Wars, the Cold War and nuclear threats, either viewed religion as a source of conflict, a stage to be overcome, or ignored it all together because it could neither be operationalized nor quantified (See Kadayifci-Orellana forthcoming).

However, collapse of the Cold War system and proliferation of ethnic and religious conflicts at the end of the last century brought major changes to the world system and the way we understand conflicts. Ethnic and religious conflicts are generally defined as identity conflicts. These conflicts are usually long-standing, much more complicated and harder to resolve than conflicts over resources because most of them take place between communities that live very close to each other, include a history of violence, hostility and grievances. They incorporate psychological, physical, social dimensions, since identity is an intrinsic element of the "self" and a perceived threat to "self", or to a sense of security based on a distinctive identity usually overrides rational thought and reason (Kadayifci-Orellana forthcoming, 22). Thus, a wider social recognition of identity and effective participation in social, economic and political processes are recognized today as basic needs of all humanity (Azar 1986). Denial of that identity may lead to a sense of victimization and conflict (Rupesinghe 1988, 45).

Although the increase of religiously motivated identity conflicts rendered the study of the relationship among religion, conflict and resolution of conflicts extremely important for the scholars of peace and conflict resolution over the last decades, the relationship between violence and religion in general, and Islam in particular, became a central concern for scholars and politicians especially after September 11 attacks on the World Trade Center and the Pentagon. Then again, religious traditions that are used to legitimize violence and war can also be sources of inspiration for peacebuilding and conflict resolution. Based on this observation, this Chapter explores how religion is used and abused to construct images of *self* and *other*, dehumanize and essentialize the *other* as enemy and characterize the *self* as *pure*, agents of God at times of violent conflict. More specifically, this Chapter explores the role of hermeneutics in the conflict resolution field by revisiting different interpretations of war and peace within the Islamic tradition and focusing on the Islamic tradition of nonviolence. Consequently, it addresses a series of new topics for conflict resolution studies, including interpretation of sacred texts during conflicts, utilization of a hermeneutical approach in conflict resolution, and religious and pragmatic motivations of behavior. Moreover, it seeks to answer the questions: how can we utilize Islam as a resource for peacemaking, and what is the best strategy to empower those groups and individuals that support a nonviolent Islamic approach to actively pursue justice?

Islamic Narratives of War and Peace

Many current conflicts involve societies where religion is integral to social/ cultural life and identity, and where religious institutions represent a significant portion of the community. Many of these communities are traumatized with the impact of colonization and imperialism, and are lagging behind the West in material, technical and scientific terms. Most of them suffer from extreme poverty and economic deprivation and the pressure of globalizing economic structures (Kadayifci-Orellana 2003, 24). A large number of these conflicts involve Muslim communities.

For Muslims, Islam is deeply implicated in individual and social conceptions of peace and conflict. Consequently, it established standards for understanding peace, justifying war, and resolving conflicts in Islamic societies. Nevertheless, since its inception fourteen centuries ago, Islamic conceptions of peace and conflict have gone through various transformations, and Islamic discourse like other religious traditions incorporates various narratives regarding when and how war is legitimated, (See Kadayifci-Orellana forthcoming, Kadayifci-Orellana 2005). All based on the same resources, namely the Quran, *Hadith* (sayings of

Prophet Mohammed) and *Sunna* (deeds and practices of Prophet Mohammed), contemporary Islamic approaches to war and peace include
offensive, defensive and *nonviolent* narratives. The "offensive" Islamic
approach to war and peace is based on the idea that Islam, as the only
'true path' towards justice, freedom, and peace, should be the religion
that governs the world and that Islam aims to expand its global influence
through various ways, possibly including offensive wars (See Kadayifci-
Orellana, 2002; Qutb, 2000; 223–245; al Banna, 1990; al-Banna, Hasan
1978; Maududi, 1980). Adherents of this approach are convinced that the
current economic, political and international system that dominates the
world only breeds oppression, injustice, and exploitation, therefore must
be replaced by God's governance. In order to achieve this goal, it is in-
cumbent upon every Muslim to "fight" with whatever means they have.
Accordingly, offensive wars and even attacks on civilian targets are seen
as necessary evils to bring God's rule to earth, as illustrated in narratives
of Al Qaeda and Taleban.

The second Islamic approach to war and peace can be called "defensive" approach. Similar to the "just war" perspective in the Western tradition, this approach is based on the belief that Islam permits violence
under certain conditions, and the most obvious one being "self-defense"
(see Kadayifci-Orellana 2003; Qurashi 1991; Hamidullah 1953; Hashimi
1996; Malik 1998; Khan 1997). However, exponents of defensive Islam
argue that in the face of oppression and persecution, Islam calls Muslims
to defend themselves and to fight for justice and restoration of harmony.
This perspective can be further divided into two sub-categories, based on
their approach regarding conducts of war (*jus im bello*). The first subgroup argues that not only the ends but also the means of war must be
based on ethical grounds, and state that, although war is permissible, it is
also limited. Those who uphold this perspective call for a strict distinction between combatants and non-combatants, and prohibit killing of the
innocent strongly. The second subgroup, on the other hand, argues that
although Islam permits war and violence under strict conditions, it also
allows Muslims to adopt all means to win the war. In that line, they argue
that killing of civilians may be necessary under certain circumstances.
Islamic groups such as Hamas and Islamic Jihad, and supporters of these
groups fall into this category.

The third approach is the "nonviolent" Islamic approach to war and
peace. Also based on the Quran, the *Sunna* and the *Hadith*, this approach
rests on the belief that nonviolent resistance is the preferred method for

fighting injustice and resolving conflicts according to Islam. This narrative holds that nonviolent struggle is the preferred response to injustice, conflict and war according to Islam. Islamic holy texts emphasize values and principles that promote nonviolence and peaceful resolution of conflicts. Although in the Quran there are verses that seem to allow war, there are also stringent rules that govern use of violence under extreme conditions. Moreover, according to these rules if violence cannot discriminate between combatants and noncombatants, it is not acceptable in any form or shape (See Kadayifci-Orellana forthcoming; 2003; Abu Nimer 2003; Satha-Anand 2001). And since the modern warfare cannot distinguish civilians and noncivilians, it is not permissible.

At this point it is important to define *discourse* and *narrative*, as they are used in this Chapter. Foucault sees *discourse* as a body of thought and writing that is united by having a common object of study, a common methodology, and/or a set of common terms and ideas. Discourse as a symbolic order is linguistically and culturally specific and makes it possible for all subjects who have been socialized under its authority to speak and act together (See McHoul and Grace 1993). Discourse always has an order but there is not necessarily a single order for all discourses (Foucault 1972). Accordingly, Islam as a discourse refers to the body of thought and writing that is united by having a common object of study, a common methodology used by Islamic scholars and a set of common terms and ideas it incorporates which is linguistically and culturally specific. Islam as a discourse makes it possible for all Muslims who have been socialized under its authority to speak and act together.

Narrative, on the other hand, constitutes part of a discourse. A discourse can contain more than one narrative within its body. A narrative, then "is a representation that arrests ambiguity and controls the proliferation of meaning by imposing a standard and standpoint of interpretation that is taken to be fixed and independent of the time it represents" (Ashley 1989, 263). This definition captures the attempts of different Islamic groups to represent the *Truth*. "A narrative typically accomplishes this structuring by adopting a perspective from which it privileges the least complex, least ambiguous elements of the text it represents" (Ashley 1989, 263). The least complex and least ambiguous elements refers to "the least-questioned constructs, the dominant tropes, the recurring heroic figures, the modal forms of subjectivity, the conditions that are then and there objectified as the necessary and fundamental structures of life" (Ashley 1989, 263). Moreover, "a narrative reasserts closure by imposing a central ordering principle whose categories and standards of interpretation are taken to express the essential and timeless truth integrating all of the historical times and places among which it discriminates" (Ashley 1989, 263).

Religious traditions are recorded in sacred texts, such as Bible, Torah, Quran, Mishna, *Hadith* etc. However, religious texts are often filled with ambiguities, contradicting statements, and are written in an ancient language. Religious texts like the Quran are proclaimed by the faithful to be direct expressions of God's Word, and thus are presumably universal, eternal, and sources of wisdom for life's important questions. But religious texts still require human interpretation, because life is constantly changing, and the texts must be responsive to new conditions, problems, needs and questions. For that reason, the dynamism of life necessitates reinterpreting sacred texts based on the ever-changing needs and social contexts. This may lead to multiple interpretations/truths that compete with one another, especially in the absence of a central authority that can legitimately interpret the texts and fix the meaning for the community of the believers.

When a political or religious leader utilizes a religious narrative, one can observe that s/he de-historicizes textual elements and take them as the fixed, identical, and self-sufficient origins of meaning. These textual elements become the basic truths, whereas other elements of a text are seen as secondary, contingent, derivative, "superstructural," or marginal. These groups present their interpretation of the religious texts, myths and symbols as the ultimate *truth* applicable regardless of time and place. Thus, construct a story in which all time, all space, all difference, and all discontinuity are cast as part of a universal project in which the ordering principle is itself redeemed as necessary, timelessly, and universally true (Ashley 1989, 263). This understanding of narrative aptly captures the treatment of religious texts by different Muslim groups and actors.

There is no central authority in Islam that establishes and sanctifies an official interpretation. Different narratives compete for legitimacy and hegemony. Yet, certain narratives acquire greater influence over others in the discursive space, depending on the constellation of cultural, social, historical, and the power relations embedded within that particular community (Kadayifci-Orellana forthcoming). Although majority of the Muslims today would support the moderate defensive Islamic narrative of war and peace, the horrific nature the acts undertaken by various Muslim terrorists and the negative media coverage, have contributed to the image of Islam as a violent religion. As such, Islamic tradition of nonviolence might seem as an oxymoron to the reader. An inquiry into Islamic history, however, would support the opposing view. In fact, nonviolence has been an integral aspect of Islamic discourse since its inception and has been employed in various occasions successfully (Kadayifci-Orellana 2003, 27). In order to understand how religion is employed to achieve particular ends as well as when a particular narrative becomes dominant, there is a need to investigate the relationship between religion, conflict resolution, and legitimacy.

Religion, Legitimacy and Conflict Resolution

Violent conflict is co-constructed through the actions of the individuals situated in relation to the discursive and institutional continuities that enable the occurrence of war and render it a legitimate human behavior (Jabri 1996, 4). Protracted violent conflict and war normalize the abnormalities of peace and can involve every individual in the society. Institutional and discursive pillars of the society, such as religious, cultural, ideological, legal, and historical discourse and structures, legitimize war and dehumanization of the *other*. Yet, these same discursive and social structures can be employed to promote reconciliation, positive images of the *other* and sustainable peace.

There are various reasons for employing religious rhetoric, myths and symbolism to legitimize policies and to mobilize the population towards certain political ends, including war. Religion, as a system of beliefs and practices relating to the sacred, and uniting its adherents in a community, has a powerful hold on people's way of thinking, acting and perception of interests (Kadayifci-Orellana 2002, 82) and touches upon deep levels of identity. Therefore, religious feelings can mobilize people faster than any other element of their identity (Abu Nimer 2001).

Religion addresses some of the most profound existential issues of human life, such as "freedom/inevitability, fear/security, right/wrong, sacred/profane," because religion is "a powerful constituent of cultural norms and values" and "embodies and elaborates upon its highest morals, ethical principles and ideals of social harmony" (Said and Funk 2002, 37-38).

Religious discourse provides meaning to the lives of the faithful, explains why the things are the way they are, and offers a language and symbolism through which human beings interpret reality as well as get comfort from the effects of trauma and injuries (Kadayifci-Orellana 2002, 88). Thus, religious discourse puts the lives of the community and the individual in perspective through construction of a cosmic universe. Moral and spiritual forces of religion can encourage people to act and change, and rituals are powerful means of communication in which followers of a religion connect to their spiritual sources and observe their values and beliefs (Abu-Nimer 2003, 17–18). Consequently, religious constructs (i.e. texts, symbols, imagery, myths, hymns etc.) become effective tools to invoke various emotions such as heroism, chivalry, bravery, and vengeance.

Moreover, the religoius discourse provides the faithful with access to "the truth," not in the scientific sense of empirically verified hypotheses, but in the theological sense of the absolute and timeless "truths" of the universe (Dicenso 1990, xiii). Religious discourse can be exclusionist, that is, can be dismissive of all other worldviews. Consequently, religious discourse establishes a sharp and seemingly fixed boundaries between in-group (us/we) and out-group (them). These lines are drawn even sharper at times of conflict, as religion becomes an effective tool for justifying violence, characterizing the *self* as pure, agents of God and dehumanizing and essentializing the *other*. Influence of a history filled with resentment, dehumanization, anger, rage as well as deep injuries and traumas sustained during the conflict also impact the perception of *self* and *other*. All of these factors contribute to the complexity of religiously motivated identity conflicts and make transition from a war-like behavior to peaceful relations extremely difficult as the parties have invested significant material, spiritual and emotional resources to continue the conflict. At the heart of matter lies the question of "legitimacy."

As "the willingness to accept domination on normative grounds on which specific beliefs this acceptance is grounded" (Steffek 2000, 4), *legitimacy* is critical for transforming negative images into positive ones and establishing sustainable peace. Because any leadership that attempts to wage war or continue a conflict needs to legitimize its discourse of war. Legitimacy is important also for defining the right conduct (e.g. using conventional weapons, weapons of mass destruction or employing terrorizing acts) during a conflict, right method of resolving the conflict (e.g. international arbitration, local conflict resolution methods based on cultural traditions, international mediation, etc.), and whose intervention is accepted (e.g. interested outsider, such as a head of another state, members of international organizations, or partial insiders, like local leaders, who know the conflict and history of the communities well). Legitimacy is also important to identify who has the right to narrate and represent the community, and finally, to define the acceptable conditions and outcomes of a peace agreement (see Kadayifci-Orellana forthcoming).

Different communities have different sources upon which their conceptions of legitimacy are built. Max Weber (1978), who is the most important modern theorist on the topic of legitimacy, identifies two main sources of legitimacy: *subjective* and *external*. Subjective sources of legitimacy may be effectual/affective, which results from emotional surrender; traditional/value-rational, which is determined by the belief in the absolute validity of the order as the expression of ultimate values of an ethical or esthetic or any type and is valid because it always has been; and finally, religious/ faith based, which is determined by the belief that salvation depends upon the obedience to the order. External sources of legitimacy, on the other hand are guaranteed by the expectation of specific external effects, or interest situations. Weber states that, legitimacy based on the sacredness of tradition is the oldest and most universal type of legitimacy (Weber 1978, 33–37).

Sources of legitimacy in Western societies are external (see Seligman 2000, 4; Kadayifci-Orellana forthcoming), based on "rational grounds, resting on a belief in the legality of enacted rules and the right of those elevated to authority under such rules to issue commands (legal authority)" (Kadayifci-Orellana forthcoming, 215). Whereas legitimacy in the majority of Muslim communities inflicted with religiously motivated conflict are based on subjective sources, a combination of religion

and custom, which rests on an established belief in the sanctity of im-
memorial traditions and religion and the legitimacy of those exercising
authority under them.

To mobilize support for their acts and policies at times of conflict,
leaders need to base their narratives on the existing sources of legitimacy
within the context of the society itself. Legitimization of narratives involves establishing a *regime of truth,* or "general politics of truth: that is,
the types of discourse which it accepts and makes function as true"
(Foucault 1980, 131). The sources of legitimacy, in turn will define the
mode of authority and the form of obedience to that authority. In times
of conflict leaders legitimize their discourse through the symbolic orders
embedded in their cultural traditions. These symbolic orders and meaning structures, which are inter-linked with structures of domination and
legitimation, are mobilized to legitimate the interests of certain groups.
In this process of mobilizing support, shared norms, such as religious
norms, myths and legends of one cultural group may be manipulated to
dehumanize the opponent and justify the oppression and destruction of
the *other,* which distances the *other* by using myths and symbols to
prove superiority of one group against another, to dehumanize the "enemy," and to justify violence (Kadayifci-Orellana forthcoming, 25).
Thus, transforming the negative perceptions of the *other* becomes necessary for establishing sustainable peace. "This requires justification for
altering the negative mind frames concerning the *other,* in addition to
addressing the needs and interests of the parties" (Kadayifci-Orellana
2003, 31).

Additionally, virtually all religious traditions embody ideals of, and
cultural and moral resources for, peacebuilding and reconciliation. Religious traditions, with their unique empowering and transforming power
can also be employed to legitimize peace and positive images of the
other and provide emotional, psychological and spiritual resources for
healing trauma and injuries. Religious leaders are often perceived as
even handed, trustworthy agents of God, thus have greater
moral/spiritual legitimacy and are highly respected. Thus, they can influence the opinions of their followers. They often know the history and
the traditions of the parties well and they know the needs (both physical
and emotional), therefore they are better equipped to reach out to the
people, mobilize them, to rehumanize the *other* using religious values
such as justice, forgiveness, harmony, among others to motivate them to
work towards peace. As a result they can mobilize and motivate their

communities to change their behaviors and attitudes effectively and can contribute to the willingness to resolve the conflict and commitment to peace as well as contribute to altering negative mind frames. Their broad community base includes committed followers who can devote the time for mediation, reconciliation or peace education as part of service to God.

Therefore, conflict resolution scholars should seek to divulge the religious basis of narratives of violent conflict and its relation to practice and recognize how war is reproduced or reinforced through shared inter-subjective meanings and images. They should develop methodologies to constructively interact with those religious leaders who justify violence and dehumanize the Other. These methodologies necessitate engaging with these groups within a conflict resolution framework and including an analysis of religious texts, myths, symbols and traditions, institutions that legitimize or delegitimize violence.

Hermeneutics and Conflict Resolution

Conflicts are real. In conflictual settings, (real) people suffer, take up arms, kill and are killed. Yet, how do people make sense of events? What makes them decide how to act, to kill or to die for, and how do they in-terpret and give meaning to wars (Kadayifci-Orellana Forthcoming, 7)? Hermeneutics as the theory of the operations of understanding in their relation to the interpretation of texts (Riceour 1982, 43) can contribute to conflict resolution field by providing methodological tools for uncover-ing the procedures through which humans interpret their surroundings world around them and act upon their interpretations. The individual gives meaning to the world and social structures enable and/or draw the boundaries of these meanings. The link between the individual and social structure is found in the processes of generating meanings and in the in-terpretation of the life-world through cultural schemes and symbols. Un-covering the link between interpretation and action is especially impor-tant to comprehend the dynamics of mass mobilization towards war or peace, since the high risks involved require the conviction of the individuals in the legitimacy of the narrative that justifies the conflict.

There are a variety of possible reasons why people choose one religious response to a conflict over another. Some of these explanations are related to cognitive and emotional needs that may be met by particular religious imagery, symbolism, and text (See Gopin 1991, 2000, 2002). Social motivations and personal experiences also play a critical role in determining affiliations with a group that espouses a certain interpretation of religious texts. The way sacred texts are used to foster peace or promote violence and destruction "seems to depend on the complex ways in which the psychological and sociological circumstances and the economic and cultural constructs of a particular group interact with the ceaseless human drive to hermeneutically develop religious meaning systems, texts, rituals, symbols, and laws" (Gopin 2000, 11). Especially under extreme conditions like war, religious texts are interpreted through deep fears and concerns. At such times various verses, ideas, or spiritual images may meet cognitive and emotional needs of the individual (Gopin 2000, 11). Accordingly, the turbulent relations with the enemy impact the way texts are understood.

Although there are different hermeneutic approaches (see Kadayifci-Orellana forthcoming), this Chapter holds that the hermeneutic approach developed by Hans Georg Gadamer offers insight into religiously motivated identity conflicts in conflict resolution because it is sensitive to the historical and cultural situatedness of the interpreting individual and captures the inter-subjective and continual process of interpretation that is conditioned by religious and cultural traditions, myths, texts and also historical experiences of the community. Gadamer (1991) argues that understanding is "concerned with knowledge, and with truth," therefore "belongs to human experience of the world in general" (1991, xxi). Yet, rejecting the possibility of reaching the eternal and objective truth (since such a perspective ignores the temporality of the individual, thus the temporality of interpretation), he focuses on historicity and argues that interpretation is an encounter between the researcher and a past that presents itself for interpretation. He argues that the historical, social and cultural context (horizon) of the agent has an effect on the way the agent experiences the world and how he interprets the texts that he/she is engaged with. Noting that the interpreter's present (hermeneutical) situation, which can never be hold at a critical distance or be objectified, shapes understanding, Gadamer argues that (Gadamer 1991, 297) people read the texts differently at different ages because different questions, prejudices, and interests move them. "The text, whether law or gospel, if it is to be understood properly – i.e., according to the claim it makes – must be understood at every moment, in every concrete situation, in a new and different way" (Gadamer 1991, 309). Thus, understanding is *"essentially, a historically effected event."*

Describing horizon as the "range of vision that includes everything that can be seen from a particular vantage point" (Gadamer 1991, 302) Gadamer conceptualizes the process of understanding as the *fusion of horizons*, where the horizons of past and present merge into one (Gadamer 1991, 304–305). Accordingly, understanding is embedded in history as it deploys the knower's effective-history, personal experience and religio-cultural traditions to assimilate new experiences. The initial structure of an effective-history constrains the range of possible interpretations, excluding some possibilities and calling forth others. This means that every agent reads the text through the lenses of his/her personal and social experiences. Contextual factors such as different historical, economic, political or social situations the recipient of the text is situated within, impact the questions, issues and problems with which she approaches the text.

Furthermore, human beings live in a world of culture/religion formed by language, providing the contextual perspectives that inform and condition participation in reality as well as their understanding of conflicts. Contextual factors go through meaning systems that are shaped by religio-cultural constructions. Construction and reconstruction of meanings occur at the nexus of event and cultural objects (e.g. religious values, myths etc.) because there is an interdependent influence of culture/religion and action on social change (ibid.) and there is a co-constructive relationship between events and narratives. This means that events affect the narratives and narratives affect the way events are perceived or rendered meaningful (Kadayifci-Orellana forthcoming, 155). Although events are shaped by some set of ideas, beliefs, or rules embodied in ritual, symbol or speech, they also transform these same cultural objects and social structures (Sahlins 1991; Sewell 1996; and Ellingson 1997). Events disrupt the operative systems of ideas, beliefs, values, roles, and institutional practices in a given society, (Sahlins 1991, 44). In return, the events change the way in which social actors think about the meaning and importance they assign to modes of actions and the rules that govern interaction, groups and their discourses, symbols, and rituals (Ellingson 1997). Thus, the effective history, filtered through religio-cultural lenses, impacts how interpreting agent views events. Especially in communities where religion plays a critical role in social life and defining identities, religious discourse and texts become critical components of this context. In other words, the *hermeneutical situation* impacts the meaning-making process and the way individuals view conflicts, perceive their enemies, and their options, as it forms their horizon.

Documents of faith contain theological statements, modes of discourse and narratives, prophecies, legislative texts, sayings, hymns, prayers, and liturgical formulas and interpretation of a religious text always involves a tension between the fixed text, the word of God and the sense arrived at by applying it at the concrete moment of interpretation in preaching (Gadamer 1991, 309). So, application of a text to a current situation, which is very different from the situation and issues when the text was first revealed, becomes a challenge. From the perspective of their lived experience, people approach religious texts and draw conclusions on how they should act under certain circumstances as they try to make sense of their lives, sufferings and ways to deal with them. Historical events that influence the experience and interpretive process of the individuals (e.g. wars, upheavals, peace agreement, etc.) may call attention to a particular problem, win credibility for a movements frame, encourage new organizations to join a movement, or serve as a model of success that foments expectations among constituents of future movement victories (See Klandermans 1992, 92-93, 77-92; Klandermans, Kreisi and Tarrow 1988, 185).

In this process, religious constructs (e.g. myths, texts, symbols etc.) become tools with which actors chart their action-plans for suicidal attacks, torture, or nonviolent demonstrations, for example. These cultural objects enable leaders to define certain issues, beliefs, and forms of action as legitimate and others illegitimate, thus either reproducing or challenging social structures and relations of power (Ellingson 1997, 269; Bourdieu 1991). Various tales, sagas, and myths are selected to support interpretations of the religious tradition that legitimize war, and construct negative enemy images. Religious actors simplify religious myths, dehistoricize religious texts, and construct a story in which all time, place, and difference are represented as meaningful parts of a divine project (Kadayifci-Orellana 2003, 28). With the aid of religious imagery and vocabulary, various sagas, myths and tales, with which the population is familiar, past, preset, and future are linked in the minds of the population (Kadayifci-Orellana 2002, 357). Religious objects provide cosmology, history and eschatology of the war and simplify the world into good and evil. This simplification distinguishes the faithful, who is on the side of God, thus good and pure, from the *other*, who is against God, thus evil, therefore must be eliminated.

As religious narratives are legitimized, mythic stories are interpreted and reinterpreted in ways that demonize an enemy and justify violence. Myths translate complex problems into manageable and comprehensive cognitive structures. In times of conflict myths become tools to make sense of human atrocities, to "explain" the reasons and sources of the conflict to the people in a "clear" way. These myths provide a deeper meaning to what is happening to the community. These myths may also be utilized to clearly separate what is considered legitimate from what is considered illegitimate. Based on these limits, these myths render various acts (which would be otherwise considered illegitimate) legitimate.

Moreover, religious imagery provides the faithful with hope of victory as well as other-worldly rewards, such as eternal bliss in heaven. Past wars and victories are interpreted from the perspective of the religious tradition, and are employed to recreate the history of the people. By locating these victories and wars in the collective memory of the population religious and political actors engage the population into the politics of interpretation. By retelling these religious myths, sagas, and stories, they rewrite the history and shape the spaces (e.g. national homeland) and events (e.g. wars, victories, massacres, etc.) that constitute the basis of religious identity. Such stories create the imaginative boundaries that contain the identity of the people and influence self-interpretations and modes of exclusion and inclusion (see Kadayifci-Orellana, forthcoming). These narratives reconfigure the imagination of the population within which the actions have meaning and thus become the contexts for action, such as defending the nation through war or suicide attacks.

Meaning-making is a dynamic process in which the narrators compete with one another for legitimacy. "Meaning is thus constructed through the ongoing process of contestation within a discursive field as speakers jockey to gain legitimacy for their position, the support of targeted audiences, and the opportunity to implement their solutions" (Ellingson 1997). When the expected outcomes are not reached, and new events occur, when the solutions fail to materialize, the audiences may alter their interests and beliefs, change the meanings of various actions and identify new ways to achieve their goals and look for ways to achieve them. In this context, Ellingson writes:

> As the horizons change, some solutions may be rejected and some diagnoses judged incorrect, while others are accorded greater authority. Speakers respond to the event and altered horizons by reworking their discourses-jettisoning arguments that are untenable, adopting those of their rivals, or crafting new ones that incorporate the event... as the ground from which to asses the viability and legitimacy of old and new arguments- to make them more resonant with their audiences' new horizons of expectations and to help speakers compete more effectively within the field of debate (Ellingson 1997, 272–273).

Leaders, who are recognized as having legitimacy to narrate, craft new arguments and adopt pre-existing ones, arrange these arguments in various combinations to pursue their goals or expected outcomes, which might include alternative conceptions of what the debate is about or what the potential consequences are. These narrators might reject solutions (e.g. peace agreement or cease-fire), change goals, or rework their arguments when they contradict or fail to resonate with their audiences. Failure to do so may undermine the legitimacy of their position or impair their capacity to mobilize their audiences (Ellingson 1997, 272).

Legitimation of narratives involves a competition for establishing a regime of truth. In this struggle, "*truth* is centered on a specific discourse/narrative and on the institutions that are linked in a circular relation with systems of power that produce and sustain the *regime of truth*" (Kadayifci-Orellana forthcoming, 253). Language is the main mode of human operation in the world (Gadamer 1997, 3). Hence, *truth* can only be constituted through a discourse/ narrative. In the process of legitimization power enables a certain narrative to be considered as *true*. Thus, power and power relations – as a set of forces that establishes positions and ways of behaving influencing people—are critical elements of legitimization of narratives (Kadayifci-Orellana forthcoming, 254).

Foucault examines the link between power and establishment of regimes of truth. He writes that "We are subjected to the production of truth through power and we cannot exercise power except through the production of truth" (Foucault 1980, 93) and "Power never ceases its interrogation, its acquisition, and its registration of truth: it institutionalizes and rewards its pursuit" (Foucault 1980, 93). Yet, power is not static but is mobile and flows from one place to another very quickly. Relations of power are immanent in all types of relationships such as economic process, knowledge relationships, etc. (Foucault 1978, 86–87). Power is first found and constituted at micro levels (such as work places, prisons, churches, mosques, schools, hospital, etc.) and later incorporated and developed into larger institutional structures. It is at these institutional sites that different narratives compete for legitimacy, insert themselves as *regimes of truth*. Again, at these sites, manifold relations of power permeate, characterize and constitute the social body (see Kadayifci-Orellana forthcoming, 41).

Narratives do not emerge in a void but develop from pre-existing fields of possibilities, which new narratives can realign and reconfigure. A field of possibilities is constituted by various horizons in which the past, the present and an image of a future is constructed. These narratives operate in a material world, against and in relation to prior and contemporary narratives, other discursive formations, and social, political, and economic material forces. In this process, power moves around and through different groups (e.g. the government, religious groups, etc.), events, institutions, and individuals. Furthermore, the way people understand the world, develop values and aspirations and the way they react to events are constituted out of various technologies of power. Hence, individuals are strongly influenced by the power of institutions, such as universities, mosques/churches/synagogues, or medical agencies.

In many conflicts involving Muslims today one can observe multiple groups attempting to mobilize the population towards their political and strategic narratives and offensive narratives compete with nonviolent narratives. Who is more successful is measured in terms of their ability to mobilize the population towards their objectives. Each group attempts to provide overall frames of meaning within the historical, cultural and religious context of their society and use symbols that can evoke strong emotional reaction. Especially, when there is not a single well-defined leadership but a number of groups that are competing for that position, this process becomes more complicated as these groups attempt to use various national or religious resources for symbols to evoke the emotions of their populations. Within this structure of meaning/culture, their narratives become effective and constitute and reproduce systems of power and authority in which they coordinate the actions of the individuals. Within this context, the constellation of power relations and leaders enables a certain narrative to emerge as the dominant one at a particular period.

The next section introduces the nonviolent movement led by Abdul Ghaffar Khan, in North Western part of British India in order to illustrate how nonviolent Islamic narrative replaced an offensive one in a conflict context. At a time when Islam is depicted as fundamentally violent, this case illustrates the long-standing commitment to peace in this religious heritage, and can offer guidance to practitioners for promoting positive change in relations among protagonists of religious conflict.

Case of Ghaffar Khan

Living in the strategically located North-West Frontier Province of British India, Pashtuns had the reputation of being extremely aggressive and violent, and were described by the British as the "most barbaric of all races" (see Easwaran 1984; Johansen 1997, 56; Crooke 1896, 167-168). The sources of legitimacy and authority among the Pashtun community were based on a combination of religion (Islam), tribal codes and customs, which emphasized vengeance (*badal*), honor, and military arts. Acts of revenge were considered a duty of honor leading to generations lasting feuds. "They also had a well-established tradition of tribal organization that constituted a military confederacy" and almost all men carried firearms, and considered war a normal aspect of life (Johansen 1997, 57).

Consequently, "the prevailing moral code emphasized Islamic beliefs justifying violence in defense of the faith" and "when some of the more vengeful customs came into conflict with Islam, the former often prevailed leading to feuds" (Johansen 1997, 58).

Ghaffar Khan, son of a religious chieftain, felt the personal religious calling to serve God by uplifting his people through social reform and education and was convinced that pervasive violence was responsible for the Pashtun society's inability to uplift itself (ibid). In order to realize his reforms and repel the British, Khan established the world's first known nonviolent army, *Khudai Khidmatgars* (Servants of God). In order to legitimize social reforms, he employed a strategy based upon traditional norms, codes and Islamic religion. For example, he utilized Islam's emphasis on social welfare, justice and service and interpreted the Islamic understanding of jihad in its broadest sense. Consistent with Islamic emphasis on justice, protection of the poor, weak and needy, they supported the needs of the oppressed by dedicating themselves to attitudinal change in which they emphasized sacrifice and relinquishment of hatred, jealousy, and personal reward for service (Johansen 1997, 59). They established schools as they considered education a sacred duty according to Islam, worked on local developmental projects, promoted hygiene and sanitation. Moreover, Khan, also established a network of committees called *jirga's,* based on the traditional tribal councils that had maintained the law for centuries (Johansen 1997, 60).

Additionally, Khan also adapted the Pashtun code of honor, so central to the society, to face a hostile army with courage and without arms rather than to fed and killing. "Ghaffar Khan deliberately employed this code's emphasis on willingness to fight no matter what the cost" (Johansen 1997, 60), arguing that only the most courageous, like the Pashtuns, would be able stand for righteousness and justice without arms and face death solemnly and "only a people prepared to fight, he said, could prove the virtue of not fighting" (ibid.). Moreover, he employed the sacredness of oath that is central to both Islamic and Pathan tribal norms. As Easwaran (1984, 112) states:

> For a Pathan, an oath is not a small matter. He does not
> enter into a vow easily because once given, a Pathan's
> word cannot be broken. Even his enemy can count on
> him to keep his word at the risk of his life.

Joining the army required an oath to refrain from violence, revenge, and
any antisocial customs and practices, and to devote at least two hours a
day to social work. They vowed to eliminate violence in their relations
with other Pashtuns as well as with anyone else (Johansen 1997, 59).
Following the code of honor in the Pashtun society and Muslim beliefs,
military recruits swore allegiance before God to give their lives for their
people. At the heart of the oath and the organization was the commitment
to nonviolence (Easwaran 1984, 112). This oath was of great importance
as Pashtun culture assumed that one's word could not be broken without
losing one's integrity and that the word must be honored with life.

Utilizing Islamic principles of discipline, obedience to leaders who
acted in accordance with God's will and an uncompromising willingness
to sacrifice in the service of God's will, *Khudai Khidmatgars* (which also
included women) was drilled and disciplined with officers, cadres, uniforms, a flag, a drum and bagpipe corps. Khan told his followers that he
was going to give them the most powerful weapon, *the weapon of the
Prophet*, and this weapon was *nonviolence* based on patience and righteousness, when standing against oppression. He stated (cited in Easwaran 1997, 59):

> I am going to give you such a weapon that the police and
> the army will not be able to stand against it. It is the
> weapon of the Prophet, but you are not aware of it. That
> weapon is patience and righteousness. No power on
> earth can stand against it... when you go back to your
> villages, tell your brethren that there is an army of God,
> and its weapon is patience. Ask your brethren to join the
> army of God. Endure all hardships. If you exercise pa-
> tience, victory will be yours.

Khan extended the Islamic notion of *sabr* (patience) to mean renunciation of all forms of violence, thus made it a key element in his religious teaching and practice. He emphasized that *sabr* is counseled to repeatedly in the Quran Prophet Mohammed in the early years of Islam,

when he did not have any political or military power. He also emphasized that, during these difficult times the Prophet and his followers held firmly to truth without retaliating violently or retreating, as the ultimate submission to God's will, which is also the true meaning of Islam (See Johansen 1997, 60; Khan 1969; Pyerelal 1966). He also stated that he understood Islam to be *"amal, yekeen, muhabat"* (work, faith and love) and that the Quran "makes it absolutely clear that faith in One God without a second and good works are enough to secure a man his salvation" (Khan 1969, 23).

Derived from the Islamic tradition, other basic principles of *Khudai Khidmatgars* included service, forgiveness, sacrifice, and gentleness. Abdul Ghaffar Khan argued that God grants to *rifq* (gentleness) what he does not grant to *unf* (violence) (See Kadayifci-Orellana 2003, 52). He based his argument on the *Hadith* which states:

> Whenever violence enters into something it disgraces it, whenever 'gentle-civility' enters something it graces it. Truly God bestows on account of gentle conduct what he does not bestow on account of violent conduct (Cited in Abu-Nimer, 2003: 43).

He noted that the word *rifq* has been used in this *Hadith* as an antithesis to *unf* (violence) and that these terms convey exactly what violence and nonviolence mean in present times. Accordingly, *Hadith* clearly shows the superiority of the nonviolent method from God's disdain of *fasad* (violence). Based on the Quranic verse (2:205): "[w]hen he turns his back, his aim everywhere is to spread mischief through the earth and destroy crops and progeny but Allah loveth not mischief," he interpreted *fasad* to mean 'mischief,' an action which results in disruption of the social system, causing huge losses in terms of lives and property. Khan concluded that God loves nonviolence and abhors violent activity in human society. Consequently, based on the Islamic teaching, Khan was able to successfully resist the British and undo culture of violence that plagued the Pashtun society, replacing it with a culture of peace and

232 S. Ayse Kadayifci-Orellana

nonviolence, based on the Islamic notions of patience, forgiveness, compassion, and sacredness of human life.

Conclusion

In spite of widespread belief that religious traditions generally, and Islam in particular, demand the use of violence against adversaries, the case of Pashtuns reminds us of the long-standing commitment to peace in the Islam faith. Islam seeks to reduce the moral space, as it were, in which Muslims can legitimize violence (see Johansen 1997, 65–67). Islamic religious identity can provide an effective basis for recruiting people to join a nonviolent movement, nurture a strong identity and discipline and that nonviolent interpretation of Islamic principles of peace can provide a clear antidote to violent conflict, encourage activists to avoid intolerance towards others to overcome use of violence against adversaries both in interpersonal and inter-group conflicts.

Accordingly, conflict resolution scholars and practitioners need to identify those religious and cultural values that promote peace and coexistence and include them in conflict resolution models. Abu-Nimer, whose experience in the field supports this position, notes also that "framing the interventions within a religious context and deriving tools from a religious narrative have made [it] possible for interveners to gain access and increase their potential impact on the parties" (Abu-Nimer 2001, 686). These values should be put into practice by engaging local religious leaders that are committed to peace and the nonviolent pursuit of justice. These narratives must be supported by religious texts and myths as:

> a close study of the sacred texts, traditions, symbols and myths that emerge in conflict situations may contribute to theoretical approaches to conflict analysis by providing a useful frame of reference for conflict resolution workshops, and interfaith dialogue groups, and by creating a bridge to the unique cultural expression of a particular conflict (Gopin 2000, 15).

This requires hermeneutically engaging with these texts and symbols.

Likewise, since institutions play a major role in the legitimization of narratives and mobilization of society, those local institutions that uphold nonviolent values and are committed to justice should empowered (See Kadayifci-Orellana forthcoming). In that line, scholars and practitioners should first identify institutional sites that could contribute to peacebuilding and reconciliation. They should then develop strategies to empower these institutions financially, technically and also by providing the necessary training for facilitating dialogue with the *other*. One way to do that would be to open channels through which these institutions could connect to wider network of peacebuilding initiatives across social, political and economic spectrum. In addition, it is also necessary to encourage them to reach out to their constituencies to change attitudes, mind frames and negative enemy images through lectures, sermons, and rituals. Consequently, religious peacebuilding could become a major tool for training, empowering, and motivating religiously oriented people towards peace and religious traditions, such as Islam, can become resources for creating a culture of peace as well as reducing violence, and dehumanization of the *other*.

Notes

1. Here, by "traditional" I refer to the dominant approaches within the conflict resolution field, especially at policy and decision-making levels in the United States and Europe.

References

Abu-Nimer, M. 2003. *Nonviolence and Peacebuilding in Islam,* Florida: University Press of Florida.
———. 2001. "Conflict Resolution, Culture, and Religion: Toward a Training Model of Interreligious Peacebuilding," *Peace Research* 38 (6): 685–704.
Ashley R. K. 1989. "Living on Borderlines: Man, Poststructuralism, and War." Pp. 259-321 in *International/Intertextual Relations: Postmodern Readings of World Politics,* edited by James Der Derian and Michael J. Shapiro. New York Lexington Books.

Azar, E. "Management of Protracted Social Conflict in the Third World," paper prepared for the Fourth ICES Annual Lecture at Columbia University (unpublished) New York 10 June, 1986.

al Banna, H. 1990. *Majmu'at Rasa'I al-Imam al-Shahid Hasan al-Banna* new legal ed. Cairo: Dar al Da'wa.

————. 1978. *Five Tracts of Hasan al-Banna (1906–1949),* Charles Wendell tr., Berkeley: University of California Press.

Bourdieu P. 1991. *Language and Symbolic Power.* Cambridge, Mass: Harvard University Press.

Crooke, W. 1896. *The Tribes and Castes of the North-Western Provinces of Oudh,* Vol. 4 Calcutta: Office of the Superintendent of Government Printing.

Dicenso, J. 1990. *Hermeneutics and the Disclosuere of Truth: A Study on the Work of Heidegger, Gadamer, and Ricoeur* Charlottesville: University Press of Virginia.

Ellingson S. 1997. "Understanding the Dialectic of Discourse and Collective Action: Public Debate and Rioting in Antebellum Cincinnati." Pp. 268–80 in *Social Movements: Readings on Their Emergence, Mobilization and Dynamics,* edited by Dough McAdam and David A. Snow. Los Angeles, CA. Roxbury Publishing Company.

Easwaran, E. 1984. *A Man to Match His Mountains: Badshah Khan: Nonviolent Soldier of Islam* Petaluma, California: Nilgiri Press.

Foucault M. 1980. "Truth and Power." Pp. 109–133 in *Power/Knowledge: Selected Interviews and Other Writings, 1972-1977,* edited by Colin Gordon, translated by Colin Gordon *et al.* New York: Pantheon Books.

————. 1978. *History of Sexuality: An Introduction, Volume I.* New York: Vintage Books.

————. 1972. *Archeology of Knowledge and Discourse on Language,* translated by A. M. Sheridan Smith New York: Pantheon Books.

Gadamer, H.-G. 1991. *Truth and Method.* Trans. Joel Weinsheimer and Donald G. Marshall. Second revised edition. New York: Crossroad.

——————. 1997. "Universality of the Hermeneutical Problem (1966)." Pp. 3–17 in *Philosophical Hermeneutics: Hans Georg Gadamer,* translated and edited by David E. Linge. Los Angeles: University of California Press.

Gopin, M. 2002. *Holy War Holy Peace,* New York, Oxford University Press.

————. 2000. *Between Eden and Armageddon: The Future of World Religions, Violence, and Peacemaking.* New York: Oxford University Press.

————. 1991. "Religion, Violence, and Conflict Resolution." *Peace and Change* 22. no.1: 1–31.

Hamidullah, M.1953. *Muslim Conduct of State, 3rd ed*, Lahore: Sh. Muhammad Ashraf.

Hannigan, J. A. 1991. "Social Movement Theory and the Sociology of Religion: Toward a New Synthesis." *Sociological Analysis* 52, no. 4: 311–331.

Hashmi, S. 1996. "Interpreting the Islamic Ethics of War and Peace." Pp. 146-66 in Ethics of War and Peace: Religious and Secular Perspectives, edited by Terry Nardin. Princeton: Princeton University Press.

Jabri, V. 1996. *Discourses On Violence- Conflict Analysis Reconsidered.* Manchester, U K: Manchester University Press.

Johansen, R. C. 1997: *"Radical Islam and Nonviolence: A Case Study of Religious Empowerment and Constraint Among Pashtuns." Journal of Peace Research* 34. No. 1: 53–71.

Kadayifci-Orellana S. A. 2005. "Muslim Perspectives of War and Peace," presented at *First Annual Conference of the Mahatma Gandhi Center for Global Nonviolenc*e at James Madison University, Harrisonburg, Virginia, on "Religion: Conflict and Peace." April 11.

Kadayifci-Orellana S. Ayse. 2003. "Religion, Violence and the Islamic Tradition of Nonviolence." *Turkish yearbook of International Relations 34.*

————.2002. "Standing on an Isthmus: Islamic Narratives of War and Peace in Palestine." Doctoral Dissertation, Washington D.C.: School of International Service, American University at Washington D.C.

————. forthcoming. *Standing on an Isthmus: Islamic Narratives of War and Peace in Palestine.* Lanham MD: Lexington.

Khan, A. G. 1969. *Aap Biti (Autobiography).* Lahore: Rohtas Books.

Khan, M. A. M. 1997. *"Peace and Change in the Islamic World"* paper presented at the conference *Islam and Peace in the 15/20th century.* Washington DC. (February 6–7, 1997)

Klandermans, B. 1992. "The Social Construction of Protest and Multior-
ganizational Fields (77–103) A.D. Morris and C. McClurg eds. *Frontiers of Social Movement Theory*. New Haven. Conn.: Yale University Press.

Malik, I. H. 1998. "Islamic Discourse on Jihad, War and Violence."
Journal of South Asian and Middle Eastern Studies 21, no. 4: 47–78

Maududi, S. A. 1980. *Jihad in Islam*. Lahore: Islamic Publications.

McHoul A. and W. Grace. 1993. *A Foucault Premier: Discourse, Power
and the Subject*. London: UCL Press.

Pyarelal, N. 1966. *Thrown to the Wolves: Abdul Ghaffar* Calcutta:
Eastlight Book House.

Qurashi, M.M. 1991. "The Concept of Islamic Jehad." *Islamic Thought
and Scientific Creativity* 2, No. 1: 57-71.

Ricoeur, P. 1995. *Figuring the Sacred: Religion, Narrative, and Imagination*. Minneapolis: Fortress Press.

———. 1982. *Hermeneutics and the Human Sciences*: Edited and Translated by John London and New York: Cambridge University Press.

Rupesinghe, Kumar. 1988.*Civil Wars, Civil Peace: An Introduction to
Conflict Resolution*. London: Pluto Press.

Said, A. A. and N. C. Funk. 2002: "The Role of Faith in Cross-Cultural
Conflict Resolution." *Peace and Conflict Studies* 9, No. 1: 37-50.

Sahlins, M. 1991. "The Return of the Event, Again: With Reflections on
the Beginnings of the Great Fijian War of 1843 to 1855 between the
Kingdoms of Bau and Rewa." Pp. 37-100 in *Clio in Oceania: Toward a Historical Anthology*, edited by Aletta Biersack. Washington
D.C: Smithsonian.

Satha-Anand, C. 2001. "The Nonviolent Crescent: Eight Thesis on Muslim Nonviolent Action." Pp. 195-211 in Said, *Peace and Conflict
Resolution in Islam: Precept and Practice*, edited by Abdul Aziz, et.
al .eds. 195-211 New York: University Press of America.

Seligman, A. B. 2000. *Modernity's Wager: Authority, the Self, and Transcendence*. Princeton: Princeton University Press.

Sewell, W.R 1996. "Three Temporalities: Toward an Eventful Sociology." Pp. 245–80 in *The Historic Turn in the Human Sciences*, edited by T. J. McDonald. Ann Arbor: University of Michigan Press.

Steffek J. 2000 *The Power of Rational Discourse and the Legitimacy of
International Governance*. Paper presented at the workshop "Analy-
sis of Discourse and Ideas in European and International Affairs"
Florence: EUI (12/12 May).

Weber, M. 1978. *Economy and Society.* Edited by Guenther Roth and Claus Wittich. Berkeley: University of California Press.

Part III: The Dynamics of Collective Axiology

Chapter 10

"Good Violence" and the Myth of the Eternal Soldier

David G. Alpher and Daniel Rothbart

A true military officer is in one particular like a true monk. Not with
more self-abnegation will the latter keep his vows of monastic obedience
than the former his vows of allegiance to martial duty.
-Herman Melville

Historically, there is a long and rich tradition of overlap between the
military and religious worlds. The Knights Templar, the Teutonic
Knights, the Knights of Malta, the Shaolin Monks and the Maccabees
exhibit explicit characteristics of both military and religious systems. The
history of soldiers who have gone on to become monks or priests is deep
and rich, suggesting a strong connection between two rarified fields.

Although comparisons between Gods and Generals reflect delusions
of grandeur—particularly when suggested by a General—there is value
in attending to the religious dimensions of military systems. Military
training demands of its recruits a personal transformation that shows
striking similarities to immersion in a fundamentalist religion. In such
fundamentalist systems, prayers, hymns, symbols and symbolic rituals
help an individual socialize or re-socialize themselves as "a member of
the tribe." Similarly, the military shapes a recruit's identity through a

sequence of cadences and slogans, physical, emotional, and mental indoctrination, insignias (a specific kind of symbol) and oaths, inculcating a new social persona that is alien to the past persona.

The new identity is characterized by a system of language and action that serves to create a "center," holding peace within and holding at bay the chaos without. Within the ordered centers are ways of knowing and ways of describing knowledge in order to give it meaning. Among the keys to understanding systems such as these is that they assume a body of knowledge, which is legitimate and can and should be validated by constructing language patterns to describe it, and a history and innate nature to be described

This identity-transformation carries commitment to a fixed worldview (differing, sometimes significantly, from that held by the general public), providing a lens through which to view current events and a spiritual resource with which to meet the sacrifices to come. In both systems of training, ingroup identity is glorified through visions of embattled relations with the Other.

Perhaps the most important question that could be asked about military training is not "why is the training like it is," but "what attracts people to military life?" Flawed though Freud's theory of the Pleasure Principle might be, human beings do not tend to seek out pain and suffering, or situations characterized by sometimes debilitating degrees of fear and moral horror, on purpose—except in the military and deeply religious worlds. The immediate follow-up question is "how does military training hold the power it does?" How does one get a human being to override every instinct of self-preservation and run *forwards* into battle? How does one get a recruit to remain and advance him or herself in a livelihood that bears a daily weight of mental and emotional strain and the risk of physical harm or death? Perhaps more poignantly, what is it about military service that has exerted such a pull on human beings throughout history, so often tearing communities violently apart? It is these questions that will guide the theory offered in this chapter.

Of course, the purpose of military training is to prepare the recruit for violent encounters, establishing in such training a rationale and an absolution for acts of "good violence" in response to the enemy's "bad violence." Both the religious and military worlds confer on adherents just such a proto-system—what will be defined herein as a "hermetic conceptual framework," based around myth-symbol systems.

The hermetic conceptual framework fosters a mindset for promoting peace within and holding at bay the chaos without; a framework that also establishes ways of knowing and ways of describing episodes of violence. The hermetic frameworks underpinning both military and religious symbols are sharply defined with only semi-permeable boundaries that delineate what is internal and what is external to the system—in other words, what is sacred and what is profane. The framework reinforces itself through institutions and practices, such as language, history, projections of future and networked connections with the past, ethics, worldview, and law that make it an independently functioning culture.

Our intent is not to explore a particular military system or religious tradition *per se*, but to examine the similar social/cognitive processes of identity transformation among them. The re-socialization in military training is necessary for the acolytes or trainees to better place themselves within the new context and achieve its rewards, offering the right and ability to attain the gifts bestowed by that system. Both military systems and fundamentalist religious sub-groups provide in their training proprietary forms of language and learning that are highly structured around powerful icons, sacred words, and conceptual models. (See Chapter 3 by Rothbart and Korostelina in this volume).

The word "military" as used within this paper refers only to professional militaries, not to paramilitary forces, mercenaries or coerced troops. Mandatory conscription does not necessarily discount an army from this argument, but the wholesale force used to "recruit" troops in many areas of the world creates an altogether different entity than does voluntary enlistment or a socially sanctioned draft. These types of paramilitary groups do form their own hermetic conceptual framework—although an altogether more dangerous and uncontrollable one than do professional militaries. This mutated form will be discussed further below, and analysis of the parallels and differences between the two is important to keep in mind.

Mercenaries have been an accepted, if rarely liked, adjunct to regular military units for the better part of recorded history, and continue thriving to this day despite United Nations (UN) sanctions. With the notable exception of such groups as the French Foreign Legion and the Vatican Guards however—both of which are technically mercenary forces, although both are extremely codified, professional forces with full governmental sanction—they comprise an entirely different set of values and traditions (or lack thereof) than do their "regular" counterparts. Militias, which have their own traditions and would be an interesting focus of study, will not be addressed below.

MoralPolitik

Military training instills in recruits moralistic categories of the virtuous national self as opposed the amoral, vicious outsider—"all enemies, foreign and domestic," as goes the oath a U.S. soldier swears. Military institutions find their roots in the distinction between inside and outside morality, conferring not only legitimacy but also honor to the act of killing—as long as it is done within proscribed limits of "civilized" behavior. Within this system, the successful killer is rewarded both professionally from above and laterally within his peer group, as long as the killing is done within the bounds of professionally sanctioned conduct.

The Treaty of Westphalia not only solidified the sovereignty of the European state system, but also conferred contractual arrangements with the ingroup public. Imposition of borders, orders and identities by sovereigns was intended to establish a distinction between the "good" national self and the "bad" foreign Other. Going to war was not simply an act of conquest for a mark of moral superiority (Mansbach, R. W. and F. Wilmer 2001, 89). Subjects would provide the state with human resources necessary for fighting in exchange for the commitment by the state to protect subjects from "enemy" attacks.

In his or her capacity as an official arm of state power, a soldier acts as surrogate for the state in violent confrontation with an Other. The state in turn legitimizes violence through the myth of a morally supreme "civilized" war as opposed the "savagery" committed by someone who kills without official sanction—or who kills with someone else's "misguided" sanction. In this way, the powerful cultural practice of sanctioned violence was, ironically, extended from the days when a military was guided by leaders who fought under a banner of divine legitimacy.

Even in post-Westphalian secularized Europe, however, old customs echoed a commitment to divinely inspired missions. For example, German soldiers of WWI wore belt buckles engraved with the legend "Gott mit uns": "God is with us."

Today, a "true soldier" acquires, through training and indoctrination, membership in a moral community, defined through reciprocal obligations to act, for example, fairly, justly, and in a civilized manner. A military "hero" is a cluster of characteristics of bravery, sacrifice, and strength, fulfilling an innermost identity through sacrifice and an almost religious devotion to a worthy, noble cause (Jabri 1996). A soldier is trained to comply with elaborate rules and mechanisms of combat, committed to humane treatment of prisoners and civilians. The military worldview is fleshed out in codes of conduct, offering legitimacy, authority, justice and especially absolution to the obedient solder—and making outcast, through the removal of these same things, for the non-compliant. The world of the military and the worlds of fundamentalist religions draw their power, absolutions and justifications for purpose and action, as well as definitions of "right life" and "good violence," from the more central construction of the hermetic conceptual framework.

Military training essentializes territorial divisions between nations. In spite of the territoriality of national identities, the cognitive mechanism for establishing, solidifying, and reinforcing nationalities are clearly *anti-territorial*, grounded instead on the devices of axiological bordering. (See Chapter 3 by Rothbart and Korostelina in this volume.) In particular, the formation of military identity rests on the cognitive instruments of axiological bordering; the icons, moral discourse and conceptual models of purity and contamination that are familiar to scholars of fundamentalist religions. That is, the kind of cognitive mechanisms that rationalize and absolve the would-be soldier perpetrating acts of "good violence," and vilify the enemy's acts of "bad violence," rest on clear categories of virtue and vice, the sanctified and the vilified, the noble cause and the demonic deed.

We argue below that the hermetic framework of the military exhibits a system of axiological bordering between the virtuous Self and the dangerous Other, as we draw upon the rich anthropological literature that documents similar kinds of bordering in the myth-symbol constructions of human societies throughout history. Although value-commitments are minimized in most social scientific investigations of aggression, we believe that the value-orientation within military training provides insight into institutionally sanctioned violence.

As religious studies scholars have documented, the various fundamentalist strains of Islam, Christianity and Judaism, albeit in radically different detail, are dominated by a sense of embattled spirituality, identifying in worldly affairs the forces of evil that threaten an apocalyptic doom (Marty and Appleby 2004, 819-820). From this viewpoint, adherents are not merely engaged in localized skirmishes among self-interested groups, adherents are immersed in a cosmic war against an enemy committed to universal destruction. Fundamentalists mythologize their enemies, situating them within the same eschatological drama in which they see themselves. Likened to savages who celebrate murder and rejoice in acts of terror, the enemy is viewed as being consumed with a zeal for killing without reason or conscience. Demonic forces are thought to be disguised as "innocent" workers in secular institutions. From the perspective of religious fundamentalists, struggles with secular institutions are conveyed as an eschatological drama unfolding in the mind of God and directing the course of human history (Marty and Appleby 2004, 819-820). Anyone associated with the enemy becomes tainted, contaminated by demonic influences. The faithful believe themselves to be crusaders for virtue, seeking to save civilization against an apocalyptic annihilation.

In setting boundaries, the faithful act to preserve their purity and protect themselves from possible contamination. Not surprisingly, the purity/danger divide comes into prominence in times of crisis, actual or perceived, promoting fear of extinction as a people or absorption into an overarching culture (Marty and Appleby 2004, 823). The enemy's perceived evil-doings promote an anger and hatred that demands a response, testing the resolve, courage, and skill of soldiers. In preparation for the sacrifices that lay ahead, the faithful are strengthened by their reliance on a sacred history, retrieving inspiration from stories of a glorious past.

Through the lens of a sacred history, their mistakes are absolved, their "soul" is pure, and their cause is just.

Such adherents are impelled by the unfolding eschatological drama to commit acts of evil, and become willing and capable of dangerous behavior. Outgroup vices acquire an aura of solidity and fixity akin to eternal truths, laying the foundation of validation for the sacrifices that lay ahead. Acts of "good violence" against members of the dangerous Other are driven in part by fears and in part by the resolve of the faithful to do what must be done. For indigenous societies, the juxtaposition of purity and danger is essential to group identity."[1] This fundamental attribution error—what we do, we do because we are forced to; what they do, they do because it is their nature—is fostered by declarations of moral superiority through a sense of universal rightness.

To the ingroup member, secular outsiders will fail to recognize the true character and capacity of insiders and enemies, because outsiders lack the redemptive identification with a transcendent source of purity in the form of God-like figures as conveyed through myths enjoyed by the insider. Once embedded in lifestyle choices of individuals and institutional commitments, self- and enemy-narratives become self-fulfilling, reinforced in the meanings given to current interactions. A church may be charged with the guardianship and salvation of souls, but an officer of the church is charged with the guardianship and salvation of *these* souls and never forgets that he has his own to mind. A military may be charged with the guardianship of a nation and its people "from all enemies, foreign and domestic," but a specific soldier is charged with guardianship during *this* engagement, against *this* enemy. In this way, definitions and charges remain relevant, not diluted by long-distant or overly broad connections.

Both fundamental religious institutions and military training promote non- or semi-porous boundaries between themselves and the larger socio-cultural matrix into which they fit and from which they draw their acolytes. During training, an episode of violence is presented through clear divisions between friend and foe, ally and enemy, disciple and heretic. In comparison to an enemy's system of values, the faithful are acting from a superior moral position. In contrast to the value-neutral realpolitik that George Kennan champions for diplomats engaged in in-

ternal relations, morally charged nationalism is essential to military training, conferring on the successful recruit the virtues of the sacred home
against the vices of the foreign land. A moralpolitik, as it were, is a pivotal aspect of military identity (Mansbach and Wilmer 2001, 76).

The official ethical system taught at the United States Military Academy (USMA) is known as the "Thayer system," after the man who formulated it. In creating the doctrine, Thayer effectively used a mixture of
classical Spartan and Athenian principles and reframed them in the context of a modern military academy, likening the new recruit to warriors
whose myth is emulated even today. The system encompasses a "high
standard of appearance, weekly attendance at chapel, and a strict enforcement of rules against lying, stealing, and other 'irregular or immoral
practices" (Ellis and Moore 1974, 33). "The Spartan ideals were those of
the noble warrior: austerity, discipline, the comradeship of arms, devotion to the state, and above all commitment to heroic deeds and a love of
glory" (Franke 1999, 69). It is no accident that the central device in the
insignia of the USMA is the silhouette of an ancient Greek military hel-
met.

Unlike in the civilian world, where standards are constantly chimeri-
cal and unclear, standards at the USMA are rigid. Failure in two classes
leads to expulsion; a recruit who fails all three chances for physical fitness is sent packing. Tests of military ability are similarly strict.

There is an official prayer at the United States Military Academy,
part of which runs: "...Strengthen and increase our admiration for honest
dealing and clean thinking... Encourage us in our endeavor to live above
the common level of life...." (Lipsky 2003, 15).[2] This exemplifies the
common desire of both fundamentalist religions and militaries to live a
life that is inaccessible to the greater mass of humanity. A special, chosen life; "many are called, few are chosen," as the recruiting slogan went.

Underlying the Thayer system is an assumption that allies and enemies are characterized by their adherence to a similar system—even
though their allegiance is to a different nation, the standards of "honest
dealing and clean thinking" and the brotherhood of military life are held
to the same standards. It has often been stated that religious adherents—
and particularly fundamentalist sects—have an easier time relating to
devout members of a rival religion than they do relating to a secular

member of their own. Similarly, the soldier will often relate better to an enemy soldier than to a civilian of his own nation.

Between members of opposing professional militaries, there has often been noted a very real, if often grudging, respect. In the act of killing an enemy, per order or by necessity, outright wrath is comparatively rare, except perhaps in the heat of battle. Deindividuation is common, and probably necessary—enemies are seen not as individuals, but as a representation of the system within which they originate. Dehumanization, however, is less common, and represents a particularly acute form of wrath saved for an enemy who kills outside the ethical and moral sanctions of uniform military codes of conduct. It is also a signal that the control mechanisms have failed, particularly when the dehumanization becomes indiscriminate.

The Second World War was fought in the Pacific with a ferocity unmatched in the European theater. Much of this had to do with terrain, but much also had to do with feelings of deep animosity between the opposing troops. Unadulterated racism was severely compounded by a mutual feeling of violation of military codes. Japanese treatment of prisoners, and their refusal to accept surrender or to surrender themselves, all contributed to an atmosphere in which Americans felt they were fighting against a "subhuman" enemy—Japanese soldiers, interviewed during and after the war, reflected a similar disdain of "dishonorable" American soldiers that was not present in most of the European theater (except after the discoveries of the concentration camps).

The historical record shows comparatively little record of hate from the members of one professional military towards the members of another, but documents intense disdain from professional military towards paramilitary and militia forces, or regular military forces that break the bounds of legitimacy and thus cross the line into atrocity (both humanitarian atrocity and the atrocity of apostasy). The inherently immoral character of these latter is evidenced by their repudiation of accepted codes (although these codes have changed over the centuries, the existence of codes has remained a constant) and lack of allegiance to a recognized source of legitimacy—combined with their willingness to endanger, and possibly destroy, the faithful. A statement from a

Legionnaire of the Legion d'Etrangere (Foreign Legion) on atrocity seen during action in Rwanda states,

> There was an atmosphere of chaos on the streets. We could hear the shouts and screams of men, enemies of the Tutsis, being tortured and then killed. I saw a body being thrown onto the street from a house. It was followed by half a dozen lightly armed men; once again I refuse to describe them as soldiers (Parris 2004, 224).

Instead of responding with the dispassion and respect given to an enemy dictated by the Legion's Code of Conduct (see Appendix 1), the Legionnaire goes on to state that he and his unit hoped for any excuse to kill these non-soldiers; however, their mission allowed them only to fire in self-defense. This is a case of dehumanization, which must be recognized by whatever name it appears; in indigenous languages, the name a people applies to themselves is almost invariably some form of "the people," "human beings," or some other combination that implies a differentiation between chosen and not-chosen, real and false. "Soldier" here is the indigenous term for "real," and equated with "human." The speaker has made a statement ("...once again I refuse to describe them as soldiers.") not of deindividuation, but of dehumanization. He is prevented from killing these not-soldiers only by the strength of his own control mechanisms and adherence to his own code.

Within the sanctioned boundaries of mutually recognizable hermetic conceptual frameworks, there is no institutional repercussion for killing, as long as the act conforms to the boundaries of the sacred rather than the profane. That is, as long as the boundaries are recognized as the "rules of warfare" within the Uniform Code of Military Justice (UCMJ) for Americans, the Geneva Conventions, and other similar protocols governing, for example, what type of weapon it is permissible to use against what type of target, how one defines non-combatants and how one treats prisoners.

The UCMJ, legitimized by the government of the United States of America, is the final authority that will tell a soldier whom it is proper to kill, what kinds of actions are justified, and why he is absolved of moral responsibility for carrying out such acts. It will tell him whom he is *not* authorized to kill, and in what circumstances, as well as what exactly will happen to him if he violates the Code and leaves the fold. The more closely and less interpretively a soldier follows this code, the better off everyone will be. To stray too far from doctrine is effectively mutiny or barratry, minor military equivalents of the Protestant schism or the current debate over an openly gay Bishop within the Episcopalian Church, and is punishable in the field by death—so that no competing source of justification may exist. The semi-permeable cultural structure that supports this, introduced in Basic Training, is constantly reinforced.

Nevertheless, even within the larger confines of a given military, there are groups such as snipers and special operations units—those used for "unconventional warfare"—that occupy a very liminal place in their universe. While powerful, useful, and operating under the same flag—and thus on the same team—these units are quite often mistrusted and held at arms reach by the "real soldiers," because they do not operate or kill according to the same rules of engagement and thus cannot be fully trusted.

To legitimize and give authority to such rules, a single, ultimate source for justification, retribution and absolution must be established. For a fundamentalist Christian, the single (and final) source is God, and His revelation the Bible (although "Christian" is hardly a monolithic concept, and the question of which edition, interpretation, interpreter, etc. of the Bible is of obvious import). For the soldier, this single source is the UCMJ and the concept of national sovereignty. According to the UCMJ, killing that is sanctioned by the governing authority is not only acceptable but "necessary," "right," or "good." This is predicated upon the premise that nation-states have the authority to make war and order soldiers to kill.

Of course, the military professional is subject to more stringent control mechanisms relating to violence compared to the non-military civilian. One reason for this is that violence is included in the lexicon of permissible and encouraged military action, which it is not in the civilian world—and thus the intellectual terminology for describing, understanding and mitigating it is necessarily richer in the military realm. In the creation of a soldier, violence must be incubated and encouraged to grow in the right circumstances and in the right directions and degrees—but having been so encouraged, it must also have strong checks and balances to guard against its misuse or loss of control. The ultimate source for these checks and balances is the sovereign nation (or defended ideal of a sovereign nation) and the idea of service to a higher ideal—the "life above the common life" referred to in the USMA prayer. Or similarly, in the Foreign Legion's Paratrooper's Prayer, "Give me God what you have left/ give me what others don't want/ but also give me courage, strength and faith."[3]

Of primacy to the soldier is the existence of a mission as a value-rational action. The soldier is expected to complete the mission despite discomfort, pain, or risk to personal survival. It would seem irrational for a civilian to continue a hike in the woods despite a twisted ankle; it would seem irrational for a soldier to quit a road march despite the same twisted ankle. It would place a civilian somewhat outside the pale of "civilized behavior" to spend extended periods of time in the same hardened circumstances in which it would place a soldier outside the pale not to endure. According to the Foreign Legion's code of conduct, "A mission, once given to you, becomes sacred. You will accomplish it at whatever cost." (See full text in Appendix 1.)

Soldiers, especially infantrymen, must be aggressive—but controllably so. In the atmosphere of basic training or combat—both concentrated microcosms within the range of military experience—arguments are common and sharp. If soldiers are overly aggressive, the unit's integrity and cohesiveness suffers, and atrocity is risked. If not aggressive enough, the soldiers won't fight with the necessary strength and decisiveness. Motivations for aggression and violence are altered situationally: the more abstract the situation (that is, classes about the purpose of the military, and the soldier's purpose within it), the more abstract the motivation... country, duty and honor.

The more acute the situation (such as, specific range trainings, exercises and the like, or actual combat), the more specific the motivation. You fight to keep yourself and your teammates alive; if you don't, you and they will die. Motivation is thus shifting and tailored so that it is never out of place or context. Violence is tied not only to killing but also to life; some of the justification for it will thus always be a positive benefit to personal emotional ties—"whom have I saved through this act of violence"—as opposed to the more nebulous and potentially questionable justification of ideology. In the context of belonging within a structure that is built by fighting units, the culture of that unit will tend to trump all others and be all but impossible to resist.

We currently see in the news some of the results of what happens when the boundaries between the prescribed center and the outside world are breached. Coalition forces in Iraq are partnered with a very high number of private security forces and non-military contractors, hired as experts in such fields as security, interrogation and intelligence-gathering. Private security personnel have fired shots in combat in efforts to protect military personnel (the distinction—or lack thereof—between "private security forces" and "mercenaries" is worth pursuing, but again, the subject for another paper), and military personnel are nervously confused as to what exactly the rules of engagement are relating to these private security forces.[4]

Interrogation contractors have been present at the Abu Ghraib prison and questions have arisen as to how much sway these personnel—not technically covered by either the UCMJ or the Geneva Conventions governing treatment of prisoners—had in the direction of regular military forces within the prison. The chain of command and delegation of responsibility are quite blurred in these cases, with resultant problems.

There are in fact cases in which orders legally must be questioned or refused. It would be illegal according to the UCMJ or Geneva Conventions, for example, to obey an order to kill unarmed civilians or a combatant who has already surrendered. The ability of any individual soldier to muster the strength to resist such an order, especially in the crucible of wartime, is not always the equal to the training to obey. One famous example of successful resistance stemmed from the incident in the My Lai massacre in Vietnam.

Helicopter pilot Hugh Thompson and door gunner Lawrence Colburn, circling over My Lai, saw what was happening and landed between the fleeing villagers and Lt. Calley's oncoming troops—with guns trained not on the Vietnamese, but on the American soldiers. Both men were awarded the Soldier's Medal (in 1998) for preventing an abhorrent slaughter, but the accolade came only decades after the incident had passed. However—the medal went to two soldiers who aimed their weapons on apostate troops of their own army; the court-martial went to the unit commander who gave an illegal order to kill in wartime.

In Abu Ghraib, confusion existed as to whether military or civilian personnel issued orders to exert the sort of pressure we have unfortunately seen on prisoners in the pursuit of confessions and information. Similar confusion emerged when guards in that prison apparently undertook—whether they were ordered to or not—jobs that should belong to intelligence/interrogation personnel. One result of this infiltration of confusion into the ordered center of military command is that aggression and violence become increasingly difficult to control.

One of the control mechanisms for the sanctioned aggression of the soldier is, perhaps ironically, the *semi*-permeable nature of the boundary between the military and society at large. What this boundary accomplishes is a sort of grounding, by which the soldier is reminded of the object of the service and self-sacrifice of his role. When the boundary becomes too impermeable, the result can be a Praetorian Guard, en entity that takes morality and action into its own hands, acting to control rather than serve. If one of the major binding agents of military culture—the sense of service to a worthy society and nation—is removed, disaster can result.

Consider for example, a statement made by a former U.S. Marine to one of the authors of this chapter that "nobody in this country sends their kids into the military anymore. We Marines feel like we aren't supported or appreciated by the rest of America, we do this and they don't care or they don't like us or what we're doing anyway, which means we're basically off there on our own, and getting pretty angry about it."[5] This is bolstered by a statement made to that same author by a company First Sergeant in the U.S. Army as the company was preparing to be dismissed for a holiday leave: "When you go out there, remember that *they* will not understand you, they will not know you, they will not like you, they will not recognize you. You will have to be a bridge between them and us."[6] The *they* in this case is the rest of the U.S., and the sense of division is obvious.

It has been a historical truism that religious fervor, once aroused, must be treated with the utmost caution—for if the fervent group feels betrayed, they will tend toward extreme retaliation. Israel spent decades inculcating an extreme Jewish nationalism in the settler movement as a tool for strategic expansion and defense; when Prime Minister Rabin began to move towards peace, "threatening" to pull the settlers out of the occupied territories, he was assassinated by one of the settlers. Osama bin Laden turned his ire against the Saudi government when, after years of support, that government changed direction and allowed U.S. troops to base on "holy ground."

It should be noted that groups such as the U.S. Marines and the French Foreign Legion swear allegiance *to their corps first*—and the nations they serve second. There is historical precedent for elite military forces, when they felt that their service and sacrifice was wasted on an unworthy ruler, to follow the pattern of betrayed fundamentalists and turn on the erstwhile source of their own legitimacy. The binding force of the unit outweighs even that of service to national sovereignty.

There is very real danger in this—and a rich historical precedent for groups united in religious or nationalistic fervor to turn violently on social hosts by whom they feel betrayed. As an example, witness the Israeli settler movement, purposely inculcated with a combination of religious and nationalistic fervor for strategic purposes; it was an Israeli settler who assassinated Rabin in 1995 in retaliation for perceived Israeli betrayal through the Oslo Accords, and at the time of writing this chapter, the settler movement is again coiling in response to the planned Gaza pullout.

While it would be alarmist to say that the U.S. Marine Corps is on the verge of going the way of the Praetorian Guard, it would be a grave mistake to forget the historical tendency of fervent hermetic groups to react badly upon feeling betrayed by their parent societies or clients. Policymakers would do well to listen carefully to statements such as those recounted above that indicate a widening perception of "us" and "them" and an increase in enclave mentality and feelings of abandonment or betrayal within military units—particularly elite units.

The House of Pain

Powerful images and icons are deployed in military and religious systems as symbols of timeless messages. The display of a national flag, for example, implies not only a loyalty to, pride in, or love of that particular nation, but also devotion to a sovereign nation-state and the supra-concept that nation-states are an entity that embodies such legitimacy. Icons are often used to separate emotion-ideas from dispassionate inspection[7]; the Christian's cross, the Marine's "Globe and Anchor."[8] The destruction of a fundamental symbol, one which has become, in the semiotical lexicon an "index symbol"—say a cross, or a national flag—is thus in both cases raised in import from vandalism to desecration, an act of sacrilege, of repudiation, or at the very least a most jarring re-examination of the symbol.

The word "sacred" must be understood as not simply relating to something literally "holy," but more broadly to anything held as exemplary and mythologically true by the devotees, a thing whose unassailable "rightness" is essential to that devotee's sense of identity.[9] During the ongoing debate about flag burning in the United States, we have had an opportunity to witness the "sacredness" of secular national symbols intrinsic to not only the military worldview, but even to the worldview of a broad national culture.

The system of military symbols gives meaning to those experiences that would be disturbing or anathema to civilians. From the moment Basic Training begins, the symbol-system functions as a major source of information for trainees. Unit patches draw attention not only to the accomplishment of the individual wearer, but also to the accomplishments of the military units to which a soldier is attached. A patch from the 101st Airborne, or the 82nd Airborne (two of the U.S. Army's most legendary units) speaks of the presence of past deeds as well as current prowess and future victory. School badges—Airborne wings, Pathfinder, SCUBA, etc.—provide not only a platform for showing ones' accomplishments, but a signifier of connections to the history and power of a school or unit.

Military institutions seek to remove ambiguity from their language. Thus the military provides its own systems of pronunciation, spelling, counting and conveying information, as well as strictly defining how one speaks to an inferior or superior (and by inference, that there is such a thing as inferiors and superiors). Language systems frame the thought by which one relates to violence and feelings about violence. Language systems also frame the ideas about violence, about heroes and cowards, legal war and just war. It may have been a joke when one U.S. military commander referred to retreat as "retrograde action," but his use of that terminology also had cognitive force.

Trainees are provided with small stages to which they can aspire, small successes that make the duration of training easier to bear. Just by receiving uniforms while still in civilian clothes makes recruits feel that they have begun the process of becoming soldiers. Nametags appear on the right chest pocket, and the "US ARMY" tag is displayed on the left. Initially, those symbols are stenciled, while "real" soldiers have embroidered ones. New recruits can observe the unit patches they see on the Drill Sergeants' shoulders, acutely aware that their own shoulders are bare. Patches also denote special training: airborne qualifications, air-assault qualifications, pathfinder, combat-experienced infantry, and the like. Not until they have these things will recruits feel that they have become "real" soldiers.

The cadences sung throughout Basic Training prod this process along. "*Let's go out and kill some commies... turn around and rape their mommies... stab their babies in the back... put 'em on a roasting rack... slap 'em with some barbeque... makes 'em tender and easy to chew...*" [remembered by David Alpher from experience.] A trainee can run along, thinking "I don't mean it, I don't think that way," but he is there and chanting it with the rest as he pounds along the road. Change occurs by complicity, therefore the trainee must be something other than purely "himself." He is aware that if he *really* wanted to, he could stop running, sit down by the side of the road and refuse. There's really nothing they could do to him at this point in his initiation, except dismiss him, but he's not doing that. With every cadence, the new recruit becomes a little more of a soldier and a little less his own. The individual within doesn't think like a killer, but the individual is complicit by his participation in the initiation. He begins to become a soldier, some other thing that is a part of history and the structure around him... shared presence equals shared responsibility.

Each trainee, indistinguishable except by skin color in uniform and without hair, could be any or all of the others. The burden of any action is lessened by being shared. The burden of thoughts that run contrary to every childhood education is mitigated by making those thoughts universal and shared; in *this* place, *this* is normal. *"When I get to hell... the Devil's gonna say... how'd you make your living boy... how'd you earn your pay... and I'll reply with a fist to his face... I made my living putting souls to waste... gimme a knife and I'll cut my way to heaven... gimme an axe and I'll hack my way down..."*

No officer or officer trainee—legally bound to "gentlemanly behavior" within the official constructs of the military—would be singing cadences about rape, infanticide and cannibalism. Such "ungentlemanly" acts would of course fall far outside the realm of "acceptable combat" as well as per military doctrine for *any* "real soldier."

It is further interesting to note, as a point of texture within these arguments, that in the American military, officers are not allowed to be interrogators. Interrogation may necessitate lying to a prisoner, and officers have taken an oath to be "officers and gentlemen." A gentleman may not lie, and is both legally and morally prohibited from doing so within a military context; therefore, officers may not be interrogators.

Initially, breaking down old patterns is as important as building up of new ones, and the two processes weave in and out of each other. To instill in the young recruit a new persona, Basic Training imposes a symbol system. Unit affiliation becomes more important than civilian identity. A ranking system dominates the social landscape, although for the trainees, rank is invisible *within* the group (among the enlisted in Basic Training—this is not true of cadets in a military academy). The land itself becomes "terrain;" fields, woods and meadows become interlocking areas of cover, exposure and concealment.

Not only are the meanings of symbols deliberately unintelligible to most outsiders, their existence can escape attention. The implications of the way a hat is folded, how sleeves are rolled, or which type of boot a soldier wears are less obvious to the outsider—although they carry a freight of meaning to the insider. Unit patches on the shoulders and the badges denoting special training, for example, are more overt. Rank designators are important to learn quickly, for obvious reasons. On dress uniforms (as opposed to BDUs, or "Battle Dress Uniforms"), there is a "salad bar" of multi-colored ribbons on the left breast. Each one denotes a duty assignment or a medal; achievements are worn in public display. In this way, each person can place himself within the system exactly; relations to others are never a mystery.

A veteran soldier of thirty years will still relate back to the experiences of the first weeks of training when beset by feelings of indecision or uncertainty. Basic Training is designed to create an "ideal world," in which all rules and structures are presumably absolute; and that initial, "pure" training will resurface time and time again.

> West Point is a full-immersion experience, what the administration calls a 'twenty-four-hour, seven-day-a-week military environment.' Cadets don't get summer vacations. Until firstie [sophomore] year, they are required to be in uniform at all times. A plebe [freshman] hitting the bathroom for a small-hours pee must slip on Army-issue sweats before stepping into a barracks hallway (Lipsky 2003, 9).

New soldiers or academy cadets are deliberately given a structured, pre-made identity that is declared to be superior to, and more valuable than, their old one. This new identity promotes the self-fulfillment of service. Through this new identity, they acquire a power beyond that of civilians. This power comes part in parcel with a sense of worth over and above those "cold, timid souls," (to borrow Theodore Roosevelt's phrase), which is tied irrevocably to the sense of service; or at the very least, to the idea that they have neither dishonored themselves nor their unit through their actions. Honor is defined as the quality of adherence to a set of ideals and code of ethics. True soldiers are not strong *against* the weak... they are strong *in defense* of the weak, and taught to destroy without compunction those who misuse the power they have been given, power that is granted for a purpose, a higher cause.

One of the mainstays of military training is the cult of shared suffering. The physical, mental, and emotional deprivations common to indoctrination into both military and religious systems convey transcendent meanings and are thus beyond condemnation unless they violate a set of *internal* precepts not common to the rest of humankind. Stoicism, in both traditions becomes a virtue as opposed to a simply survival trait.

By the time they complete their training (which in both cases is viewed as the beginning of a longer journey and belonging—not as an ending), recruits have acquired experiences that few people will ever know or understand. Just as a religious ascetic renounces worldly things for a life of privation, tied irrevocably to a culture and group eternally removed from the rest of a society, so too a soldier who suffers in the mud, the rain, the heat, the dust, the sleepless nights, and the endless fear and tension will forever be linked to everyone who has ever become a soldier in the same manner. The shared trials of training or combat are rewarded and justified by a sense of service to a "higher purpose."

> Just stand in the middle of Fort Bragg in the middle of the day—there's such a sense of *urgency*. Airplanes are flying over. Everybody's camoed up, going out to train. Artillery rounds are being shot on the range; the windows rattle...at Bragg I realized what real brotherhood was like—kind of a fire that melds people together. You're doing tough, challenging, dangerous things, for a good reason. It's just an awesome feeling... and that's exactly what I was feeling: part of something that is big and powerful and inherently good—and I believe the Army is inherently good. You're not chasing money or anything like that. I think it's a noble profession. That's why they call it the service. I literally would wake up in the morning... when you see U.S. Army, it's a good feeling. It's a good feeling to be part of that organization (Lipsky 2003, 12).

Each stage of the training provides further segregation and tighter bonds to circumstances and comrades. "We all bleed OD [olive drab] green," the saying goes in the military. The infantry, however, is a separate case—the "real" military. The entire military structure exists to support them, and they are reminded of that at every opportunity; pilots bomb targets, "softening" them so that the infantry may occupy ground more efficiently and safely. Artillery pounds the guns that might cut them down, intelligence tells them where to go, cooks feed them, the Navy transports them across the water. Nobody else in the Army goes through the same training that they do. Throughout each branch of the military, this pattern of differentiation and competition is repeated.

The opening phase of Basic Training is known as "total control." Trainees are never away from the presence of the Drill Sergeants unless asleep or in the bathroom, and even then they are close by. Except for a few hours on Sunday when those who want to go are marched to church, every hour of every day is ordered by the Drill Sergeants. This phase, for non-infantry, normally lasts two weeks. It is longer in the infantry, but even the five battalions of infantry training are further sub-divided and set in competition with each other. In the "House of Pain," (the 2/58 regiment) this initial phase lasts for five weeks. Trainees in this regiment are constantly reminded that they are the House of Pain. After Basic Training, they are told again and again that they will never be the same as people who have not experienced this training, including the rest of the infantry.

In the House of Pain, civilian clothes are locked away, watches are taken. Trainees are told what time it is if it is necessary for them to know. They have no access to magazines, newspapers, radio, TV, telephones, or anything that would provide them contact with the rest of the world except for the mail, which cannot legally be intercepted.

There is only one book to read, known as the "smart book." It details all the minutiae a soldier must know: weapons maintenance and technical details, squad and individual movement and tactics, marksmanship, rules and regulations, military etiquette, and always, the meanings of symbols. Recruits are known collectively as "troop" or by any of a list of epithets; if some individual reference is needed, recruits are called by their number. Travel from the Starship—what the barracks buildings are known as—to any of the various ranges where the recruits train is either by pre-dawn march or by means of a nearly windowless truck appropriately called a "cattle car." Either way, they can't see where they're going and the landscape remains a mystery. The only point of reference, the only place that can be considered familiar, is the Starship and the symbolic and cultural system around them, an anchor when all else is disrupted. When in garrison (at the Starship), trainees move at attention wherever they go, and run unless specifically marched at a cadence.

From the first day, House of Pain trainees chant cadences when they march: "One, two, three, four, train... to kill. One, two, three, four, kill... we will." (This is replaced, in other infantry battalions, with "one, two, three, four, train... to *win*. One, two, three, four, *win*... we will.") The constant subdividing among units is largely functional. During the Vietnam war, Ranger units[10] were removed from their place alongside "regular" infantry troops because it was felt they demoralized the ones who did not live up to their rarified Ranger status, and the "real soldiers"—often not on good terms with the liminal special operations troops—were rarely sorry to see them go. The simultaneous presence of two separate "forms" of military personality and methods of waging war was not conducive to controlling of the troops.

The Rangers were therefore separated and aloof, held up variously as giants among giants or as "fringe whackos" who did things no sane person would even consider. In the former incarnation, they provided something to which the regular troops could aspire. In the latter, the contrast of their extremism produced a sense of reassuring normalcy in the "regular" infantry. In neither case were they available for close examination by the general military population. In Basic Training, a fringe group segregated from the larger body of infantry trainees provides the same balance as in the example cited above: the House of Pain derives its motivation and cohesion from being the toughest of the tough; the other four units draw their strength and cohesion from having a fringe group nearby—but not too nearby—who seems, they hear, worse off than they are.

There are parallels to be made here. The relationship between enclave fundamentalist groups[11] to the mainstream faiths from which they spring is an apt analogy; liminality is not a one-way accusation, but a dialectical one. Similarly, special operations troops often regard themselves as the most pure form of the ideal of soldiering, however liminal they may appear to the mainstream from which they spring.

Mythic Time

The notion of good violence is framed through categories of heroic figures and agents of evil, and draws upon comparisons to the eschatological myths of fundamentalists. Military training is anchored in some sacred "truths" of primordial origins. The origin is generally a mythic war, not necessarily a specific one, neither singular nor locatable in one place in time. Rather, this mythic war recurs in all generations with new heroes and new creators (seen as supernatural beings). Heroes who define the ideals *of* the temporal world are created and reinforced through engagements *in* the temporal world, and contemporary soldiers draw power and motivation not only from their mythic-symbolic connection to the heroic past, but also by the possibility that they themselves can become new avatars.[12]

The dismantled limitations of time and space in the mythic war provide resources for overcoming the fear of giving one's life for the cause. Military training is a way of achieving a very real kind of sacred immortality—not immortality literally, but immortality of the soul after the physical body has died[13]. Through shared training, shared experience and shared suffering, a soldier does not merely emulate those past, but becomes them; an avatar, temporary in this body, eternal in this spirit.

"We do not only have weapons,/ but the devil marches with us./ Ha! Ha! Ha! Ha! Ha! Ha! Ha!/ Because our elders of the Legion/ are fighting there, we follow in their footsteps./ For this destiny of knights,/ honour, loyalty./ We are proud to belong/ to the 2eme REP [parachute regiment]."[14] Note here the transposition of time; "elders" of the legion, images of past heroes, that precede the current soldier into battle, present following in the footsteps of a past that also exists and has effect in the future.

General George Patton wrote at various points of negating his fear of death through the belief that his was a reincarnated soul, always to be a soldier. Death was unimportant, for his lot would be the same in the next life. He drew strength from his position not as an individual, although his individual accomplishments were his to claim, but from his position as a temporary link within a continuum, a facet of an eternal being. [15] Or, in another example:

> Each U.S. Marine, past and present, has entered more than just the Brotherhood of Marines. He has become, and will always remain, part of a mystical fellowship of valor. He must comply with hallowed rituals. He must conform to an uncompromising code of honor, discipline, and personal integrity. Commitment to his Corps—that's right, *his* Corps—and moral strength become the norm. Throughout the history of the Corps, these virtues have sustained Marine Warriors during the chaos and perils of combat (Sturkey 2001, 1).

A soldier draws power and justification from knowing a history of sacred events, from knowing the origins of military rituals, assimilating into an unbroken symbolic pattern of memory, and thus becoming virtually indistinguishable from any element of its past, present or future. This assimilation provides an individual destiny and pattern within the larger whole, a necessary element of maintaining motivation both in religions and in armies. The pain of the afterlife, for the ancient Greeks, was not active punishment, but the inability to affect the world of the living; irrelevance. It is this that indoctrination into a military system offers escape from, and this that takes the form of immortality of the soul.

"Chronological time," as viewed by the general population, is time in which each given moment occurs in a transitive sequence of units, and the infinite series of moments that preceded it vanished in their turn, forever lost except in representation. Mythic time, on the other hand, contains moments drawn from primordial sources that can be replicated in the events of "ordinary" chronological time. Thus, any given chronological moment can be viewed in relation to a primordial or mythic event, as opposed to being seen as a temporal event. Successive wars are akin to primordial "origin myths," and are reiterations of the original—that is, the first war, the first soldier. Rather than an account that purports to outline the creation of the universe, origination myths instead relay the beginnings of specific things within the greater cosmogony, the time when heroes performed their great deeds. A time of origin is considered a "strong" time "precisely because it was in some sort the 'receptacle' for a new creation" (Eliade 1963, 34).

The primordial history referred to here is the history of the events and actions experienced and performed by those past members of the group that the individual has now joined by becoming a soldier, providing a foundation for becoming "supernatural" in the temporal world. What those supernatural characters did, can be done again—but only by those born into the "authentic" life[16]. Indoctrination into any hermetic system includes the taking of oaths that mark official acceptance of an unbroken line and the crossing of a boundary from one life into the next.

There is a sense of continuation within the system of an essential part of oneself even after the individual has left the system or died. The overt display of personal symbols—"salad bars," unit insignia and the like—preserves a sense of immortality to which the individual is attached. Even after leaving the service, individuals remain part of that ongoing history, which in turn remains a part of them. Companies may come and go, governments rise and fall, but the soldier is eternal.

The soldier is in the position of not having to reject the irreversibility of time in order to access the worlds of Gods and heroes. Mythic war, occurring in transcendent time, recurs endlessly in chronological time—that much is sadly certain. Military rituals prepare soldiers for its re-emergence while reinforcing the presence and shield of the sacred. "Freedom is not free. The tree of liberty must be watered from time to time with the blood of patriots." This quote from Thomas Jefferson illustrates a conception of warfare as an act of regeneration even in the midst of its destructive effects.

Each successive war is a "baptism of fire" (no accident in that language) for new soldiers. Parris points out that the time between the origin and the present (considering time historically) is "neither 'strong' nor 'significant,' (except, of course, for the periods during which the primordial Time has been re-enacted)" (Parris 2004 236-237). In light of this, there is no mystery why soldiers—in particular, the infantry—who have NOT seen war first-hand feel such a disassociation, a sense of incompleteness and inadequacy with their compatriots who have. War is a crucible in which the human spirit is put to one of its ultimate tests, and the spirit of a soldier meets its *specific destiny*. To be denied the opportunity to perform in war leaves a soldier with a profound sense of loss. In the hermetic context, the essential being of their military identity is threatened, never actualized in their lifetime. They feel they have not been baptized, that they retain the smell of the profane.

> After the claustrophobic hell of the jungle and the excitement of Rwanda, there had been a creeping sense of anti-climax for some time… From talking to older Legionnaires, I had to class myself as fortunate to have seen so much in a relatively short career. Some Legionnaires had never been off [the island of] Calvi and the only action they had seen was in the bars of their adopted town" (Parris 2004, 236-237).

Eschatological myths project the time of beginnings to a future. Destruction is inevitably intertwined with new hope and new beginnings, and each new beginning carries within it the seed of its own destruction. In the new thing is power and perfection; the baptized is called reborn and blameless in the eyes of the Lord; the soldier has burned away his past and gained a new self. It is this baptism under fire that draws upon techniques of advanced religious training.[17]

In some cases this shedding of self is more literal than in others—in the French Foreign Legion, for example, an inductee symbolically casts away his civilian name upon enlistment. Fulfill of the obligation to the Legion can replace, if the Legionnaire wishes, the old self with a new one and French citizenship. Monks and nuns, upon taking their vows, often take a new name. In any case, "the individual's return to the origin is conceived as an opportunity for renewing and regenerating the existence of him who undertakes it" (Eliade 1963, 79).

So, moral absolution for an act of "good violence" is achieved when certain social encounters in the mundane world of human beings mimic interactions among idealized figures in a transcendent realm. Even "dying for the cause" can be proof of one's sacred identity defined by categories from the narrative structure of a sacred myth.[18] This conference of sacredness is especially meaningful given conditions of mental, emotional and physical deprivations that both the fundamentalist and the soldier deliberately undertake.[19]

To the faithful, the world within hermetic cultures offers more than the usual rewards available to the general population.[20] The military myth offers individuals far more than a livelihood; it offers purpose and meaning in life, and the hope or dream of becoming supernatural—the hero reborn.[21] The actions of soldiers within war become the exemplary models for all other soldiers, present, and future—either positively or negatively. Judas Iscariot and Benedict Arnold might find something in common in the latter sense. Audie Murphy[22] and St. Peter, the unbelievers turned faithful, might find commonality in the former.

Part of the lure of both military and religious hermetic centers is the opportunity to lift the common person to the realm of the extraordinary, offering transcendence to the faithful above the directionlessness and opacity of the "regular" world into a meaningful and illuminated place. Through the absorption of a system of symbol and language, a soldier or religious fundamentalist achieves more meaningful communication than he could ever have outside that framework. The randomness of joint action in the larger culture, whose causes and results so often seem pointless, misdirected or counterproductive, in this place, this center, become ordered, directed and productive. The reward is fellowship, community—"We few, we happy few... we band of brothers," as Shakespeare said, describing those who would fight together on St. Crispin's Day. There are many mirrors to this "band of brothers" within religious communities. By taking on this mantle of meaning and expression, a road to the transcendence of everyday meaninglessness is revealed.

Appendix 1

The Code of Honor of the Legion d'Etrangere

1. You are a volunteer serving France faithfully and with honour.
2. Every Legionnaire is your brother in arms, irrespective of nationality, race or creed. You will prove this by according him the

    unwavering loyalty that will always bind members of the same family.

3. Respectful of the Legion's traditions and honouring your superiors, discipline and comradeship are your strengths, courage and loyalty your virtues.

4. Proud of your status as a Legionnaire, you will display this pride in your turn-out, always impeccable, in your behaviour, ever worthy and modest, and in your living quarters, always tidy.

5. As an elite soldier you will train vigorously. You will maintain your body at a peak of physical fitness and your weapon as if it were your most prized possession.

6. A mission, once given to you, becomes sacred. You will accomplish it at whatever cost.

7. In combat you will act dispassionately and without anger. You will respect the vanquished enemy. You will *never* abandon your dead, wounded or arms. [emphasis in the original]

The Paratrooper's Prayer (also from the Legion d'Etrangere)

God, give me what you have left,
give me what no one ever requests.

I am not asking you for a rest,
nor tranquility,
neither that of the soul nor the body.

I am not asking for wealth,
nor success, or even health.

You are asked for all these so often,
that you must have none left.

Give me God what you do have left,
give me what no one wants.

I seek insecurity and disquiet,
I seek torment and combat,
and God, give them to me indefinitely,
that I am sure to have them always,
because I won't always have the courage to ask you.

Give me God what you have left,
give me what others don't want,
but also give me courage, strength and faith.

Chantes de 2eme REP (Regiment Etranger de Parachutistes)
(Cadence of the second Foreign Paratroop Regiment)

The Legion marches towards the front,
singing we follow,
heirs to its traditions,
we are with her.

We are the men of the assault troops,
soldiers of the old Legion,
tomorrow brandishing our flags
as victors we will parade.

We do not only have weapons,
but the devil marches with us.
Ha! Ha! Ha! Ha! Ha! Ha! Ha!
Because our elders of the Legion
are fighting there, we follow in their footsteps.

For this destiny of knights,
honour, loyalty.
We are proud to belong
to the 2eme REP

Appendix 2

West Point Cadets Prayer
by Clayton Wheat

O God, our Father, thou Searcher of men's hearts, help us to draw near to thee in sincerity and truth. May our religion be filled with gladness and may our worship of thee be natural.

Strengthen and increase our admiration for honest dealing and clean thinking, and suffer not our hatred of hypocrisy and pre- tense ever to diminish.

Encourage us in our endeavor to live above the common level of life.

Make us to choose the harder right instead of the easier wrong, and never to be content with a half truth when the whole can be won.

Endow us with courage that is born of loyalty to all that is noble and worthy, that scorns to compromise with vice and injustice and knows no fear when truth and right are in jeopardy.

Guard us against flippancy and irreverence in the sacred things of life.

Grant us new ties of friendship and new opportunities of service.

Kindle our hearts in fellowship with those of a cheerful countenance, and soften our hearts with sympathy for those who sorrow and suffer.

Help us to maintain the honor of the Corps untarnished and unsullied and to show forth in our lives the ideals of West Point in doing our duty to thee and to our Country.

All of which we ask in the name of the Great Friend and Master of men.

Rules of Engagement
Joint Task Force for Somalia Relief Operations

Ground Forces
Nothing in these rules of engagement limits our right to take appropriate action to defend yourself and your unit.

1. You have the right to use force to defend yourself against attacks or threats of attack.
2. Hostile fire may be returned effectively and promptly to stop a hostile act.
3. When U.S. forces are attacked by unarmed hostile elements, mobs, and/or rioters, U.S. forces should use the minimum force necessary under the circumstances and proportional to the threat.
4. You may not seize the property of others to accomplish your mission.
5. Detention of civilians is authorized for security reasons or in self-defense.

Remember
The United States is not at war.
Treat all persons with dignity and respect.
Use minimum force to carry out the mission.
Always be prepared to act in self-defense.

[Note some of the problematic incongruities within this document, issued as a laminated card to U.S. troops on a peacekeeping mission: soldiers who have been trained on a platform of "maximum violence" (an axiom used within the U.S. Army) are told they are "not at war" and are being instructed to use "minimum force;" the rules do not specify how, as in point 2, troops can be on a peacekeeping mission and also be forbidden to use force in order to stop a hostile act that is not aimed at they themselves; the card also does not provide instructions relating to ambiguous situations in which a soldier may be confronted with, for example, a child carrying a firearm—a sadly common occurrence in this day and age. The ordered center of the soldier is being blurred with the "outside world," with dangerous ambiguities as a result.]

Appendix 3

THROUGH A GLASS, DARKLY
by Gen. George S. Patton, Jr.

Through the travail of the ages,
Midst the pomp and toil of war,
Have I fought and strove and perished
Countless times upon this star.

In the form of many people
In all panoplies of time
Have I seen the luring vision
Of the Victory Maid, sublime.

I have battled for fresh mammoth,
I have warred for pastures new,
I have listed to the whispers
When the race trek instinct grew.
I have known the call to battle
In each changeless changing shape
From the high souled voice of conscience
To the beastly lust for rape.

I have sinned and I have suffered,
Played the hero and the knave;
Fought for belly, shame, or country,
And for each have found a grave.

I cannot name my battles

For the visions are not clear,
Yet, I see the twisted faces
And I feel the rending spear.

Perhaps I stabbed our Savior
In His sacred helpless side.
Yet, I've called His name in blessing
When after times I died.

In the dimness of the shadows
Where we hairy heathens warred,
I can taste in thought the lifeblood;
We used teeth before the sword.

While in later clearer vision
I can sense the coppery sweat,
Feel the pikes grow wet and slippery
When our Phalanx, Cyrus met.

Hear the rattle of the harness
Where the Persian darts bounced clear,
See their chariots wheel in panic
From the Hoplite's leveled spear.
See the goal grow monthly longer,
Reaching for the walls of Tyre.
Hear the crash of tons of granite,
Smell the quenchless eastern fire.

Still more clearly as a Roman,
Can I see the Legion close,
As our third rank moved in forward
And the short sword found our foes.

Once again I feel the anguish
Of that blistering treeless plain
When the Parthian showered death bolts,

And our discipline was in vain.

I remember all the suffering
Of those arrows in my neck.
Yet, I stabbed a grinning savage
As I died upon my back.

Once again I smell the heat sparks
When my Flemish plate gave way
And the lance ripped through my entrails
As on Crecy's field I lay.

In the windless, blinding stillness
Of the glittering tropic sea
I can see the bubbles rising
Where we set the captives free.

Midst the spume of half a tempest
I have heard the bulwarks go
When the crashing, point blank round shot
Sent destruction to our foe.
I have fought with gun and cutlass
On the red and slippery deck
With all Hell aflame within me
And a rope around my neck.

And still later as a General
Have I galloped with Murat
When we laughed at death and numbers
Trusting in the Emperor's Star.

Till at last our star faded,
And we shouted to our doom
Where the sunken road of Ohein
Closed us in it's quivering gloom.

So but now with Tanks a'clatter
Have I waddled on the foe
Belching death at twenty paces,
By the star shell's ghastly glow.

So as through a glass, and darkly
The age long strife I see
Where I fought in many guises,
Many names, but always me.

And I see not in my blindness
What the objects were I wrought,
But as God rules o'er our bickerings
It was through His will I fought.

So forever in the future,
Shall I battle as of yore,
Dying to be born a fighter,
But to die again, once more.

Notes

1. An indigenous community enlivens memory of heroic figures and discovers sources of danger (Douglas 1996, Chapter 1).
2. The whole text of the prayer appears in Appendix 2
3. For full text of the prayer, see Appendix 1
4. For a further example, see the commentary on rules of engagement in Somalia, Appendix 2
5. Recalled from conversation
6. Recalled from conversation
7. C. Geertz wrote: "men do not care to have beliefs to which they attach great moral significance examined dispassionately, no matter for how pure a purpose: (Geertz 1973, 195).
8. The insignia of the USMC, comprised of a globe, foul anchor (an anchor with one or more turns of rope or chain twisted around it) and spread eagle

9. "Sacred symbols function to symbolize a people's [or group's] ethos... its moral and aesthetic style and mood—and their world view—the picture they have of the way things in sheer actuality are, their most comprehensive ideas of order... World view is rendered emotionally convincing by being presented as an image of an actual state of affairs peculiarly well-arranged to accommodate such a way of life" (Geertz 1973, 89-90).

10. The oldest of the American special operations groups—they predate even George Washington's Army of the Potomac, originating with a group known as Rodger's Rangers in the French and Indian wars.

11. A concept was coined by Appleby, Marty and Almond in *Strong Religion: the Rise of Fundamentalisms Around the World*, characterized briefly by groups who feel themselves embattled and exiled by the very societies from which they spring (Almond, Appleby, and Sivan, 2003).

12. The 327th regiment of the 101st Airborne Division, for example, takes as its name the "Bastogne Bulldogs," referring to a famous battle that unit fought in World War Two. Besieged by the German army in the French town of Bastogne, in the winter of 1944, General McAuliffe (the 101st's commander) received an offer to surrender from the German commander. On the back of the note, he wrote one word—"nuts"—and sent it back. The 327th was one of the units of the 101st that held out for weeks despite severe casualties from both action and weather until they were rescued by General Patton—although to this day, no member of the 101st has ever described it as a "rescue."

13. "The dead are those who have lost their memories... certain privileged mortals... preserve their memory after death" (Eliade 1963, 121).

14. From the "Cadence of the 2nd Parachute Regiment," French Foreign Legion. For full text, see Appendix 1

15. In his poem Through a Glass Darkly, Patton wrote: "So as through a glass and darkly, the age long strife I see/ Where I fought in many guises, many names, but always me." The full text of the poem appears in Appendix 3

16. "For *homo religious* real, authentic existence begins at the moment when this primordial history is communicated to him and he accepts its consequences" (Eliade 1963, 92).

17. "In order for something genuinely new to begin, the vestiges and ruins of the old cycle must be completely destroyed" (Eliade 1963, 51).

18. "Myth assures man that what he is undertaking has already been done, in other words, it helps him overcome doubts as to the results of his undertaking" (Eliade 1963, 141).

19. There is a reason, perhaps needless to say, why the word "spartan" now means what it does; the soldiers of that city-state are still, millennia later, legendary for their stoicism in the face of hardship, their prowess in battle and their adherence to their own rigid code of military conduct.

20. "The man of the societies in which myth is a living thing lives in a World that, though 'in cipher' and mysterious, is 'open.' The World 'speaks' to man, and to understand its language he needs only to know the myths and decipher the symbols...The World is no longer an opaque mass of objects arbitrarily thrown together, it is a living Cosmos, articulated and meaningful"(Eliade 1963, 141).

21. "Myths describe the various and sometimes dramatic breakthroughs of the sacred (or the 'supernatural') into the world" (Eliade 1963, p. 6), which among other things includes the actions of otherwise normal human beings who are given the opportunity to become something more.

22. Audie Murphy was America's most decorated World War Two veteran. He initially opposed all war before being convinced of the rightness of enlisting.

References

Almond, G., Appleby, R. S. and Sivan, E. 2003. *Strong Religion: The Rise of Fundamentalisms Around the World*, Chicago, IL Chicago University Press.

Douglas, M. 1996. Purity and Danger: An Analysis of the Concepts of Pollution and Taboo. London: Routledge.

Eliade, M. 1963. *Myth and Reality*, New York: Harper & Row.

Ellis, J. and Moore, R. 1974, "School for Soldiers: West Point and the Profession of Arms," Oxford: Oxford University Press.

Franke, V. 1999. *Preparing for Peace: Military Identity, Value Orientations, and Professional Military Education*, Westport: Praeger Publishers.

Geertz, C. 1973. *The Interpretation of Cultures*, New York: Basic Books.

Jabri, V. 1996, *Discourses of Violence*, Manchester: Manchester University Press.

Lipsky, D. 2003. *Absolutely American: Four Years at West Point*, New York: Vintage Books.

Mansbach, R. W. and F. Wilmer 2001. "(B)orders and (dis)orders: the role of moral authority in global politics," Pp. 73-90 in *Identities, Borders, Order: Rethinking International Relations Theory*, edited by Albert, D. Jacobson, and Y. Lapid. Minneapolis: University of Minnesota Press.

Marty, M. E. and R. S. Appeby, eds., 2004. *Fundamentalisms Comprehended.* Chicago : University of Chicago Press.

Parris, B. 2004. *The Making of a Legionnaire*, London: Weidenfeld and Nicolson.

Sturkey, M. F. 2001. *Warrior Culture of the U.S. Marines*, Plum Branch: Heritage Press International.

Chapter 11

Gender and Violence: Redefining the Moral Ground

Sandra I. Cheldelin

Introduction

When Phyllis Chesler asked her male colleague "What comes to mind when I say the phrase, 'woman's inhumanity to woman'?" he replied, "Nothing much. Jealousy, maybe." She then went on to ask him, "And what do you think of when I say 'man's inhumanity to man'?" "Oh," he responded, "That's a big one. War. Fratricide. Slavery. Greed. Evil." (Chesler 2001, 9). Why is his response so different in the context of women versus men? Does "inhumanity" evoke different images that are gender-specific? Is Chesler's colleague's response extra-ordinary?

In the exploration of violent conflict we cannot ignore the significant role of gender. This chapter examines circumstances when one group—women, usually—becomes demonized as the *other*, permitting justifiable violent acts against them. As dichotomous groups emerge with "self as good" and "other as enemy", hostile scripts, corresponding threats and violent behaviors result and get reinforced. This denigration process consistently occurs around the world during times of war with well documented cases of genocide, rape, torture and other gender-related violence. Our challenge is to both fully understand the intersection of gender and violence, analyzing it carefully—the essential first step—and to consider intentional and sustainable strategies to intervene. Is it possible to demonstrate effective ways to lessen or stop gender-based violence? Are there techniques or strategies to acquire new gendered moral ground?

This chapter explores these issues and suggests answers to these questions.

Violence against Women

The pervasiveness of violence against women during times of peace is remarkable. Considering just sexual violence (as defined by the World Health Organization 2002)—rape (within marriage, in dating relationships and by strangers), unwanted sexual advances, forced marriage, forced abortion, denial of the right to use contraception or protection against sexually transmitted diseases, female genital mutilation, obligatory inspections for virginity, forced prostitution and trafficking—has its own stigmas and methods of coping. At least one in four women (range 10-69%) experience sexual violence by an intimate partner during her life (WHO 2002, 2). Each year hundreds of thousands are forced into prostitution. Sexual violence is rooted in a culture of discrimination denying women equal rights with men, and which "legitimizes and sexualizes the violent appropriation of women's bodies for individual gratification or for political ends." (Amnesty International 2005, 2) Sexist policies and practices aggravate women's vulnerability to further violence, denying women recourse and forcing women to remain in violent situations. (2)

In peacetime women, compared to men, rarely have the same economic and political power, or the authority to meet their needs or control their environment. The unevenness of these rights and privileges is only exaggerated under conditions of armed conflict, and gender-specific violence takes on a special horror during conditions of war. Why is this still the case? It is not a new phenomenon. As Sharon Frederick (2001) documents, in ancient Greece "rape was socially acceptable behavior well within the rules of warfare, an act without stigma for warriors who viewed the women they conquered as legitimate booty, useful as wives, concubines, slave labor or battle camp trophy". (11) Over the centuries women were thought of as "reimbursement" for the grave conditions soldiers experienced during wartime. (13) Both World Wars had massive rape incidents in Belgium, France and Japan (the most famous being the

Rape of Nanking) (Frederick 2001, 15). Does history give permission for rape to be an understood condition of war?

As we explore genocide, rape, war systems, misogyny and trauma we realize the impact of war requires us to think years beyond—to the oppression structured into militarized societies. These societies' economic and political institutions deeply influence women's identities as well as men's attitudes and behaviors against them.

Genocide and Rape

The most severe gender-based violence has been documented under conditions of genocide. In her efforts to learn why rape and violence were both commonly used and especially effective tactics in genocide, Murdock (2004) researched the transcripts from the United Nations Genocide Convention. In the text of the convention, Hinton (2002) reports genocide as deliberately inflicting on a group conditions of life calculated to bring about physical destruction, imposing actions on them intended to prevent births within the group and forcibly transferring their children to another group. This criminal behavior becomes institutionalized violence when it is legitimized through social structures: not just the act of genocide but also the tactical planning for genocide and the cultural and structural failures wherein reproductive systems become weapons against the victims and their community (Murdock 2004). In fact, Appadurai (2002) found no cases of genocide without evidence of state collusion or participation. Amnesty International (2004a) says this about Rwanda:

> The legacy of genocide and war in Rwanda lives on ten years after the events in which as many as one million lost their lives. Between April and July 1994, Rwanda was the site of a horrifying litany of human rights abuses—mass killings of unarmed civilians, rape and numerous other acts of torture.... For those raped or tortured, or whose family members were killed, justice and redress remain elusive. The United Nations estimates that between 250,000 and 500,000 rapes were committed

during the genocide. Degradation was integral to the physical violence, with some women being made to parade naked or perform various humiliating acts at the bidding of soldiers and militia. (1)

The act of rape—when the aggressor penetrates the intimate being of the victim—violates the most personal elements of both her (or his) cultural and personal identity. The degradation of rape victims' roles and statuses within their community in terms of social values and their understanding of themselves in terms of cultural determinants of self esteem and worth have multiple examples. In the Middle East women are perceived as objects of value, based on perceptions of "purity". Rape violates purity and renders women unable to fully participate within their culture. Violations of cultural rules regarding purity result, too, in the loss of honor for the families (Agger 1994). This cultural value is rooted in women's reproductive responsibilities. The autonomy of men, at the same time, includes the responsibility to protect the social mechanism of reproduction (Black 2003). The purpose of rape as a gendered tactic in genocide is to "dominate, humiliate, and control behavior" within the larger collective culture (Swiss and Geller 1993, 612). Its intentionality is especially vicious.

For many women their dominant identity connects to family identity. When women are valued primarily for their reproductive capabilities and their social responsibility is to protect their sexuality, rape is an effective way to annihilate their personal identity and potentially remove them from reproducing the socio-cultural identity. This phenomenon is called 'spoiling'. Spoiled women have been sexually violated outside the boundaries of marriage or by persons outside their cultural group. They are "damage" and no longer legitimate within the social structures of their community (Medecins Sans Frontieres 2004).

War Systems

Nearly all war systems are rape systems. As Ramphele (2000) declares, "when we accept the war system, men and women alike tacitly agree to sanction the violation of the flesh—the rape of women and men who have been conditioned to be 'warriors'". (117) Rape, then is one of several strategic tools of combat. "Planned rape, commanded by higher authorities, used in order to enable men to fight better...and to humiliate and demoralize the enemy, has become a major strategy for a number of armies." (Barstow 2000, 8) Many rape survivors report their lives were threatened if they were to expose their rapists. If discussing sexual violence would result in their death or death of a family member, then any successful attempt to obtain testimonies for the purposes of justice is clearly impaired.

There are endless examples of war/rape systems. In Armenia, 1.5 million died by starvation, dehydration, beatings, rape and execution (Chapman 2003). Women and children were abducted and taken to villages of their captures to be their sexual prisoners (Reid 1992). The Somalian war is renowned for rape and murder of children and women with victims as young as age 4. Victims were beaten, stabbed, robbed or shot by their aggressors before, during or after their assault (Human Rights Watch 1993, 1995). In Sudan militiamen systematically raped women and girls in villages in front of family members to "spoil" them. Laws prohibit women to be treated for rape without referral from police, yet it was not uncommon for militiamen and police to jointly attack and rape whole villages (British Broadcasting Company 2004; Martin and Mutchler 2004; Alvarez, 2001).

In their report *Mass Rape—Time For Remedies*, Amnesty International (2004b) says tens of thousands of women and girls (ages 6-70) were victims of systematic rape by combatant forces during the armed conflict in the Democratic Republic of Congo (1). Humanitarian and NGO staff reported they had never come across as many victims of rape as they had in the DRC. Systematic gang rapes were committed by the majority of the armed groups—up to 20 men per group. Collective rapes of groups of women were also common, accompanied by beatings, threats, and extreme acts of torture such as having "rifles, knives, sharpened pieces of wood, glass, rusty nails, stones, sand, and peppers inserted into their vaginas or were shot in their genitals". (1) The unavailability of health care infrastructures—collapsed during the war—along with no water, electricity or means to sterilize instruments left victims dying unnecessarily.

Bosnia has its own story. There were thousands of documented cases of rape for the purpose of impregnation. Bosnia women were forced to give birth to rape-conceived babies, again, rendering the mothers spoiled, and in addition, altering the ethnic composition of their community, and deconstructing their ethnic and gender identity. Some mothers killed their children at birth because of the social stigmas and psychological traumas (Alvarez 2001; Becivbasic and Secic 2003). Rape camps are also common tactics of war. Violations occur by gang rapes, rape by men with HIV/AIDS, rape with inanimate objects, by dogs, and forced rape and sexual violence between prisoners. (Ahmed 2002)

To understand the tactical nature of a rape system we must consider ways that rape is used in various conflict situations. Bloom (2001) suggests it varies. Rape and torture can be preemptive actions, early on as a strategy to shorten a potentially long and drawn-out war and therefore lessen the number of casualties. Or, more common, it can be used as a tipping point to escalate the war when there appears to be a stalemate and when the parties are relatively equal in both power and access to resources. This occurred in the Iran-Iraq war. Iranian women (and children) were recruited as soldiers and suicide bombers. "In Iraq, Kurdish women were raped during the periods when *Peshmerga* (those prepared to die) rebels were making headway *vis a vis* the Iraqi state". (Bloom 2001, 2) Finally, rape and torture may well occur at the end of wars to "signal a type of revanchismo against civilian populations who have aided and abetted the other side." (2) It can also help deter potential witnesses to war crimes from being forthcoming.

Misogyny

In profound ways misogynous systems rear their ugly heads particularly during wartime. In most wars civilian casualties far outnumber the armed combatants. Both women and men both suffer human rights violations. The unique ways in which women are targeted for violence or are otherwise affected by armed conflict, though, are usually overlooked. The impact of war weighs heavy on them—as civilians, refugees or displaced people. They face significant obstacles to obtaining justice:

> The rhetoric, institutions and processes of war and militarization have been described as inherently male-centered, premised on values which prize male aggression and devalue characteristics associated with women. The gender-stereotyping often used in arguments for war has very real consequences for the way conflict is conducted. Women's bodies, their sexuality and reproductive capacity, are often used as a symbolic and literal battleground. (Amnesty International, *Lives Blown Apart* 2004c)

Instrumental misogyny uses women in place of men to achieve men's goals. In the US during World War II women became the backbone of the economy running factories and helping produce war-time equipment, only to be sent home immediately following the war to allow returning warriors employment and status. Differences in men and women's roles and relationships are not uncommon but it is the subordination of women to benefit men that reflects misogyny.

Traditional misogyny is the assertion of a conservative political agenda at the expense of women. There were countless numbers of female Muslim refugees in Bosnia sent to fundamentalist Arab countries where women had to conform to traditional customs and rules of dress and role. And, if she was a victim of rape or torture, her "spoiled" nature would render her an outsider.

Psychological Trauma

Victims of institutionalized rape suffer psychological trauma years following. Signs of this trauma include attempts of suicide, severe depression and even psychosis (Swiss and Geller 1993). Copelon (1995) found that violations of women's social identity result in violations of their personal identity. The identity loss from rape renders a woman "homeless within her person" to the same extent that she is "homeless in her culture" in her loss of self-value (202). Rape survivors encounter widespread discrimination and rejection by their communities, receive threats and insults, and have been abandoned by their husbands and left as sole caretakers of their children.

As reported by Amnesty International (2004b) about victims in the Democratic Republic of Congo, rejection based on moralistic attitudes that women are responsible for what has happened to them can result in feelings of shame and uncleanliness. If they have children as a result of the rape, they will endure similar humiliation and rejection. Social rejection always carries economic consequences.

Many rape victims have to endure chronic severe pain, bleeding, and incontinence. The nature of their injuries makes it difficult to heal physically as well as psychologically. Common themes from interviews of victims are recurring nightmares and flashbacks of the horror.

When Gender Identity Matters

Why are women—and sometimes men—targeted for such violence? To understand this we must understand identity formation *as it relates to gender*. Identity takes on different meanings in different cultures but across all, personal identity—a sense of who we are as individuals—emerges and solidifies. Not in isolation though, it is in constant negotiation with collective, cultural identities. The negotiations reflect cultural and social changes and role requirements over time and provide templates to understand individuals' uniquenesses and similarities with members of their own groups.

The illusive notion of gender, its difficulty in pinning down, and its lack of visibility make it hard to discuss. Defined in contrast to sex, gender includes the socially constructed roles associated with sex. (Sex refers to males and females and is differentiated by chromosomal, anatomical and physiological differences.) Social constructs such as gender are categories we create to identify who does and who does not belong. Born from the stories we tell and have been told, our *gendered identities* unfold as social constructions that are deeply shaped by our culture and social networks. Gendered roles are learned, have historical and cultural bases that define masculinity and femininity, and are influenced by other variables such as ethnicity, class and age.

Jasmine Tesanovic, born in Belgrade, sat with male friends in a restaurant when the former Yugoslavian war began in 1991. The police—tracking down draft dodgers—came to their table and the men showed their identity cards. When she offered the police her papers they responded abruptly: "These men are answering for you. This is a matter of life and death. This is war!" (Tesanovic 2003, 80) She wondered why the men were responsible and the women were excluded.

The former Yugoslavia had multiple wars—ethnic, religious and civil. Mixed marriages and families were common and most were not nationalistic in terms other than "Yugoslavs". The war forced citizens to make unwanted choices. This was a particular problem for women. Tesanovic writes, "National, state and public identity in women are second-hand identity. Women take their names from their father, they change it to their husband's, and very often they are supported or protected by a son after their spouse's death, or adopt a new identity with the next husband". (81)

There are countless stories of Serbian women married to Croatian men living in Muslim-dominated towns or cities across Bosnia. When the war began and alliances between Croats and Muslims started to break down, a number of families moved to Croatia. However, the women—not Croatian born even though they might have converted to Catholicism—were rejected at the borders. As Tesanovic (2003) says, "the problem is that she has no single one-way identity. She has a multiple identity that is only exposed by a critical situation". (82)

Figure 11.1 reflects the complexity of gender identity formation. It includes only some of the significant actors involved in the process.

To begin (and reflected in the central core of the figure), children learn the folkways, mores, and traditions of their culture relating to roles, statuses and values that have been passed down through generations. Moving clockwise around the circle—nested in these cultural and social influences—are the social institutions

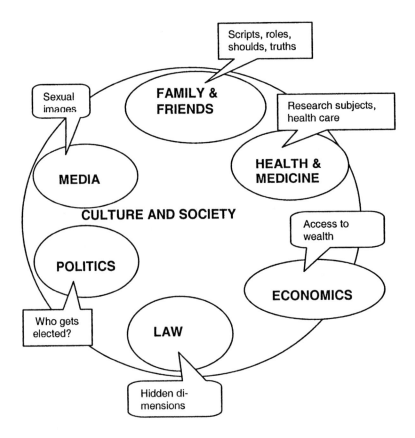

Figure 11.1: Gender Identity Influences

of family, medicine, economics, law, politics, and media. These are merely representative spheres of influence on the internalized educational process of gender identity formation. What emerges is our understanding of our *gendered selves* in terms of culturally developed determinants of esteem and worth and its relation to the *gendered 'others'*.

Experiences with each of these institutions reflect how we think of our gendered selves, how we observe and interpret our world, and how we think of gendered 'others'. Scripts we learn and corresponding role expectations are the seeds to the development of dichotomous thinking in terms of what is "masculine" and what is "feminine". Sadly, we usually stay with these dichotomies rather than understand gender as a dynamic and interactive phenomenon.

In the family, children learn acceptable gender-related rights, expectations, privileges and behaviors. The stories we are told significantly impact our impressions of what it is to be male or female. Chesler (2001) carefully documents many gender-based myths and fairytales common across cultures. Mother-daughter relationships are often tragic and common themes of their mutual insecurity include jealousy, rage and a need for a male hero. Stories of Harems have mothers responsible for selecting the prized women for their sons. Women rule other women cruelly as female slaves. Stories of infertile women's rage and hostility towards fertile women, and the wickedness of stepmothers are also common themes (175). What do these stories teach boys and girls about the demeaning behavior acceptable towards women? Various psychological theories give explanation for gender identity differences. Most agree that navigating family-based conflicts from early childhood creates a blueprint for ways of developing and maintaining relationships throughout adulthood. Boys and girls learn about their differences and incorporate the differences into their own identity—separate from the *'other'* gender.

Examined closely we can find patterns in which gender and voice become—or not—institutionalized. In the social institutions of medicine, law and politics there are learned gendered roles including who have access to resources and power. In the US, prior to the uprising of feminists, the legal system largely reflected and supported the public/private separation of social roles with women being denied access to serve on juries, enter law schools or be admitted to the bar (Belknap 2000). It did not protect women from domestic violence or sexual assault (Robinson 2002). On a regular basis laws that do support women and their rights for privacy—Roe vs. Wade, for example—are under continuous attack, scrutiny and political and legal challenge.

Medicine and politics in the US have similar checkered histories with the legal system, beginning with lack of access. Women waited for decades to be eligible to enroll in medical and law schools, were denied voting privileges until the 1900s, and even today have few political positions of significant influence. There continue to be exaggerated power differentials between the sexes.

Bunting (2001) presents evidence of the gender differences between men and women in the media in England in her article *Women's Voices Silenced in the Enthusiasms for War.* Following the terrorists' attacks on the US on 9/11, the world was transfixed at that moment and men and women equally spoke only of the event—on buses, at corner shops, in offices and schools, and in their homes. Yet they had dramatically different responses towards a US initiated military attack on Afghanistan shortly thereafter: the first two days following the attack there were no women writing about the crisis. It took more than a week before women found their voice of opposition. Why were women silenced? Who silenced them?

The powerful narratives that get repeated to us through the media reinforce expectations and shape minds and attitudes towards or against current gendered paradigms. The stereotypes of women within the media as sexual objects created for, by and under men, continue the subordination of women and encourage violence toward women by objectifying them. Most magazines designed for women across cultures focus on physical beauty, sexual ambitions and capabilities, fashion, and home and domestic design. Film usually adheres to and reinforces the social norms concerning beauty and gender stereotypes. Pearson (2000) claims that scenes in movies of rape portray violence as "sexy" and "acceptable", creating another generation who support a rape culture and who believe that rape is not violence but merely sexual intercourse that sometimes went "wrong".

Sexuality and sexual-appropriate gender roles and behavior are difficult to separate. Consider the incident at Abu Ghraib prison where the pyramid-high blindfolded and naked men were at the mercy of a fully dressed woman in military attire. The scene highlights the shocking nature of sexual humiliation of men. Why is it so humiliating for men? Myerson and Northcutt (2005) believe it "flies in the face of (constructed) notions of masculinity, male as actor/agent/doer and of heteronormativity. Indeed, these images play into our tacit yet socially sanctioned homophobia". (3) Lukic (2000) studied the media representation of women and men in the Serbia crisis and concluded that mass media was enormously important in creating and sustaining an atmosphere of intolerance and hatred that favored war and violence. In the early 1990s women were more absent than present. The two kinds of women that attracted most attention in the media were politicians—Mirjana Markovic, wife of the late President Slobodan Milosovich as "the most beautiful of all"—and those in the entertainment sector.

Can We Stop the Violence?

We cannot intervene until we fully understand why violence occurs—its history, sources, dynamics, culture, traditions, and so on. We know the formation and sustainability of identity, gender and violence. It is at the intersection of these three that we are provided a platform to conduct an analysis of such violent acts as rape, torture and genocide. Figure 11.2 is a framework adapted from Cheldelin and Lucas (2004) to focus the analysis. It depicts three nested levels common to all conflict systems.

The inner core—the micro-level—attends to the types, sources and dynamics of the violence. This includes identification of the parties, their issues, and how their conflict unfolds. The middle circle—the meso-level—considers the identity and situationally related aspects of the violence. The outer circle—macro level—attends to issues specific to culture, traditions and structures. Each level considers at least a minimal series of questions. Only when the analysis is complete can we design appropriate and sustainable interventions.

Redefining a moral ground regarding gender and violence must begin with fully understanding the interrelationships within and between these three nested levels. Genocide and rape cannot occur without the dichotomous spheres of *us* vs. *them*. Victims are subjected to tactics of dehumanization that are informed by the cultural gendered traditions of both parties in order to legitimize the horror. This process reinforces the dichotomous spheres.

Taking a gendered perspective about such violence through changing social relations and institutional practices is essential to lessen the violent behaviors to which victims are subjected. It requires a gendered *repositioning* and a change in the gender narrative as to what is acceptable and

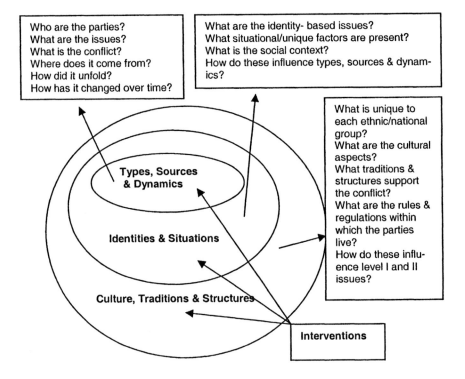

Figure 11.2: A Framework for Conflict Analysis
(Cheldelin and Lucas 2004)

sanctioned—and what is not—by the social and cultural order. A useful first step is to support what Reimann (2001, 7–27) refers to as "gender mainstreaming" and implement her proposed strategies. Her design is adapted from the World Health Organization's *Madrid Statement* (2001) on mainstreaming gender equity in health. [I have located the mainstreaming strategies within the three nested levels—micro, meso and macro—as they are presented to demonstrate how to use the framework.]

Gender Mainstreaming

Both a political and technical process, gender mainstreaming requires shifts in organizational cultures and ways of thinking. The goal is to insert gender into the *analyses, formulation and monitoring* of all policies and programs [macro] relating to a conflict and its corresponding violence, and to develop initiatives that would enable women and men— shoulder to shoulder—to formulate and express their views and to participate in decision-making processes [macro] that could intervene in the violence. (Reimann 2001, 7)

Women and men have different access to power and resources [macro] during and after violent conflicts. The majority of peace negotiations do not consider women's situations [meso], and gender equality has not been adopted as an explicit aim [macro]. Peace settlements become "gendered deals" whereby patriarchal structures [macro] are perpetuated in the political and economic institutions [macro] as well as in gender relations [micro]. (Reimann 2001, 9)

Reimann's strategies for gender mainstreaming also consider interventions at pre-, during-, and post-conflict phases. She offers a creative range of activities for women and men to be empowered in different ways at each phase. As a method of *prevention*, women should be identified and supported for potential leadership roles [meso]; women's organizations should be trained in conflict resolution techniques [micro], and separate support should be provided for new women's organizations working on non-traditional issues such as the development of new businesses and community services [macro]. She suggests creating platform-building activities for women to meet, network and strategize [micro];

and design "cultures of peace" that include political and legal changes, minority voting and constitutional rights provided to the disenfranchised [macro].

During a crisis existing women's organizations that have wide membership or large social networks [macro] should be empowered so that their impact at peace conferences and linkages with other decision-making bodies can be increased [micro and macro]. The most difficult challenge, of course, is changing the masculine culture of most organizations in charge of peace negotiations [macro]. It is essential to include women in the negotiation process.

Post-conflict situations require gender-sensitive training programs for health and trauma [micro]. Reintegration programs must account for crisis-based health problems such as HIV, sexually transmitted diseases, alcoholism, domestic violence and suicide [micro]. Programs for social inclusion and readjustment should be initiated as well as support for self-help groups [micro and meso]. Business loans and credit mechanisms must be put into place to support economic stability [macro]. (Reimann 2001, 21–27)

Violence against women occurs because of the interpersonal, cultural and structural power differentials [micro, meso and macro]. It involves "ownership" of the "weaker" gender, placing women as reproductive tools and victims of enforced violence [micro]. Acts of rape and genocide impact the formation and deconstruction of identity [meso]. Violating the female—spoiling—also violates male identity as her protector. Because rape is an intentional tactic that results in a violation of identity [meso] and an attempt to destabilize the social order [macro], it is necessary to recognize victims as people with rights and establish programs wherein women are valued beyond their reproductive capabilities. Condemning victims as spoiled and removing them from their sociocultural unit results in a culturalized dehumanization of victims, their families, and community members [macro]. This kind of institutionalized violence uses political structures to permit large-scale gendered violence. Therefore, these very structures must move toward equal rights by instituting international laws, institutional accountability regarding gender crimes, and position equality in such social structures as health care, education, law, politics and the media [macro].

Changing the Position and Narrative

Healing individuals traumatized by political violence must take into account the unspoken and indirect positioning of the perpetrator. The psychological and action boundaries we develop—what we possess and what we are willing (or not) to do—are challenged under conditions of violence such as war. Feelings of shame, revulsion, contempt, anger and terror serve to destabilize our core identity. Because our collective categories of what is (and is not) unthinkable are social constructions, they can be deconstructed. This is possible by providing victims agency outside themselves—support systems via legal, economic and equity sanctions and opportunities—at the micro to macro levels.

Third parties can help create new cultural and social stories with moral grounding in legitimate and rights-based positions that reflect what will be acceptable. They can assist in the evolution of new storylines based on a framework of personal, social and cultural responsibility and accountability that is supported by and reflects global networks, international courts, United Nations sanctions, transnational expectations and pressures, as well as other social agencies—family, healthcare, economics, law, politics and the media—to change the moral narrative. This is essential to provide strategies for long-term shifts in national and global definitions of what is morally acceptable (and what is not) for men and for women. As Czarniawska (1997) points out, we are never the sole authors of our narratives—every conversation involves positioning that is accepted, rejected, or improved upon by the parties in the conversation (14). Stopping intentional violent acts toward women (and men) requires narrative shifts with sanctioned endorsement of what will—and will not—be acceptable. New narratives will be reinforced and, hopefully, sustained when women are positioned in the family, organization and society to co-influence women's rights and privileges equal to those of men.

References

Agger, Inger. 1994. *The blue room. Trauma and testimony among refugee women: a psychosocial exploration.* Tran. M. Billie. New York: St. Martin Press

Ahmed, A.S. 2002. "'Ethnic cleansing': a metaphor for our time?" Pp. 211–230 in *Genocide: an Anthropological Reader,* edited by A. L. Hinton. Malden, MA: Blackwell Publishers, Inc.

Alvarez, A. 2001. *Governments, Citizens and Genocide.* Indianapolis: Indiana University Press.

Amnesty International, *Stop Violence against Women: Fact Sheets.* 2005, <http://www.amnestyusa.org/stopviolence/factsheets/sexualvilence.html> (18.Nov. 2005)

Amnesty International, *Women of Rwanda Marked for Death.* 7 April 2004a, <http://web.amnesty.org/web/web/nsf> (18.Nov. 2005)

Amnesty International Media Briefing, *Democratic Republic of Congo: Mass Rape—Time for Remedies.* AI Index: AFR 62/022/2004, News Service No: 257, 26 October 2004b, <http://web.amnesty.org/library/print/ENGAFR620222004> (18.Nov. 2005)

Amnesty International, *Lives Blown Apart: Crimes against Women in Times of Conflict.* 8.12.2004c, <http://web.amnesty.org/library/print/ENGACT770752004> (18.Nov. 2005).

Appadurai, A. 2002. "Dead Certainty: Ethnic Violence in the Era of Globalization." Pp. 286–304 in *Genocide: An Anthropological Reader,* edited by A. L. Hinton. Malden, MA, Blackwell Publishers Inc.

Barstow, Ann Llewellyn, Ed. 2000. *War's Dirty Secret: Rape, Prostitution and Other Crimes against Women."* Cleveland: The Pilgrim Press

Belknap, J. 2000. *Invisible Woman: Gender, Crime and Justice* (2nd ed.). Belmont, CA: Wadsworth.

Becivbasic, B. and Secic, D. 2003. "Invisible Casualties of War" in *Bosnian Institute series,* 32–34, December-July 2003.

<www.bosnia.org.uk/bosrep/report_format.cfm?articleid=9503reporti d=157> (8.Nov. 2004).

British Broadcasting Company News. 2004. *Testimonies of Rape in Sudan*, <http://news.bbbc.co.uk/go/pr/fr/-/2/hi/africa/3900777.stm> (28 Sep. 2004)2/hi/africa/

Black, Peter. 2003. "Identities." Pp. 120-139 in Cheldelin, Druckman and Fast, *Conflict*, New York and London: Continuum.

Bloom, Mia M. 2001. "War and the Politics of Rape: Ethnic versus Non-ethnic Conflicts. Unpublished manuscript.

Bunting, Madeleine. 2001. "Women's voices silenced in the enthusiasms for war" *Guardian*, London, England, 20 September 2001.

Chapman, M. 2003. "Never forget the Armenian Genocide" 5/6/2003 *Genocide1915.info: Armenian Genocide.* <http://222.genocide1915.info/articles_view.asp?crypt=%86u%A1% 85a%7D> (8 Nov. 2004) (M. Chapman is the editorial director at the Cato Institute)

Cheldelin, Sandra and Lucas, Ann. 2004. *Conflict Resolution.* San Francisco: Jossey-Bass

Chesler, Phyllis. 2001. *Woman's in Humanity to Woman*, New York: Penguin Putnam Inc. (Plume)

Copelon, R. 1995. "Gendered War Crimes: Reconceptualizing Rape in Time of War." Pp. 197–214 in *Women's Rights, Human Rights: International Feminists Perspectives,* edited by J. Peters and A. Wolper. New York: Routledge.

Czarniawska, Barbara. 1997. *Narrating the Organization: Dramas of Institutional Identity.* Chicago: The University of Chicago Press.

Frederick, Sharon and Aware. 2001. *Rape Weapon of Terror.* New Jersey: Global Publishing Co.

Hinton, A.L. Ed. 2002. United Nations "Text of the UN Convention." Pp 43-47 (reprinted) in *Genocide: An Anthropological Reader.* Malden, MA: Blackwell Publishers Inc.

Human Rights Watch (HRW) 1993. "Somalia Refugees is Kenya" in *A Human Rights Watch Short Report,* Volume 5, No. 13, October 1993 <www.hrw.org/about/projects/womrep/general-73.htm> (8 Nov. 2004)

Human Rights Watch (HRW). 1995. "Rape in Somalia" in *A Human Rights Watch Short Report,* Volume 7, No. 2, April 1995 <www.hrw.org/about/projects/womrep/general-73.htm> (8 Nov.2004)

Lukic, Jasmina. 2000. "Media Representations of Men and Women in Times of War and Crisis: the Case of Serbia." Ch. 14 in G. *Reproducing Gender: Politics, Publics and Everyday Life after Socialism,* edited by Gal, S. and Kigman. Princeton, New Jersey: Princeton University Press.

Martin, S. and Mutchler, M. 2004. "Sudan: for Raped Women in Darfur: Access to Reproductive Health Services Limited" in *Refugees International.* <http://www.refugeeinternational.org/content/article/detail/4260/> (8 Nov.2004).

Medecins Sans Frontieres, 2004, "MFS In Somalia." (September 2, 2004) <www.mfs.org/countries/index.cfm?indexid=22ODZE-BECF-11D4-8522059027891873> (8 Nov.2004)

Murdock, Elizabeth. 2004. Unpublished research paper for Conf 723 course on Gender and Conflict at the Institute for Conflict Analysis and Resolution, George Mason University, Sandra Cheldelin, professor.

Myerson, Marilyn and Northcutt, Susan. 2005. *Globalizing Sexual Humiliation*, presented March 4, 2005 at the International Studies Association (ISA) annual meeting, Honolulu, HI

Pearson, Alyn. 2000. "Rape Culture: Media and Message" in *Off our backs.* August/September issue.

Ramphele, M. 2000. "Teach Me How to Be a Man: an Exploration of the Definition of Masculinity." Pp. 102–119 in *Violence and Subjectivity,* edited by V. Das, A. Kleinman, M. Ramphele, and A. Reynolds. London and Berkeley: University of California Press.

Reid, J.J. 1992. "Total War, the Annihilation Ethnic and the Armenian Genocide." Pp. 21–47 in *The Armenian Genocide: History, Politics, Ethics,* edited by R. Hovannisian. New York: St. Martin's Press.

Reimann, Cordula. 2001. *Towards Gender Mainstreaming in Crisis Prevention and Conflict Management: Guidelines for the German Tech-*

nical Co-operation. Federal Republic of German: Deutsche Gesellschaft für, Eschborn, <http://www.gtz.de>

Robinson, M. 2002. *Justice Blind?: Issues and Realities of American Criminal Justice.* Upper Saddle River, NJ: Prentice Hall.

Swiss, S. and Giller, J. E. 1993. "Rape as a crime of war: a medical perspective." *Journal of the American Medical Association* 270, no. 5: 612–615.

Tesanovic, Jasmine. 2003. "Women and Conflict: a Serbian Perspective." Pp. 80–86 in *Women on War: an International Anthology of Writings from Antiquity to the Present*, edited by Groseffi, Daniela. New York: The Feminist Press at the City University of New York.

World Health Organization World Report on Violence and Health. 2002, <http://www.euro.who.int/eprise/main/who/mediacentre/pr/2002/200 21002> (20 Nov.2005)

World Health Organization. 2001. The Madrid Statement: Mainstreaming gender equity in health. The need to move forward.

Chapter 12

Psychocultural Interpretations and Dramas: Identity Dynamics in Ethnic Conflict

Marc Howard Ross[1]

Throughout the "marching season" in Northern Ireland, Protestant men in dark suits and bowler hats assemble at local lodges, attend church services, and hold parades celebrating past victories, such as the Battle of the Boyne in 1690 (when William of Orange's Protestant forces defeated the army of Catholic King James II), and commemorating losses, such as the deaths of many soldiers at the Battle of the Somme during the First World War. Protestant accounts of these parades emphasize the solemn, religious nature of the parades and the occasions they mark (Lucy & McClure 1997). Banners celebrate key events in Protestant history, especially those of the Williamite period, and emphasize important religious themes, symbols, and persons. Bands playing familiar music accompany the marchers, and important politicians may address the crowd (Bryan 1997; Jarman 1997). Catholic accounts, in contrast, express resentment because of the narrow sectarian nature of these same events and what they see as their stress on Protestant triumphalism and domination, the aggressive music of the "blood and thunder" bands (often clad in paramilitary symbols), and the anti-Catholic lyrics of many of the songs.

Jarman (1997, 119) reports that as of 1995, there were 3,500 parades each year in Northern Ireland, a region with a population of 1.5 million. The vast majority are exclusively Protestant (74%) or Catholic (9%) events that mark, celebrate, or commemorate events of significance to each community.[2] Much less common are parades that bring members of the two communities together around a shared experience or underscore the common fate of the region's population. Parades are typically celebrations of ingroup solidarity and are perceived as statements about domination and resistance (Bryan 1997; Jarman 1997).

Parades offer occasions where political and cultural differences are emphasized and the tensions and anger produced mobilize loyalties along sectarian lines. As a result, any parade in Northern Ireland can easily become an emotionally charged, sectarian political expression. Although the vast majority of parades each year take place without incident, there are about 60 parades that are considered contentious. Particularly when Protestant parades are routed through Catholic working-class neighborhoods, they are often strongly resented by local residents, while Protestants contend that restrictions on parading along "traditional" routes are an infringement of their religious and political rights. In recent years there have been confrontations with police, and violence and death were associated with parades in South Belfast and Portadown. To address such contentious parades in 1997, the government appointed a Parades Commission charged with making decisions about the routing, structure, and organization of potentially problematic parades.[3]

Conflicts about parades in Northern Ireland are not fundamentally about freedom of speech or religion or protection from intimidation, but about the threatened identities of people in the region: "Put simply, the parades issue goes to the heart of the deeply fractured society that, sadly, Northern Ireland represents" (North 1997, 41). I argue that because identity issues are at the core of the larger conflict—here as elsewhere—ethnic conflict is often bitter and prolonged. Understanding the importance of identity in such ethnic conflicts draws attention to what social identity means to both ingroups and outgroups, how it is symbolized and communicated, and how it affects political behavior and beliefs (Ross 1997a). Focusing on identity is especially useful in explaining the intensity of ethnic conflict and the circumstances in which identity's content and salience may resist or yield to change (Ross 1993a, 1997a).

My attention to identity in ethnic conflict is rooted in the failure of interest theories (from neo-Marxist to rational choice) to adequately account for ethnic conflict, especially its intensity (e.g., Banton 1983; Hardin 1995). Whereas interest theories see shared identity as arising from common interests, identity theories stress that shared identity defines and creates the perception of the interests over which ethnic conflicts are fought. Although I emphasize identity dynamics in this article, I do not claim that only identities matter in ethnic conflict; interests count too, and the interrelationship of identity and interests is complex and not always appreciated.

Central to my analysis of identity and ethnic conflict are psychocultural interpretations and psychocultural dramas. Psychocultural interpretations are the shared, deeply rooted worldviews that help groups make sense of daily life and provide psychologically meaningful accounts of a group's relationship with other groups, their actions and motives (Ross 1995). They are at the core of shared systems of meaning and identity that define cultural communities (Ross 1997a) and are revealed in a group's narratives recounting their origin, history and conflicts with outsiders, as well as in the community's symbolic and ritual behaviors. Understanding a group's psychocultural interpretations (or worldviews) analytically means making sense of their origin, intensity, and significance for political action. Although it is often easy to dismiss ingroup explanations as incorrect or irrational and therefore irrelevant "just-so" stories, to do so would be as foolish as for a psychoanalyst to tell a patient he or she had just recounted a stupid dream

Psychocultural dramas are conflicts between groups over competing and apparently irresolvable, claims that engage the central elements of each group's historical experience and identity and invoke suspicions and fears of the opponent Psychocultural dramas are polarizing events about non-negotiable cultural claims threats, and/or rights that become important because of their connections to group narratives and core metaphors central to a group's identity. My development of the concept of psychocultural drama builds on Victor Turner's (1957) concept of the social drama. The social dramas Turner analyzes are conflicts that are not ever fully resolved, but they are settled for a time when the conflict is redefined away from incompatible principles to the symbolic and ritual domain, where disputants can emphasize shared concerns and superordinate goals. I suggest that the psychocultural drama is an excellent tool for the analysis of identity in ethnic conflict and for understanding new possibilities for managing ethnic conflicts constructively Psychocultural dramas, such as the conflict over parades in Northern Ireland are found in all long-term ethnic conflicts. By examining their development, escalation and termination (but not necessarily successful resolution), we can better appreciate the central role of culture and identity in ethnic conflict.

Identity in Ethnic Conflict

Ethnic identity connects individuals through perceived common past experiences and expectations of shared future ones. It entails a sense of common fate, including expectations of common treatment, joint fears of survival/extinction, and beliefs about group worth, dignity, and recognition. Identity involves group judgments and judgments about groups and their motives. For example, Horowitz (1985, 147–192) discusses the power of assigning the labels "backward" and "advanced" to ethnic groups in colonial and post-colonial settings, and the claims of entitlement that groups may make as a consequence of such a designation.

Social Identity Development

Social identity begins to develop at the earliest stages of the life cycle, and its intensity is crucial to explaining why people are willing to make the greatest personal sacrifices in its name (Stern 1995). People with the same identity share targets of externalization—common enemies—which reinforces a shared view of a world filled with enemies and allies (Volkan 1988). High emotional salience is attached to group differences that are emphasized through symbolic and ritual behaviors binding individuals to their own groups. As Volkan writes:

> The psychoanalytic view indicates that ethnicity or nationality originates much as other emotional phenomena do in clans or tribes. The sense of self is intertwined at a primitive level with the identity of the group. Membership in these groups is not like that in a club or professional organization, since it is tinged with raw and primitive affects pertaining to one's sense of self and others and to their externalization and projections (Volkan 1990, 36).

Humans clearly have an evolved predisposition for sociality and a well-developed capacity to form cohesive social groups (Howell & Willis 1989), and ingroup identity provides the basis for a fundamental paradox of human existence. It facilitates both physical and emotional survival within groups; at the same time, strong ingroup solidarity can promote outgroup competition and conflict, although we are unclear about exactly how the two dynamics are related (LeVine & Campbell 1972).[4]

Modern psychoanalytic writing is particularly helpful for understanding identity development and the relationship between individual and ethnic identity (Ross 1995). Unlike older, drive-based theories of psychodynamic functioning, contemporary object relations theory, with its emphasis on linking a person's inner and outer worlds, focuses on the social development of attachment (Bowlby 1969; Greenberg & Mitchell 1983). This work sees early social relationships as providing a template for ones that develop later in life, and it is especially concerned with the parts of the outer world brought inside and with inner parts projected outward (Stern 1985; Volkan 1988). Normal development, facilitated by what Winnicott (1965) calls the good-enough mother, encourages both the attachment of the individual to others and separation-individuation as a person builds a sense of self connected to a progressively wider circle of attachment (Mahler, Pine, & Bergman 1975).

Winnicott (1958) describes the importance of transitional objects— teddy bears, soft towels, and other treasured objects that link a child's inner and outer worlds and are infused with high emotional significance. It is easy to extend this linkage process to social and cultural objects— significant symbols and rituals that are first encountered in safe, within-group contexts (often in childhood), revisited in adolescence when peer groups and wider social attachments are especially salient emotionally, and embedded in daily practices and their culturally specific sights, smells, and sounds.

Understanding ethnic identity is also complicated by the fact that human groups range widely in form and content, and that any one person has multiple identities whose salience varies across situations. Identity involves the capacity to distinguish in specific settings between people who are like oneself and those who are different, and depending on the context the same people may be variously classified as alike or different.

To analyze identity, we need to examine what it is that people believe they have in common, and to consider how a sense of shared fate develops and is reinforced within a group.

Psychocultural interpretations are critical to this dynamic. Several factors shape the interpretive process. One is the human predisposition to make sense of experience. This capacity is at the core of our ability to learn and to act upon our environment. Yet the same factors that push actors to make sense of a situation also lead to cognitive and perceptual distortion in identity conflicts, because the desire for certainty often is greater than the capacity for accuracy. Not only are disputants likely to make systematic errors in the "facts" underlying interpretations but homogeneous social settings and the presence of cultural amplifiers reinforce these distortions (Mack 1983). What is most crucial, however, about subjective interpretations of a conflict is the compelling, coherent account they offer to the parties in linking discrete events to general understandings. Central to such interpretations is the attribution of motives to parties (Jones & Nisbett 1972; Pruitt & Rubin 1985, 103). Once identified, the existence of such motives seemingly makes it easy to "predict" another's future actions and, through one's own behavior, to turn such predictions into self-fulfilling prophecies.

A second factor that makes the interpretive process possible is the ambiguity and complexity of the situation in most ethnic conflicts. Although participants in any dispute can often tell someone "just what the conflict is about," this precision is usually illusory (Roy 1994). Opposing parties operate from very different frames of reference; as a result, they don't agree on what a conflict is about, when it started, or who they consider to be involved. External events can be interpreted in a number of ways; as a result, groups turn to internal frameworks and perceptions, which then shape subsequent behavior. This, of course, is what makes ethnic conflict so difficult to contain and manage. Ambiguous events are easily selectively interpreted as confirming evidence for preexisting beliefs. Furthermore, because many disputes involve parties with a long history of conflict, older grievances can easily be appended to newer ones as political conditions warrant. For all of these reasons, it is appropriate to suggest that, rather than thinking about particular objective events that cause conflicts to escalate, we ought to be thinking about the *interpretations* of such events that are associated with escalation and those that are not.

A striking feature of many identity-based ethnic conflicts is the parties' emotional investment in what outsiders may view as unimportant matters. The fact is, however, that any matter invested with emotional significance is no longer trivial, and intransigent intergroup disputes quickly become characterized by perceived threats to group self-esteem and legitimation (Ross 1995). The dynamic is one in which the parties feeling threatened place identity issues at the core of their concerns (Northrup 1989). Such emotion-laden conflicts can be especially difficult to settle. When each side feels the same intense emotions, it may be difficult to recognize what is, in fact, shared. For example, although both Protestants and Catholics in Northern Ireland each see themselves as a threatened minority, each has trouble acknowledging the other side's view. One party's own emotional concerns make it very difficult to accept another's account, especially when their own action may be the root cause of an adversary's feelings and behavior.

Identity is linked to shared images of the world. Group members often go through common developmental experiences, including shared events, that are incorporated into one's own personal identity (Ross 1995, 526-531). Anderson (1991) wrote of imagined communities, which link personal and collective identities. The process of within-group identity formation overemphasizes what it is that group members actually share, giving greater emotional weight to the common elements, reinforcing them with an ideology of linked fate, and frequently over-estimating within-group uniformity (Turner 1988). There is also a shared, and usually exaggerated, conception of the differences between one's group and outsiders. The strong, and opposing, identities involved in intense conflicts emphasize the homogeneity of each party, sometimes using what are small objective differences to mark large social distinctions (Volkan 1988). Outsiders then can serve as objects for externalization, displacement, and projection of intense negative feelings while dissenting perspectives present inside the group are denied (Fomari 1975; Volkan 1988).

Identities and Interests for Motives or Action

In examining the role of identity in ethnic conflict, it is important to acknowledge that interests also drive conflict in general and ethnic conflict in particular (Ross 1993a). If interests and identities are two imperatives that drive ethnic conflict, then each can provide motives for political organization and action. At first glance, interests seem more straightforward motives, are easy to articulate as political claims, and provide a basis for group (or individual) goals. Interests are generally quite concrete, and given the pervasive use of economic metaphors in our culture, it would seem reasonable to say that people are pursuing, or are motivated by, their own interests. Indeed, public discourse in most democracies legitimizes interest-based claims, such as "We are seeking more and better jobs for our people." However, even when interests are presented as objective, they have important subjective dimensions as well. For example, when groups make claims concerning such things as jobs, seats on government boards, or positions in universities, they are also invoking implicit notions of justice derived from an assessment of what they feel entitled to receive. Specific entitlement demands—involving, for example, high-level political positions or the public display of flags or street signs—are often "tests" to gauge how a political system views a group, and any analysis that ignores the intense subjective elements of such demands is going to be incomplete.

Identity is a more complicated basis for political claims. The members of a group, for example, may not be fully aware of the group's identity concerns. Often operating at a subconscious level, perceived threats and deeply rooted fears can be difficult to talk about or to specify. As a result, groups frequently assert identity claims in strident and hard-to-hear ways, emphasizing firm positions, when in fact the deeper underlying needs remain diffuse and implicit. When identity-based demands do become explicit, however, their emotional meaning can cause them to be stated in all-or-nothing, moralistic terms, which makes them difficult to address through the give-and-take of everyday political life.

Interests and identities are often quite interconnected. The distinction between the two is analytic, but people caught up in conflicts intuitively understand their empirical linkage. For example, it is easy to see how the achievement of certain interest goals, such as gaining a political office or improved job opportunities, can address a group's identity and recognition concerns at the same time. To the extent that interest claims are "tests" of a group's acceptance as a legitimate political player, achievement of the interest claims also addresses concerns about identity. However, there are times when a group may be ready to drop or alter an interest claim if identity needs can be met in another manner. Similarly, when identity-based fears of exclusion diminish, groups may alter the kinds of interest claims they make. Understanding intense ethnic conflict as involving both interests and identities thus increases not only our analytical understanding but also our options for constructive conflict management (Ross 1993a, 1993b).

Psychocultural Interpretations and Psychocultural Dramas as Analytic Tools

Psychocultural Interpretations

Psychocultural interpretations are found in many forms, including formal written materials, historical documents, public discourse, government records, law cases, videos, plays, music, systematic observations, and survey data. In addition, data on psychocultural interpretations are available in ethnographic field research, in-depth interviews and life histories, structured interviews, extended case analysis of what legal anthropologists call trouble cases, popular culture, and public and semi-public myths and rituals.

Survey Data

Good survey data are a valuable tool in the analysis of ethnic conflict. Because it is so easy in public discourse to emphasize polarizing identity labels and to adopt the language of the most strident political actors, data from surveys that offer respondents more nuanced options can be more complex and preferences less polarized than is often thought. Such data can also provide important evidence at odds with the claims of political leaders and groups.

In Northern Ireland, survey data have consistently offered important insights into public understanding of the conflict. For example, they show that while Catholics in the North prefer a united Ireland, many have also been consistently willing to accept solutions short of reunification, provided they gain a real political voice and significant protection for minority rights. Surveys have also shown the complexity of Protestant identity, revealing great diversity in self-identification. At various times and in different proportions, Protestants choose the labels British, Northern Irish, Anglo-Irish, "sometimes British and sometimes Irish," and Irish (Rose 1971; Ruane & Todd 1996, 57–60; Whyte 1990, 65–71).

In the Middle East, survey data reveal important features of Israeli and Palestinian identity. They show that although there is greater Palestinian acceptance of the state of Israel—even before the Oslo Accords in 1993—than is often believed (Smooha 1997), the Arabs who are residents and citizens of Israel prefer to be called "Palestinians in Israel" or "Palestinian Arabs" rather than Israeli Arabs, the term the Israeli government uses most often (Rouhana 1997).[5] Surveys also show that among Jews in Israel, self-designation as religious or secular is highly correlated with a large number of political attitudes concerning the organization and structure of the state, its appropriate size, access to state resources, and citizenship (Arian & Shamir 1995; Shamir & Arian 1999).

Survey data can provide a good look at the distribution of opinions in a group and can reveal important sources of variation. What they are less able to offer are insights about the broader context in which particular dimensions of identity are embedded, or why it is that specific identities are so salient. To address these issues, we can use group narratives and psychocultural dramas to supplement the broad-based, but thin, data good surveys provide.

Group Narratives

How do individuals and groups explain a conflict to themselves and to outsiders? Listening to and analyzing the narratives shared by activists and their communities can reveal a great deal about the deep fears and threats to identity that drive ethnic conflict. Particularly important are the implicit and explicit assumptions about motives—one's own and those of others—that these stories contain.

Consider this brief excerpt from a longer conversation I had with Denis Watson, the grand marshal of the Orange Order in County Armagh and a newly elected Protestant Unionist member of the Northern Ireland Assembly in October 1998. We were discussing the stand-off in Portadown over the Parades Commission's refusal the previous July to permit the Orange Order to march from Drumcree Church to their lodge headquarters though a Catholic neighborhood (other routes were available but were quickly dismissed as unacceptable and nontraditional by the local lodge). I asked Watson why the conflict in Drumcree has been so bitter and hard to resolve. He replied by reminding me that the area was the site of a Catholic massacre of Protestants ... in 1641. Clearly this image frames the recent conflict in a broad historical context, conveying the Protestant view of what Catholics will do to Protestants given the chance, and invoking the siege metaphor, which emphasizes Protestant vigilance and self-protection as necessary to defend their rights and interests (Buckley & Kenney 1995).

Narratives are accounts groups develop to address both the substantive and emotional levels of a conflict. Important themes in a group's narratives link past experiences to strong emotions, providing support for certain courses of action (Roy 1994; Scott 1985). In Northern Ireland, Protestant narratives, for example, continue to invoke the theme of siege and the value of collective resistance (Buckley & Kenney 1995, 41–57) and the idea of a sacred covenant rooted in the Exodus story (Akenson 1992). Serbian narratives are full of images of marauding Turks (Volkan 1997, 50–80), and Jewish narratives contain themes of the destruction of the Second Temple and the Holocaust. All powerful narratives build on collective memories of what are believed to be actual events, but their significance lies in the way the elements are put together into authoritative accounts that trigger strong emotional responses.

Culturally defined narratives express group identity for the parties locked in struggle as they recount past encounters, present difficulties, and future aspirations (Ross 1997a, 1997b). Obviously, there can be a huge gap between the elements and structure in actors' narratives and how a researcher understands political action, just as there is a great difference between the content of a patient's dreams and the psychoanalyst's interpretation of their structure and significance. Bridging this gap requires an understanding of the culture sufficient to build interpretations that both make sense to cultural insiders and can be appreciated by outsiders.

Narratives are valuable for showing how participants think about and characterize a conflict. As we listen to them, it is important to consider the differences in the stories each community uses to explain what is apparently the same conflict without necessarily contradicting each other directly. In these "separate histories," each side selects key events that come to have central meaning for their own community. For example, in Northern Ireland, Protestants find great meaning in the story of William of Orange and the Battle of the Boyne in 1690, whereas Catholic accounts say little about King Billy or the battle. In contrast, Catholic Nationalists emphasize the meaning of the 1916 Easter Uprising, which for Protestants is far less significant than their sacred pact committing themselves to resist Irish self-rule four years earlier. Even when an event enters into both sides' narratives, such as the hunger strikes of Republican prisoners in 1980–1981, the metaphors and meanings associated with the event can be so different that a person hearing the two narratives may not immediately realize that they concern the same event.[6]

Narratives about a longstanding conflict contain the culturally rooted aspirations, challenges, and deepest fears of ethnic communities. One particularly poignant kind of narrative is what Volkan calls a "chosen trauma," referring to specific experiences that symbolize a group's deepest threats and fears through feelings of helplessness and victimization (Volkan 1988, 1997). He provides many examples of such events, including the Turkish slaughter of Armenians, the Nazi Holocaust, the experience of slavery and segregation for African Americans, and the Serbian defeat at Kosovo by the Turks in 1389 (Volkan 1997). When group members feel too humiliated, angry, or helpless to mourn the losses suffered in the trauma, Volkan argues that the group then incorporates the emotional meaning of the traumatic event into its identity and passes on the emotional and symbolic meaning from generation to generation.[7]

In escalating intergroup conflicts, key metaphors, such as the chosen traumas, serve both as a rallying point and as a way to make sense of events that evoke deep fears and threats to existence (Horowitz 1985; Kelman 1987). Only when the deep-seated threats these stories represent are addressed is a community able to begin to imagine a more peaceful future with its enemies.

Psychocultural Dramas

Psychocultural dramas are intergroup conflicts over competing and apparently irresolvable claims that come to engage the central elements of each group's historical experience, contemporary identity, and suspicions and fears about an opponent. They are polarizing events whose manifest content involves non-negotiable cultural claims, threats, and/or rights that become important because of their connections to core metaphors and group narratives that embody a group's identity.

The manifest focus of a psychocultural drama can be over the allocation of material resources, or can involve differences about cultural questions such as language, religion, social practices, or music and popular culture. As the drama unfolds, the conflict becomes connected to a central element of a group's identity. Unless there are dispute resolution mechanisms (such as a judicial system, administrative process, or legislative process) that are recognized as legitimate by the parties, the scope and intensity of the conflict escalate and the initial conflict becomes a crisis.

The social dramas Turner (1957, 89–90) describes occur within a society that shares key values when (a) competing principles, which groups or individuals in conflict invoke to support their positions but which do not take precedence over each other, lead to a serious breach in the social order; and (b) there is a common norm that each side contends the other has broken.[8] The social dramas Turner presents, which arise from structural contradictions between Ndembu norms of inheritance and residence, result in marital and village instability and tension, which increase during contests for succession to village headmanship.

Turner (1957, 91–92) defines four phases through which social dramas pass: breach of social relations, mounting crisis, redressive action, and reintegration or recognition of schism. As a social drama unfolds, tensions mount and the conflict escalates as each side works vigorously to strengthen its position and to draw in new allies. New issues are often interjected as social dramas develop, and in addition past events and feelings resurface. When it is possible to use jural mechanisms to resolve the crisis, the community may do so, but Turner emphasizes the importance of ritual mechanisms of redress, especially when jural mechanisms either do not exist or are inadequate because none of the competing principles is clearly more important than any of the others.

The Ndembu rituals Turner describes are responses to a high level of social tension and often focus on matters (such as fertility) that are ostensibly unrelated to the ongoing crisis. In addition, they bring in participants from neighboring communities who are related by principles such as cult membership or age. Mobilization of the wider community for the performance of reparative rituals refocuses people's emotional energy and puts the original conflict in a context where disputants emphasize shared norms and goals, because ritual activity links the disputants through affiliations (such as ritual cults or age organizations) that cut across existing communities and lines of cleavage. As a result, it is not so much that the original conflict is resolved in any profound sense, because the competing norms are still present. Rather, either the emotional significance of differences diminishes sufficiently so that people find a solution they can accept and return to their daily routines in relative harmony, or there are outcomes such as the fission of a village into smaller ones.

In ethnic conflicts, psychocultural dramas arise over competing claims that evoke deeply rooted dimensions of the conflict and cannot be settled by reference to more general rules or higher authority. As a result, although psychocultural dramas have great political significance, they are not narrowly political events, particularly in their early stages. This is because the contending parties emphasize competing rights in such a way that negotiation, redefinition of goals, or compromise is not possible. For example, when a group believes it is fulfilling God's commands, compromising its goals and modifying behaviors becomes blasphemy. Turner observes that the intensity of social dramas can be diffused through the transformation of disputes over competing interests into ritual actions emphasizing what the parties share. Of course, this is difficult to achieve through political processes in cases where there has been prolonged ethnic conflict. The discussion on parades below suggests, however, that when it is possible for symbolic redefinition and political action to go hand-in-hand, constructive settlement of psychocultural dramas becomes possible even in bitter ethnic conflicts. What constructive conflict management involves is not the denial of the divergent narratives; rather, it involves redefining the substantive issues, such that the parties feel there is something they could talk about with an opponent (Kelman 1992), and finding ways to reframe or redefine the symbolic and emotional aspects of the conflict.

Examples of psychocultural dramas I am investigating are disputes about such matters as Israel's opening of an archeological tunnel under the Moslem holy sites in Jerusalem; Muslim girls who wear head scarves in French schools; the use of English in public signs, businesses, and government in French Canada, and the rules about who can send their children to English-language schools there; the flying of the confederate flag over the South Carolina state capitol; and ethnically based land claims in Kenya's Rift Valley.[9] In long-term ethnic conflicts such as those in Northern Ireland, the Middle East, or Sri Lanka, there are a number of psychocultural dramas that could be analyzed.[10]

Psychocultural dramas produce reactions that are emotionally powerful, clearly differentiate the parties in conflict, and contain key elements of the larger conflict in which they are embedded.[11] In psychocultural dramas, identity is linked to a group's core symbols, although these symbols can take a variety of forms: historical narratives, key leaders, ritual actions, places, or objects. Their powerful emotional meaning merges time and space and stresses ingroup solidarity and outgroup hostility (Volkan 1997).

Loyalist Parades in Northern Ireland as a Psychocultural Drama

Parades disputes in Northern Ireland are psychocultural dramas that begin with Catholic objections concerning some aspect of Loyal Order parades, such as their routes, size, or music.[12] A crisis begins when the authorities are asked to decide whether the parade can go forth. It escalates as each side makes its case to the public and mobilizes supporters. Appeals emphasize competing rights, and the conflict evokes powerful images of domination, resistance, historical suffering, and identity in each group's core narratives. In its first three years of existence, the Parades Commission has found that simple reference to a single higher principle or authority cannot provide an avenue for settlement of these conflicts— or even an agreed-upon framework for addressing them—because either these do not exist or their existence is not widely accepted.[13] Most psychocultural dramas arising from parades disputes do not effectively invoke redressive mechanisms and remain stuck in the crisis stage.

As an illustration, consider Portadown, a small town southwest of Belfast near where the Orange Order was founded. In 1985 and 1986 there were six major riots and many violent incidents associated with the Orange Order parades when the Royal Ulster Constabulary (RUC) rerouted the July parades away from a narrow road through a Catholic nationalist working-class area (Bryan 1997, 374–375). Between 1995 and 2000 there has been a series of yearly psychocultural dramas surrounding the Portadown parade. In five of those years, first the RUC and later the Parades Commission prohibited the marchers from parading from Drumcree Church outside the town through a Catholic neighborhood to return to their lodge hall. Escalation and expansion of the conflict took place each year as hard-line Orange Order members and their supporters burned businesses and cars, clashed with police, intimidated Catholics, committed murders, and since 1998 camped out on the church site, insisting they would leave only when they could complete the march. In 1999 and 2000, with the protest still continuing from 1998, the Parades Commission again banned the march and the security forces braced for violence, erecting both barbed-wire and steel-and-concrete barriers and flooding a local stream to create a moat. The Orangemen responded with a symbolic contingent of a handful of marchers who protested to the police verbally but turned back peacefully to avoid a confrontation. Despite numerous efforts by various third parties to mediate the conflict in Portadown, no settlement has been reached.

Parade conflicts become psychocultural dramas when each party's core narratives and the symbols associated with the parades invoke intense feelings, and each side respectively defends and attacks these symbols (North 1997, 41–52). As Bryan wrote, "Orange parades are ritual events and are cited by both those inside and outside the community as pivotal to local Protestant 'tradition,' defining the ethnic boundary between Protestant and Catholic communities" (Bryan 1997, 375). He added that "much of their power comes from their ability to give identity and historical meaning to the world" (392). For Catholics too, Loyalist parades are associated with powerful (and in their case negative) symbols. As a result, confrontations are regarded in win-lose terms and a middle ground is hard to find.

In 1995 the psychocultural drama in Portadown began when the RUC's chief constable refused to allow the Orangemen to parade down the Garvaghy Road to their lodge after their service at Drumcree Church. The crisis mounted during two days of protests, and Protestants evoked images of earlier sieges they had endured; the police then reversed their decision at the last minute, removed the Catholic protesters installed on the route, and permitted the Orange parade—joined by prominent Protestant politicians, including current leader David Trimble and Ian Paisley—to take place. Again in 1996, the RUC first banned the Orangemen from marching on the Garvaghy Road but then reversed their decision after five days of protests and violence throughout the North. Next, the police ousted nationalist protesters critical of the reversal of the original decision. In 1997 the police and army secured the area to allow the parade to occur. These outcomes were hardly an effective resolution, however, and when in 1998 the Parades Commission refused to let the Orange Order march on the Garvaghy Road, thousands of Orangemen and their allies gathered in Drumcree, hoping that once again they could pressure a reversal of the original decision. This time, however, on the eve of the march, the house of a Protestant man and his Catholic wife (living elsewhere in the province) was firebombed, killing her three children. The fervor of the protesters then dissipated and the ban stayed in place, leaving a hard core of protesters camped at Drumcree for months, unable to get permission to finish their march and unwilling to call off their protest.

These powerful psychocultural dramas gain the full attention of the region (and beyond) and evoke strong feelings from each community. They displace other concerns; in 1998 the parade conflicts clearly slowed down, and distracted from, efforts to implement the recently signed Good Friday agreement. In the psychocultural dramas arising from contentious Loyalist parades, the movement from crisis to redressive mechanisms is most often slow or ineffective and the crisis remains unresolved. However, it is possible to view the responses from both Protestants and Catholics to the death of the Quinn children and the powerful, common reactions to the large car bomb that exploded in the city of Omagh in August 1998 as a shared symbolic response that emphasized common values, especially the rejection of violence and a commitment to build a peaceful future. Were these responses effective as redressive mechanisms? Probably not by themselves, but they were not insignificant after the political agreement reached a few months earlier. It is reasonable to hypothesize that what the responses did was to isolate the perpetrators of violence on both sides more effectively than was possible in the past, and to underline values that had widespread cross-community support. Certainly in 1999 there were louder voices in the Protestant community calling for non-confrontation, including important church leaders insisting that Orangemen adhere to good-behavior pledges to attend church services. Protestant political leaders also realized that another violent confrontation would not serve their cause. Perhaps these played an important role in discouraging a violent confrontation at Drumcree in 1999 and 2000.

Interestingly, a quite different situation has evolved in Londonderry/Derry he region's second largest city, where the psychocultural dramas arising from the parades' disputes during the same period have invoked more powerful redressive mechanisms that have led to much more constructive outcomes (Kelly & Nan 1998). In 1995 the psychocultural drama in Derry began when, after the paramilitary cease-fires in 1994, the Apprentice Boys of Derry—whose marches marking the beginning and end of the city's siege in 1688-1689 dominate the annual parading calendar—petitioned to be allowed to parade the entire circumference of the city's walls, as they had been able to before 1970 when the British Army set up positions on the walls overlooking the Catholic Bogside neighborhood. The Apprentice Boys' request produced strong protests from the Bogside Residents Group (BRG) and the course of conflict could have resembled Portadown, but over the next few years multi-party negotiations and redefinition of the parade within the context of a broader cultural festival in Derry provided important redressive mechanisms.

In the days before the August 1995 parade, members of the BRG occupied sections of the walls. When negotiations proved unsuccessful, the RUC finally removed them by force and the Apprentice Boys paraded the full circuit of the walls. In addition, there were incidents during the parade in the afternoon (Kelly & Nan 1998, 50–51). In 1996, after the Drumcree standoff in July, civic leaders and local MP John Hume arranged negotiations in which both the Apprentice Boys and the BRG took part. The sticking point was the BRG's insistence that any agreement concerning Derry also contain limits to parading in other nationalist areas of Northern Ireland. However, issues such as the time of the march on the walls, the number of marchers, who the marchers would be, bands to accompany the marchers, and the music they would play were discussed before the talks eventually collapsed. The government then banned any parading on the walls in August, although the march took place in other parts of the city. In October the Apprentice Boys marched the walls without incident (Kelly & Nan 1998, 55–56).

The following year, the Apprentice Boys refused to enter into direct negotiations with the BRG but did agree to participate in proximity talks in Derry City Hall. Once again the situation was complicated by events in Portadown, although cancellation of an Orange Order parade scheduled for Derry in July eased tensions considerably. Linkage to parades in other areas was still a sticking point, but the mayor, the head of the Chamber of Commerce, and a member of the Parades Commission proved to be effective mediators, and an agreement was eventually reached to permit the parade to take place without violence in 1997 and 1998. In 1999, relations in Derry were tense, a reflection of the uncertain outcome of the political negotiations over the implementation of the 1998 Good Friday agreement. The BRG demanded face-to-face talks with the Apprentice Boys and insisted that the negotiations include a discussion of feeder parades in other cities. When the indirect negotiations broke down, there was rioting and significant property dam-age in South Belfast and Derry. However, Derry Catholics were hardly united behind the rioters, and shortly after the August parade negotiations resumed, there was an agreement around the important Apprentice Boys' December march well before it was held.

The Catholic-dominated City Council was important in the process that led to changes in the structure of the celebration, including agreements regarding the time of day and the number of marchers on the city walls, the parade's organization and route, control over the bands that accompanied the march, and the musical selections they were to play. Certainly some of the changes resulted from each side acknowledging the other's most basic concerns, although there were pragmatic self-interests at work as well.

From the perspective of identity theory, an even more noteworthy point is that the agreement was, in part, made possible by the redefinition of the celebration as a broad, more inclusive cultural festival focusing on the city's history. Each year the festival, partially financed through municipal funds, has expanded to include an exhibition at City Hall, a talk by a Catholic historian, contests involving both Protestant and Catholic schoolchildren, a mini-bluegrass festival and a street fair. Although there are still plenty of tensions and unresolved issues around the Apprentice Boys' parades, the lines of cleavage in the city have been blurred, and the deep threats to or attacks on group identity associated with the marches have diminished in many ways.

Psychocultural dramas reveal important fault lines in relations among ethnic groups. They identify points of emotional fissure in the relations between groups; they can reveal both the specific interests around which ethnic conflicts are waged and the deeper identity dynamics at work, which often make it so hard to find effective redressive mechanisms and to settle these conflicts constructively. Turner's idea that effective redress requires performance of public ritual is fully consistent with what psychoculturally oriented theorists such as Kelman, Montville, and Volkan propose. Ritual is significant because it emphasizes what groups (even those in conflict) share, and it provides reassurance that future relationships will be less threatening than past ones. To the extent that it can achieve this, ritual is an important mechanism for redefining ethnic conflict away from incompatible differences and threatened identities, and toward agreed-upon relations under which groups live together or recognize separation as the best solution.

Signed agreements between longstanding opponents, such as Protestants and Catholics in Northern Ireland, Jews and Palestinians in the Middle East, or whites and blacks in South Africa, are only one step in the peace process. Implementation of agreements forces us to consider how ritual and symbol are a significant part of peacemaking and peacebuilding. An important aspect of implementing agreements involves either developing inclusive rituals that link different communities or redefining older rituals so they are no longer highly threatening and exclusive. This is not easy where group identity and group celebration is often defined in opposition to another community. Even legitimating divergent identities can be an important part of this process. For example, in the Derry city museum, both Protestant and Catholic accounts of history are presented without favoring either.

Conclusion: Examining Identity and Ethnic Conflict

In conclusion, I want to raise three additional questions—puzzles if you like—whose answers would be especially useful to understand the significance of identity in ethnic conflict. I suggest that the framework offered here for examining ethnic conflict, with its emphasis on psychocultural interpretations and psychocultural dramas, will help provide good answers to them.

1. What does identity provide us? Short-run sacrifice for the group is rarely in an individual's self-interest, unless we stretch the concept of self-interest in a tautological direction to include whatever it is that a person happens to do, or have a theory such as sociobiology that explains such behavior at the genetic level (while still failing to explain the proximate mechanisms by which it works) (Ross 1991; Stern 1995). So how is it that young (mainly male) soldiers fight, and older (mainly male) political leaders devote incredible resources (including their sons) to group struggles, and emotional support for the group is often so great that dissent is cause for death? The answer probably lies in complex psychocultural dynamics that systematically confound individual and group interests, and in the power of, and insecurity about, an individual's connections to the group (Campbell 1983).

2. Why is it that there is a striking contrast between the social, contextual, and constructivist character of ethnicity—widely documented in recent social research (e.g., Cohen 1969; Eller & Coughlan 1993; Waters 1990) and popular and political discourse that sees ethnic groups as fixed, unchanging, and often biological entities that fight over "ancient hatreds" (e.g., Kaplan 1993)? I suspect that this gap is far more than just the time lag between what social research has discovered and what the public knows. Rather, I would hypothesize that the gap tells us something about how people understand the social world, our powerful needs to see social categories as "real" and stable, and the threats posed to individual identity by a constructivist view of the social universe. Rituals are

important because they variously reinforce group   boundaries and content, but they also can be significant in changing group identity as well.

Although ethnicity and nationalism are often viewed in terms of enduring and unchanging ingroups—fixed, indelible, almost "biological" categories—we can also view them as mutable and changing over time. But we need to be careful not to go so far as to argue that all categories are arbitrary social constructions. As Smith (1991) argues, although group definition is more socially constructed than popular images hold, it is not as easily altered in the short run, as some constructivist accounts suggest. Rather, we need to explain the social, cultural, and political dynamics that determine how enduring specific identities are, and how they change. In examining ethnic identity over a relatively long (and even medium) term, I hypothesize that terms such as modification, refocusing, broadening, narrowing, incorporation, redefinition, and merging, which can describe changes in the categories themselves and their content, will gain in importance.

3. How can we incorporate identity dynamics into efforts to manage ethnic conflict constructively? To do so, we must begin with the parties' frames of reference, and recognize that cognitive approaches that try to persuade parties that they are wrong, or efforts to change the ethnic categories groups use (governments try to do this all the time), almost always fail. A more productive approach acknowledges groups' perceptions of threats to their identity and seeks to diminish them. For example, recognition and acceptance of the power of a group's narratives can create new possibilities for cooperation. Linking identity (and threats to identity) to new metaphors, or rearranging the content of old ones in culturally acceptable ways, is another possibility for creating new patterns of group interaction.

Volkan (1988, 1997), Montville (1991), and others argue that a crucial dynamic involves mutual acknowledgment of prior loss and processes of collective mourning. Kelman (1987, 1992) stresses the importance for the parties in conflict of coming to believe that acknowledging the other's right to exist is not tantamount to denying their own existence. Such emotional and ritual—not just cognitive—re-definition of a conflict situation is needed for new more complex, and less directly opposed, identities to emerge, such as the emergence of a European identity after the Second World War.

Consider Northern Ireland, where much analysis of the conflict has (appropriately) focused on the long-term discrimination against, and threats to Catholics (Whyte 1990). During the period of direct rule since 1974, the government has addressed the most blatant abuses from the past, and the 1998 Good Friday agreement goes a long way toward giving Catholics both some power in the North and formal links to the Republic in the South. An identity-focused analysis recognizes that a crucial problem to address now concerns Protestant identity: their own uncertain self-definition, and how the Catholic community in Ireland (both North and South), the British, and Europe see them (Bryson & McCartney 1994; Ruane & Todd 1996). After all, it is not clear to many exactly who these people are. Are they colonial usurpers? The "niggers of Britain," as some have described them? Ulsterpersons (whatever that is)? British? A powerful challenge to peace-building is whether Catholics can acknowledge Protestant heritage and identity in the North, so that Protestants no longer feel the need to impose themselves on Catholics as aggressively as they do in marches each summer.

Notes

1. Earlier versions of this paper were presented to the International Society of Political Psychology, the International Studies Association, and a seminar of the Program for Interactive Conflict Analysis and Resolution (PICAR) at Harvard University. I thank the United States Institute for Peace for supporting the research reported in this paper, and Katherine Conner for extensive discussions that helped me to conceptualize the role of psychocultural dramas in ethnic conflicts.

2. The remaining 617 parades are not classified as either loyalist or nationalist; they include such events as May Day parades held by trade unions and Salvation Army parades (Jarman 1997, 118-120).

3. The Loyal Orders, which sponsor the parades, have been hostile to the Parades Commission, and no members of any of the Loyal Orders have agreed to serve on it to date.

4. Campbell (1975) proposed that cultural institutions such as religion have been important in extending cooperative behavior beyond small related kin groups to far larger social aggregates. One could compile a long list of cultural practices that have effectively built upon this propensity to form groups even among individuals who have no prior first-hand knowledge of each other.

5. It should also be recognized that wording and contextual factors (such as recent political developments) affect responses to this question, and the responses show a good deal of variation among Palestinians (Rouhana 1997; see also Smooha 1989).

6. Jewish and Palestinian accounts of events in the 20th century, such as 1948, are similarly different in both content and affect.

7. The flip side is the chosen glory in which a group perceives triumph over the enemy; this is seen clearly in the annual Northern Irish Protestant celebration of the Battle of the Boyne on 12 July.

8. Turner also described social dramas involving individuals competing for a single position for which both are eligible, but they are not my focus here.

9. Although I focus on intergroup psychocultural dramas here, one can fruitfully apply the concept to differences between subgroups in a larger ethnic community, such as the conflict between secular and religious Jews in Israel over military service or the use of cars on the Sabbath.

10. In Northern Ireland one could look at the late 1960s civil rights marches, internment, Bloody Sunday, the Protestant general strike in 1974, and the 1980-1981 hunger strikes in these terms. In many ways, O'Malley (1990) analyzes the hunger strikes as a psychocultural drama without using the term.

11. Not all conflicts are psychocultural dramas. Hence, these three criteria exclude disputes that fail to mobilize intense feelings and those that do not divide a community on group lines.

12. The Loyal Orders are Protestant organizations—the Orange, Purple, and Black orders and the Apprentice Boys of Deny.

13. Using civil servants to resolve divisive values disputes is difficult even in a society with a strong tradition of legitimate authority. In Northern Ireland, this mechanism is especially problematic and fails to gain support from large segments of society.

References

Akenson, D. H. 1992. *God's peoples: Covenant and land in South Africa, Israel, and Ulster*. Ithaca, NY: Cornell University Press.

Anderson, B. 1991. *Imagined Communities: Reflections on the Origin and Spread of Nationalism,* rev. ed. London: Verso.

Arian, E. A., & Shamir, M. 1995. "Why 1992 was not 1977." In *The Elections in Israel: 1992*, edited by E. A. Arian & M. Shamir. Albany, NY: State University of New York Press.

Banton, M. 1983. *Racial and Ethnic Competition*. Cambridge: Cambridge University Press.

Bowlby, J. 1969. *Attachment and loss (vol. 1)*. New York: Basic Books.

Brown, R. 1985. "Ethnic Conflict." In *Social Psychology: The Second Edition*. New York: Free Press: 531-634.

Bruce, S. 1994. *The Edge of the Union: The Ulster Nationalist Political Vision*. Oxford: Oxford University Press.

Bryan, D. 1997. "The Right to March: Parading a Loyal Protestant Identity in Northern Ireland." *International Journal on Minority and Group Rights* 4: 373-396.

Bryson, L., & McCartney, C. 1994. *Clashing symbols? A report on the use of flags, anthems and other national symbols in Northern Ireland*. Antrim, Northern Ireland: Baird.

Buckley, A. D., & Kenney, M. C. 1995. *Negotiating identity: Rhetoric, Metaphor, and Social Drama in Northern Ireland*. Washington, DC: Smithsonian Institution Press.

Campbell, D. T. 1975. "On the Conflicts between Biological and Social Evolution and between Psychology and the Moral Tradition." *American Psychologist* 30: 1103-1126.

———. 1983. "Two Distinct routes beyond Kin Selection to Ultrasociality: Implications for the Humanities and Social Sciences." Pp. 11-41 in *The Nature of Prosocial Development: Theories and Strategies*, edited by D. L. Bridgeman. New York: Academic Press.

Cohen, A. 1969. *Custom and Politics in Urban Africa*. Berkeley, CA: University of California Press.

Eller, J. D., & Coughlan, R. M. 1993. "The Poverty of Primordialism: The Demystification of Ethnic Attachments." *Racial and Ethnic Studies* 16: 183-202.

Fornari, F. 1975. *The Psychoanalysis of War*. Champaign, IL: University of Illinois Press.

Greenberg, J. R., & Mitchell, S. A. 1983. *Object relations in Psychoanalytic Theory*. Cambridge: Cambridge University Press.

Hardin, R. 1995. *One for All: The Logic of Group Conflict*. Princeton, NJ: Princeton University Press.

Horowitz, D. T. 1985. *Ethnic Groups in Conflict*. Berkeley, CA: University of California Press.

Howell, S., & Willis, R. Eds. 1989. *Societies at Peace: Anthropological Perspectives*. London: Routledge.

Jarman, N. 1997. *Material Conflicts: Parades and Visual Displays in Northern Ireland*. Oxford: Berg.

Jones, E. E., & Nisbett, R. E. 1972. "The Actor and the Observer: Divergent Perceptions of the Causes of Behavior." Pp. 79-94 in *Attribution: Perceiving the Causes of Behavior*, edited by E. E. Jones et al. Morristown, NJ: General Learning Press.

Kaplan, R. D. 1993. *Balkan Ghosts: A Journey through History*. New York: Vintage.

Kelly, G., & Nan, S. A. 1998. "Mediation in Practice in Northern Ireland." Pp. 50-61 in *Mediation in Practice: A Report of the Art of Mediation Project*, edited by G. Kelly. Deny/Londonderry: INCORE.

Kelman, H. C. 1987. "The Political Psychology of the Israeli-Palestinian Conflict: How Can We Overcome the Barriers to a Negotiated Solution?" *Political Psychology* 8: 347-363.

———. 1992. "Acknowledging the Other's Nationhood: How to Create a Momentum for the Israeli-Palestinian Negotiations." *Journal of Palestinian Studies* 22: 18-38.

LeVine, R. A., & Campbell, D. T. 1972. *Ethnocentrism: Theories of Conflict, Ethnic Attitudes and Group Behavior*. New York: Wiley.

Lucy, G., & McClure, E. 1997. *The Twelfth: What it Means to Me*. Lurgan, Northern Ireland: The Ulster Society.

Mack, J. 1983. "Nationalism and the Self." *Psychohistory Review* 2: 47-69.

Mahler, M. S., Pine, F., & Bergman, A. 1975. *The Psychological Birth of the Human Infant: Symbiosis and Individuation*. New York: Basic Books.

Montville, J. V. 1991. "Psychoanalytic Enlightenment and the Greening of Diplomacy." Pp. 177-192 in *The Psychodynamics of International Relationships, Volume 2*, edited by V. Volkan, J. V. Montville, & D. A. Julius. (Unofficial diplomacy at work). Lexington, MA: Lexington Books.

North, P. 1997. *Independent Review of Parades and Marches*. Belfast: The Stationery Office.

Northrup, T. A. 1989. "The Dynamic of Identity in Personal and Social Conflicts." Pp. 55-82 in *Intractable Conflicts and Their Transformation*, edited by L. Kriesberg, T. A. Northrup, & S. J. Thorson. Syracuse, NY: Syracuse University Press.

O'Malley, P. 1990. *Biting at the Grave: The Irish Hunger Strikes and the Politics of Despair*. Boston: Beacon.

Pruitt, D. G., & Rubin, J. Z. 1985. *Social Conflict: Escalation, Stalemate, and Settlement*. New York: Random House.

Ross, M. H. 1991. "The Role of Evolution in Ethnocentric Conflict and its Management." *Journal of Social Issues* 44: 167-185.

———. 1993a. *The Culture of Conflict: Interpretations and Interests in Comparative Perspective*. New Haven, CT: Yale University Press.

———. 1993b. *The Management of Conflict: Interpretations and Interests in Comparative Perspective*. New Haven, CT: Yale University Press.

———. 1995. "Psychocultural Interpretation Theory and Peacemaking in Ethnic Conflict." *Political Psychology* 16: 523-544.

———. 1997a. "Culture and Identity in Comparative Political Analysis." Pp. 42-80 in *ComparativePolitics: Rationality, Culture, and Structure*, edited by M. I. Lichbach & A. S. Zuckerman. Cambridge: Cambridge University Press.

———. 1997b. "The Relevance of Culture for the Study of Political Psychology and Ethnic Conflict." *Political Psychology* 16: 523-544.

———. 1998. "Cultural Dynamics in Ethnic Conflict." Pp. 156-186 in *Culture and World Politic*, edited by D. Jacquin, A. Oros, & M. Verweij. Basingstoke, UK: Macmillan.

Rouhana, N. N. 1997. *Palestinian Citizens in an Ethnic Jewish State: Identities in Conflict*. New Haven, CT: Yale University Press.

Roy, B. 1994. *Some Trouble with Cows*. Berkeley, CA: University of California Press.

Ruane, J., & Todd, J. 1996. *The Dynamics of Conflict in Northern Ireland: Power, Conflict and Emancipation*. Cambridge: Cambridge University Press.

Scott, J. C. 1985. *Weapons of the Weak: Everyday Forms of Peasant Resistance*. New Haven, CT: Yale University Press.

Shamir, M., & Arian, A. 1999. "Collective Identity and Electoral Competition in Israel." *American Political Science Review* 93: 265-278.

Smith, A. D. 1991. *National Identity*. Reno, NV: University of Nevada Press.

Smooha, S. 1989. *Arabs and Jews in Israel: Conflicting and Shared Attitudes in a Divided Society (vol. 1)*. Boulder, CO: Westview.

————. 1997. "The Viability of Ethnic Democracy as a Mode of Conflict Management: Comparing Israel and Northern Ireland." Pp. 267-312 in *Comparing Jewish Societies*, edited by T. M. Endelman. Ann Arbor, MI: University of Michigan Press.

Stern, D. N. 1985. *The Interpersonal World of the Infant*. New York: Basic Books.

Stern, P. 1995. "Why Do People Sacrifice for Their Nations?" *Political Psychology* 16: 217-235.

Tajfel, H. 1981. *Human Groups and Social Categories*. Cambridge: Cambridge University Press.

Turner, V. W. 1957. *Schism and Continuity in an African Society: A Study of Ndembu Village Life*. Manchester, UK: Manchester University Press.

Volkan, V. D. 1988. *The Need to Have Enemies and Allies: From Clinical Practice to International Relationships*. New York: Aronson.

————. 1990. An Overview of Psychological Concepts Pertinent to Interethnic and/or International Relationships. Pp. 31-46 in *The Psychodynamics of International Relationships. Volume 1: Concepts and theories*, edited by V. D. Volkan, D. A. Julius, & J. V. Montville. Lexington, MA: Lexington Books.

————. 1997. *Bloodlines: From Ethnic Pride to Ethnic Terrorism*. New York: Farrar Straus Giroux.

Waters, M. 1990. *Ethnic Options: Choosing Identities in America*. Berkeley, CA: University of California Press.

Whyte, J. H. 1990. *Interpreting Northern Ireland*. Oxford: Clarendon.

Winnicott, D. W. 1958. "Transitional Objects and Transitional Phenomena." *International Journal of Psychoanalysis* 34: 89-97.

————. 1965. *The Maturational Process and the Facilitating Environment*. Madison, CT: International Universities Press.

Chapter 13

Coping with Collective Stigma: The Case of Germany

Edward A. Tiryakian

Introduction

The crumbling and seeming overnight implosion of communism in both Yugoslavia (FRY) and even more in the Soviet Empire, the marked expansion of the European Union bringing a number of countries with limited experience in political democracy, the changing demographic composition of Europe in the combined wake of population decline of host populations and immigration from outside Europe, the problematic of tomorrow's Muslim states within Europe, and accelerated economic challenges of globalization have altogether provided in less than two decades vast forces for a major phase of the modernization if not radical transformation of Europe, one as far-reaching as that of the sixteenth century, and again of the latter part of the eighteenth. Integral to this multi-dimensional development is the (re)construction of national identities in Eastern and Western Europe. For most of this post-1989 period, in Europe economic growth has been more stagnant than buoyant increasing the difficulty of achieving national consensus.

In the East (the occidental part of the Soviet world system), both old and new successor states have appeared with a heterogeneous population having to adjust to new and old ethnic minorities, and with varying degrees of ethnic conflict (Alexseev 1999; Cordell 2000), particularly intense and violent in the Transcaucasus (secessionist movements within Georgia, warfare between Armenia and Azerbaijian) and the ex-FRY (which had developed a semblance of national unity under Tito in the 1970s), the latter the scene of violent warfare in the 1990s between Orthodox Serbs, Catholic Croats and Muslim Bosniaks. In several ex-communist countries (Estonia, Latvia, some of the central Asian republics), a Russian-speaking immigrant population (mainly but not exclusively ethnic Russian) that had been privileged elites in professional, military, and bureaucratic strata, now find themselves in a status reversal as something like European "guest workers" and their home language, Russian, which yesterday was the official *lingua franca*, now takes a backseat to the host language, Latvian or Estonian.[1] Elsewhere in East Europe, significant minority groups (e.g., Hungarians in Romania and Slovakia, Turks in Bulgaria, Albanians in Serbia and Macedonia, and Serbs in Croatia) found themselves in the revived and/or constructed nation-state with an ambiguous minority status, if not perceived by the indigenous majority as an "alien" population.

And further on the European periphery, though spared of the enormous challenges of economic and political modernization faced by East Europe, Western Europe has also undergone a major period of transition since 1990 that bears on national identity. The restructuring of internal and external aspects of nation-states is arguably as extensive as after the Treaty of Westphalia.

On the one hand, are internal *centrifugal tendencies* away from the centrality and dominance of the state. A primary centrifugal tendency is the regional devolution of authority in Europe's oldest states (Scotland and Wales in the United Kingdom, the Basque region and Catalonia in Spain, and at present, a similar devolutionary movement in France's troubled Corsica). It is new (and old) immigrant minorities which seem most supportive of the central state, at least in Great Britain and Spain, as multiculturalism becomes increasingly in evidence of the "socioscape". A second such tendency is an apprehension that the evolving European Union is becoming in Brussels a top-heavy bureaucracy, viewed by the conservative right as secularist and viewed by the left as shifting its ethos from the traditional state responsibility for social welfare to the liberal "Anglo-American" model of economic individualism. A disturbing new negative identity for the European Union provoked the unexpected rejection in 2005 of the European Constitution by France and Denmark, their respective "No" vote owing to the alliances of various groups.

Complementing the above are *exogenous centripetal tendencies* of integration into a larger whole, the "new Europe". This is most visible at the socioeconomic level, with the ease of adopting in 2002 a carefully planned single currency having multiple national symbols (Shore 2000); other successes for European integration transcending the nation-state are the dramatic accession of ten new member states in 2004 for example, the increased role of the European Parliament and a rejuvenated mutual security organization, NATO, reenergized by its "humanitarian" intervention in Kosovo/Serbia (though strains may be arising by having NATO's mission extended well beyond its frontiers to an ancillary role in Afghanistan). Perhaps the greatest success of European integration is the absence of interstate warfare on the continent in the past 60 years.

German Identity

Amidst challenges of transformation, this paper focuses on Germany, as having a distinct and complex set of issues involving changes in national identity. First, it rose rapidly to imperial unification 1870-1914, then following the loss in WWI, it became a weak republic in the 1920s, followed by a short resurgence as a military power which lost a disastrous war in the 1940s, leading to a drastic separation into two antagonistic regimes after World War II, with the country as a whole seen as a potential battlefield for World War III. Second, the unexpected collapse of the Soviet Empire led in 1990 to the equally unexpected opting of the German Democratic Republic to (re)join the German Federal Republic. *This is the only instance of an ex-communist state losing its territorial identity and autonomy by becoming part of a Western state.* The political reunification of Germany happened practically overnight; the economic, psychological, and social reunification is a much longer term process that illustrates the complex dynamics of national identity.

What makes Germany the more interesting for comparative analysis is that post-war German identity and development, first for the FRG and then, in the wake of reunification, for the GDR, has been profoundly marked by a double *negative identity*. The primary base has been that of the image of Germany outside of Germany and the internalization of that image within Germany. The secondary base, after reunification, has been a certain negative identity of the "East" by the "West". Taken as an entity, *negative identity* as a feature of national identity has received scant if any attention in the vast literature on national development (including "nation-building") and modernization, and the equally impressive literature on social identity. Yet it contains a very powerful matrix of meanings and values which may reinforce antagonistic or dysfunctional behavior and inhibit more amicable, cooperative activities between the collectivity and its "Other".

Utilizing conceptual tools derived from a social psychological literature based on the seminal writing of Erving Goffman, I will consider how this negative identity has been structured and manifested. In keeping with a frame of reference that might be termed "neo-modernization analysis"[2] (Tiryakian 1991), a complementary focus of attention will be given to collective *coping strategies* of dealing with a negative identity: assuming that social actors wish to discard or overcome the *stigmatization* of a negative identity, how do nation-states as collective actors seek to upgrade their image? I will point out several courses of action taken by Germany in this endeavor, including the most recent "stepping out" at the international level. To conclude on a note of cautious optimism, the new century brings to a reunified Germany the structural factors and opportunities to work out, both on the home front and the international front, a new positive identity.

Conceptualizing National Identity

Ultimately any notion of identity, including national identity, entails a social context; however, the extensive social psychological literature on identity/identities has been predominantly biased toward the identity of *individuals*. Even where that points to group or *collective* identity, the discussion tends overwhelmingly to treat of an *individual's* cognitive mappings and actions (Stryker, Owens and White 2000; Howard 2000; Tajfel and Turner, cited in Howard 2000: 368) as a function of her/his group membership and/or the status of that group relative to other groups. The unit of analysis in the social psychology literature on social identity, a topic that has come in vogue in recent years, then, is still predominantly a micro, subnational referent, individuals and small groups. I begin with the notion of "national identity" as it has developed from a more macro cross-disciplinary focus on nationhood (Calhoun 1993).

Following Renan (1990), I treat "nation" as an intersubjective, interpersonal and dynamic social entity, which entails a collective memory of the past and collective projects of the future. Further, Renan's approach touches on the voluntaristic element of nation by signaling that ultimately, it is "a daily plebiscite," which connotes that in everyday social actions and institutional practices, in commemorations (from holidays to monuments), and in more dramatic historical moments (of heroism as well as infamy) the nation qua "societal community"(Parsons 1969: 254) is validated and revalidated by the engagement and commitment of actors. The nation is not a fixed "fact" (nor, as in some perspective, a "fiction") but an on-going con-struction. [3]

Complementing Renan's frame of nation as a collective enterprise, tacitly in a becoming process, the more micro American approach launched by George Herbert Mead and Charles Cooley also views the identity of the self as arising in the interactive process of self with others. Howard's summary statement of a vast body of recent literature on the social psychology of identities captures this macro-micro convergence: "Identities are thus strategic social constructions created through interaction, with social and material consequences," (Howard 2000: 371). One caveat needs to be kept in mind: if identities as definitions of selfhood are products of action, and thus ultimately partake of the "creativity of action" (Joas 1996), they are not constructed independently of "the other", where "other" may be individuals, groups or entire collectivities such as nation-states. Identities—individual and collective—are constructed in situations by the actor and by the "Other". Furthermore, "situations" are not morally neutral, as Rothbart and Korostelina emphasize in their introduction to this volume: there is an "axiological" grounding of situations, and a "national identity" as experienced by those who identity themselves as members of a given societal community *and* by those on the outside has an important value component which may be very "positive" for insiders or very "negative" for outsiders. In some circumstances, it is possible that a "negative" moral judgment of "outsiders" becomes internalized by the self, individual or collective. While psychology (psychoanalysis and psychiatry) has given attention to the internalization process, there is little comparative research regarding the dynamics of internalization of collective identities.

Absent such empirical research, it may be argued theoretically that national identities, as a distinct species of social identities, may well have multiple meanings and different horizons. The latter implicitly contain different programs of social action for different sets of actors in the same (objective) territory—including actors of the same *ethnie* (Smith, 1987). Even if there is a consensus definition articulated in public life, such a consensus cannot be taken as a "constant" but rather as a variable (no "plebiscite" is carved in stone). Not only individuals but also groups (such as women, blacks, etc.) change their collective identities, including collective names and terms of address by the "others") over time. And this "instability" of identities is also manifest in national identity changes, even from a healthy state of national identity to a bellicose, aggressive nationalism (Smith 1991), or alternatively, from an aggressive nationalism to a more reflective, inward national identity. To unearth the multiple meanings of a given national identity and the latent projects they entail, in any case, is an important direction for comparative empirical research on nationhood in the post-Soviet world.

To extend the conceptualization one step further, I propose, in keeping with a basic presupposition of social identity theory (Mummendey *et al* 1999, 260), that, *ceteris paribus,* a modern national body of persons—whether Americans, Germans, or Gellner's "Ruthenians"—seek a positive national identity, to evaluate themselves and be evaluated by other nations positively. Obviously there are various components to such an evaluation and one might think of a continuum ranging from very high self-esteem as seen by members of the societal community and by "other" national communities to a very low or negative evaluation internally and/or externally. Measurement or observation of where on this continuum of national evaluation a given population stands is obviously difficult with any degree of rigor. What is heuristic is to seek conditions or instances of a *negative national identity*, as the obverse of a positive one. We shall shortly seek to indicate where and how Germany as a collective entity has in the past half century been viewed by Germans and by others.[4]

German National Identity

As Le Gloannec (1994), Fulbrook (1994), Schwartz (1994) and Giesen (1998), among others, have observed, the question of national identity has been a momentous one for much of the course of modern Germany, from the early nineteenth century to our contemporary setting (Giesen 1998). As indicated previously, in the course of successive modernization from the late 18th century to the post-1989 world, Germany has had an exceptional set of changes in national identity: (1) from the laggard if not backward quasi-feudal states, trampled by Napoleon (who wittingly or unwittingly provoked a new generation to think and act "German" with the forging of a new national identity on the battlefield, in the university classroom, and in economic union), to the Bismarck/Wilhelmine great European power; (2) from the unsuccessful endeavors of the Weimar "middle" at constructing German democratic identity in the brief period 1919-1933 to a new collective identity grounded in both an archaic reconstruction of a Teutonic past and a modern shaman who willed himself the crucible of a new millennial Germany; and (3) from the postwar disaster setting of a wrecked nation whose surviving wartime leaders were placed on trial for a new category of crimes, to the radical differentiation of Germany into two sharply opposed states, each becoming a satellite of superpower antagonists.

Now, less than two decades after a brief effervescent moment (Zelikow and Rice 1995; Tiryakian 1995), the reunited Germany faces new challenges of modernization, some of which are shared by other European countries: for example, challenges of integrating Third World immigrants and their children, of globalization limiting the financial autonomy of the state, of an aging population and of government deficit facing cutbacks in welfare expenditures. But some challenges—and particularly for the purpose of this essay the *negative identity* bestowed by remembrances of things past—are rather unique to Germany. Responding to these past and present challenges may well provide the matrix for a new modern national identity.

Germany has been tainted with a strong negative identity, not because of *present* deeds—indeed its behavior as a political democracy and its economic performance have been near exemplary—but because of the stigma of the *past*. To acknowledge and overcome that negative identity has been perhaps a greater challenge for Germany than for any other country, including successors to anterior regimes whose past actions were odious and morally reprehensible. A closer examination of the dynamics of *stigmatization* is in order before examining the strategies of seeking to establish a positive national identity.

Germany's Negative National identity

Although the military adventurism of Kaiser Wilhelm II and above all of Germany's invasion of Belgium at the start of WWI provoked in much of the West an image of a war-like nation in the first decades of the last century, it was the actions of the German state in the 1930s and 1940s which provided the foundation of a negative national identity, certainly for other countries but also for its own post-war citizens. Despite far-reaching transformations of social structures and collective mentalities, the negative identity still leaves its imprint in various manifestations, as will shortly be seen.

In the 1940s Germany was viewed by the outside world as the chief culprit of World War II, as an "aggressor" nation-state that had for the second time in history precipitated a brutal war of expansion. The negative identity was given vivid international display in the Nüremberg trials, which established "crimes against humanity" as a new juridical category. The Nazi treatment of Jews and other minority groups (religious, political, ethnic, and cultural) both within and without the borders of Germany—driven by their racist ideology which sought not only to propagate a "master race" but also to rid the "impure" from the Volk—tainted not only the Nazi regime but the entire country. As a shorthand summary of the negative national identity which attached to Germany for most of the post-war period at least, it is a *"Holocaust identity"* that perhaps best expresses it:

> ... the Holocaust identity drew a border against the past, and founded identity on an attempt to prevent a repetition of the catastrophe... irrespective of political camps, the Holocaust past is accepted in contemporary German public discourse as the reference of national identity, because appealing to it provides an unchallengeable value commitment. The Holocaust identity serves as the reference for entirely different political positions, and is no longer the exclusive project of a particular social carrier (Giesen 1998: 152-60).

To a sociological "outsider", Germany has been replete with the following signs of a negative national identity.

1. National Pride. In terms of country comparisons, Eurobarometer public opinion surveys conducted on behalf of the European Union (EU), consistently show Germany at the bottom of member states on the issue of national pride (Tables 13.1 and 13.2).

While the survey data shows a climb to 67% of the population survey saying they were "very" (15%) or "fairly" (51%) proud to German, that was still below the next country (Belgium with a combined 73%), and below the EU average of 83%. Moreover, the 2000 survey found 32%— one out of three—"not very proud" or "not proud at all", higher than the next country, Belgium (24%), and much higher than the EU average.

2. Discourse. Negative identity is expressed in various ways by German "insiders" (most frequently intellectuals) such as:

> . . . the German postwar identity arose more from an orientation by the demonic and catastrophic than by conceptions of the sacred, or of fulfillment of collective happiness. The new encodings consisted less of a

catalogue of national virtues than of collective avoidance imperatives. This construction of national identity *ex negativo*, accomplished through an exclusion of threat instead of a positive symbolization... left to Individuals a free space in which to design their own identity (Giesen 1998, 146).

Sociologist Wolf Wagner saw this post-war identity as a sort of blanket security... "The Federal Republic I grew up in was not Germany, onlyWest Germany. Over all these years, I had build up an anti-heroic and, asI understood it, an anti-German identity" (cited in Heneghan 2000: 151)."German-bashing" (critically examined by Collins 1995 and by Knöbl 1995) is also frequently used by "outsiders". The most

Table 13.1.
1996 Levels of National Pride, Germany vs. European Union Aggregate
(15)

Would you say you are very proud, fairly proud, not very proud, not at all proud to be

(NATIONALITY AS SPECIFIED IN QUESTIONNAIRE)?
a= Sympathizers   b- Positive Pragmatics   c= Skeptics

	Germany			European Union Aggregate		
	a	b	c	a	b	c
Very proud	6	9	11	22	24	26
Fairly proud	33	33	34	48	47	41
Not very proud	31	38	30	17	18	17
Not at all proud	15	12	16	6	5	9
Don't know	17	9	10	7	6	6

*Source: Eurobarometer 28-04-*99. Results taken from Standard Eurobarometer No. 45.1,
Fieldwork 12th April-18th May 1996.

Table 13.2.
2000 Levels of National Pride, Germany vs. European Union Aggregate

Would you say you are very proud, fairly proud, not very proud, not at all proud to be

(NATIONALITY AS SPECIFIED IN QUESTIONNAIRE)?

Union Aggregate	Germany			European
	West	All	East	(N=15 countries)
Very proud	17	17	17	37
Fairly proud	51	50	46	46
Not very proud	18	20	25	10
Not at all proud	6	6	7	3
Don't know	7	7	5	3

Source: Eurobarometer 54.1, release April 2001. Fieldwork November-December 2000.

common aspect is in popular culture representations (television, plays, movies, novels, etc.), especially in the United States and Great Britain, which depict not only the Nazi abominations of the period 1933-1945 but also frequently suggest that just slightly beneath the placid portly German surface even today lurks the unrepentant Nazi tendencies of the 1930s.

It is also found in public pronouncements alluding to the past as a background factor to be wary of. Thus, the expansion eastward of NATO was justified by both a German member of Parliament and by former American national security adviser Zbigniew Brzezinski as a way of "preventing the power and influence of a united Germany from being used in a 'destructive way'," (*New York Times,* December 7, 1997).

One further instance is invoking the specter of the Nazi stigma to suggest its presence or the threat of its presence in present government actions. This was used by marginal sects in Germany, none more so than the controversial "Church of Scientology", which the German federal government and the state government of Bavaria have not considered as a legitimate mainstream religious organization; consequently, Scientology has been kept under surveillance and has not received state financial subsidies that other mainstream religious organizations receive. In response, the Church of Scientology sought international condemnation of the constraints on their freedom of action, such as taking out a full page ad in the New York Times[5] that juxtaposed the situation of Germany 1995 with that of Germany 1934. The page suggested an identification of Scientologists today with the Jews of the 1930s, and with parallel excerpts from Nazi leaders and from present German officials today, such as the following: "The striving of the Jewish people for world domination"—Adolph Hitler, *Mein Kampf*; "Scientology is striving for world domination"—Claudia Nolte, Minister for Youth and Family Affairs, April 1996." Aside from the excerpts, one reads in the text of the advertisement, "Why are German officials discriminating against Scientologists? There is no legitimate reason, just as there was none for the persecution of the Jewish people. And, let us not forget, Germany has no tradition of religious freedom as in the United States."

3. Signs and Symbols. How to remember the past, how to remember the dead, and what if any would be appropriate national memorials have posed acute dilemmas for Germany for the past half century, as Schlie has well documented (2000, 109-47). Nazi symbols are outlawed in Germany, which has led to a dismantling of most monuments and buildings of that period, though some constructions of the Nazi period, like Berlin's Tegel Airport and its massive style, have remained because they serve a useful public function (Tegel, however, is scheduled to close down in five years with the modernization of airport facilities).

The deep-seated ambivalence regarding expressing and expressions of national identity is particularly marked in Berlin: its designation as capital of a reunited Germany came after spirited discussion in the German parliament. The appropriate architecture for the new parliamentary *Reichstag* was itself vigorously debated (should it be a new modern building or a replica of the one burned in the mysterious fire of 1933?); the Käthe Kollwitz statue of a pietà (a mother holding her dead son in her lap) in the Memorial Hall generated in 1993 a major controversy as a war memorial (Wobbe 1995); the question of razing or renovating the Olympiastadion, site of the 1936 Olympics built by Hitler as a colossal bit of public relations, launched new public acrimony and debate (Steinmetz 1998), and even the design and location of the Holocaust Museum was mired for years in "endless discussions and recriminations," (Markovits and Noveck 1996).

How to evoke the past without evoking its demons has been a slippery rope for Germans, with a negative national identity always threatening to drag down Germany's standing in the global community. Perhaps it is telling that the murals in the Berlin underground— at least those that stand out to a visitor—are scenes from the second half of the 19th Century, evoking a strong but politically neutral appeal of *nostalgie*. A stark alternative to *nostalgie* is what is emptied of the past altogether, such as the desolate open terrain called today the "Topography of Terror" (located at what has been renamed Niederkirchnerstrasse) that housed a set of buildings forming the government district of the most malefic administrators of Nazi Germany—the very navel of an "evil empire".

German university students, who may be taken as surrogate for the rising educated elite, have difficulty in identifying national symbols. A survey of 577 students enrolled in eleven universities in West Germany, East Germany, and Berlin asked "What is an appropriate symbol(s) for Germany in the 21st Century? Why?" The largest category of open-ended responses was the 46% who "refused to answer", with another 9% explicitly stating that Germany should *not* have a national symbol or task; only 11 per cent expressed "traditional national" (national buildings, the flag, the national anthem) or "traditional cultural" symbols, such as German poetry, music, etc. (Ezell *et.al.* 2001).

4. The special case of East Germany. A geopolitical disaster in the wake of WW II was the dismembering of Germany into West and East. It was an arrangement that for the West made the DDR a sort of disturbing "phantom limb". Whether to seek regrafting that "phantom limb", and if so, how, was the subject of much postwar debate in Western Germany. The de facto amputation of Eastern Germany—which had been the geopolitical center of modernization in the unification of Germany in the 19th Century—contributed to the postwar negative identity of the country, in the sense that without the "East", something was missing, at least in the idea of Germany.[6] How to regraft the limb, to extend the metaphor, is an important question still requiring attention.

In the interim, the aging generation in East Germany, those that had formed their career in the DDR, experienced a negative identity after reunification; this is in stark contrast to the positive national identity they had experienced for several decades of a socialist Germany which had triumphed over fascism and became a prized state within the Soviet orbit. If feelings of national pride are still fragile for West Germans, they are even more so for East Germans. Note, for example, a statement of one of the teachers in the 1996 Neuruppin study (discussed *infra*). In response to the questionnaire item, "What do you think should give your students a sense of national pride?" the poignant (anonymous) response was, "Our national pride has been destroyed twice, in 1945 and 1989; first of all, we have to develop it."

Having provided indications of what may be termed a negative national identity, shared for different reasons by West and East Germany, how can the various facets of this identity be tied up in a more analytical fashion?

Conceptualizing Stigmatization

An analytical frame of Germany's negative collective identity may be provided by the microanalysis of *stigma* undertaken years ago by Goffman (1963) and subsequently expanded by others (Hunt 1966; Katz 1981; Heatherton 2000). Goffman used stigma to denote an attribute of the person that is deeply tainting, disgracing; it is above all some visible mark of deformation—of body, from which inferences are made of deformations of character: whatever the particular kind of stigma, the person or group stigmatized tends to be totally devaluated.

> Earlier it was suggested that a discrepancy might exist between an individual's virtual and actual identity. This discrepancy, when known or apparent, spoils his social identity; it has the effect of cutting him off from society and from himself so that he stands a discredited person facing an unaccepting world (Goffman 1963, 19).

Goffman's analysis also considered how stigmatized individuals used *coping strategies* to attenuate damages to their public identity set off by the stigma. We shall see shortly how this part of the analysis of stigmatization relates to post-war Germany.

Though nation and national identity do not figure in the respective studies of stigmatized individuals by Goffman and his followers , the condition and process of stigmatization may be readily applied. Germany, in fact, has been the scene of not one but two instances of stigmatization. During the Nazi regime, Jews were stigmatized with the yellow Star of David, and concentration camp victims were further branded.[7] Exactly as noted by Goffman, this was to totally discredit those so marked from the community of "real" Germans (of Aryan ancestry, of good moral character, etc.). By the dialectic of history, however, what the Nazis used as their badge of honor, the Swastika, has itself become the stigma of the century. It is with the latter instance as relevant for the dynamics of a negative national identity that this paper is concerned. I will now proceed to make further use of the earlier studies of stigma and stigmatization, because much of what the early studies discussed regarding stigmatized individuals may be taken as fitting the German case in the past half-century.

Katz brought out that Goffman's discussion of "impression management" in coping with stigmatization has as a variable just how "evident" is the stimulus. In most instances, the stigma is a source of threat, that is, of bringing about disorder. It may also stimulate sympathy arousal, albeit the deprivation "is often taken as a sign of badness and guilt," (Katz, 1981: 4). And stigmas also differ as a function of perceived responsibility: "the extent to which the possessor is likely to be held responsible by judges for his or her deviance" (ibid.). The significant thing about this is that the Nazi stigma has persisted well beyond the Nazi era, attaching itself even today to a Germany which has repudiated in all ways possible (public apologies, restitution of property, monuments to Nazi victims, etc.) its historic ties.

In connection with this, Katz discussed the stigmatization process as having as one component a "negative attribute model" in the sense that a single attribute (which can be any feature of the stigmatized's physical makeup, social behavior, or familial heritage) may act as a sufficient cause in discrediting, in the eyes of others (i.e., arousing strong feelings of repugnance, disdain, fear, etc.) "The whole moral being of the possessor," (1981, 118). In Nazi Germany, being a Jew discredited all other qualities of the person, even those of say, being a world-class artist, scientist, etc. Today, having been found to have had a Nazi attachment of any sort acts in the same way to discredit all other endeavors, even in non-political activities such as philosophy and literary studies (Gottfried 1996).

Elaborating the stigmatization process, Katz invokes the labeling perspective.This is grounded in the premise that a "deviant" individual is devalued because others, for various contextual reasons, regard the attribute he has as deviant and act toward him accordingly (ibid.). In reference to blacks, for instance, Katz suggest that this increases the chances of being assigned a range of other labels, such as criminal, unemployable, mentally retarded, etc. By the same token, being identified as a Nazi (either a real person or a popular culture character) increases one's chances of being assigned other labels such as sadist, pervert, etc.[8]

Coping Strategies

Goffman, Katz, and Hunt do not stop their respective analyses with stigmatization as conferring a potent deviancy on actors.[9] In keeping with the subtitle of Goffman's seminal essay—"Notes on the Management of Spoiled Identity"—attention is also given to the *coping strategies* of actors having imputed a negative identity. Though lying beyond the scope of this essay, a comparative analysis of how different countries cope with the stigma of past or present action, including as a strategy *denial* that a collective action was a breach of international morality (or even more, denial that the action took place despite what others say), would be an important addition to the study of national identities.

We may suggest three areas that provided space for post-war Germany to develop a positive identity, one for itself, and two for "significant others". This relates to Townsend's observation that the stigmatized show a "powerful . . . desire for integration with ordinary social groups," (Hunt 1966, vii)—in this instance, a stigmatized nation wishing to be accepted by the international community in general and more specifically, by the democratic West and by a community which has particular cause with the basis of the stigmatization.

Democratic transformation

In a remarkably brief period, (West) Germany shed its old clothes and put on new garbs of modernity: the *Wirtschaftswunder* of German economic reconstruction from being a battered war loser became the strongest economy in Europe with high social expenditures. Though intellectuals did not rejoice, the majority of (West) Germans took satisfaction in a new monetary-based "DM identity" and the achievement of socioeconomic reconstruction in two decades, and this without recourse to militarization, which had been the Nazi regime's thrust in coping with the economic stagnation of the Great Depression.

NATO alliance

A second source of positive identity emerged from new alliances with democratic countries. On a one-to-one basis, the Adenauer-DeGaulle amity marked a major turning point in Germany's relation with France, and a postwar generation of Frenchmen grew up without suspicion of Germany. On a wider basis, the Cold War, which offered a significant role for the FRG to play in the new NATO concert of Europe: as a strategic buffer zone that would absorb the first blows of any attempted overrunning of the West coming from the East. Demilitarized by its new republican constitution, Germany was of vital military significance should the need arise. Thus, (Western) Germany sought and found a positive ego-political identity that enabled it to have some sense of belonging and acceptance with the "free world". The price was steep, made even more so in 1983 with the deployment on German soil of missiles that would be themselves prime targets, making Germany a sort of deterrent Maginot Line for the 1970s and 1980s; but this is in keeping with the stigmatized seeking "to attempt to buy acceptance on any terms," (Hunt 1966: 151). The ultimate post-war accolade of being viewed favorably by others was the commitment of the West to the

Berlin airlift and the symbolic solidarity of President Kennedy's famous identification of the world of freedom with West Berlin in his felicitous phrase, "Ich bin ein Berliner!"

Atonement vs. Denial

An actor with a spoiled identity (one caused by past actions) can choose as a general cause of action *denial* as a strategy. A successor state to an anterior regime may deny that it is responsible for the stigma of a past odious action by either blaming it on previous actors or altogether by publicly denying the action took place . Thus the Turkish government successor to the Ottoman Empire, which long had a negative identity in Europe as successor of Islamic invasions and perpetrator of harsh repression of Christian minorities (Delanty 1995) has not only steadfastly refused to acknowledge the oft-documented genocide of Armenians in 1915 (Hovannisian 1999), but also in 2005 placed in the new Turkish Penal Code Article 305 which criminalizes public acknowledgement of the genocide.

Similarly, the post-war Japanese government has been loath to acknowledge the war crimes of the Hideki Tojo government, including the forced prostitution of "comfort women" (Hicks 1995); visits to the Shinto Yasukini Shrine and its War Museum by the Japanese prime minister have aroused condemnation by countries like Korea and China as a blatant denial of war guilt (Shibuichi 2005).

Even the United States, with a moral self-identity as a "city unto the Hill" and a lead prosecutor of international war crimes, backed down in 1995 from the proposed Smithsonian Institution's National Air & Space Museum exhibit of the *Enola Gay,* the plane that dropped the atomic bomb on Hiroshima. In the latter instance, it was not a denial that a raid had taken place but a denial that the Japanese were "victims" of atomic bombing "atrocities" (*Encyclopedia Britannica Online*). One could readily point to earlier conditions of Blacks and certainly Native Americans that are equally stigmas on the historical record of the United States that have not been adequately addressed at the governmental level. And some might view as perhaps an even more egregious source of stigmatization the American declaration of war on Iraq in 2003 for allegedly having weapons of mass destruction, which seem as of this writing (2006) to result more in the mass destruction of the country than in finding such weapons.

(West) Germany has in this respect followed quite a different strategy of coping with the stigma of nazification, what may be called a strategy of *atonement*, of a successor government assuming responsibility for the guilt of its predecessor and seeking to make amends. After an initial period of denial, Germany, especially under Adenauer and later Kohl, has opted for a vigorous, multidimensional atonement.

Although Nazi Germany had been equally repressive of the Roma (Gypsies) and homosexuals, it was Jews who bore the heaviest brunt of the Nazi desire of "purification". Correspondingly, the post-war German government's endeavor of atonement, of accepting guilt and responsibility for the Shoah, has given priority to materially and psychologically redressing the image of Germany in the international Jewish community. This is more than a symbolic gesture; it is also an attempt to validate the significance of the Jewish heritage in German history, which the Nazis had sought to obliterate.

Materially, for example, substantial financing of the Jewish Museum, the Holocaust Museum and the Jewish synagogue in Berlin, the city with the largest Jewish population (8,000) in Germany. And Berlin's Culture Ministry between 1997 and 1999 provided 30% of its religion budget for the Jewish community, which represented 0.58% of the city's population and the community receives over 90% of its annual expenditures from the Berlin government (Laurence 2001, 38). But there are other and equally significant ways.

At one level, ever since the Six-Day War, which saw 59% of Germans showing decidedly pro-Israeli sympathies and only 6% pro-Arab (Markovits and Noveck 1996: 411), Germany and Germans (excepting the far left) have been strong supporters of Israel. Many Germans find it *de rigueur* to make a visit to Israel, part of a "new mania about Jewish everything", including in Germany the popularity of Jewish studies. Giesen's observation is apposite: "This attempt to connect somehow—to find a way to understand what Jews were and are—is an essential part of the intellectual culture of today's Germany," (Giesen 1998: 148). Other indications at the cultural level are worth noting. The publication of an American doctoral dissertation became the sensation of 1996 in asserting the general support in German culture and its entire population for the Nazi policy of exterminating Jews (Goldhagen, 1996), and as much to his surprise as anybody else, its author received an unexpected triumphal tour in Germany (Joffe 1996). In terms of popular culture, Steven Spielberg's *Schindler's List* had immense appeal at German movie theaters, on a per capita basis far outdistancing any other European country, while Yiddish literature and poetry are taken up in cities and university towns (Markovits and Noveck 1996, 439).

Modernizing National Identity in the 21st Century

The new century, the new decade offers challenges and opportunities for a reunited Germany to reconstruct for itself and for others a positive national identity, something which has been elusive in the previous century.

Certainly, like France, Germany is facing a profound socioeconomic malaise that is having a negative impact on its carefully developed "D-Mark identity". Sharp budget reductions for higher education leading to new student unrest, grave problems regarding labor market reforms and cutbacks in social welfare, massive funding for the reconstruction of East Germany, and high unemployment rates[10] have significantly altered the socioeconomic climate, including the security felt by German workers, from one decade to the next. I do not want to minimize the gravity of the downturn in the material conditions, which are having a negative impact on labor and educational relations. Nonetheless my basic view is that Germany can come out of this socioeconomic morass, or at least, that it is not an insurmountable problem.

What nurtures my optimism in this regard is a set of personal observations. In 1996 during a stay in Germany, I visited Dresden, which had become a sea of flames and subsequent ruble of ashes during the terrible and wanton Anglo-American bombardment of Ash Wednesday, February 14/15, 1945 (Taylor 2004). I was very struck with the meticulous care with which all the fragmented remnants of the noted Frauenkirche have been numbered and stored, with the target of having the entire religious edifice rebuilt in ten years (with the help of individual contributions from all over Germany).[11] Later, a visit to Leipzig gave me the occasion to see an equally monumental reconstruction in progress at the Hauptbanhof, with the intention of restoring it to its former Wilhelmine grandeur as the largest railway station in Europe. Together with the equally enormous construction in Berlin of the Potsdamerplatz and the rebuilding of the infrastructure of Eastern Germany, these impressions of a collective will and determination to rebuild, regardless of the immensity of the task, suggest that Germany is capable of reestablishing in short order an impressive material infrastructure.

While this material renovation is important for its positive national identity, there are other equally significant challenges of further modernization. Although "modernization" may be applicable for any social unit of analysis, it is here treated as a general process of development and upgrading of the societal body for environmental fitness; it entails both processes of structural differentiation and integration (Parsons 1960). To focus on the latter, Germany in the new century faces the challenges of integration in three important areas: (1) European integration, (2) the integration of the Turkish minority group, and (3) the integration of East Germany.

European integration

In an insightful discussion of the Maastricht Treaty, Cavazza and Pelanda argued that until 1989, it was the United States, which played the role of prime agent, and engine of European integration, but that with the end of the Cold War that role "passes, inevitably, to Germany," (1994, 67). Although the United States and US-led NATO took a strong military role in the civil wars of ex-Yugoslavia in the 1990s, the overall security concerns of the United States do seem to have shifted away from Europe to more troublesome Third World settings (notably the Middle East, and particularly those that may be sites of terrorism). Neither France, with both left and right internally divided and having in a referendum said "No" to a constitution drafted by the Convention of the European Union chaired by a Frenchman (Giscard d'Estaing) nor is Great Britain under its long-serving Labor leader Tony Blair showing much leadership potential, much less interest in joining the eurozone.

In the present vacuum, Germany finds itself in a pivotal position to shape the future of Europe (not the old *Mitteleuropa* but Europe *tout court*). To accept the responsibilities that attend being de facto the strongest democracy in Europe, and because of its geographical location being the vital bridge between Western and Eastern Europe—which implies providing continuing support for the democratic transition of the latter vast region—constitute an awesome challenge for the German state and for German national identity. What may well be the dilemma of the decade for Germany is how much militarization and how much of an overseas military role to accept in the new global war on terrorism. Short-term this can gain a positive image of being "part of the team" against a common foe (or conversely, refusing to go along with the United States war on terrorism as defined by the Bush administration, led Germany and France to be derisively called "Old Europe" with an implicit financial sanction in the form of redeployment of American military bases out of Germany to more cooperative "New Europe" countries).

Turkish integration

A visitor to Berlin cannot fail to be impressed with the large-size Turkish community, for example, around the Kottbusser Tor area; the Turkish presence is not confined to a single location, if only because the "Doner Imbiss" snack bars seem to be a welcomed popular eatery everywhere in the capital. Public settings where Germans and Turks encounter one another give the impression of strangers sharing the anonymity of life in the metropolis, so well dissected by Simmel (1950b). Highly publicized racist incidents and violence did occur in the wake of unification (some allegedly involving Kurdish attacks on Turks in reprisal of Turkish government attacks on Kurdish separatists), but on the surface at least, a visitor today is unlikely to observe hostility or hear disparaging remarks on the part of ordinary Germans toward Turks, nor anxiety or apprehension on the part of Turks. Still, the challenge for German national identity is very real because "guest workers" as a designation, or even "immigrant", is less and less applicable as Berlin (and other parts of German) is now "home" for a growing segment of the Turkish population: the German-speaking children and grandchildren of the first generation "guest workers". How can one reconcile the German identification of German as a modern democracy with an ascribed status delimiting citizenship?

The distinction which has been made between countries that define citizenship in terms of *jus soli* and those in terms of *jus sanguinis* (Brubaker 1992) seems less and less important in recent years as all industrially developed, affluent countries have converged to severely restrict immigration in the face of a combination of an economic downturn of recent years and/or a conservative political backlash (for the United States, see Jencks 2001). What is a challenge for Germany and for other (Western) European countries as well is the change from being historically lands of emigration to having become lands of immigration, and this becoming more acute as the would-be immigrants are more likely to come from cultural areas (especially different parts of the Third World) very different from those of the "native" population, particularly from sub-Sahara Africa, the Maghreb, and the Middle East.

Still, the Turkish population in Germany seems economically integrated and not just in menial and blue-collar occupations but increasingly in higher-paid service industries, albeit cultural and political integration are at lower levels [see also Gillmeister, Kurthen and Fijalkowski (1989) and Kurthen (1991)]. To accept as Germans those Turks who are willing and committed to being German is not an easy matter—witness that other "democracies", the United States included, have had spotty records of accepting "others" as "us".[12] What is involved in the question of Turkish integration leads to rethinking the model of citizenship appropriate for the new Germany and the new Europe, including rethinking the boundaries of inclusion/exclusion (Müller 1995); this is a critical research area for German social scientists to undertake.

East Germany integration

Undoubtedly, what was the German Democratic Republic is better off materially than would have been the case had unification not taken place, and public opinion surveys have repeatedly shown that East Germans would not want to turn the clock back politically or economically. The contrast today between, say, Dresden, Leipzig or Jena, on the one hand, and Kaliningrad (ex-East Prussia), on the other should convince anyone of the benefit of unification versus isolation. Granted that, economic and political integration are nonetheless juxtaposed with what seems to be social separation.[13]

The social-psychological integration of East and West into a single Germany is the key to the future; the German West really needs to seek the active participation of the East in the reconstruction of a new Germany. The educational sector is critical since it plays a major role in imparting collectivity identity in the nation-building process. In the post-1990 years, many East German educators felt they had been unfairly cast aside in the hiring process, and that the Westernization of East Germany education was as much a "take-over" as a "take-off" process of modernization (Meier 1994).[14] In essence, East German teachers and professors that I met (admittedly, this was ten years ago) felt stigmatized for having been functionaries of the socialist regime; some might have had low professional qualification levels for what they taught (in areas like the social sciences where ideological conformity was paramount), but many were as well if not better qualified than the West Germans who replaced them. One result of this stigmatization is a deep-seated ambivalence regarding the benefits of reunification, although at the time East German academic were guarded about expressing it.

As a supplement to these observations, I had the occasion of administering a questionnaire to a small sample of East German secondary school teachers of English in the region around Neuruppin (Brandenburg). Relevant to this discussion are some questionnaire items. Asked whether they have more than, one, or no contacts (defined as "people you see at least once a year, that you know by first name, that you might visit or meet if you went where they lived and vice versa") with teachers in West Berlin, 24% indicated more than one contact, 18% one, and 55% none (one declined to answer). While 70% felt it was important for their students to have more contacts with students from West Germany, only about half (52%) felt it important for teachers from East Germany to have more contacts with West German teachers. Perhaps even more disturbing are responses to questions pertaining to trust, trust that teachers have in elected officials, as indicated in Table 13.3: it is the very low level of trust across the board that is patent.

Table 13.3
Trust in Elected Officials, Neuruppin Teachers (Brandenburg) (n=33).

Do you have trust that elected officials in Brandenburg are doing the best job they can to improve conditions, given their resources? Do you have trust that elected officials in the federal government are doing the best job they can to improve conditions, given their resources?

	Yes	No	NA/DK
Trust in Brandenburg officials	21%	64%	15%
Trust in federal officials	3	88	9

Undoubtedly, it is not peculiar to East Germany that actors have greater trust in their local officials than in the more distant national representatives. Distrust of authorities is a further precipitate of former socialist regimes, as Sztompka (1996) has forcibly argued in the case of Poland. And East Germany under Communist rule had, as noted by Garton Ash (Venclova 1997), about one of every 50 adult with direct connection to the State Security Service (Stasi)—a much larger number than in the heyday of the Gestapo—which induced not only distrust of authorities but a general climate of distrust.[15] As a legacy of this past, if we assume that students pick up important cues from teachers (as well as parents) regarding their larger sociopolitical environment, the distancing if not alienation of East German teachers from political authorities, especially at the federal level, is indicative of a fault line in an important segment of the German population feeling "not at home" in the new Germany.[16]

There is an encouraging sign of the breaking down of what has been called "the wall in the mind" separating "Wessies" from "Ossis". A study of university students in West Germany, East Germany, and Berlin found little if any regional differences on evaluations of national identity issues; there seems to be an interesting majority convergence toward what might be termed "post-national" or even "post modern values", with emphasis on Germany taking a leadership role in areas such as the environment, enforcing human rights, and promoting world peace (Ezell, *et. al.* 2001).

Conclusion

A few years ago, sociologist Hans-Peter Müller proposed a new "agenda of intellectual creativity" as a visionary critique to counter possible complacency resulting from Western triumphalism over socialism (1996). While I applaud his attentiveness to the Third World (which did not disappear with the demise of the Second World of socialism), I would also stress that the agenda should include the creative efforts of German intellectuals to modernize German national identity by working on the problem areas discussed earlier in this essay. The socio-political integration of ethnic minorities and of the East with the West is crucial areas for the new phase of Germany's modernization, one that requires modernizing mentalities of all parties (even, ultimately, of "German bashers") as necessary "costs" of modernization. They are problem areas which in different guises other countries face. Constructive and courageous efforts to meet these challenges will not only enable Germany to take leadership in making the European Union more than a monetary union, and more than a surrogate for American hegemony. It will also, in the process, recast German national identity away from the past, or the identity of Germany as heartland of the Third Reich, to an authentic emergent present, a heartland of a new pan-European identity.

The start of a new century is a critical transition for West, East, and ethnic Germany to bury definitively the totalitarian stigmas (Nazism and Communism) of the past in the modernization (and "reinvention") of a new common, democratic and inclusive national identity. And this identity is not a self-contemplative one of a German *Sonderweg* but one open and responsible to the world with new European and international initiatives and responsibilities, such as most recently the German government indicating willingness to lead a European Union military mission to protect polling in the June 2006 elections in the Democratic Republic of the Congo; beyond on the horizon, is the real possibility of

Germany taking a seat on the UN Security Council., which would enhance its acceptance as a valued member of the international community. In accepting the challenges of a broad European leadership and becoming a leader of a new inclusive Europe, Germany can cast off both its post-war negative identity and its makeshift D-Mark identity. This, I would propose, is one way to a post-modern positive identity.

An even more recent positive development in the reconstruction of German national identity has taken place in 2006 with Germany hosting the FIFA World Cup of soccer. For the millions of spectators in Germany and the many times larger television audience around the world, Germany was most successful, not only in its surprising third place finish but also in providing the right ambience for an international sporting event. In stark contrast to the 1936 Olympics which Hitler staged to display the swastika, the 2006 football achievements of German coach Klinsmann's *Nationalmannschaft* enabled German citizens for the first time in the post-war world to feel real pride at the black-red-gold tricolor national flag as a valued part of the international community.

In closing this essay on negative identity, and the part of stigma and coping strategies, history provides some interesting ironies. On the one hand, East Germany, which in the West before 1990 had been stigmatized as an oppressive Communist regime threatening the democratic Bonn government and in the years after reunification as both backwards and an economic drain on West Germans, while still something of a "second-class" entity, may in fact be showing West German the way for necessary social and economic reforms (Williamson 2006).

On the other hand, if Germany in the second half of the 20th Century was a salient instance of an inherited negative identity because of its bellicosity and drastic violation of human rights in a previous regime, that mantle in the first part of the 21st Century may be falling on the United States because of its unilateralism, particularly its war on Iraq and treatment of alleged terrorists and other prisoners, in violation of the Geneva convention. Whether the present or a future American administration will seek coping strategies to deal with this new stigma is an open chapter.

Notes

1. On a comparison of the crucial language issue in Latvia and Quebec, see Schmid, Zepa and Snipe (2005).

2. The prefix "neo" attached to "modernization" implies modifications made to the basic modernization paradigm that stresses the capacity of societies to "upgrade" their adaptation to changing environmental conditions. Adaptation is neither linear/unlimited (as had been an earlier tacit assumption of continuous development after "take-off") nor without costs, since the processes of development do not preclude human degradation: there is a "dark side" to the "civilization of modernity" as part of the Jacobin legacy (Eisenstadt 1998). For a fuller discussion of the presuppositions of this paradigm, see Tiryakian (1992).

Of relevance to the present study, neo-modernization analysis takes the area of collective mentalities as an important component of the development process: a new set of actors, a new generation, may have the ability of bringing about new institutional arrangements that are more efficacious (including being more inclusive of the societal community) in improving the general performance of the society. Hence, if modernization brings new strains to social actors, they can also respond with new *coping strategies* (Coelho and Ahmed 1980). This will be taken up in this paper in a discussion of Germany coping with the stigma of a negative identity.

3. To be sure, a nation is a "social fact" in Durkheim's sense of objectivity and external constraint to individual actors (Durkheim 1988: 103-107).

4. The present article may be considered a case study in a more comparative aspect of nations that have been stigmatized with a negative national identity. The case of the "Black Legend" of Spain is prototypical (Gibson 1966; Keen 1985).

5. "Practicing Hate Propaganda," *New York Times*, November 8, 1996, A9.

6. A lesser physical amputation of historic Germany was the taking over by the USSR and its successor, Russia, of Eastern Prussia. Visiting oblast Kaliningrad (ex-Königsberg) in 1996, I was impressed, besides the tomb of Kant, with the vestiges of its glorious Wilhelmine and pre-Wilhelmine days *and* with the terrible isolation of this Russian enclave, from its neighbors (Lithuania and Poland), from the rest of Germany, and even from *its* metropole, Moscow.

7. Claudia Koonz, a noted historian of Nazi Germany, informs me that starting in 1941, Jews had to display stars when outside their home. In the concentration camps each type of "enemy of the state" had to display a distinct color triangle: besides the yellow for Jews, pink was for homosexual, red for political, green for criminal (personal communication, October 2, 1997).

8. And in the United States, to be found to have had a Nazi past may be subject to deportation, even in the case of octogenarians who have led an otherwise normal American life for forty or more years.

9. Neither Goffman nor Katz after him not spend attention on the moral or spiritual elevation of persons receiving the stigma, as noted in the Christian tradition, for example the exemplary receiving of the stigma by Francis of Assissi. In this tradition it may be said that bodily condition is a mark of moral elevation, not one of moral depravity.

10. At year-end 1997, a post-war record 11.3% for Germany as a whole and 18.3% for eastern Germany (*Wall Street Journal,* December 10, 1997, A18). In October 2001 this had declined to 9.4% for Germany as a whole, but still above the average EU figure of 8.3% (*The Economist,* October 27, 2001, p. 100).

11. In fact, the church was reconstructed and reopened a year in advance, in November 2005, a remarkable triumph of peaceful restoration bringing about reconciliation, since for the opening came a delegation from the Coventry Church in England which had been destroyed by German bombardment during the blitz earlier in World War II (Apthorp 2005).

12. "Nativism" has cast a long dark shadow in American history, recast today in various right-wing organizations seeking to make English the official language of the United States and turning back the immigration of Hispanics from Latin America.

13. I observed at East German universities that I visited a lack of informal interaction between West German and East German academics. West German scholars that I talked to who were teaching in East Germany universities told me they opted to live in Berlin and commute to their respective institution because they could not be accepted neither in the East German communities nor by East German colleagues and students.

14. Hagemann-White reports (1997: 559) that in October 1995 of 49 professors of sociology in East Germany, half were from West Germany where they previously lacked tenure, and only eight of the total were "native" to East Germany. In a sense, the political "cleansing" of East German academics that took place after 1990 was the third time this has taken place in 60 years: in the 1930s the universities had to submit to Nazification, and after 1945 to de-Nazification.

15. In his review of Ash, Venclova (1997: 14) notes about the Stasi, "it spied on everybody, first and foremost on the country's own citizens, making virtually everyone suspicious of everyone else."

16. My visit to Neuruppin took place around the time (May 1996) that a referendum was held in Brandenburg regarding consolidation of the province with Berlin (this had been proposed to save money and avoid the duplication of government functions, like in the United States voting on the merger of city and county governments in a given locality. Though Berlin voted for` unification, the countryside rejected it. The Neuruppin teachers were heavily against the unification proposal, in part, some confided, because they were afraid their jobs might be taken over by Berlin schoolteachers.

References

Aho, J.A. 1994. *This Thing of Darkness. A Sociology of the Enemy.* Seattle and London: University of Washington Press.

Alexander, J. and P. Colomy, eds. 1990. *Differentiation Theory and Social Change: Comparative and Historical Perspectives.* New York: Columbia University Press.

Alexeev, Mikhail A., ed. 1999. *Center-Periphery Conflict in Post-Soviet Russia. A Federation Imperiled.* New York: St. Martin's Press.

Anderson, B. 1991. *Imagined Communities: Reflections on the Origin and Spread ofNationalism.* London: Verso, rev. ed.

Apthorp, Shirley, 2005. "Dreden's Heart Reclaimed from the Ashes," *Financial Times*, November 22.

Brubaker, R. 1992. *Citizenship and Nationhood in France and Germany.* Cambridge, MA: Harvard University Press.

Brustein, W. 1996. *The Logic of Evil: The Social Origins of the Nazi Party, 1925-1933.* New Haven: Yale.

Calhoun, Craig. 1993. "Nationalism and Ethnicity," *Annual Review of Sociology,* 19: 211-39.

Cavazza, Fabio Luca and Carlo Pelanda. 1994. "Maastricht: Before, During, After," *Dædalus*, special issue "Europe through a Glass Darkly," 123 (Spring): 53-80.

Church of Scientology International. 1997. *Religious Apartheid 1997. Volume 2: Continuing Official Repression of Minority Rights in Germany.* Los Angeles and Washington: Church of Scientology.

Clogg, Richard. 1991. *A Concise History of Greece*. Cambridge: Cambridge University Press.
Coelho, George V. and Paul I. Ahmed, eds., 1980. *Uprooting and Development: Dilemmas of Coping with Modernization.* New York and London: Plenum Press.
Collins, R. 1995. "German-Bashing and the Theory of Democratic Modernization," *Zeitschrift fηr Soziologie,* 24, 1 (February): 3-21.
Cordell, Karl, ed. 2000. *The Politics of Ethnicity in Central Europe.*Houdmills, Basingtoke (UK): Macmillan; New York: St. Martin's Press.
Delanty, G. 1995. *Inventing Europe: Idea, Identity, Reality.* Houndmills, Basingstoke (UK): Macmillan.
Durkheim, Emile. 1988 (1894). *Les Règles de la Méthode Sociologique,* Jean-Michel Berthelot, ed. Paris: Flammarion.
Eisenstadt, Shmuel Noah. 1998. *Fundamentalism, Sectarianism and Revolutions: The Jacobin Dimension of Modernity.* Cambridge: Cambridge University Press.
Etzioni, Amitai, ed. 1998. *The Essential Communitarian Reader.* Lanham, MD: Rowman & Littlefield.
Ezell, Elizabeth Dietrich, M. Seeleib-Kaiser, and E.A. Tiryakian. 2001. "The Future German Elite and National Identity: A Study of German University Students."
Freudenheim, Tom L. 2001. "Confronting Memory and Museum," pp. 143-66 in Todd
Herzog and Sander L. Gilman, Eds. *A New Germany in a New Europe.* New York & London: Routledge.
Fulbrook, Mary. 1994. "Aspects of Society and Identity in the New Germany," *Dædalus*, special issue, "Germany in Transition," 123 (Winter): 211-34.
Gerhardt, U. 1996. "Talcott Parsons and the War Effort at Harvard University." Paper presented at the International Sociological Association, Research Committee on the History of Sociology Conference, Amsterdam, 16-18 May.
Gibson, Charles. 1966. *Spain in America.* New York: Harper & Row.

Giesen, Bernhard. 1998. *Intellectuals and the Nation. Collective Identity in a German Axial Age.* Cambridge and New York: Cambridge University Press.

Gillmeister, H., H. Kurthen, and J. Fijalkowski. 1989. *Ausländerbeschäftigung in der Krise?* Berlin: Edition Sigma Bohn.

Goffman, E. 1963. *Stigma: Notes on the Management of Spoiled Identity.* Englewood Cliffs, N.J.: Prentice-Hall.

Goldhagen, D. 1996. *Hitler's Willing Executioners. Ordinary Germans and the Holocaust.* New York: Knopf.

Gottfried, Paul. 1996. "Postmodernism and Academic Discontents," *Academic Questions,* 9 (Summer): 58-67.

Hagemann-White, Carol. 1997. "Current Debates in German Social Science," *Contemporary Sociology,* 26, no. 5 (September): 556-59. note to editors: I use this reference in footnote 14 – restore?

Handl, Vladimir and Charlie Jeffery. 2001. "Germany and Europe after Kohl: Between Social Democracy and Normalisation?" *German Studies Review,* 24, 1 (February): 55-82.

Heatherton, Todd F., R.E. Kleck, M.R. Hebl, and J.G. Hull, eds. 2000. *The Social Psychology of Stigma.* New York: The Guilford Press.

Heneghan, Tom. 2000. *Unchained Eagle. Germany after the Wall.* London: Reuters.

Hicks, George. 1995. *The Comfort Women: Japan's Brutal Regime of Enforced Prostitution in the Second World War.* New York: W.W. Norton.

Hovannisian, Richard G., ed. 1999. *Remembrance and Denial: The Case of the Armenian Genocide.* Detroit: Wayne State University Press.

Howard, Judith. 2000. "Social Psychology of Identities," *Annual Review of Sociology,* 26: 367-393.

Hunt, P., ed. 1966. *Stigma, the Experience of Disability.* London: Geoffrey Chapman.

Jencks, Christopher. 2001. "Who Should Get In?" *The New York Review of Books,* 48 (November 29): 57-63.

Joas, Hans. 1996. *The Creativity of Action.* Chicago: University of Chicago Press.

Joas, H. 1999. "Decline of Community? Comparative Observations on Germany and the United States," pp. 55-66 in Josef Janning, Charles

Kupchan, and Dirk Rumberg, eds., *Civic Engagement in the Atlantic Community*. Guterslch: Bertelsman.

Joffe, J. 1996. "Goldhagen in Germany," *New York Review of Books* (November 28): 18-21. Note to editors: I use this reference on page 24—restore?

Katz, I. 1981. *Stigma: A Social Psychological Analysis*. Hillsdale, NJ" Lawrence Earlbaum Associates.

Keen, Benjamin. 1985. "Main Currents in United States Writings on Colonial Spanish America, 1884-1984," *Hispanic American Historical Review*, 65, no. 4 (November): 657-682.

Knőbl, W. 1995. "Kommentar zu Randall Collins' 'German-Bashing and the Theory of Democratic Modernization,' *Zeitschrift für Soziologie*, 24, 6 (December): 465-68.

Kurthen, H. M. 1991. "Ethnic and Gender Inequality in the Labour Market: The Case of West Berlin and Germany," *Studi Emigrazione* (Rome), 28 (March): 82-111.

Laurence, Jonathan. 2001. "(Re)Constructing Community in Berlin," *German Politics and Society*, 19, 2 (Summer): 22-61.

Le Gloannec, A-M. 1994. "On German Identity," *Dædalus*, special issue on "Germany in Transition," 123 (Winter): 129-48.

Luhmann, N. 1982 *The Differentiation of Society*. New York: Columbia University Press.

Markovits,Andrei S. and Beth Simone Noveck. 1996. "West Germany," pp. 391-46 in David S. Wyman, ed., *The World Reacts to the Holocaust*. Baltimore: Johns Hopkins University Press.

Meier, A. 1994. "Take-off or Take-over? The Westernization of East German Higher Education." Paper presented at the RC 04 session 11, World Congress of Sociology, Bielefeld, July 1994.

_____. 1995. "The Political Construction of Curricula: Comparing Re-education Programs in Germany after 1945 and 1990." Paper presented at the ISA RC 04 conference, "Educational Knowledge and School Curricula—Comparative Sociological Perspectives," Jerusalem, December 1995.

Miller, Carol T. and Brenda Major. 2000. "Coping with Stigma and Prejudice," pp. 243-72 in Heatherton *et. al., The Social Psychology of Stigma, op. cit.*

Müller, H-P. 1995. "Citizenship and National Solidarity," in Kenneth Thompson, ed., *Durkheim, Europe and Democracy.* Oxford: British Centre for Durkheimian Studies, Occasional Papers #3.

_____. 1996. "Intellectuals—aprīs la lutte? The role of critique in the knowledge society." Paper presented at the ISA Research Committee on the History of Sociology conference, Amsterdam, 16-18 May.

Mummendey, Amélie, *et al.* 1999. "Socio-structural characteristics of intergroup relations and identity management strategies: Results from a field study in East Germany," *European Journal of Social Psychology,* 29, nos. 2-3 (March-May): 259-285.

Murphy, D.E., S.A. Kondrashev, and G. Bailey, 1997. *Battleground Berlin. CIA vs. KGB in the Cold War.* New Haven: Yale University Press.

Nairn, Tom. 1977. *The Break-Up of Britain. Crisis and Neo-Nationalism.* London: NLB.

Olick, Jeffrey K. and Joyce Robbins. 1998. "Social Memory Studies: From 'Collective Memory' to the Historical Sociology of Mnemonic Practices," *Annual Review of Sociology,* 24: 105-40.

Osmond, John, ed. 1985. *The National Political Question Again. Welsh Political Identity in the 1980s.* Llandysul, Dyfed: Gomer Press, and London: Routledge & Kegan Paul.

Parsons, T. 1960. *Structure and Process in Modern Societies.* New York: Free Press.

_____. 1969. *Politics and Social Structure.* New York: Free Press.

Peck, Jeffrey M. 1996. "East Germany," pp. 447-72 in David S. Wyman, ed., *op.cit.*

Renan, E. 1990 (1882). "What is a Nation?" pp. 8-22 in Homi K. Bhabha, ed. *Nation and Narration.* London and New York: Routledge.

Rossteutscher, S. 1997. "Between normality and particularity—national identity in West Germany: an inquiry into patterns of individual identity constructions," *Nations and Nationalism* 3 (December): 607-30.

Salazar, José Miguel. 1998. "Social Identity and National Identity," pp. 114-123 in Worchel, Steven, J.F. Morales, D. Páez and J-C Deschamps, eds., *Social Identity. International Perspectives.* London and Thousand Oaks, CA: Sage.

Schmid, Carole, B. Zepa, and A. Snipe. 2005. "Language Policy and Ethnic Tensions in Quebec and Latvia," pp. 100-26 in Edward A. Tiryakian, ed., *Ethnicity, Ethnic Conflicts, Peace Processes: Comparative Perspectives.* Whitby, Ontario: de Sitter Publications.

Schwarz, H-P. 1994. "Germany's National and European Interests, *Dædalus,* special issue on "Europe Through a Glass Darkly," 123 (Spring 1994): 81-106.

Schlie, Ulrich. 2000, *German Memorials.* Timothy Nevill, trans. Bonn: Goethe-Institute Inter Nationes.

Seeleib-Kaiser, Martin. 2001. "Globalisation and the German Social Transfer State," *German Politics,* 10 (December): 103-18.

Sheehan, J.J. 1992. "National History and National Identity in the New Germany," *German Studies Review.* Special issue: German Identity. 15 (Winter): 163-74.

Shibuichi, Daiki. 2005. "The Yasukini Dispute and the Politics of Identity of Japan: Why All the Fuss?" *Asian Survey,* 45, 2 (March-April): 197-215.

Shore, Cris. 2000. *Building Europe. The Cultural Politics of European Integration.* London and New York: Routledge.

Simmel, G. 1950a. "The Stranger," pp. 402-08 in Kurt H. Wolff, ed., *The Sociology of Georg Simmel.* New York: Free Press.

———. 1950b. "The Metropolis and Mental Life, " pp. 409-24 in Kurt H. Wolff, ed., *The Sociology of Georg Simmel.* New York: Free Press.

Smith, A.D. 1987. *The Ethnic Origins of Nations.* Oxford and New York: Blackwell.

———. 1991. *National Identity.* Reno: University of Nevada Press.

Steinmetz, Greg. 1998. "What if They Put Sky Boxes Where Hitler Once Stood?" *Wall Street Journal,* January 9, 1998, A1.

Stryker, Sheldon, Timothy J. Owens, and Robert W. White, eds. 2000. *Self, Identity, and Social Movements.* Minneapolis & London: University of Minnesota Press.

Sztompka, P. 1996. "Trust and Emerging Democracy: Lessons from Poland," *International Sociology* 11 (March): 37-62.

Tajfel, Henri and J. Turner. 1986. "The Social Identity theory of intergroup behaviour, pp. 7-24 in S. Worchel and W.G. Austin, eds., *Psychology of Intergroup Relations.* 2nd ed. Chicago: Nelson-Hall.

Taylor, Fred. 2004. *Dresden, Tuesday February 13, 1945.* New York: Harper Collins.

Thies, J. 1994. "Observations on the Political Class in Germany," *Dædalus*, 123 (Winter 1994): 263-76.

Thunem, Judith. 1966. "The Invalid Mind," pp. 47-53 in Paul Hunt, ed., op. cit.

Tiryakian, E.A. 1991. "Modernisation: Exhumetur in Pace (Rethinking Macrosociology in the 1990s)," *International Sociology*, 6 (June): 165-80.

————. 1992. "Pathways to Metatheory: Rethinking the Presuppositions of Macrosociology," pp. 69-87 in George Ritzer, ed., *Metatheorizing*, Newbury Park and London: Sage.

————. 1995. "Collective Effervescence, Social Change and Charisma: Durkheim, Weber and 1989," *International Sociology*, 10 (September): 269-81.

Venclova, T. 1997. "State of Snitch," review of Timothy Garton Ash, *The File. A Personal History, in New York Times Book Review,* October 12: 14-15.

Werz, Michael, 2001. "Instituting Europe: Germany, the Union, and the Legacy of the Short Century," *German Politics and Society.* 19, 2 (Summer): 1-21.

Williamson, Hugh. 2006. "From Burden to Beacon: How Eastern Germany is Becoming an Unlikely Pace-Setter for Reform," *Financial Times*, March 9, p. 9.

Wobbe, T. 1995. "Distorted Memory: Germany's New National Memorial," paper presented at the international conference, "Memory and the Second World War in International Comparative

Perspective," April 26-28, Netherlands State Institute for War Documentation, Amsterdam. *der gesellschaftl*

Zapf, W. 1996. "Die Modernisierungstheorie und unterschiedliche Pfade ichen Entwicklung," Leviathan, 24, 1: 63-77.

Zelikow, P. and C. Rice. 1995. *Germany Unified and Europe Transformed*. A Study in Statecraft. Cambridge, MA: Harvard University Press.

Chapter 14

Reconciliation as *Realpolitik*: Facing the Burdens of History in Political Conflict Resolution

Joseph V. Montville

Introduction

In the lexicons of most foreign affairs professionals, "reconciliation" is a soft word. It has a religious flavor. In fact, one of its early definitions was the restoration of a penitent sinner to the church. "Reconciliation" is not a word ordinarily used by diplomats, journalists or professors of international relations when plans are discussed to deal with the enduring crises between Greece and Turkey, the Tamils and Sinhalese in Sri Lanka, Protestants and Catholics in Northern Ireland, Israelis and Palestinians, even Quebeckers and Anglophones in Canada. The diplomats work first to prevent violence and then to patch together a deal that will get the adversaries—and the mediators—through the short term until, they hope, some unforeseen actor or event comes along to resolve the conflict once and for all.

And that is the problem. Traditional peacemaking approaches by and large avoid the normative issues that nourish and drive the so-called intractable ethnic and sectarian conflicts. The demands for justice by the warring sides are considered self-centered, emotional and not susceptible to the rational process of bargaining for advantage and the art of arranging trade-offs. But the toughest conflicts are those where one or, usually, both sides have suffered traumatic losses in the past and in recent times. The people in the groups or nations in conflict are predictably and unavoidably emotional, irrational and obsessed with issues of justice. They are victims, and they display all of the symptoms of victimhood psychology. They feel vulnerable to attack. They fear and loathe their adversaries. Building trust between the parties is a Sisyphean task.

The thesis of this chapter is that any conflict resolution strategy that does not address the psychological needs of the victims and victimizers can only have a superficial effect on the resolution especially of ethnic and sectarian conflict. Thus the only practical approach to the so-called intractable conflicts is one that aims for the actual reconciliation of peoples and nations. Relationships need to be changed for the better. Ways have to be found to help adversaries face the historic burdens on their relationship, to help them present their historic grievances but also, especially, acknowledge the wrongs they have inflicted on the other side. A process must be established in which the losses of victims are recognized and made part of the public record for all to see.

The parties to the conflict need to be led to accept moral responsibility for their behavior and that of their predecessors. Only then will some sense of justice begin to emerge among the people who have suffered. And when a sense of justice emerges, so too will the possibility for real peace. For there is an inescapable link between justice and peace that is documented in human psychology but to date eludes professional diplomacy and statecraft which tend to cling nostalgically to a scientifically unjustifiable concept of power politics and cynicism, the traditional *realpolitik*.

Today there is a new, much more realistic, *realpolitik*, based on new knowledge acquired through the synthesis of political analysis and the scientific study of human behavior, or psychology, in the enriched discipline of political psychology. There is impressive evidence of the dominance in universal human needs not only for food, shelter, and physical safety, but also for recognition, acceptance and respect, the iron laws of human nature. The most persistent evidence of the sources of continued antagonism and inclination toward violence comes from documentation of wounds to the self-concept or self-esteem of identity groups—ethnic, religious, linguistic, indeed, whatever trait a group considers its most noteworthy characteristic. Thus the new *realpolitik* recognizes that conflict resolution and peace building can succeed only if the circumstances that originally produced a people's sense of victimhood are recognized and dealt with. There is a need for healing processes that go far beyond training in problem-solving skills.

Theorists and practitioners of international conflict management and resolution have a moral obligation to understand and respect the depth of hurt of the peoples we propose to help. We must proceed with modesty, great care, professional skill and commitment to the analysis of the historic and psychodynamic dimensions of what is essentially a task in healing in the relationships between the groups and nations whose conflict we approach. Conflict resolution theory and practice have evolved to the point where there can no longer be ambiguity about this obligation. This chapter attempts to outline the dimensions of this task.

The Dimensions of Political Reality

For some academics and professionals in the field of international affairs, the idea that they need to understand the psychodynamics of political conflicts is unwelcome or even intimidating. Indeed, psychology offers explanations as to why the study of emotions and human motivation is something many of us avoid with some energy. (Psychology even explains why we use the psychological mechanism of avoidance to insulate us from unwelcome information.) Thus it may be useful to hear from a person who is neither a psychologist, an academic theorist, nor a conflict resolution practitioner. He is, however, one of the most respected jurists in the world, whose recent responsibilities have included service on commissions of inquiry in South Africa and the international war crimes tribunals on former Yugoslavia and Rwanda.

Justice Richard Goldstone was already a distinguished lawyer and jurist when President De Klerk asked him in 1991 to head a new Commission of Inquiry Regarding Public Violence and Intimidation, in South Africa. Between 1991 and 1994, Justice Goldstone emerged as a powerful influence in South Africa's transition from an apartheid regime to a new experiment in democracy. In 1994, President Nelson Mandela named him to the newly established South Africa Constitutional Court but allowed the Justice to accept a two-year appointment as prosecutor at the International Criminal Tribunal in the Hague with responsibility for war crimes in Bosnia and Rwanda. This was the first such war crimes tribunal since the Nuremberg and Tokyo tribunals after World War II. On January 27, 1997, Justice Goldstone spoke at the U.S. Holocaust Museum in Washington, D. C. He entitled his speech, "Healing Wounded People." The following is a synthesis of relevant portions of the speech based on an audiotape of the event. The text that follows may be considered verbatim from Justice Goldstone's speech:

> The most important aspect of justice is healing wounded people. I make this point because justice is infrequently looked at as a form of healing—a form of therapy for victims who cannot really begin their healing process until there has been some public acknowledgment of what has befallen them. How one deals with the past, with a series of egregious human rights violations, is a problem that has come to the fore since the end of World War II. How is it that there has been more genocide since World War II than before? How do we explain that people seem not to have learned the lessons of history?
>
> Obviously, the problem after World War II for many European countries was how do we deal with our own part in the human rights violations. This affects not only Germany but also the Netherlands, Belgium, and Scandinavian and East European countries where there was collaboration with the Nazis. Certain Latin American countries began to deal with their post-World War II past through establishment of various truth and reconciliation commissions. In South Africa, how would we deal with the past? Should we brush it under the carpet? Why reopen the sores? In Rwanda, how can we deal with a country that suffered one million dead in genocide? In attempting to answer these questions, the people who should be consulted more than anyone else are the victims. What do they want and need for themselves and

their families?

Justice is one aspect of what must clearly be a multi-faceted approach to healing a wounded people—a wounded nation. One must not expect too much from justice, but my experience has shown me that justice can play a very material role in bringing about an enduring peace. The link between peace and justice was seen by the UN Security Council in 1993 with resolution 827 that established the first international war crimes tribunal since Nuremberg and Tokyo. And it must be noted that these latter were not international, but rather multinational tribunals made up of the victorious powers in the war.

It must be noted that it was the photographs of emaciated prisoners in Bosnia that mobilized public opinion internationally and especially in the West so that the UN Security Council was moved by the member states to make the link between peace and justice by establishing the international war crimes tribunal. Without making that specific linkage the Security Council would not have set up the Hague tribunal. However, this key point was forgotten at Dayton. There was a conflict between the peace and justice linkage and the politics of negotiation. In The Hague, we decided that we had a mandate that could not be compromised by diplomats. We would press on with our task. The link between peace and justice is not a link between peace and cease-fires, but between justice and enduring peace.

One thing I have learned in my travels in former Yugoslavia, Rwanda and South Africa is that where there have been egregious human rights violations which have gone unaccounted for, where there has been no justice, where the victims have not received any acknowledgment, where they have been forgotten, where there has been national amnesia, the effect is a cancer in the society and is the reason that explains the spiral of violence that the world has seen in former Yugoslavia for centuries and in Rwanda for decades, as obvious examples.

There are five important contributions justice can make to the process of peace building. First, it can expose the guilt of individual perpetrators, thus avoiding the human tendency to assign collective guilt to an ethnic group or a religion. In the areas I have visited, individuals have not been blamed, but an entire people have been. For example, Serbs tend to blame Croatians as a people for the genocide of Serbs, Jews and Gypsies by the Ustashi regime during World War II. One of the main contributions of the Nuremberg tribunal was the identification of individual criminals.

Second, it can record the truth in the public record. This makes it extremely difficult for perpetrators or their sympathizers to deny the truth, as, for example, people who attempt to deny the reality of the Holocaust. It is a matter of fact that perpetrators work very hard to cover up evidence of their dirty work.

Third, it can provide acknowledgment of crimes against the victims. I have learned especially in South Africa, the importance to victims of public, official acknowledgment. This is not because the victims do not know that happened to them. Or do not know their perpetrators. They do. But they still want their story brought to a court or tribunal because they want public, official acknowledgment of what happened to them. Thousands of victims of apartheid have been coming to the Truth and Reconciliation Commission in South Africa. They have left a better people. The same is true at the Hague tribunal. Many terrified, broken people have made their way to the war crimes tribunal to give evidence in public. Even when given the option of private testimony, they insist on doing it in public. When they left The Hague, they were different people. Their healing had begun.

Fourth, truth and justice help in the dismantling of the institutions of society that have played a role in injustice and oppression.

And, fifth, criminal justice is a deterrent to further human rights violations. There are direct links between the efficiency of policing and low crime rates. What deters criminals is the fear of getting caught, not the penalties established. It is no different with wartime and political crimes. If political leaders think they will be brought before an international tribunal, they will think twice before committing a crime. I am not speaking only of criminal justice *per se*, but also of public exposure by truth and reconciliation commissions.

Our commission [Inquiry Regarding Public Violence and Intimidation, 1991–94] in South Africa was able to expose terrible deeds within days of their occurrence. Television news broadcast our findings usually in less than a week after the event. This had a calming effect on people who might have taken to the streets without the psychological relief provided by exposure of the truth about the crimes.

After the political transition in South Africa, President Mandela ruled out a Nuremberg-type tribunal because it would have caused uproar in the white community. But there were too many victims who needed public acknowledgment of their losses. He decided on the compromise between amnesia and criminal trials. The Truth and Reconciliation Commission, his choice, has received over four thousand applications from South African police, security forces and other perpetrators of "political" crimes for indemnity from prosecution. Can one imagine what it would have been like to put four thousand plus people on trial?

The Truth and Reconciliation Commission [whose two year life is coming to and end] will have an important impact on South African society. It has served as a bridge between the past of human rights violations and a future of a democratic country in which a human rights culture could be built. It is saddening to note that the international war crimes tribunal at The Hague has not been able to have the same effect in former Yugoslavia. Without the political will of the international community to pursue indicted war crimes suspects, the body's healing effect in that region has been severely limited.

Justice Goldstone's Holocaust Museum speech is remarkable in its clear and unambiguous support of the psycho-political approaches this writer and his colleagues have developed in more than twenty years of work with victims and victimizers in conflict resolution processes. And because the Justice claims no status as a researcher or theoretician–he just calls it as he sees it in his real world, tribunal work–his beliefs and conclusions influence others. His speech is a rousing overture to the body of this chapter.

Acknowledgment and Justice in Conflict Resolution Strategies

Training seminars and problem-solving workshops are a basic tool in conflict resolution theory and practice, but the approach to reconciliation and peace building taken here goes well beyond the question of how to design an effective workshop. In fact, it challenges the assumptions of many practitioners of conflict resolution who get involved in political disputes that conflict resolution training is the essence of the process. The emphasis here fully reflects Justice Goldstone's themes of the burdens of history on contemporary political relationships and the specific, non-negotiable psychological tasks history imposes on those who would design a conflict resolution strategy. Thus political diagnosis must be the first step in a strategy, followed only then by the choice of the most appropriate problem-specific conflict resolution techniques and processes.

There are a variety of approaches available for improving political and social relationships between groups that have endured protracted conflict and violence. Some focus on the task of helping leaders define steps forward in a discreet, creative way. Still others focus on the challenge of helping to shift public belief systems in a way that supports leadership initiatives toward compromise for peace building. Others emphasize practical relief and development. In this approach conflict resolution workshops and training can have important, but only partial, roles in the grand strategy. The conceptual conviction here is that political conflict resolution is made up of a set of strategic challenges, and the inevitably complex nature of conflicted inter-group and international relationships requires a politically sophisticated approach. For example, the task of organizing a third party facilitated council of historians from each side in a conflict to "walk through history" is fundamental to eliciting an inventory of unacknowledged and unatoned wounds from the past. Then one must consider and build into strategic planning the healing potential of enlightened political leaders as well as the critical importance of non-political leadership from various sectors of involved communities, groups and nations.

Integrated conflict resolution strategies will almost always include the stimulation and encouragement, including perhaps partial funding, of inter-ethnic networks organized to pursue super-ordinate goals, for example, clean water or the mobilization of community services. The potential roles of interfaith clergy and networks of women drawn from groups in conflict in promoting the habit of collaboration and non-violent resolution of conflict must also be considered. Here traditional negotiation and mediation training for interethnic teams that have specific tasks to perform can be put to very good use. For example, Mercy Corps International, an American relief and development agency, successfully trained Muslim, Serbian and Croatian employees in post-Dayton Bosnia who worked together rebuilding houses and laying water pipes.

The concept of integrated strategies in a comprehensive approach to ethnic conflict resolution is attracting important attention in world capitals, the United Nations and the Organization for Security and Cooperation in Europe (OSCE), among other international organizations. And in 2005, in what could be seen as a revolutionary initiative by the United States government, the Agency for International Development committed itself to a five-year, $400 million program to deal with Instability, Crisis, and Recovery (ICRP) that will recruit and direct outside specialists in conflict mitigation and management using integrated strategies in fragile states in need of help.

This chapter is an exposition on the broader theory and practice of complex conflict resolution acquired by the writer in over twenty-five years of evolving practice. It is based on an appreciation of the burdens of history, specifically of continuous insult from and the infliction of traumatic losses on one people by another. The losing side's resultant psychology of victimhood sets up the enormously difficult barriers that impede traditional conflict resolution and peacemaking approaches. It requires a healing process that is not provided for most of the current schools of conflict management and resolution.

Victimhood in History

There are three major characteristics of victimization. First, the individual, group or nation has experienced a major traumatic loss of freedom, physical or mental capacity, life, property, territory, security and/or faith in the future. Second, the violence or aggression that caused the loss cannot be justified by any sense of law or morality. And third, there is an enduring, if not always conscious, fear among the victims that the victimizers, or their descendants, by refusing to acknowledge their injustice and to express contrition, are only waiting for a chance to return and attack again.

History, of course, is the story of victims and victimizers. Indeed, the advent of ethnic and sectarian conflict resolution theory and practice, unofficial or "track two" diplomacy (Davidson and Montville 1980–81, Montville 1986), and the concepts of preventive engagement (Dellums 1993), or constructive engagement (Perry 1994), and preventive diplomacy (Boutros Ghali 1993), represent conceptual initiatives designed to head off the tragedies which engender victimization and the perpetuation of political violence.

The critical first step in an international conflict resolution process that aims at genuine reconciliation is acknowledgment by the aggressor group or nation or its successors if current leaders have no direct responsibility for the unjust actions. Acknowledgment is the act of explicitly describing and accepting moral responsibility for the violent acts or events, which caused the traumatic losses to the victims. Explicit description of the acts for which guilt is acknowledged is necessary so that the victims can be assured that none of the violations are overlooked in the subsequent contrition and forgiveness transaction which is the ultimate aim of the healing process and which is the psychological foundation of genuine reconciliation (Montville 1993).

Richard Hovannisian, a historian at UCLA, interviewed five hundred survivors of the wartime massacres and forced march of Armenians in Anatolia in 1915 and 1916 by the last of the Ottoman regimes. He compiled a tragic record of victimization of a people and said, simply,

> We want Turkey to admit its guilt. We want acknowledgment. Our homeland, our property was all taken.... The major grievance is the indifference of the world community. That this slaughter remained unpunished, and so did not serve as a preventative (Rosenfeld 1985).[1]

Acknowledgment may require detailed preparation. One of the most dramatic and morally responsible acts of acknowledgment occurred in 1991, when the Chancellor of Austria, Franz Vranitsky, citing exhaustive research by an Austrian historian, accepted responsibility for Austria's complicity in the Holocaust. The historian had used state archives and other sources to unequivocally document the complicity of Austrian officials and non-governmental organizations, businesses and individuals in the Nazi campaign of persecution of the Jews in the late 1930's and of participation in the execution of the genocide during the war.

Up to the time of Vranitzky's revelation, in a speech televised live to the nation on July 6, Austrians had denied any complicity in the Holocaust, and, indeed, claimed that Austria had been Hitler's first victim. To his enduring credit, Vranitsky said in his speech,

> Austrian politicians have always put off making this confession. I would like to do this explicitly, also in the name of the Austrian government, as a measure of the relationship we must have to our history, as a standard for the political culture of our country (quoted in Montville 1993).

Taking a Walk through History

It should be apparent from the discussion above that literally and in the therapeutic sense, taking a history of a political conflict is a fundamental step in designing a reconciliation strategy. The medical metaphor is apt when the idea of healing is introduced into the discussion of the methods of international conflict resolution. In the psychodynamic approach, the third party team designing and executing and integrated strategy should ideally have at least one member with clinical experience in individual and small group psychotherapy. This could be critical in a problem-solving workshop setting where an interethnic leadership group is being developed, for example. The job of the clinically trained person is to tact-fully help participants express *inter alia* basic anxieties about national identity, rage over past assaults and losses, fears about present and future safety and security, and perceptions of the adversary side.

People coming from violent conflict experiences often go to great lengths to avoid honest expression of basic emotional preoccupations. They use well-known psychological defenses. Yet it is only expressions of feelings that can reveal the agenda for healing in a conflict resolution process. And without searching discussion of healing needs, workshops can go on for days, weeks or even years without providing insight about how to end violence and genuinely resolve the conflict. The specific techniques and dynamics of the psychologically sensitive problem-solving workshop are described extensively in Volkan, Montville and Julius, *The Psychodynamics of International Relationships* (Lexington 1990 and 1991), and they need not be repeated in this chapter. However, it would be useful to outline some general guidelines.

Recruiting Participants

The first step in planning a workshop for a leadership group or a council of historians is the careful selection of the representatives of the groups or nations in conflict for participation in the process. They should have keen intellect, knowledge of history, emotional maturity, moral courage, leadership qualities and the ability to influence high-level, official political thinking and decision-making.

Senior political leaders in intense conflict situations are rarely the best candidates for psychodynamic work and membership in a "leadership" group, because they are generally emotionally deeply invested in their public image if not survival and therefore not susceptible to change simply through new insight; and they are also limited in their room to maneuver by the negative emotions of their constituencies. Their ability to "learn," acknowledge and articulate new and potentially healing insights gained in workshops is limited by the need for the insights to be acquired also by their mass of followers.

Senior political leaders are also unlikely to risk their positions by getting out in front of their followers with moral or peacemaking initiatives toward the enemy. This is a political reality that careful conflict resolution strategies must take into account. Intellectual or spiritual leaders from other sectors of a community or nation may have to undertake the moral responsibility, paving the way for politicians to "catch up" with and hopefully transform this fundamental leadership by others into official policy. These non-political leaders could be academics, clergy, business people, trade union officials, poets or playwrights. What make them leaders are their courage, wisdom and capacity to show the way.

The Psychodynamic Workshop

The early presentation of fears, grievances and political demands by the more victimized group is predictable and normal in a problem-solving workshop. After initially creating a sense of safe space for the participants, psychologically sensitive third parties will attempt to make room for them to walk through history with each other, if and as the group dynamic indicates it is appropriate. "Walk" is the operative term. We prefer not to "run," with a torrent of accusations and condemnations, but rather encourage the thoughtful expression by representatives of each side of the unhealed wounds in their historical relationship.

This is almost always a profound learning experience for each side, since victimizers traditionally employ the psychological mechanisms of avoidance and denial of unpleasant truths about their behavior and that of their forebears. And victims are ordinarily so intensely absorbed by their own losses that they rarely understand the complexities and moral ambiguities their oppressors might have experienced in the past. It is especially important to take into account the fact that the victimizers may also have been victims at some point. This is why revision of history books—getting the story straight—is common in successful political reconciliation processes (Willis 1965, Montville 1986, 1990, and Luttwak 1994).

Taking a reasonably accurate history of a conflicted relationship in effect sets out the agenda for healing in a psychologically informed conflict resolution strategy. Participants in a leadership group or workshop or council of historians will lay out what Volkan (1992) calls their "chosen traumas", those losses in history which have greatest symbolic meaning for their profound sense of victimhood and which continue to nourish their feeling of unacknowledged injustice. We have dealt theoretically with the critical importance of acknowledgment in ethnic and sectarian conflict resolution. It might be useful at this point to look briefly at two case studies for the impact of historic loss on contemporary violent conflict.

Understanding the Mind of Serbia

Most observers of the Serbian leader Slobodan Milosevic credit a speech he gave in Kosovo in April 1987, as the beginning of his climb to dominant power. In the speech, he implored the Serbian minority to stay in the province even though it was economically distressed. Kosovo's population was 90% ethnic Albanian, but the province was also the birthplace and symbolic center of Serbia's national identity. The Serbian Orthodox monasteries of Kosovo are a legacy of a tribal chieftain Stefan Nemanja, who established the first independent Serbian state in the twelfth century CE.

On June 28, 1989, Milosevic returned to Kosovo to celebrate the 600th anniversary of Serbia's national day that, ironically, marks the defeat of Serb forces by the Ottoman army at the Battle of Kosovo. Hundreds of thousands of Serbs from Yugoslavia and around the world gathered at the site for the event that commemorated the loss as an enduring sacrifice of the Serbian nation for the benefit of Christian Europe. "Six centuries ago," Milosevic said, "Serbia defended itself on Kosovo, but it also defended Europe. She found herself on the ramparts for the defense of European culture, religion and European society as a whole."

The Serbian epic poem declares "Whoever is a Serb and of Serbian blood and comes not to fight at Kosovo...Let nothing grow from his hand...until his name is extinguished forever." Thus Kosovo represents for modern Serbs not only the signature event in the establishment of national identity, but also a gift for which Europe shows no gratitude. Furthermore, Serb leaders rationalized their contemporary genocidal violence in Bosnia as the continuation of their struggle against Islamic "fundamentalism," again in the face of an ungrateful Christian Europe.

Psychologically, there is a direct link between the pro-Nazi, Roman Catholic Croatian Ustashi genocide that killed hundreds of thousands of Orthodox Serbs during World War II, and the loss at Kosovo, five centuries earlier. Indeed, there is also a direct link between the Catholic Fourth Crusade's destruction of Orthodox Constantinople in April, 1204 CE, in Serbian memory.

Each case, the Serbs perceived Latin Europe as indifferent to their sacrifices. And each case nourished the profound sense of victimhood that tells Serbs that the world cares nothing about their well being, sacrifices and losses. The majority of Serbs who kept Milosevic in power until his overthrow in 2000 appeared until then to live in an awesome loneliness in which they concluded that they may use any means to defend their identity from extinction. The new democratically elected Serbian government has made important and psychologically healthy strides towards connection with Europe and the West.

The Uncivil War in Northern Ireland

Unlike Milosevic, The Irish Republican Army (IRA) has not come close to majority support either in the Republic or among the Catholics in Northern Ireland, but it has endured as a lingering symbol of Irish Catholic victimhood in the historic relationship with England, even after the 1999 Good Friday peace agreement signed by Northern Ireland political party leaders through the mediation of former Senator George Mitchell.

When one understands the psychology of victimhood and its capacity to flourish generation after generation unless dealt with, it becomes easier to comprehend the meaning of the IRA's attempt to blow up Margaret Thatcher and her cabinet in Brighton in 1984, car bombs in the British Parliament's parking garage, the rockets fired at No. 10 Downing Street and every other incidence of IRA terrorism. And terrorism it is, denounced vigorously by the Irish government and the great majority of Irish Catholics in the Republic and in Northern Ireland.

But there has been a remarkable persistence and determination in the hatred of the tiny minority of IRA militants against Britain, cease-fires notwithstanding. A symbolic walk through the history of the Anglo-Irish relationship helps to explain why. Such a walk could be a valuable stimulus to English memory and a contribution to current peacemaking efforts for Northern Ireland.

By all available evidence, official Britain has persisted in avoiding or denying its historic moral responsibility to the Irish people for a centuries-old record of extraordinary violence and repression. This contemporary resistance to acknowledgment of and contrition for past aggression kept alive an Irish instinct toward defense of the collective self expressed, among other ways, in IRA violence.

Any number of historical works could be used to "take the history" of English oppression of the Irish people, but *The Story of the Irish Race*, by Seamas McManus (1993), first published in 1921 and still in print is representative. In a chapter called "Suppressing the Race," the author begins by saying, "Through these many dread centuries England's energies were concentrated upon an effort, seemingly, to annihilate the Irish race (1993, 399)." McManus quotes a letter from the eminent English conservative statesman and political philosopher, Edmund Burke:

> All [of Cromwell's penal laws. . . were manifestly the effects of national hatred and scorn towards a conquered people whom the victors delighted to trample upon and were not at all afraid to provoke...every measure was pleasing and popular just in proportion as it tended to harass and ruin a set of people who were looked upon as

enemies to God and man; indeed, as a race of savages who were a disgrace to human nature itself (McManus 1993, 399).

Oliver Cromwell landed at Dublin in 1647, with 17,000 men in a vengeful Puritan passion, "Bible-reading, psalm-singing soldiers of God—fearfully daring, fiercely fanatical, papist hating....and looking on the inhabitants as idol-worshiping Canaanites who were cursed of God, and to be extirpated by the sword (McManus 1993, 423)." Cromwell's Christian soldiers slaughtered thousands of men, women and children at Drogheda, "in the streets, in the lanes, in the yards, in the gardens, in the cellars, on their own hearthstone" (McManus 1993, 424). At Wexford Cromwell made no distinction between defenseless civilians and armed soldiers. Britain through the 17th century had conducted a policy of active genocide against the Irish race. In the 19th century there was a policy that could be called passive genocide.

By the 19th century, the potato was the primary food of the Irish peasant majority. Cereals, meat, and dairy products were produced, but they were sold largely to England. When the potato blight hit in 1845, followed by complete crop failures in 1846 and 1848, the export pattern of other foods to England was maintained. Peasants died of starvation. Sir Charles Trevelyan, permanent head of the English Treasury said that to feed or clothe the dying would be to interfere with the free market.

The Irish population was estimated at 8.5 million in 1848. By 1851, emigration and starvation had reduced it to 6 million. (Today the population stands at about 4.5 million.) The famine had a powerful psychosocial impact. There was a sense of cumulative degradation in both those who remained and those who immigrated to North America.

Yet there has been a significant development in the centuries old Anglo-Irish antagonism. In November, 1997, British Prime Minister Tony Blair formally expressed regret at London's role in the Irish famine. Further, Blair came out in support of a memorial to Irish famine victims in Liverpool where many of them were buried. He also promised to explore sources of government funding for the memorial. The Irish News said on November 20, the prime minister's powerful and sympathetic letter [of support] will be seen as an act of reconciliation and acknowledgment of the hurt that was caused in those terrible years. There is no question that the arrival of Mr. Blair at No. 10 Downing Street has had a major impact on the peace process in Northern Ireland.

Poland, Russia and the Katyn Forest Massacres

Yet another very important example of detailed work to fill in the blank pages of history is the case of Russia's acknowledgment of its moral responsibility for the murder of 26,000 Polish officers and other imprisoned citizens in March, 1940. The event is known as the Katyn massacres for the name of the forest in Belarus where most of the Poles were held. The Polish-Russian collaboration on archival research, Gorbachev's partial and then Yelstin's complete and unqualified acknowledgment of Soviet government responsibility for the order to execute the Poles stands an impressive model of a psychologically sensitive conflict resolution process.

Poland and Russia have had a historical relationship burdened with violence, conquest and accumulated grievance, the balance of which has been clearly on the Polish side. When Mikhail Gorbachev proposed to rehabilitate the Polish relationship with the Soviet Union during his revolutionary campaign of glasnost and perestroika, he found a willing response in the Polish Communist Party and also the intelligentsia. But a representation of the latter–writers, artists, journalists, philosophers and social scientists–published open letters to Gorbachev insisting that before his initiative toward Poland could be accepted, the Soviet Union must acknowledge responsibility for the murder of the Polish officers whose bodies had been found in the Katyn Forest. The murders were seen as a cold-blooded act by Stalin to destroy the young leadership generation of an independent country, a selective, class genocide.

The Soviets had always admitted that the Poles at Katyn were part of a contingent of 15,000 reserve officers seized by the Red Army in 1939, when the Soviet Union absorbed eastern Poland under the Molotov-Ribbentrop pact. But Moscow insisted from the beginning that the massacre had been carried out by Hitler's troops in 1941, after the German Army overran the Soviet camp where the officers were interned. Successive Communist governments in Warsaw had backed the Soviet story, but accumulating evidence pointed to the NKVD as the murder instrument, acting on Stalin's orders.

In 1987, General Wojciech Jaruzelski announced that a joint Soviet-Polish commission was being established to examine the "blank spots" in the record of bilateral relations. Also to be studied were the 1939 Soviet-German treaty dividing Poland and the 1944 Warsaw uprising, in which many Polish and Western observers believe that Soviets paused to let the Nazis finish off the pro-Western Polish leadership before occupying the city.

Gorbachev eventually accepted Soviet responsibility for Katyn in April 1990, after the Communist government in Warsaw had collapsed. But the admission was only partial, limiting the blame to the NKVD. It was not until October 14, 1992, that President Boris Yeltsin sent a special envoy to President Walesa with two sets of photocopied secret Soviet documents which proved that Stalin and several Politburo members signed Resolution number 144, dated March 5, 1940, instructing the NKVD to execute 14,700 Polish officers and other prisoners of war. The order included 11,000 other Polish civilians and state officials who were imprisoned by the Red Army in 1939. There were numerous other documents in Yeltsin's package including handwritten reports and memoranda from the Khrushchev period. Later, Moscow released other documents on Soviet-Polish relations including secret protocols from the Molotov-Ribbentrop agreement.

There is no suggestion that this unprecedented act of revelation of the most damning of state secrets was entirely an act of moral compulsion. Yeltsin's gift of documents also embarrassed Gorbachev by revealing critical material that Yeltsin said he withheld from the Poles. And the act also served to further discredit the Communist Party in Russian and international opinion, a continuing goal of Yeltsin in his political struggles. Nonetheless, the release by Yeltsin, the successor to the victimizers, and, almost as important, the delivery by special envoy of the Katyn documents to Lech Walesa, the formal representative of the victimized Polish nation, in a ceremony of acknowledgment and contrition was existentially an act of vision and extraordinary political courage. Certainly the reactions of Walesa attest to this judgment.

American journalist Louisa Vinton (1993) reported that publication of the Politburo resolution had an enormous impact in Poland. President

Walesa was visibly moved by the revelations and, wiping tears away, handed the microphone over to the poet Czeslaw Milosz during the announcement of the transfer of the documents (Vinton 1993, 21).

One Polish journalist wrote that the release had "epochal significance." The weekly "Politkya" said that "contemporary Polish-Russian relations in the moral sphere now have the chance to throw off the burden of the past." Walesa said that Yeltsin hade made a "heroic decision" which none of his predecessors had the courage to make. Vinton showed admirable insight into the critical need for acknowledgment, writing that:

> Many outside observers were puzzled by the strength of the Polish reaction, as the facts of the case had long been known, especially in Poland. The relevant point for the Poles, however, was moral and political, rather than historical. *A truth known to them but denied public confirmation for fifty years had at last been acknowledged.* [italics added.] The revelations reinforced the sense that Poland's relations with Russia could only become normal once all the facts about the past had been revealed (Vinton 1993, 24, emphasis added).

Justice in Times of Transition

It is encouraging to note that an American non-governmental organization that is neither self-consciously associated with conflict resolution nor psychodynamically-oriented has had a psychologically important conflict resolution impact in several countries in transition from authoritarian rule to democracy. The Project on Justice in Times of Transition, originally founded in New York, is now an inter-faculty program at Harvard University. Conceived by Timothy Phillips, a Boston-based businessman and public policy activist, the Justice Project brings together political leaders, policy makers, jurists, human rights activists and writers to confer on basic issues of civil liberties, human rights and national reconciliation in former Communist countries of Eastern Europe, the former Soviet republics, the Baltic states as well as South Africa and in Latin

America.

The original focus of the Justice Project was the protection of civil liberties and respect for the rule of law during the transition from totalitarianism to democracy in the former Communist countries of Europe. The Project soon came to focus on the fundamental task of "coming to terms with the past" which included confronting the legacy of human rights abuses. The use and function of truth commissions was explored with Eastern Europeans being briefed *inter alia* by former Argentinean President Raul Alfonsin and former Chilean Truth Commission member Jose Zalaquett on the experience of their two countries. Launched at a major conference in Salzburg in 1992, the Project helped organize an unprecedented three day meeting in January, 1993, in San Salvador called "Reconciliation in Times of Transition" which involved President Christiani and FMLN military chieftain Villa Lobos, Defense Minister Ponce and senior representatives of the military, business, government, labor, NGO and former guerilla sectors of Salvadoran society. The very presence of former bitter enemies in one conference hall caused veteran observers of Salvadoran politics and warfare to shake their heads in wonder.

While the importance of acknowledging historic wrongs was emphasized by some of the plenary speakers, including this writer, and all Salvadoran presenters spoke of the need for healing the wounds of the past, there were no acknowledgments of responsibility for specific acts of aggression. Unlike the Katyn Forest case, the deaths in El Salavador were perhaps too recent, and the perpetrators too concerned about criminal liability to be frank about their roles. However, acknowledgment had been carried out by two truth commissions, one international and one domestic, whose findings had been generally known to the public and were to result shortly after the conference in public condemnation of senior military officers and certain guerilla leaders. The former were slotted for early retirement and the latter were declared ineligible for political office.

The Project on Justice in Times of Transition became a moveable consultation in steady demand. Czech President Havel and Hungarian President Goncz were strong supporters of the Justice Project as a mechanism for reconciliation. The Project was invited to South Africa by Nelson Mandela to assist in a post-election healing process, paving the way for creation of the South African Truth and Reconciliation Commission. In 1997, it convened a meeting in London of significant leaders of the Muslim, Serbian and Croatian communities in Bosnia that the participants believe was an important contribution to the building of alliances in support of the civilian goals of the Dayton peace accords.

The Justice Project also mounted an extraordinary public meeting in the previously much-bombed Europa Hotel in Belfast in June, 1995. The gathering brought Catholic and Protestant politicians and militants together with British and Irish cabinet ministers. Poets and writers evoked the tragic past of Ireland with a poignancy that riveted the audience. It was an experience of profound mourning. Several of the Northern Ireland participants in the Belfast meeting took part in the negotiations leading to the Good Friday peace agreement in 1998.

Contrition and Forgiveness

Clearly one of the most daunting tasks in the psychodynamic approach to international conflict resolution is to persuade victimizers or their descendants to offer meaningful, unambiguous and unqualified apology to the victimized group or nation. There have been inspiring cases such as President Yeltsin's initiative with the Katyn documents, Chancellor Vranitsky's speech to the Austrian people, and President Walesa's formal apology to the Jewish people for Polish anti-Semitism and complicity in the Holocaust offered in the Israeli Knesset and other examples at lower or non-official levels (Montville 1989, 1993).

Beyond the fact that meaningful apology requires moral courage, there is the fear that the victimized individual, group or nation might use the apology as a weapon to exact crippling reparations or to visit political revenge upon the leaders or body offering the apology. Many observers of the Turkish-Armenian case believe one of the obstacles to unambiguous acceptance by Turkey of responsibility for the 1915–1916 massacres of Armenians is the fear that Armenians would demand massive financial compensation. An official of the Russian Foreign Ministry who supported a Katyn-style turn-over of incriminating Politburo documents on Stalin's Baltic annexation decisions told this writer in April 1994 that

Moscow could not do so because of fears that Latvia and Estonia would use the acknowledgment to justify the forced repatriation of their large Russian-speaking minorities.

Despite the difficulties in carrying out contrition/forgiveness transactions between perpetrators and their victims, there are signs that the idea is becoming more powerful in the public discussion of the resolution of protracted ethnic and sectarian conflict. The American writer, Cynthia Ozick, joined the debate in the wake of the murder of Muslim worshipers by Baruch Goldstein, a deranged Israeli settler from Brooklyn, at the Tomb of the Patriarchs in Hebron in February 1994. In an op-ed piece in the "New York Times," Ozick urged contrition as a primary assertion of effective leadership, an example of the political power of sorrow, shame and grief.

> What is required...as an element of *realpolitik* is an understanding that mutual contrition, even more than the resolution of issues of acreage and border patrols, must be the next step in the [Israel-Palestinian] peace process....Hardheaded politicos will no doubt scoff at the notion of mutual contrition as a way of...enhancing the negotiations. They will think it too soft a proposal, smacking of the useless high ground, unserious, devoid of pragmatism. But no way...can be more serious, more allied to truth-telling, more effective and more profoundly practical (Ozick March 2, 1994, A15).

No less a student of the meaning of Jewishness in the modern era than Hanna Arendt (1958) wrote that forgiveness was essential to human freedom. "Only through this constant mutual release from what they do can men remain free agents, only by constant willingness to change their minds and start over again can they be trusted with so great a power as that to begin something new." Lawrence Weschler, a staff writer for "The New Yorker," and participant in the Project on Justice in Times of Transition, quoted Arendt and in an eloquence of his own wrote:

> True forgiveness is achieved in community: it is something people do for each other and with each other–and,

at a certain point, for free. It is history working itself out as grace, and it can be accomplished only in truth. That truth, however, is not merely knowledge: it is acknowledgment, it is a coming-to-terms-with, and it is a labor (Weschler April 5, 1993, 4,6).

Cynthia Ozick, the late Hannah Arendt and Lawrence Weschler each, in their distinct way, have played a leadership role–literally showing the way–in trying to instruct the broad public in the essence of peacemaking. Each has recognized the difficulty for senior political leaders of consistently or even intermittently exerting moral leadership in the raucous and sometimes violent arena of politics. And so there seems to be a constant need for moral–lifesaving–leadership from other sectors of society.

As the pioneers of the new field of international conflict management and resolution walk toward the outstretched arms of groups and nations seeking help to escape their past and present tragedies, it seems clear that a moral task devolves on them in the process. And that task is to respect the suffering of their clients by learning what must be learned about their history and their losses and helping them to walk through the processes necessary to come to terms with their past. If conflict resolution practitioners go about their work with a compassion informed by profound knowledge and skill, they can help people and nations to heal and get on with their future. And they will be able to take justifiable satisfaction with their accomplishments.

Note

1. The Turkish government acknowledged the occurrence of "a great tragedy" in 1915 but denied there was a deliberate Ottoman policy of genocide against the Armenians.

References

Boutros-Ghali, Boutros. 1992. "Agenda for Peace", New York: United Nations.

Davidson, William D. and Montville, Joseph V. 1981–82. "Foreign Policy According to Freud," *Foreign Policy* 45, Winter/Spring: 145–157.

Dellums, Ronald V. 1993. "Preventive Engagement: Constructing Peace in a Cold War World," *Harvard International Review* Vol. XVI, No. 1: 24–27.

Luttwak, Edward. 1994. "Franco-German Reconciliation: The Overlooked Role of the Moral Rearmament Movement." Pp.37-63, in *Religion: The Missing Dimension and Statecraft*, edited by Douglas Johnston and Cynthia Sampson. Oxford and New York: Oxford University Press.

McManus, Seamus. 1921, 1993. *The Story of the Irish Race*, Old Greenwich, CT: The Devin Adair Company.

Montville, Joseph V. 1993. "The Healing Function in Political Conflict Resolution." Pp. 112-128, in *Conflict Resolution Theory and Practice*, edited by Dennis Sandole and Hugo Van Der Merwe. Manchester and New York: Manchester University Press.

Montville, Joseph V. 1987. "The Arrow and the Olive Branch: A Case for Track Two Diplomacy." Pp. 7-25, in *Conflict Resolution: Track Two Diplomacy*, edited by John W. McDonald, Jr. and Diane Bendahmane. Center for the Study of Foreign Affairs, Foreign Service Institute, GPO.

Montville, Joseph V. 1989. "Psychoanalytic Enlightenment and the Greening of Diplomacy," *Journal of the American Psychoanalytic Association*, 37/2.

Ozick, Cynthia. 1994. "Mutual Sorrow, Mutual Gain," *New York Times*, March 2, 1994

Perry, William J. 1994. Address by the Secretary of Defense at George Washington University, March 14. Washington, DC: Department of Defense.

Rosenfeld, Stephen. 1985. "Armenian Memories," *Washington Post*, April 11, 1985, p. 4.

Vinton, Louisa. 1993. "The Katyn Documents: Politics and History," *RFE/RL Research Report* 2, No. 4, January 22: 1993.

Volkan, Vamik D. 1992. "Ethnonationalistic Rituals: An Introduction," *Mind and Human Interaction* 4, No. 1: 3–19.

Volkan, Vamik D., Montville, Joseph V., Julius, Demetrios A. 1990, 1991. *The Psychodynamics of International Relationships*, 2 vols., New York: Lexington Books.

Weschler, Lawrence. 1993. "Getting Over," (unsigned), New Yorker, April 4: 4, 6.

Willis, F. Roy. 1965. *France, Germany and the New Europe, 1945-1963*, Stanford, CA: Stanford University Press.

About the Authors

David Alpher

David Alpher is a Masters' graduate and current PhD student at the Institute for Conflict Analysis and Resolution. His studies there focus on asymmetrical conflict, particularly with ethnic and religious components, and on bridging theory and practice to advance the study and implementation of conflict resolution in its various forms. Regionally, he is a specialist in the Middle East, where he has worked on track-two dialogues within Israel and Palestine. He comes to the field of conflict resolution with a diverse background as a US Infantryman, writer, technical journalist, documentary filmmaker and backpacker.

Sandra I. Cheldelin

Sandra Cheldelin is the Vernon M. and Minnie I. Lynch Professor of Conflict Resolution at the Institute for Conflict Analysis and Resolution (ICAR). A psychologist and expert in organizational conflict, she facilitates large and small scale mediations, coaches senior executives, helps resolve interpersonal, intergroup and inter-organizational conflict, designs institution building mechanisms and supports collaborative leadership. She has worked with more than 150 organizations and is often a keynote speaker or invited lecturer on workplace issues of violence, change, race, gender and conflict. She facilitates large-scale interethnic and interfaith community dialogues on topics of fear, terrorism, violence and suspicion. She is coauthor (with Ann Lucas) of *Conflict Resolution*, (Jossey Bass, 2004) co-editor (with Daniel Druckman and Larissa Fast) of *Conflict: from Analysis to Intervention* (Continuum, 2003) and serves on a variety of conflict resolution related boards. Previous appointments include Provost at the McGregor School of Antioch University, Academic Dean at the California School of Professional Psychology (Berkeley campus), and Director at Ohio University College of Osteopathic Medicine, holding faculty appointments at each.

Rom Harré

Rom Harré began his academic career in mathematics and physics, teaching in New Zealand and Pakistan. Later, at Oxford, he turned to philosophy physics and chemistry developing the case for scientific realism in such books as *Varieties of Realism*. More recently he has applied linguistic analysis to the analysis of the everyday construction of social reality, conceived on the model of a pan-human conversation in such books as *Social* and *Personal Being*. He currently works at Georgetown and American Universities in Washington DC.S.

Ayse Kadayifci-Orellana

Born and raised in Turkey, Dr. Kadayifci-Orellana received her Ph.D. at the American University in Washington D.C. in the field of International Peace and Conflict Resolution and her M.A. at the University of Kent at Canterbury, England in the field of International Conflict Analysis. Her doctoral dissertation looked at different interpretations of war and peace in the Islamic tradition and explored the reasons behind the rise of extremist interpretations in the West Bank and Gaza. Dr. Kadayifci-Orellana' research interests include religion, culture and conflict resolution, sources of peace building and conflict resolution in the Muslim world, mediation and negotiation from a cross-cultural perspective, and sustainable development and peace building, among others. She is currently a Temporary Assistant Professor at the School of International Service at American University in Washington D. C. and Associate Director of Salam Institute for Peace and Justice, a nonprofit organization that focuses on conflict resolution, peacebuilding, human rights, democratization and development in the Muslim world. Dr. Kadayifci-Orellana has co-authored the edited the volume, "Anthology on Islam and Peace and Conflict Resolution in Islam: Precept and Practice" as well as various journal articles on Islam and nonviolence, conflict resolution, and mediation. She is currently working towards publishing her dissertation entitled: Standing on an Isthmus: Islamic Narratives of War and Peace in Palestine.

Karina V. Korostelina

Karina Korostelina is a Research Professor at Institute for Conflict Analysis and Resolution, George Mason University and Professor in the Psychological Department at National Taurida University. She is a Fellow of European Research Center of Migration and Ethnic Relation (ERCOMER). She conducts research on the topics of national and ethnic identity, ethnic conflict resolution and ethnic relations, reconciliation and peacebuilding. She has been Fulbright New Century Scholar, Research Fellow at the Kennan Institute, Woodrow Wilson Center, and Fellow at the Curriculum Resource Center of the Central European University. She has received grants from the MacArthur Foundation, Soros Foundation (Research Support Scheme, Managing Multiethnic Communities Project, Renaissance Foundation), the United State Institute of Peace, US National Academy of Education, Bureau of Educational and Cultural Affairs of USDS, INTAS, IREX and Council of Europe. She is authored the following books: *The system of social identities: The analysis of ethnic situation in the Crimea*, *The social identity and conflict*, *Psychodiagnostic of interethnic relations in the Crimea, Social identity: Structure, dynamic and implications or conflict* (forthcoming). She is editor of *Interethnic coexistence in the Crimea: the ways of achievement* and co-editor of *Identity, Morality and Threat: Studies in Violent Conflict*. She conducts seminars, round tables and trainings for leaders of NGOs, community activists, teachers and government officials, organized by Danish Refugee Council, OUN and other international organizations.

Joseph V. Montville

Joseph Montville is currently a Diplomat in Residence, American University, Senior Fellow, Center for World Religions, Diplomacy and Conflict Resolution, George Mason University and Senior Associate, Center for Strategic and International Studies. He founded the preventive diplomacy program at CSIS in 1994 and directed it until 2003. Before that he spent 23 years as a diplomat with posts in the Middle East and North Africa. He also worked in the State Department's

Bureaus of Near Eastern and South Asian Affairs and Intelligence and Research, where he was chief of the Near East Division and director of the Office of Global Issues. Montville has held faculty appointments at Harvard and the University of Virginia Medical Schools for his work in political psychology. He defined the concept of Track II, nonofficial diplomacy. Educated at Lehigh, Columbia, and Harvard Universities, Montville is the editor of *Conflict and Peacemaking in Multiethnic Societies* (Lexington Books, 1990) and editor (with Vamik Volkan and Demetrios Julius) of *The Psychodynamics of International Relationships* (Lexington Books, 1990 [vol. I], 1991 [vol. II]).

Marc Howard Ross

Marc Howard Ross is William R. Kenan, Jr. Professor of Political Science at Bryn Mawr College where he has taught since 1968. He received his degree in political science at Northwestern University and in addition he spent a year studying at the Philadelphia School for Psychoanalysis. He has done research in East Africa, France, Northern Ireland, the Middle East, and most recently in Spain, and South Africa. His current work has two major themes (1) the role that cultural performance and memory play in the escalation and deescalation of ethnic conflict and.(2) social science theories of conflict and their implications for conflict management He has written or edited six books including *The Culture of Conflict* and *The Management of Conflict* and over 50 articles that have appeared in books and academic journals. The topic of tonight's presentation is draws from his forthcoming book, *Cultural Contestation in Ethnic Conflict* to be published by Cambridge University Press in 2007.

Daniel Rothbart

After receiving a Ph.D. in philosophy from Washington University, St. Louis, Daniel Rothbart was visiting research scholar at the University of Cambridge, Dartmouth College, and the University of Oxford, Linacre College. He is currently associate professor of conflict analysis at the Institute for Conflict Analysis and Resolution, as well as professor in the

Department of Philosophy at George Mason University. In the area of conflict analysis, he teaches philosophy of social science, the epistemology of conflict theory, and conceptions of practice. His current research centers on models and methods for analyzing identity-based conflicts. He is co-editor of *Identity, Morality and Threat: Studies in Violent Conflict*. Rothbart is also a leading scholar in philosophy of science, with expertise in the philosophical aspects of research, the centrality of modeling to scientific inquiry, and the relationship between science and technology. His work has appeared in major interdisciplinary journals and scholarly volumes. He authored *Explaining the Growth of Scientific Knowledge: Metaphors, Models, and Meanings*, as well as *Philosophical Instruments: Minds and Tools at Work*. His edited volumes include *Science, Reason and Reality and Modeling: Gateway to the Unknown by Rom Harré*. His pedagogy was recognized in the Excellence in Teaching Award, given by the Provost of George Mason University in 2000.

Dennis J. D. Sandole

Dennis J.D. Sandole, Ph.D. (University of Strathclyde, Glasgow, Scotland, 1979) is Professor of Conflict Resolution and International Relations at the Institute for Conflict Analysis and Resolution (ICAR), at George Mason University in Arlington, Virginia, where, as a founding-member, he has been for 25 years. A former U.S. Marine and police officer, he has lectured worldwide on various aspects of conflict analysis and resolution, especially with regard to the necessity of identifying and responding to the deep-rooted causes of why some people are motivated to kill themselves in order to kill others, including Americans. Among Dr. Sandole's publications is, *Capturing the Complexity of Conflict: Dealing with Violent Ethnic Conflicts of the Post-Cold War Era* (1999). His upcoming book, due to be published later this year by Routledge (Taylor & Francis), is *Peace and Security in the Postmodern World: The OSCE and Conflict Resolution*.

Peter N. Stearns

Peter N. Stearns was named Provost of George Mason University effective January 1, 2000. He also regularly teaches courses in world history and social history. Stearns received his Ph.D. from Harvard University, and previously attended Harvard College. Prior to coming to George Mason University, Stearns taught at Harvard, at the University of Chicago, at Rutgers University (where he chaired the New Brunswick History Department), and Carnegie Mellon University, where we was Heinz Professor of History. He served as Dean of Carnegie Mellon's College of Humanities and Social Sciences from 1992 to 2000. Past Vice President of the American Historical Association, in charge of the Teaching Division. Stearns currently serves as chair of the Advanced Placement World History committee. He founded and continues to serve as editor-in-chief of the *Journal of Social History.* Author or editor of over 90 books, Stearns has also published widely on world history and on related teaching issues, including several texts and readers, thematic books on industrialization, on gender, and on consumerism; and three recent books include *American Behavioral History, Childhood in World History,* and *American Fear.*

Lena Tan

Lena Tan is a doctoral candidate in Political Science at the University of Massachusetts, Amherst where she is working on a dissertation that examines the role of identities, identity contestation and domestic political structures in the decisions that states make in disengaging from their colonial and territorial possessions. Her research interests include constructivist International Relations theory, the role of identity and issues of race and empire in world politics.

Edward A. Tiryakian

Edward A. Tiryakian, an alumnus of the Fulbright Program, is Professor of Sociology at Duke University, Durham, North Carolina. He received his Ph.D. from Harvard and held faculty positions at Princeton and Harvard before joining the Sociology Department at Duke in 1967, where he has served as departmental chair and as Director of International Studies. He has held visiting professorships at Freie Universität Berlin, at the Institut d'Etudes Politiques in Paris; and at the Sorbonne (where he is *docteur honoris causa*), among others. Professor Tiryakian is recognized internationally for his contributions in several fields of sociology. His prolific scholarship encompasses the history of sociology, sociology of development, sociology of religion, and nationalism and ethnicity. He has six times been the Director of a National Endowment for the Humanities Summer Seminar for College Teachers, including one on "New Nationalisms and Modernity." He has also directed a year-long Mellon Foundation seminar on "New Nationalisms, New Identities, New Perspectives." Professor Tiryakian has served as president of both the American Society for the Study of Religion and the Association Internationale des Sociologues de Langue Française and twice elected chair of the Theory Section of the American Sociology Association.

Index